MUSLIM FRIENDS

CONCORDIA
SCHOLARSHIP
Today

MUSLIM FRIENDS
Their Faith and Feeling

An Introduction to Islam

Roland E. Miller

CPH.
SAINT LOUIS

Copyright © 1995 Concordia Publishing House
3558 S. Jefferson Avenue, St. Louis, MO 63118-3968
Manufactured in the United States of America

Library of Congress Cataloging-in-Publication Data

Miller, Roland E.
  Muslim friends : their faith and feeling / Roland E. Miller.
      p.   cm.   — (Concordia scholarship today)
  Includes bibliographical references (p.   ) and index.
  ISBN 0-570-04624-6
  1. Islam I. Title. II. Series.
BP161.2.M49   1996
297—dc20   96-13901

  2 3 4 5 6 7 8 9 10   05 04 03 02 01 00 99 98

To my wife, Mary Helen,
my companion on the road,
with love and gratitude

Contents

CONTENTS

Transliteration System

Although this volume is prepared with the general public in view, Arabic transliteration has been used for two reasons: the first is out of respect for the tradition of Islāmic studies, while the second is to provide the reader with the flavor of the original Muslim religious language. The system used is that of the *Encyclopaedia of Islam* as modified in the usage of *Muslim World*. As usual in this matter, arbitrary decisions have been made. Muhammad, Ḥadīth, and Sūfi are all spelled in this manner; Qurānic is used as the adjective of Qurʾān. Shīʿa is employed for both the noun and adjective. Some terms are borderline English usage, but the volume leans in the direction of pointing such words, for example, *jihād* and *ʿulamāʾ*. Names of places are unpointed, but names of individuals are generally pointed. The writer recognizes that other approaches are equally possible.

As for dates, for convenience reasons, the common Western dates are used instead of the Muslim lunar calendar, or a combination of both.

In endnotes, *E2[1]* refers to the first edition of the *Encyclopaedia of Islam*, *E2[2]* to the second edition, and *SE2* to the *Shorter Encyclopaedia of Islam*.

Preface

There are many outstanding academic introductions to Islām. This introduction is not intended to compete with those valuable works, but rather to provide a supplement with particular emphases.

My first intention is to provide a work that is academically sound but is written for the general reader. It is my impression that there is a growing need to make the Islāmic reality more accessible to the public. The second emphasis is the rather personal form of communication that I have employed. In part this represents an effort to personalize the data; and in part it results from the writer's experience of 24 years of living in a Muslim town in India. The third aspect is the attempt to present Islām imaginatively from a Muslim perspective, yet at the same time keeping non-Muslim readers in mind. I hope that through this process both non-Muslims and Muslims can share this material with some benefit.

This is a delicate task. It seems to me that it places at least four requirements upon a scholar and writer:

(1) The material must be factually trustworthy;

(2) It must be generally acceptable to ordinary Muslims;

(3) It must be understandable to ordinary non-Muslims; and

(4) It must express the spirit of friendship.

I cannot pretend to have met such demanding requirements, but I have tried to adhere to them as closely as possible.

It will be easy for the reader to sense the influence of my great teachers in this art: Wilfred Cantwell Smith, Kenneth Cragg, Daud Rahbar, and Willem Bijlefeld. It is the Mappila Muslims of Kerala who have deepened for me the meaning of friendship, joined by Muslims in Regina and St. Paul. The University of Regina and Luther College that have provided a stimulating context for developing these materials, and the enthusiastic support of students and encouragement of academic colleagues is a warming memory. Finally, Luther Seminary in St. Paul has been more than gracious in providing assistance.

The primary purpose of this volume is to enable non-Muslims to understand Islām more easily and to help foster friendly relations between non-Muslims and Muslims. It is my hope that this intention will have been at least modestly served by this volume.

There is an old Arab proverb that I like to quote: "What comes from the lips reaches the lips; what comes from the heart reaches the heart!" Whatever the merits of this material, perhaps it will be clear to the reader that it has come from the heart.

Roland E. Miller
St. Paul, Minnesota
1996

1

Meet My Muslim Friends

As I consider my Muslim friends, and their faith and feeling, I recall a recent visit to a Muslim village where my family and I lived for a quarter century. Some distinguished Muslim leaders had invited me to a delicious meal. After the dishes were removed one of the men asked me, "When did you become our friend?" The question was totally unexpected, but it was also very straight forward and I had to answer. I considered it for a moment, and then replied with a simple story.

We had recently come to the area of a Muslim community that we had been informed was "dangerous." All the reports about the people whom we came to love had assured us of that, with a liberal sprinkling of the word "fanatic." We could not help but be influenced by these descriptions even as we tried to form our own independent impressions.

It was now the middle of a typical monsoon. The rain was coming down with machine-gun sounds and startling force. The time was midnight. I was working late on the outside veranda of our small home. Three tall figures loomed out of the darkness and advanced into the dim circle of light cast by my flickering kerosene lamp. They beckoned me to come to them. My language ability at that point was totally inadequate to the task. I had no idea where they wanted me to go or why. They seemed friendly, but the situation was forbidding and I was very nervous.

I resolved to go with them. We drove as far as we could into the interior and then began walking. We seemed to walk for miles along mud ridges separating the rice paddy fields, although later I realized it was not as far as it seemed. Guided only by the uncertain light of a torch, I frequently slipped into the irrigated field. I knew we were at the very core of a notorious center of alleged religious communalism.

At last, and seemingly out of nowhere, a teashop loomed ahead of us, and we gladly entered its welcome protection from the heavy rain. Inside an unusual scene greeted our eyes. A group of Muslims had seized a man whom they were holding fast. The story unfolded from the owner of the teashop, told in broken

English. A wandering man had come into the teashop. The shopowner had noticed a red packet in the stranger's pocket and had forced him to remove it. On examination it was found to be the registration book for my trusty Vanguard car. The stranger was a thief. The people in the teashop had seized and held him, while others walked three miles in driving monsoon rains at midnight to inform the Canadian missionary what had happened! I was overwhelmed, and deeply moved. The experience made a profound and lasting impact.

I turned to my Muslim hosts at the lunch and said simply, "That is when I became your friend." They were pleased. They liked the story, sensed its sincerity, and our bond became closer.[1]

This is a book about Islām, but its context is the experienced relation of friendship. The book introduces the religion of Islām, but I prefer that the reader view it as an attempt to clarify the faith and feeling of some Muslim friends. What do they believe, how do they see life, and what moves their emotion? In short, I invite you to meet my Muslim friends.

It may be argued that friendship has nothing or very little to do with the study of Islām. The study of Islām deals with facts that can be learned like any other facts—scriptural facts, doctrinal facts, historical facts, legal facts, cultural facts, artistic facts—facts of all kinds. The study of Islām begins by honoring the facts. The friendship relation between the observer and the observed has little to do with the acquiring and learning of such evidence. It may even interfere with the effort to be impartial and objective.

It is clear that the objective study of the facts is essential for the understanding of Islām. It is probably more important for the understanding of Islām than it is for the study of any other religious tradition, simply because the facts of Islām are so often distorted. Muslims themselves yearn for more factual presentations of their religion on the part of others, even as they struggle to understand the realities themselves. Let a truer picture, based on genuine facts, emerge from the current fog of misrepresentation! This is certainly a desirable goal.

At the same time it may be argued that friendship has everything to do with the study of Islām. What is involved is the truth that every religious fact has a double dimension—the bare fact itself, and what it means for the believer. For example, a bare fact is that Muslims go on the pilgrimage to Mecca, where they follow certain rituals and become very emotionally involved. Why are they so excited? What does the experience mean for the

14

individual pilgrim? What is he or she feeling at the Ka⸱ba? To the extent possible, that meaning must be penetrated if we are to speak of real "factuality." On the human level it is friendship that provides the most ready access to the realm of personal meaning. It is to friends that we ordinarily express our deepest feelings, our hopes and fears, our inner faith. With friends we move past the casual "Hi!" and share what is in our hearts. We can insist, therefore, that apart from its own intrinsic merit, friendship plays a key role in the sensible study of Islām.

It is Wilfred Cantwell Smith, respected scholar of the Muslim world, who has made this point most persistently:

> The study of religion is the study of persons. Of all the branches of human inquiry, hardly any deals with an area so personal as this... The study has to do not with religious persons; or at least, with something interior to persons.[2]

He goes on to say:

> To understand what is in his heart, therefore, the student must not merely listen to or read what a believer affirms, but must come to know those qualities of the believer's life that can become known only in that two-way relationship known as friendship.[3]

Professor Smith links the words "friendship" and "persons." If the best way to understand Islām is through friendship with Muslims, this in turn means dealing with Muslims as persons, and not merely as representatives of a system. It is now both easier and harder to view Muslims as persons. On the one hand, two factors have helped to personalize the understanding of Islām. The first is the tremendous movement of people in the world. The globalization of life has inevitably put people from different backgrounds into living contact with each other. The second is the impact of the media that has brought different people into our living rooms. There is now a human face to Islām.

There are also, however, three factors that have made it harder for non-Muslims to view Muslims as persons. They are the creation of superficial images, the creation of stereotypes, and the creation of caricatures. Let us look first at the problem of superficial images. Superficiality represents a common dilemma of our time related to the 30-second clip approach of TV knowledge. That gives us the sense of learning and not its substance, resulting in a kind of stick-figure imagery. Moreover, the great abundance of various materials makes us rather content with what we receive, since we have neither the time, energy, or patience to delve more deeply into the labyrinth of issues that confront us. Muslims, with others, suffer from this process. Dealing superficially with fellow human beings trivializes them, and frequently warps their reality. *To understand the reality of Islām* means to penetrate beneath these surface impressions to the deeper levels of Muslim faith and emotion.

The second difficulty relates to the creation of stereotypes. A stereotype is a standardized image. The cowboy, for example is a North American stereotype. We create standardized images partly because of our lack of deeper knowledge, partly to bridge the vastness of human diversity, and partly because of our romantic or antagonistic attitudes. Perhaps the primary reason is that it is easier to think in such categories. It is simpler for us if all Muslims are the same, so we make them the same. A relatively innocent example of stereotyping is the inaccurate identification of Muslims with Arabs and of Islām with the Middle East. It is true that the vast majority of Arabs (not all) are Muslims, and that Arabia as the home of historical Islām and its religious language will always have a special place in Muslim affection. Nevertheless, it must be recognized that well over eighty per cent of the world's Muslims are non-Arabs, who represent many cultures and opinions. Although there are common factors in Muslim faith and life, there is no standardized image that fits all Muslims. *To understand the reality of Islām* means to move past lazy generalizations to a deeper engagement with the lively diversity of the Muslim world.

The third difficulty, caricature-creation, is the most serious one. A caricature is a ludicrous exaggeration of some peculiarity or defect that we assume to be present in someone or something. Caricaturing is the bread and butter of cartoonists, and it can produce humorous and educational results. In the field of human relations, however, persistent caricaturing is nothing less than a disaster. It is not only Muslims who suffer from this process, but they do suffer very much indeed. The most common example is the image of Muslims as unremittent militants or as outright terrorists. Some years ago I happened to write an article for a national journal, commemorating the beginning of a new Islāmic century. The editors chose to place an illustration at the head of the article. It was an old engraving of a warrior on a horse charging directly at the reader! The article was trying to help the reader to understand the broad reality of Islām; the illustration did not support that intent. Janice, a character in John Updike's *Rabbit at Rest,* says: "And even baseball players, she has noticed, looking over Harry's shoulder at the television, don't bother to shave, like Arab terrorists."[4] Caricatures distort reality. *To understand the reality of Islām* means to shatter the unreality and to move past its broken fragments to a serious engagement with the essential humanity of Muslims.

Dealing with the problems of superficiality, stereotyping, and caricature creation is not as difficult as it may seem. Superficial knowledge yields to the learning that comes from personal relationships. Stereotyping and caricaturing fall before the onslaught of common sense. The dispelling of distortions and the allowing of people to emerge in our own experience as the persons they are may be the greatest gift of friendship in our time.

Meet Abdulla and Amina

Abdulla and Amina are a composite of many friends. I am introducing them to the reader as representative Muslims. Abdulla is a lawyer in a Muslim town. His wife, Amina, is a teacher in a Muslim elementary school. They have three children—Ashraf who is in college, and two younger children, Rashid and Fatima. Abdulla's father, Ahmad, also lives with them. The family home is in a crowded semi-urban area. Their house is a small but pleasant building that Abdulla is inheriting from his father. It is surrounded by a small compound that contains several coconut trees and some beautiful bougainvillea bushes. In the course of this book we will be visiting them in imaginative ways.

Ordinarily Abdulla and Amina lead a restrained and normal life that is marked by the usual routines and the common joys and sorrows of family experience. If you would ask them what is the most important thing in their life, they would hover between their faith and their family, and finally decide on both. They take their faith seriously and try to be loyal to its requirements. At the same time they love and care for their family. They hope for the blessing of God, and beyond that they carry on as best they can. They make good friends, as many have come to know.

My Muslim friends are people who define their personhood by the term *islām*. The word is music to the Muslim soul. It suggests everything that a Muslim holds dear in life. It declares a believer's faith and obligations, and it signals the hopes that he or she cherishes for this life and the next. The words *islām* and *muslim* are two sides of the same coin. Islām is the religion and Muslim is the one who follows the religion.

The term *islām* has a telling meaning. It comes from a root verb *salama* that carries a double significance:

> to surrender
> to be at peace

Thus when you ask a Muslim friend for the meaning of the term *islām*, you may get either of two answers. He may say, "Islām means submission." Or he may say: "Islām means peace." In either case he would be right for the word bears both meanings. A human being surrenders to God, and thereby obtains peace and satisfaction. Such a person is a *muslim*.

From this basic starting-point a major religion and a huge civilization developed. The word *islām* did not remain at the basic level of a spiritual attitude. The term was capitalized and used to describe both the religion and the civilization that grew out of the commitment and proclamation to surrender to God. The religion is called Islām and the civilization is described as Islāmic.

The religion of Islām can be viewed in two ways. On the one hand, it is an *ideal*, that is a vision exemplified by the faith and life of the Prophet Muhammad and the first Muslims. It is the religion as it should be and as it was meant to be. Again and again the voices of Muslims are raised today calling upon believers to return to that principle of life. On the other hand, the religion of Islām is also a *practicum*, the religion as it actually is. In the latter sense Islām is a mosaic of many ideas, varying levels of commitment, and a tremendous variety of expression. What it really is, is different from what it ideally is, and Muslims struggle to bring the ideal and the actual together.

The term Islām also denotes a civilization. The civilization of Islām is the cultural product of Muslims over the years. It is immense in its compass and content—including a great deal of history, a variety of institutions, impressive learning in law and theology, and a splendid body of literary, artistic and scientific achievements.

Abdulla and Amina are involved in all of this. At the simplest level they are surrenderers to God, but at the same time they are also the members of a fully developed religion and a complex civilization. In summary we may suggest that Muslim persons

have, as it were, four Islāmic roles:
- —they are persons committed to the principle of surrender to God alone;
- —they are persons committed to an ideal religion of beliefs and practices that is based on that principle;
- —they are members of some actual, real-life expression of that ideal, which varies from place to place; and
- —they are persons who are the heirs and makers of a major civilization.

In one way or another all Muslims participate at each of these four levels of Islāmic experience. In this work we will concentrate on the first three. We begin with a brief summary of Muslim faith.

A Muslim holds that life in this world is to be lived in surrender to the one and only God, who is named as Allāh, *The God*, and one who is called the Most Great, and the Merciful and Compassionate. God has graciously given His guidance to humanity through his prophets and scriptures. The final prophet is Muhammad and the final sacred book is the Qurʾān. Through the Qurʾān God's will is clearly revealed. The task of human beings in this world is to be obedient to that revelation.

The relationship of obedience is fundamental to the Muslim self-understanding, and it flows naturally from the attitude of surrender. The nature of an individual's faith and obedience to the law of God in this life will determine that person's eternal destiny, whether it be in Paradise or in Hell-fire. Therefore Muslims must dedicate their life to God as His representatives on earth. They must also unite in a common family and strive together in a common effort to bring all human society into a surrendering relation to God and His will. "So remember the name of thy Lord and devote thyself with a complete devotion" (Qurʾān 73:8).[5]

The basic Islāmic faith (*imān*) that arises from this worldview is expressed in five beliefs: God, angels, prophets, books, and Day of Judgment. The Muslim life that emerges is expressed in five primary practices (*dīn*): confession, prayer, fasting, almsgiving, and pilgrimage. These basic beliefs and primary practices together comprise *islām* at its fundamental level.

Muslims believe that Islām is the final truth and that they are the privileged bearers of its precious message to the world. It is this message that makes them different from the rest of the world and at the same time useful to the rest of the world.

What we have described above is what draws all Muslims together. It makes it possible for us to speak of representative

Muslims. But Muslims are not only a community of faith—they are also unique individuals with their own ideas and their own feelings. Many people suffer from a serious eye disorder when they study members of another faith. The disease may be called "Solid Blockitis." Those who suffer from it conclude that everyone who calls himself or herself a Muslim is the same. The very opposite is the truth. There is an almost endless variety among Muslims. Professor C. Naim, a Muslim scholar, has put it this way:

> There is such a thing as Islām, of course, and there are many Islāms as well. There is one Islām in the sense that there is one revealed book and one Prophet to whom it was revealed. There are many Islāms in the sense that there are many different traditions of interpreting that book and understanding that Prophet.[6]

The variety that exists among Muslims stems from three factors. The first is that Islām is a global religion. It is spread across all continents in many lands and in many cultures. Each of these cultures has its own indigenous traditions, language and music, art and folklore. Muslims in Bangladesh, China, Indonesia, Senegal and Turkey are really very different from each other. The second reason is that Islām does not have a single individual or group who have the authority to decide what every Muslim must believe or practice in order to be a true Muslim. The basic Muslim principle of spiritual equality means that no one is in a position to systematize the cultural diversity of Muslims around the world. But it is the third factor that is the most important.

The third factor is that Abdulla and Amina are particular persons who are marked by the miracle of human individuality. There are things in their lives that are common to all humans. To some extent you can understand Abdulla and Amina because they are human persons. Furthermore, there are things in their lives that are common to all Muslims. To some extent you can understand Abdulla and Amina because they fit the general pattern of "Muslim." But there are also some things in their lives that are distinctly their own, and they must also be understood in terms of their personal faith and their special feelings as individuals. Abdulla is like no other man and like no other Muslim. Amina is like no other woman and like no other Muslim. They cannot be arbitrarily classified and then defined by the classifications. They can, however, be discovered, and the discovery road is the friendship road. That discovery will be as unique as their individuality. It will bear testimony to the truth that every new friendship with a fellow human is a fresh and exciting experience.

Salaam aleikum!

Muslims have a special greeting that they normally use with fellow Muslims. It is a common greeting in the Muslim world: *Salaam aleikum!*

The first word in the phrase, "salaam," has become an acceptable English term and is listed in English dictionaries. In ordinary use it carries the same general meaning as "hello!" Its real meaning goes much deeper. The word "salaam" comes from the same root as *islām* (look at the *s, l,* and *m*) and hence it also means "surrender-peace." The second word in the phrase, *aleikum*, signifies "to you." *Salaam aleikum* therefore means "peace be to you!" or more fully "I wish you the peace that comes from surrendering to God." It is a profoundly meaningful wish.

Salaam aleikum is very much a family greeting that is used within the Muslim community. When on rare occasions it is extended to a non-Muslim, it is reserved for one whom the Muslim community regards as truly a friend. There is a tingling sensation of elemental surprise and mutual appreciation when the *salaam aleikum* becomes the bridge between Muslim and non-Muslim. Abdulla and Amina will not use this phrase to greet you until you come close to each other. Its sound is like the light at the end of the midnight walk through the rain.

We have emphasized the role of friendship in understanding Islām, and the need to deal with Muslims as persons who are both similar and different. We have said that we will allow Abdulla and Amina to represent both the typical similarity and the personal differences that exist in the religion of Islām. As we introduce that religion we will first examine how many "Abdullas and Aminas" there are in the world, and where they are located. Then we will look more closely at their religious faith and practice.

Notes

[1]One of the products of the relationship was Roland E. Miller, *The Mappila Muslims of Kerala*, 2nd rev. ed. (Madras: Orient Longman, Ltd., 1992).

[2]W. C. Smith, "Comparative Religion: Whither and Why?", *The History of Religions. Essays in Methodology*, ed. by M. Eliade and J. Kitagawa (Chicago: University of Chicago Press, 1959), pp.34f. Bishop Kenneth Cragg put the same thought in a different way in a prayer that he consistently used to open his stimulating classes on Islām: "Help us so to enter into the minds of men so that ..."

[3]Ibid., fn.18, p.39.

[4]*Rabbit at Rest* (New York: Fawcett Crest, 1990), p.118.

[5]The English translation of the Qurʾān used in this work is Marmaduke Pickthall, *The Meaning of the Glorious Koran* (New York: New American Library, Mentor ed., 1953). Reference will also be made to translations by Yusuf Ali and E. H. Palmer. In the writing of the text I have preferred the spelling Qurʾān and Qurānic, which is now generally replacing the older Koran and Koranic. The figures 73:8 means chapter [*sūra*] 73, verse [*āyat*] 8.

[6]C. M. Naim, "Getting Real about Christian-Muslim Dialogue," *First Things*, No. 57, November 1995.

2

Muslim Population:
A World of Peoples,
A Community of Faith

When Muslims assemble at the holy city of Mecca in Arabia for the great pilgrimage of Islām, it is an incredible sight. Once a year one to two million people gather at the central shrine of Islām. By the tens of thousands they stream in from every corner of the globe, representing a myriad of races, languages, and cultures. The word immensity defines the scene. In terms of sheer numbers it is the greatest of all religious festivals. In terms of character it is like a United Nations of all Muslim peoples. They are individually different, yet they are all together at the same place and with the same purpose. They seem to know each other even though they have never met. In this chapter we will try to give a sense of the numerical and geopolitical range of Islām that explains this graphic phenomenon, and with it the feeling of family that helps to hold Islām together.

Abdulla and Amina are part of a very large family indeed. By 1995 there were about 1,122,661,000 Muslims in the world.[1] This figure represents 19.3 percent of the population of our globe. Thus about one out of every five people in the world is a follower of Islām. At least 42 nations of the world have a Muslim-majority population. Muslim authorities argue that these figures should be even higher.[2] In addition there are more than 77 other countries that have at least 100,000 Muslim citizens. Islām is the second largest religion in the world today.

A. The Global Extent of Islām

The story of how this vastness came about is a tale as fascinating as it is complex. Since it involves the history of many nations and peoples, however, we will not attempt in this work to deal with the details of that development.[3] We will be content with noting a few key points, the first of which has to do with the beginning of Islām.

Muslims believe that Islām began with Adam. In other words, it started when God created the first humans, and Adam and his wife were the first Muslims. The principle of surrendering to one God (*islām*) goes back to the birth of humanity. Moreover that birthright continues as the natural endowment of every human being. Everyone is a Muslim at birth. An individual may become something else as a result of upbringing and cultural conditioning, but that is contrary to God's creative intention. This basic principle of *islām* was witnessed to by a succession of prophets between Adam and Muhammad. Finally, concluding that development, the formal religion of Islām took its shape in history.

Historical Islām began with the appearance of the Prophet Muhammad (A.D. 570–632). Muslims believe that he was sent as a warner and as a messenger to urge humans to worship God alone and to follow the straight path of obedience to His will. At first Muhammad followed a lonely road, and the number of Muslim believers was only a handful. Conditions changed in the last ten years of his life, and as the result of his dynamic leadership Islām became the religion of Arabia.

Immediately after Muhammad's death Islām entered a remarkable period of growth. By every count it was a startling development. Within one hundred years Islām had become the dominant religious power from the Atlantic Ocean in the West to the River Oxus eastward in Russia, from Tours in France to the north all the way to Sind in India to the south. Over the succeeding centuries Islām expanded eastward to the whole sub-continent of India, to southeast Asia, Indonesia and China; southward into Africa and northward into the Balkans and Eastern Europe. In modern times—chiefly through immigration and conversion—Islām has become a major presence in Europe and North America. In fact, within two decades it is possible that Islām will have become the second largest religion in the U.S.A. Islām is the latest of the large world religions, but it has travelled very fast indeed! Let us look at a statistical profile of its adherents.

As we have already noted, the majority of the world's Muslims live beyond the Middle East. Only 16.3 percent of Muslims are Arabs. A total of 68.3 percent of all Muslims live in Asia, 27.4 percent are in Africa, and 4.3 percent live elsewhere. It is clear that the world of Islām is multicultural. Its ethos is strongly influenced by its religious rooting in Arabia, but the bulk of its members are situated within other cultures. One Asian country alone, Indonesia, has a full 15 percent of the world's Muslims. Three South Asian countries, namely Bangladesh, Pakistan and India, together contain 31 percent of the world's Muslims. Thus these four Asian nations in combination constitute 41 percent of the Muslim population of the world.

The following eight countries together hold 68 percent or two-thirds of the world's Muslims:[4]

Indonesia	171,702,000
Pakistan	127,450,000
Bangladesh	113,186,000
India	107,118,000
Iran	64,859,000
Nigeria	62,910,000
Turkey	6l,554,000
Egypt	56,283,000

These statistics reveal the concentration of Muslim peoples, but there is another set of figures that shows the spread of Muslim populations across a breadth of nations. In the following tables we see the global nature of the Islāmic reality. It is dispersed across the world. This fact has profound implications for Muslims and causes them to reflect: What does it mean to be a family of this kind, and how can we retain our sense of family?

1. A total of 25 countries have 90–100 percent Muslim population:

Maldives	100	Pakistan	97
West Sahara	100	Iraq	96
Afghanistan	99	Gambia	95
Algeria	99	United Arab Emirates	95
Comoros	99	Djibouti	94
Mauritania	99	Jordan	94
Saudi Arabia	99	Qatar	93
Somalia	99	Tunisia	92
Yemen	99	Egypt	91
Iran	98	Kuwait	91
Morocco	98	Senegal	91
Turkey	98	Mali	90

2. Eleven other countries have 80–90 percent Muslim population:

Syria	89	Indonesia	85
Gaza/West Bank	88	Tajikistan	84
Oman	86	Uzbekistan	81
Bahrain	85	Niger	80
Bangladesh	85	Turkmenistan	80
Guinea	85		

3. Six other countries have 50–80 percent Muslim population:

Azerbaijan	78	Brunei	63
Sudan	72	Lebanon	53
Kyrgyzstan	67	Malaysia	53

4. The following 22 countries have 10–50 percent Muslim population:

Nigeria	45	Ivory Coast	20
Chad	44	Suriname	20
Kazhakastan	44	Malawi	16
Burkino Faso	43	Singapore	16
Sierre Leone	43	Benin	15
Tanzania	33	Israel	14
Ethiopia	31	Liberia	14
Guinea-Bissau	30	Mauritius	13
Cyprus	23	Mozambique	13
Cameroon	22	Togo	12
Albania	21	India	11

The former Yugoslavia had 10 percent Muslim population. In the area of Bosnia-Herzegovina the ethnic group known as Bosnian Muslims numbers 2,006,028 (1985),[5] but its final stage as a separate nation has not yet been reached.

5. The Central Asian Nations:

The former Soviet Union had 12 percent Muslim population. Six new and independent countries, frequently referred to as Muslim republics, have come into being after the breakup of the Soviet Union in 1991. There is some question about the exact number of Muslims in each, not only because of the general unreliability of Soviet religious statistics, but also because of the movement of peoples taking place in that area since the dissolution of the U.S.S.R. It is estimated (1993) that there are about 41,456,000 Muslims in the six republics combined, or 70 percent of their total population. This means that about 3.8 percent Muslims remain in Russia proper or in other new nations. The percentage of Muslims in the six republics is as follows:[6]

Republic	Total Population	Percentage of Muslims
Azerbaijan	7,146,000	78
Kazakhastan	16,947,000	44
Kyrgyzstan	4,506,000	67
Tajikistan	5,272,000	84
Turkmenistan	3,856,000	80
Uzbekistan	21,301,000	81

6. Countries with Muslim percentages between 5–10 percent include: Ruwanda (9), Guyana (8), Sri Lanka (7), Central African Republic (6), Kenya (6), and Uganda (6).

Countries with a low percentage but a significant number of Muslims include: Philippines (4): 2,580,000; Burma (3): 1,560,000; China (2.4): 28,789,000; and the U.S.A. (1.9): 4,936,000. Former U.S.S.R. without the Central Asian nations has about 5,771,000 Muslims.

Statistically problematic nations where Muslim estimates vary greatly include: Albania, Bulgaria, Burkino Faso, Cameroon, Central African Republic, Ethiopia, Guinea, Ivory Coast, Madagascar, Nigeria, and Mali.

From the above it is clear that there is an almost bewildering range of humanity associated with the religion of Islām. From the religious leader who raises peanuts in Senegal to the woman who acts as chief minister of Bangladesh, from the young man who studies law in Canada to the female gynecologist in India, from the rice farmer in Indonesia to the oil worker in Iran, from the nurse in Nigeria to the shopkeeper in London, there are all sorts of persons who make up what we call the Muslim world. What holds them together is as important as their individuality. The binding factor is their sense of being one religious family. Muslims view themselves not only as individual persons but also as members of a community of faith. We must turn to that point briefly.

B. The Muslim Sense of Religious Family

In a primary textbook in Syria the fifth-year class is addressed with the following exhortation:7

> They shall make petition with awe and silence, for themselves and for the Muslims; raising their hands together to heaven, for heaven is the qibla [direction] of petition.

The prayer is full of Islāmic meaning. The word *qibla* means direction. We direct our prayers to heaven. When we pray to the Almighty, awe and silence are better than a lot of talk. Above all, when petitioning God, the children should remember their fellow Muslims as well as themselves. The exhortation makes clear the double-sidedness of Muslim emotion. Up to this time we have emphasized one side, the importance of viewing Muslims as individual persons. However, to understand the reality of Islām, we must also consider Muslims as members of a worldwide community of faith. "They shall make petition ... for themselves *and* for the Muslims."

At the bottom of this urging is the Muslim sense of togetherness. That feeling is best captured by two English words and a hyphen: *community-family*. The word *community* suggests a commonality of concerns. The word *family* points to a personal relationship. The hyphen could be interpreted by a third word: *oneness*. The hyphen is a bridge, the bridging spirit of oneness. Muslims are bound together by their faith. That bond is to express itself in mutual support. The binding element is the principle of unity that bridges the diversity of Muslims in the world. It compels Muslims to think of themselves as a single family whose members are to deal with each other in the same way that brothers and sisters would.

All this is summed up by the word *umma*, the term for Muslim community. This almost magical word in terms of emotive power, really means "mother." The Muslim community, in one sense, is the mother of all Muslims. It gives the individual members of the community a sense of fellowship and security. In every religion, no matter what it is, its members feel that they have a special relation with each other. In Islām that feeling runs very powerfully. The fellowship with other Muslims transcends all other forms of human relationship. Within its embrace, individual

Muslims feel as though they are part of a family, a family of familiar friends. In turn, it is the Muslim's duty to love and to support the whole community of Islām.

The principle of sacred community is affirmed by the Qur²ān, the Muslim scripture. The Qur²ān says:

> Ye are the best community that hath been raised up for mankind. Ye enjoin right conduct and forbid indecency; and ye believe in Allah (3,110).

> And hold fast, all of you together, to the cable of Allah, and do not separate. And remember Allah's favour unto you: how ye were enemies and He made friendship between your hearts, so that ye became as brothers by His grace ... (3,103).

The teacher of Islām, who is acknowledged by most Muslims as the greatest of all Muslim scholars is al-Ghazālī (d. A.D. 1111). He reinforced these injunctions of the Qur²ān with the following advice:

> God's Messenger [referring to a reported tradition of Muhammad] ... said: "Two brothers are likened to a pair of hands, one of which washes the other." He chose the simile because the pair are of mutual assistance towards a single aim. So it is with brothers ... In a sense the two are like one person. This entails a common participation in good fortune and bad, a partnership in the future as in the present moment, an abandonment of possessions and selfishness.[8]

Again, al-Ghazālī said:

> The duties of a Muslim to a fellow-Muslim are that you say, "Peace be upon you" if you encounter him, and respond if he gives you an invitation, that you bless him if he sneezes, visit him if he is ill, and attend his funeral if he dies. They are to honour his oath if he swears something to you, to advise him when he seeks advice, and take care of his interests when he is absent; to want for him what you want for yourselves, and to dislike for him what you would dislike for yourself.[9]

Sayyid Qutb, a well-known modern Egyptian religious thinker and revivalist, put the whole matter simply and clearly when he stated: "The whole Muslim community is one body, and it feels all things in common."[10] The principle is all-encompassing. It is to be expressed not only in personal relations, but in social organization, common decision-making, and a single political structure.

Muslims realize that Sayyid Qutb is stating an ideal, and the reality often conflicts with it. Muslims are supposed to "act as one body," and they are supposed to feel "all things in common." In practice, it doesn't always turn out that way. Human realities take over, and Muslim societies fail to live up to the noble theory of one community and one family. Muslims know that the spirit of division contends with the spirit of unity, that hatred too often subverts affection, that ethnic loyalties take precedence over pan-Islāmic commitment, and that selfish national and personal interests even produce wars between Muslim countries. The principle of oneness is constantly threatened, and Muslims too feel the stress and strains of the divisive pressures of modern life.

That pressure may be something so simple as the cultural divisions that mark the Muslim world, which our statistics have highlighted. There are comfort zones between human beings related to cultural background. It is not everyone who is relaxed with a person from another country, even though they belong to the same religion. Language and custom are important factors in determining natural relations. In North America, Muslims have immigrated from a great variety of world areas. They have attempted to maintain inter-Muslim togetherness through a variety of Muslim associations. Ideally, these associations draw their members from all cultures; in fact, those from Arab, South Asian and African background tend to gather in separate groups because the comfort level is higher. The oneness of the *umma* is pressured by cultural differentiation.

The pressure to division is felt in the behavioral realm. This relates to the simple fact that there are some Muslims who take their faith more seriously than others. Some have a light attitude toward religious observance, and others are quite secularized. These realities cause a psychological division in the community. The greatest problem relates to the feelings that sincere Muslims harbor toward nominal Muslims. Secularization is a reality of life that causes them deep distress. I recall a conversation I once had with a taxi driver in Cairo. His name was Ali. I asked Ali regarding his approach to religion. He said, "Now I am a fifty-fifty Muslim. When I get old, I will be a hundred percent Muslim!" Ali typifies that problem that has led some Muslims to make a distinction between Muslims and *mu'min* (believers). The latter are defined as persons who really practice their faith. The oneness of the *umma* is threatened by behavioral patterns.

The pressure to division is felt in the realm of ideas. Differences of opinion regarding the correct understanding of Islām have resulted in the development of a number of different groups within the Muslim family. The most well-known difference is between Sunnī and Shīʿa Muslims. When Islām began, it was assumed that one person would head the *umma*, and for some years after the prophet Muhammad died, the Muslim community was able to maintain a single social and political organization under one leader. That leader was known as the *khalifa* (caliph), the successor of the prophet Muhammad. Very soon, however, a difference of opinion surfaced as to who that leader should be. One group took the moral-democratic view, namely, that the leader should be selected on the basis of his piety and adherence to the custom of the prophet Muhammad. This group of Muslims are called Sunnīs, that is, those who follow the *sunna* (custom) of the prophet Muhammad. The second group took the position that the leader of the community should be chosen from the descendants of the family of Muhammad. The people who hold to this hereditary view of leadership are called Shīʿa (party), the partisans of the family of the prophet Muhammad. Thus, at a very early stage, a major division developed in the body of Islām. Today Sunnī Muslims represent above 85 percent and Shīʿa more than ten percent of the world's Muslims. They recognize each other as Muslims, but at times the relationships are uneasy. The oneness of the *umma* is threatened by differences in doctrine.

Finally, the pressure to disunity is also felt, we may say especially felt, in the realm of political relationships. The modern spirit of nationalism is a powerful challenge to the *umma* ideal. We have noted that there are as many as 42 Muslim-majority nations in the world, many of whom have obtained their freedom and status after World War II. Each of these countries has its own identity and interests, even though their respective citizens may be united by a common spiritual faith. The unity of the Muslim family has not been able to survive all the pressures of these differences. Pakistan and Bangladesh have gone to war with each other. So have Iran and Iraq,and so have Morocco and Mauritania. In modern times, nothing has threatened the Muslim principle of family-community so seriously as the spirit of nationalism.

Yet, despite these strong challenges, and the stresses and

strains that they have produced, Muslims nevertheless retain their sense of oneness. They know that despite the cultural differences that tend to make them gravitate to separate groups, at a deeper level they are one. They know that despite the ideological and theological differences of opinion, their relationship within a common faith creates an indissoluble bond. It is not by accident that when Jamāl al-Dīn al-Afghānī, a great modern revivalist, started a newspaper in Paris, he called it "The Indissoluble Bond." They know that despite the differences in behavior, the instinct of Islām has been in the direction of mutual acceptance and general toleration within the family. They know that despite the political problems between Muslim families, Muslim hearts around the world continue to throb with a feeling of connectedness.

When the Gulf War between Iraq and Kuwait took place in 1991, many non-Muslims puzzled over the fact that ordinary people in Muslim countries around the world sympathized with Iraq. After all, they wondered, were not the leaders of the Muslim nations committed to the allied forces of the United Nations? What could account for the massive demonstrations of common Muslims in favor of Iraq, especially in view of the behavior of its ruthless leader? The primary reason for that development was the Muslim sense of family. The members of the *umma* around the world had come to the conclusion that part of their family was being harassed by a phalanx of Western enemies and a group of wealthy and oppressive Muslim leaders. They felt a kinship with the suffering people of Iraq, even though they did not like its leader. There is a kind of uncanny spiritual electricity that runs through the Muslim world and gets turned on, either when the faith of Islām seems threatened or when a part of the *umma* is endangered. The spirit of Muslim oneness is demonstrably alive.

We started this chapter with a review of the statistics of Muslim world population. The statistics are the statement of both a triumph and a problem. The triumph relates to the fact that Islām has grown into such a massive religion and powerful social force. The problem, for Muslims, is how to keep alive the Islāmic ideal of unity as the community grows in numbers and often divides over issues. Abdulla and Amina share both the triumph and the problem. But the fact is that they do not spend much time thinking or worrying about either.

For Abdulla and Amina the sense of family is immediate, down to earth, practical. The end of the fasting season has just arrived. It is the Feast of ᶜĪd al-Fiṭr, the breaking of the fast. After thirty days of strenuous fasting, the moment of joyous release has come. The restaurants in Abdulla's town are absolutely jammed. Up and down the streets the people are moving, with happy hearts and faces and sounds. Abdulla and his friends mingle with the crowds. There is a community of joy that follows the sharing of strenuous spiritual endeavor. They are glad to be part of this family. They whole-heartedly agree with the words of the Qurʾān: "You are the best community brought forth to man!" And in their home, where the festivities have begun, they advise their children to make their petition with awe and silence, "for themselves and for the Muslims, raising their hands together to heaven."

Let us now consider the One to Whom their hands are raised.

Notes

[1]Cf. Appendix A for detailed statistics of Muslim population to 1990. Religious statistics are notoriously difficult to compile because of affiliation questions and reporting problems. Muslim statisticians routinely give higher figures. M.A. Kettani, *Muslim Minorities in the World Today* (London: Mansell, 1986), lists the 1990 world Muslim population as 1,330,220,000, making one out of every four persons in the world of Muslim faith. In compiling Appendix A, I have combined several sources of information.

[2]Kettani, ibid., adds Benin, Burkino Faso, Cameroon, Chad, Gabon, Guinea-Bissau, Nigeria, and Sierra Leone to the Muslim-majority listing.

[3]For a balanced Muslim historical survey, cf. S.F. Mahmud, *A Short History of Islām* (Karachi: Oxford University Press, 1960). A standard western work is *The Cambridge History of Islām*, ed. by P. Holt, A. Lambton and B. Lewis (Cambridge: University Press, 1970).

[4]M.A. Kettani, op.cit., p.241.

[5]For the 1993 populations I am dependent on "Russia and the Newly Dependent Nations of the Former Soviet Union," a map of the National Geographic Society, Washington, D.C., March, 1993. For the Muslim percentages I have extrapolated from ethnic populations reported in *The Europa World Year Book, 1991*, Vol. II (London: Europa Publications, Ltd., 1991). These figures are higher than the 1970 Soviet Union Census figures of 1990, reported in D. Barrett, ed., *World Christian Encyclopaedia*, p. 699, and they are much lower than the estimates of I. and L. Faruqi, *Cultural Atlas of Islām* (New York: MacMillan, 1968), p. 268.

[6]Barrett, ibid., p. 789.

[7]Constance Padwick, *Muslim Devotions* (London: S.P.C.K., 1961), p. 57.

[8]Al-Ghazālī, *On The Duties of Brotherhood*, tr. by Muhtar Holland (Woodstock, N.Y.: The Overlook Press, 1976), pp. 21f.

[9]Al-Ghazālī, "The Duties of a Muslim to a Muslim," from *Revivification of the Sciences of Religion*, quoted in J.A. Williams, ed., *Themes of Islāmic Civilization* (Berkeley: University of California Press, 1971), pp. 16f.

[10]Williams, ibid., p. 50. Qutb died in 1965.

3

My Muslim Friends
Believe in God

A well-known scholar once wrote a book that he entitled *Alive to God*.[1] I wish to make use of Kenneth Cragg's excellent title, for I do not know any other phrase that so clearly describes my Muslim friends. They are alive to God. One of the most remarkable scenes in all religion is the sight of thousands upon thousands of Muslims at Mecca simultaneously touching their foreheads to the mat in homage to the Almighty. Islām is a forehead-touching-the-ground-before-God world view, and Muslims are people who are alive to God. This simply means that a sense of God pervades Islāmic life and dominates Muslim thought and behavior.

The common Muslim term for God, as we have seen is Allāh. It has been properly said that Allāh is the reason for the existence of Islām. He is also the dominant reality for the individual believer. The name of my friend, Abdulla, means servant of God. The phrase "I am Abdulla, a Muslim," therefore signifies: "I am a servant of God who is a surrenderer to God." Surrendering to God implies both faith and obedience. The name Amina also has significance. It means "trust-filled and trust-worthy." The phrase "I am Amina, a Muslim," therefore suggests: "I am Amina who trusts God and leads a trustworthy life." Thus the very names of my friends, Abdulla and Amina, declare the Muslim aliveness to God.

The entire religious context of Muslim life underlines the Reality of God, and is designed to make and keep Muslims aware of that Reality. The creed, the fivefold call to prayer, the annual fast, the steady mutual exhortation of Muslims, in short, the whole of Islām emphasizes the place of God in human life. Immediately after Abdulla was born, sacred words were breathed into his ear. From the age of five to thirteen years he attended a religious school to be educated in the Word of God (Qurɔān). As a youth he listened to the night lectures of religious leaders that he attended during the month of fasting (Ramaḍān). As adults, Abdulla and Amina share in the activities of the community of believers that is dedicated to carrying out the will of God, and they strive to share this vision with their children, against the alternate visions that come to them from modern life. And when they die, the authority and power of God will be proclaimed over their graves. "From it [earth] we created you, and out of it will we bring you forth a second time" (20:55). The spiritual rhythm of Muslim life makes Muslims alive to God.

In the home of one of Amina's relatives there is great rejoicing. A new baby boy has just been born. The delivery was a difficult one, but God has blessed both mother and child, and they are safe and well. The women of the family are ecstatic. The Muslim midwife leans down and whispers the name of Allāh in the child's ear.

In another part of the same town a funeral procession is slowly wending its way down the main street. It is a long process of men, in single file, accompanying the body of a friend. Only one solemn word can be heard. Like a dull drum-roll the sound goes forth: "Allāh ... Allāh ... Allāh!"

As this is going on, in the market area of the town, four other men are attempting to handle a cart laden with huge bags of rice. Two are pulling the handcart and two are pushing. As they exert themselves against the heavy load, a rhythmic utterance escapes their lips: "Allāh ... Allāh ..." The words mingle, as it were, with the very sweat that pours from their brows.

From birth to death, and in all that lies between, the Reality of God encompasses Muslim life. We may put it this way: Muslim faith and life are marked by an *overwhelming* sense of God. That is not the same as saying that Muslims are emotional about God. Generally they are not, and in that regard Abdulla and Amina are typical. They are pretty quiet about their faith, and do not go around waving a flag with the word "Allāh" emblazoned on it. They are rather people who simply believe that God is Real, and really to be feared. They live like people who are standing in the Presence of God. The ordinary Muslim sense of God may be defined as an attitude of deep respect rather than emotional extravagance. The TV clips of masses of excited Muslims do not represent the religious norm, nor do they reflect the response of Abdulla and Amina. Their attitude toward the Almighty is deferential rather than presumptuous, austere rather than excited, devout rather than passionate.

Behind that attitude of restraint lies the Muslim understanding of the utter greatness of God. The whole feeling could be summed up by the exclamation "Oh God!" It is what some scholars might call a numinous feeling. To confess the words *lā ilāha illā Allāh*, "there is no god but God," or even to simply say "I believe in God," is to make statements of profound respect for the Most High, The High and Lofty One. Abdulla and Amina might not say it this way, but they would unhesitatingly agree to the sentiment of the Muslim saint:

> He who plunges deep into meditation on Thy Creative Activity and Thy high praise finds that his glance returns to him blinded and exhausted, his intellect stunned, and his thoughts bewildereed and paralyzed.[2]

These words apply to faithful Muslims, to people like Abdulla and Amina. As we have already noted there are many Muslims who do not show much interest in religion. They are nominal Muslims, secularized Muslims, partially committed Muslims, Muslims whose primary attention is diverted to the material world, even corrupted Muslims. Their sense of God has been covered over in some way, diluted, casual, formalistic, or virtually out of sight. In this problem Islām faces the same situation that also prevails in other religious traditions.

Yet it is true to say that the great majority of Muslims maintain a strong faith in God, and in the period of the 1990s the Muslim God-awareness seems to be strengthening rather than weakening. Therefore with some confidence we may say that most Muslims are people who are *alive to God*, and it is quite certain that there is no Muslim whose spirit does not thrill to the eloquent words of the Qurɔān (2:255)[3]:

God
there is no god but He,
the Living, the Everlasting
Slumber seizes Him not, neither sleep!
to Him belongs
All that is in the heavens and the earth.

Who is there that shall intercede with Him
save by His leave?
He knows what lies before them
And what is after them,
And they comprehend not anything of His knowledge

save such as He wills.

His throne comprises the heavens and the earth;
the preserving of them oppresses Him not;
He is the All-high, the All-glorious!

A. The Mosque

It is the mosque that focusses this intense awareness of God. The word mosque stems from *masjid*, an Arabic term that means "a place for prostrating"; in other words, it means "a place of prayer." It now signifies the building where Muslims meet for worship and other activities. It functions the same way as a church or temple. The mosque, however, is not only a building. It is also an important symbol suggesting that the whole world should be a house of prayer, and that all human beings should acknowledge God and worship Him alone. This attitude that the mosque symbolizes is called *ʿibādat*. The word really means service, coming from the same root as *ʿabd* or servant. It points to the truth that the first and proper service of humans is the worship of God, not the construction of buildings. The worship may go on anywhere, for "unto Allāh belongs the East and the West, and whithersoever ye turn, there is God's countenance" (2:115).

This underlying principle means that there is great liberty in the form of a mosque. There is no fixed set of rules controlling mosque architecture, and there are many different kinds of mosques in the Muslim world. Two factors are especially important in determining the style of mosque—the first is the financial capability of the local Muslim community, and the second is the depth of appreciation for the local culture. Thus there may be great structures like the Mosque of the Prophet in Medina to pagoda-like edifices in Indonesia and China, or simple, white-washed single rooms in West Africa to upstairs rented buildings in New York City. The Middle Eastern style of mosque architecture dominates the Muslim world, and with the help of financial grants from oil-rich Gulf countries that form is being adopted ever more widely. It features the dome and the minaret. The minaret is the tall tower attached to the mosque from which the call to prayer issues five times daily. Whatever the form, all mosque builders strive for a feeling of lightness, spaciousness and, if possible, elegance in order to enhance the worshipper's sense of God, and His oneness and majesty.

The mosque has traditionally been utilized for many purposes besides worship. It may be a home for clergy and students, an educational institution, a hostel for travelers, a center for poor-feeding, and in older times it even served as a hospital. It is frequently used as a meeting place to discuss the internal affairs of the Muslim community. None of this is viewed as a lack of reverence for the sacred space, but rather witnesses to the truth that the service of God encompasses all of life. The various activities of the mosque are frequently funded by endowments (*waqf*) or by the voluntary offerings of people of the area. The appointment of staff and the management of the affairs of the mosque are the responsibility of a local committee led by senior members of the community.

The central function of the mosque, however, is to be a house of prayer. The best way to understand that function is to visit a mosque. In many places Muslims welcome non-Muslims to visit a mosque or to observe a mosque service, although in other places it is not permitted. Abdulla is happy to take a friend with him on Friday noon which is the time for the weekly congregational service (*khutba*). Before he enters the mosque he performs the required ablutions and removes his shoes as a mark of respect. He will also cover his head before he prays. Amina has made her way to the section of the mosque that is reserved for women.

What may strike you first as you enter the mosque is its utter simplicity. Although there may be lamps hanging from the ceiling, there is no furniture such as altar or benches. The emptiness of things is intended to convey a sense of the Presence of God. The lamps symbolize that "Allāh is the Light of the heavens and the earth" (24:35). To avoid any suggestion of idolatry there are no images or paintings, although passages from the Qurʾān may be inscribed on the walls. The absence of any pictorial art points to the basic Islāmic principle that God cannot be represented by any human forms and cannot be "captured" or "brought down" in any way.

Set into one of the walls of the mosque a large indentation (*miḥrāb*) may be seen, marking the direction (*qibla*) in which the city of Mecca is located. That, of course, is the city in Arabia where the prophet Muhammad was born, and when Muslims pray they are to face in that direction. Spiritually the *qibla* signifies that the human heart should always be turned in the direction of God. Since this is a rather large mosque, you can also see a raised platform (*mimbar*) where the mosque preacher (*khaṭīb*) stands and from which he delivers a mediation based on one of the passages of the Qurʾān. The sermon is commonly in Arabic, although it may be spoken in the local language if it is a progressive mosque. Since Arabic is the language of the Qurʾān, it is loved by Muslims everywhere and is used in many contexts. The sermon is generally rather formalistic, and is quite often read from a standard sermon book. It is really the prayer that matters most in the mosque service.

In a succeeding section we will take up the Muslim prayer in detail. For the moment it is sufficient to say that the central point of the prayer occurs when the worshippers prostrate themselves before Allāh. As their foreheads descend to the carpet together, they recite the familiar phrase *Allāhu akbar!* God is greater, it declares. Yes, God is greater than anything that can be imagined. God is the greatest! Thus the mosque and the prayer join in helping the Muslim to remember God. For every Muslim, the universal Islāmic awareness of God must issue in the active remembering of God (*dhikr*), and the remembering of God in turn must express itself in a life that is wholly committed to the service of God (*ʿibādat*). But who is this God, this Overwhelming One Who so dominates the consciousness of Muslims? What can be said of Him? How can He be described? We turn to that question next.

There are some things in life that are important but we do not talk about them very much. They are private or sacred matters, and we are reserved about them. A practical example is marriage. If we are happily married, we simply enjoy the relationship. Speaking about it would be inappropriate and, in any event, words could not possibly explain it. That is a humble analogy of how many Muslims feel about God. They regard it as a little inappropriate for God's creatures and servants to throw around His name in common discussion. Moreover, no human words are capable of defining or explaining God, the Utterly Beyond, the Almighty. God is rather Someone to be believed in, to be surrendered to, and to be obeyed. Beyond that it is enough to say "O God!"...Allāh ... Allāh ... and to bow before the mystery. The Mystery is declared in these words (24:35):

Allāh is the Light of the heavens and the earth. The similitude of His light is as a niche wherein is a lamp. The lamp is in a glass. The glass is as it were a shining star. [This lamp is] kindled from a blessed tree, an olive neither of the East nor of the West, whose oil would almost glow forth [of itself] though no fire touched it. Light upon light. Allāh guideth unto His light whom He will. And Allāh speaketh to mankind in allegories, for Allāh is the Knower of all things.

B. The Nature of Allāh

Despite a careful reticence produced by awe and humility, Muslims cannot and do not remain completely silent on the topic of God. It is impossible to do that because God is a revealing God Who has spoken in His Word. It is also practically impossible because the subject of God must be taught to children and explained to the world. So Islām also has a doctrine of God, even though it is not elaborated beyond certain limits.

There are three primary affirmations that a Muslim makes about God. The first is that God is one, the second is that God is almighty, and the third is that God is the Lord of Life—creating, ruling and judging the world. As a typical study book for Muslim children puts it: "Belief in God means to believe that He is one and that there is no other power besides Him which rules over the world and man."[4] We will examine these three affirmations in order, realizing that they essentially belong together and can be separated only for the sake of discussion.

The unity of God (*tawhīd*) is a fundamental Islāmic concept, one which Muslims regard as absolutely critical and primary. It is expressed in a straightforward manner by the first part of the Muslim confession: *"There is no god but God."* The little word *but* (*illā*) in the confession is important because it points to the two essential meanings of the word "one." It may be understood in a double manner: "There is no god *except* God," and "there is no god *like* God." This double connotation discloses the two basic ideas in *tawhīd*—the first is that God is single, one in number; the second is that God is singular, unique in quality.

God is one in the sense of single. That means there is no other being in the category of deity. God has no partners, no associates, no coequals. There is only one God, and you must worship Him alone. "You alone! You alone!" a poet once cried. The opposite is to believe that there are several or many gods, which is the principle of polytheism. Polytheism, however, is the most abhorrent of all ideas to Muslims. It is called *shirk*, associating another being with God, and is regarded as the greatest sin of humans. It is, in fact, the unforgivable sin:

> Lo! Allāh forgiveth not that a partner should be ascribed unto Him. He forgiveth [all] save that, to whom He will. Whoso ascribeth partners to Allāh, he hath indeed invented a tremendous sin (4,48).

Dualism, tritheism, polytheism, and all idolatries ancient and modern—anything that threatens the oneness of God and creates a rival to Him, is rejected by Islām.

When the prophet Muhammad began his preaching in Arabia, the native religion of the area was nature worship and polytheism. But a few people called *hanīfs* had turned away from idolatry. They were worshipping the most high God whom they called Allāh, and Whose name was known even in that period of darkness (*jāhiliyya*). Allāh, as we have seen, is the same as *al-ilāh*, which means THE DEITY, the One beside Whom there is no other. The Prophet commended these early monotheists and called upon everyone to worship and follow the one God only. The Qurʾān declares (59:23):

> He is Allāh, than whom there is no other God, the Sovereign Lord, the Holy One, Peace, the Keeper of the Faith, the Guardian, the Majestic, the Compeller, the Superb. Glorified be Allāh from all that they ascribe as partners [unto Him].

At the end of his career the prophet Muhammad entered the Kaʿba, the sacred shrine of Mecca, and threw down the idols it contained. This he viewed as the true prophetic function—to establish the Soleness of God against all false rivals. The Qurʾān makes this clear (3–2–4):

> Allāh! There is no God save Him, the Alive, the Eternal. He hath revealed unto thee [Muhammad] the Scripture with truth, confirming that which was revealed before it, even as He revealed the Torah and the Gospel aforetimes for a guidance to mankind.

In conformity to that vision Muslims are to surrender to God alone, and to join together in maintaining the principle of divine unity.

The second aspect of the unity of God is His incomparability. There is no one like God, and there is nothing to which He can be properly compared. He is unique in His being and in His characteristics. He is described in human language because there is no other language for humans, but God is beyond description. The 112th chapter of the Qurān, called the Unity, sums up this point. It is greatly revered by Muslims. In earlier times believers said of it that the heavens and the earth are founded on it, and it is worth one-third of the entire Qurān! It declares:

> Say He is Allāh, the one!
> Allāh, the eternally besought of all!
> He begetteth not nor was begotten.
> And there is none comparable unto Him.

The *lā ilāha illā Allāh* means that God is incomparable. This principle helps to explain the Muslim hesitation about representational art. I use the word hesitation because in many Muslim cultures artistic achievement abounds. The hesitation is primarily centered on the use of representational art in relation to God. A painting or sculpture is dangerous because it may become an object of worship. But its greatest danger is a more subtle one, and that is its inherent *inadequacy*. How can God, or anything about God, be pictured? God Who is incomparably divine in quality cannot be compared to what is creaturely in origin or form. And human language suffers the same deficiency as art. It also is inadequate to describe the Being and Character of the Almighty, and all human statements about God must therefore be regarded as having a provisional quality. There is one thing, and only one thing that can represent God truly, and that is God's own message and His own revelatory language in the words of the Qurʾān. Hence the words of the Qurʾān in their Arabic form are the only safe vehicle for expressing the Reality of the Incomparable God. For this reason calligraphy—beautiful writing and inscription—has become the supreme art form in Islām, and it is to be found everywhere, in mosques, in public buildings and in homes.

The *lā ilāha illā Allāh* means two things. It means that God is the only God and it means that the only God is the Incomparable God. The practical implication for Muslim believers is that they must worship and obey God alone, and that all of life must be brought into a unity of obedience to God. For mystically inclined Muslims there is a further implication, namely, that the human spirit must be unified in some way with the divine spirit. But we will deal with that point later. Let us now turn from *tawhīd* to a consideration of the second Muslim affirmation about God, namely, that God is all-powerful.

Muslims confess the oneness of God, but they *celebrate* the power of God. One of the ways they do so is by the repetition of familiar phrases that extol the Almighty. The three most common of such expressions are the following:

> *Allāhu akbar!*—God is great!
> *Subḥāna ᶜllāhi!*—Glory be to God!
> *Al-ḥamdu lilāh!*—Praise to God!

The first of the three phrases, *Allāhu akbar!*, is called the *takbīr*, "the making God great," and it holds a special place in Muslim devotion as the most appropriate term for expressing God's greatness and power. The second phrase, *Subḥāna ᵓllāhi!*, is a liturgical praise used especially in the five-fold prayer. *Al-ḥamdu lilāhi!* is an everyday expression that falls very frequently from Muslim lips. Abdulla says, "My father has recovered from his illness—*al-ḥamdu lilāhi!*" Amina declares, "The wedding went well indeed—*al-ḥamdu lilāhi!*"

The association of power with God is normal in religion. Power and deity are naturally associated together. What makes the Muslim view of God's power special, however, is its elevation to the heights where it stands alone. Divine power is the Mt. Everest of Muslim thinking about God; it looms high above all other mountains around it. Power is not just one of the several characteristics of God, but rather power is the primary element that humans must acknowledge in the divine. It is the characteristic of the overwhelming God that overwhelms all other characteristics.

> To God belongs all that is in the heavens and the earth. Whether you publish what is in your hearts or hide it, God shall make reckoning with you for it. He will forgive whom He will and chastise whom He will. God is powerful over everything (2:284).[5]

God is powerful over everything, and His power is absolute and unquestionable.

There are two major elements that make up power: ability and authority. Both of these elements are equally important in the Muslim understanding. On the side of pure ability, there is nothing impossible for God. Thus, Marmaduke Pickthall translates "God is powerful over everything" as "Allāh is able to do all things." On the side of authority, there is nothing that God is not free to do. It is not for humans to call God into account. No one can say that God *must* do this or that. The word *must* is inappropriate. No one can say that God *should* do this or that. The word *should* is equally out of place. God cannot be limited by human ideas or opinions about Him that constrain His absolute authority or freedom, and no human can charge God with injustice or inconsistency. An old popular song had this catchy line in it: "Don't fence me in!" Humans cannot fence God in. God is greater than human concepts, rational or moral. *Allāhu akbar!*

The Islāmic emphasis on God's transcendent power produces attitudes of awe, respectful fear, and solemn praise among believers. Most Muslims are not very interested in attempting to probe further into the transcendent mystery of God's being. They prefer to bear witness to the greatness and mystery. The most common response of the Abdullas and Aminas of the Muslim world to the Almighty One before Whom they bow is deferential praise. A Muslim who is alive to God is alive to the praise of God and His power. The thought is caught up in the following poetic declaration:

> All laud to the Lord of greatness and magnitude, Lord of the great throne.
> All laud to the Lord of power and abidingness, Lord of the noble throne.
> All laud to Him whom all things praise, the Exalted, the August.
> All laud to Him whose knowledge contains all things, the Everlasting, the Eternal.
> All laud to Him to whose glorious Face such praise alone is due.
> All laud to Him who alone knoweth the mode of his Being, the Powerful, the All-Wise.
> All laud to Him the depth of whose eternal greatness is unthinkable by the minds of men.[6]

From the declaration of the power of God flows the third primary Muslim affirmation about the Almighty—that is, the One, Almighty Lord directs and governs the world according to His will. The God Who is one and the God Who is great is also the God who rules. The controlling will of God is supreme and absolute in the universe. A favorite Muslim description of God is drawn from the first chapter of the Qurʾān. It declares that God is *The Lord of the Worlds* (*rabb al-ʿālamīn*). The word *rabb* implies Lord or Master. As Lord, God is the effective Master of what He has created. As Lord, God will be the final Judge of what He has created. As Lord, He Who is at both the beginning and the end is also the God of the middle, the active ruler of life. Since this will be the subject of the next chapter, where we will take up the implications in detail, we will be brief at this point.

In Muslim thinking God is not at all like a watch-maker who has made a clock and set it in motion, but then loses interest in it and has no more connection with it. God is a connected and active Ruler. Let us use a homely example. Allāh is not a constitutional monarch like the queen of England, who is only a symbolic ruler. Nor is He quite like a forceful president, such as may be found in France or in the U.S.A. He is much more like the head of a giant corporation, whose will is supreme and who has absolute authority in company affairs. The universe, as it were, is God's company, and He is the President, Chairman of the Board, and Chief Executive Officer, all together. These are only poor human analogies meant to illustrate. Abdulla would be uncomfortable with them because of their human quality. For him "God is great" simply means that "God is in charge." God's will is the first and final factor in everything. As He wills, He commands; and as He commands, so it is done. Nothing can happen apart from the will of God, and so everything in universal history and in personal life is in some way God's will. He is *The Lord of the Worlds!*

The obvious human response to the doctrine of God's absolute, controlling will is that men and women must strive to know that will and to obey it. The emotion runs deeper, however. Abdulla's and Amina's underlying feeling is stronger than a rational or ethical response. It is summed up in the powerful little phrase *in shāʾ Allāh*, which means "if God wills." This phrase belongs to the inner core of fundamental Muslim religious expressions. The words are added to every serious Muslim decision. They are the other side of the coin of *Allāhu akbar*. When Abdulla casually says to Amina, "I will be home for lunch today," he does not usually add, "if God wills." But if he is engaged in a serious case at the court, he will say, "I will do well in the case today, *in shāʾ Allāh!*" Or, if he is saying farewell to a friend, he will likely say, "We will meet again, *in shāʾ Allāh!*" The words are not always spoken, but every Muslim *feels* the underlying condition that the words imply. All that we are, and all our affairs, ultimately depend upon the sovereign will of the Almighty God.

In the foregoing we have dealt with three basic Muslim affirmations about God: God is one; God is great; and God is sovereign. Do these affirmations sum up the whole Muslim teaching about God? Is there more that can be said? Muslims answer that question in different ways. Some say, yes. There is more that can be said because the Qurʾān itself says more. It has a great deal to say about how God thinks and acts. Other Muslims say, no. Essentially, you cannot say more than the above. To say more is to introduce a set of problems related to describing God with human concepts and languages. In one way or another such descriptions place an unacceptable restraint upon God. We will deal more with that issue in a moment. Let us first look at what are called "The Beautiful Names of God." Much of the discussion revolves around the implication of those names, and out of those discussions flow the Muslim teaching about the divine attributes.

C. The Beautiful Names of God

The Qurʾān and the Muslim traditions are full of names that describe the qualities and actions of God. Although there are a variety of collections of these names, they are commonly referred to as the 99 beautiful names of God. The phrase itself comes from the Qurʾān:

> He is Allāh, the Creator, the Shaper out of naught, the Fashioner. His are the most beautiful names. All that is in the heavens and the earth glorifieth Him, and He is the Mighty, the Wise (59:24).

The use of the names of God is important in Muslim devotional practice. Abdulla's aged father, Ahmad, is an example. He is a pious man, and if you observe him carefully, you may at times observe him fingering a string of beads or "rosary." Although it is now somewhat out of fashion; the use of a rosary is still a common sight in some parts of the Muslim world. Ahmad uses one on which there are 99 beads, one for each of the beautiful names of God. As he fingers a bead he calls to mind one of the beautiful names and meditates on it; the whole point of the exercise is the remembering of God (*dhikr*). On another type of the rosary there are only 33 beads. As you finger a bead, you call to mind three of the names of God and thereby awaken within your heart a deeper consciousness of God, Whom to remember is the greatest privilege and duty of a humble believer.

Although there is no agreement on the exact makeup of the 99 names of God, the figure of 99 is commonly accepted. Muslims point to a simple way of confirming that number. The evidence is in the palms of the hands! If you look at your left palm, you will see a mark like this: ʌ. This is the figure for the Arabic number eight. Beside it is another mark like this: (. This is the Arabic number one, which of course, has come into the English language. Put the two together like this ʌ(, and you have 81. Now look at your right palm. There you will see the figure) followed by the mark ʌ. Put these two together,)ʌ and you have 18. 81+18 = 99. Thus on the palms of your hands is the reminder of God that He has 99 beautiful names, and through His names He is to be remembered.

The list of God's names is sometimes divided into two categories: "the glorious names" and the "terrible names." In the following listing I have consolidated 99 commonly accepted names and divided them, arbitrarily, into nine categories, according to their primary significance. The majority of names are found in the Qurʾān, although the Qurʾān has more names than are included here; some of the names, however, are drawn from tradition. The name Allāh is said to gather up and incorporate the significance of all the other names. It is sometimes added as the hundredth name or is included in the list of 99. As you read the names, you will appreciate the fuller content and the great breadth of the Muslim teaching about God.[7]

I. *Names that deal with God's Nature*

One (aḥad)	Independent (ghanī)
Existing (wājid)	First (awwal)
Living (ḥayy)	Last (ākhir)
Self-subsisting (qayyūm)	Hidden (bāṭin)
Eternal (ṣamad)	Manifest (ẓāhir)
Enduring (bāqī)	Hearing (samīʿ)
True Reality (ḥaqq)	Seer (baṣīr)
Comprehensive (wāsiʿ)	Knower (ʿalīm)

II. *Names that deal with God's Glory*

Grand (ʿazīm)	Majestic (jalīl)
Exalted (ʿaīl)	Laudable (hamīd)
Very Exalted (mutʿālī)	Incomparable (badīʿ)
Glorious (mājid);	
or unique (wāhid)	Lord of Majesty and Glory
Most Glorious (majīd)	(dhūʾl jalāl waʾll ikrām)

48

III. *Names that deal with God's Power and Knowledge*

Mighty (ʿazīz)	All-powerful (qādir)
Great (kabīr)	Prevailer (muqtadir)
Very Great (mutakabbir)	Aware (khabīr)
Strong (qawiī	Subtle (latīf)
Firm (matīn)	Wise (hakīm)

IV. *Names that deal with God's Rulership*

Creator (khāliq)	Governor (wālī)
Maker (bāriʾ)	Ruler (malik)
Fashioner (muṣawwir)	Dominant (qahhaā)
Joiner (jāmiʿ)	Compeller (jabbār)
Ruler of the Kingdom (mālik al-mulk)	

V. *Names that deal with God's Absolute Will*

Opener (fattāḥ)	Originator (mubdiʿ)
Abaser (khāfiḍ)	Restorer (muʿīd)
Exalter (rāfiʿ)	Deferrer (muʾakhkhir)
Restrainer (qābiḍ)	Advancer (muqaddim)
Spreader (bāṣiṭ	Honourer (muʿizz)
Quickener (muḥyī)	Destroyer (muzill)
Killer (mumiī)	

VI. *Names that deal with God's Providence*

Faithful Guardian (muʾmin)	Generous (karīm)
Protector (muhaimin)	Protecting Friend (walī)
Manager (wakīl)	Enricher (mughniī
Preserver (hāfiz)	Giver (muʿṭi)
Repeller (maniʿ)	Answerer of Prayer (mujīb)
Bestower (wahhāb)	Guide (hādī)
Provider (razzāk)	Director (rashīd)
Bounteous (shakūr)	Strengthener (muqīt)
Benign (barr)	

VII. *Names that deal with God's Mercy*

Merciful (raḥmān)	Clement (ʿafū)
Compassionate (raḥīm)	Kind (raʾūf)
Forgiving (ghafūr)	Patient (ṣabuū)
Very Forgiving (ghaffār)	Loving (wadūd)
Relenting (halīm)	Favorable (tawwāb)

VIII. *Names that deal with God's judgment*

Watcher (raqīb)	Judge (haktm)
Witness (shahid)	Equitable (muqsit)
Counter (muhhs;i	Resurrecter (bāᶜith)
Reckoner (hasīb)	Inheritor (wārith)
Just (ᶜadl)	

IX. *Other Names*

Perfect (qaddūs)	Profiter (nāfiᶜ)
Peace (salām)	Avenger (muntaqim)
Light (nuū)	Distresser (dārr)

D. The Divine Attributes

Muslim teachers say that behind these Names, summarized by them and conveyed by them, are the attributes (*ṣifāt*) of God. They, in turn, are divided into eternal qualities and essential attributes. The eternal qualities are really only a restatement of God's unity and uniqueness. A common listing is the following:

Eternal Qualities

1. Existence — God exists, without origination
2. Priority — God is before anything else
3. Continuance — God is eternal
4. Uniqueness — God is different from anything else
5. Self-subsistence — God is independent
6. Unity — God is one

At the same time as these qualities are affirmed, their opposites are rejected.

The essential attributes are really an explanation of God's power and how that relates to the world. As we have already noted, they do not claim to describe God's inner nature which is hidden. To try to describe God's essential nature would be presumptuous, limiting, and distorting. The attributes are rather descriptions of how God customarily wills to act. A common listing is the following:

Essential Attributes:

7. Power   - God is omnipotent. He can raise the dead.

8. Will   - God is the Controller. He can do what He wills, and whatever He wills comes to pass.

9. Knowledge - God is omniscient. The past and future are known to him, and the thoughts of the human heart.

10. Life   - God is the Source of all life. He Himself does not beget and is not begotten.

11. Hearing   - God hears all things, from the rustling of the grass to the roar of the rockets.

12. Sight   - God sees all things, even the progress of a black ant on a black stone on a dark night.

13. Speech   - God communicates His will; this attribute is also identified with the Qurʾān.

Longer lists of attributes include such characteristics as possibility and creating; sustaining and renewing. In contemporary times, however, there are three other characteristics of God that have received greater attention than many of the attributes on the classical lists. These are the characteristics of mercy, justice, and truth. The attribute of God's justice has come under consideration in connection with modern ethical issues, and in that connection Muslims are discussing the justice and righteousness of God. The attribute of God's truth has also become important in relation to current intellectual issues, especially those connected with scientific discovery. The characteristic of *mercy*, however, is the one that has received the greatest attention. The mercy of God appears very frequently in current Muslim writings and discussions. That is not surprising, for the attribute of mercy is very present in the Qurʾān.

At the beginning of every chapter of the Qurʾān, except the ninth, stand these strong words: "In the name of God, the Merciful, the Compassionate!" This is called, in common language, the *bismillāh*. It completes the set of fundamental phrases that reveal the religious attitude of Abdulla and Amina. The term *bismillāh* stems from the first section of the Arabic original: *bismillāhi raḥmāni raḥimi*. The term *Raḥmān* in this phrase means "The Merciful One," while the related term *Raḥīm* means "The Bestower of Mercy." The *bismillāh* may therefore be translated as: "In the name of God, the Merciful One Who bestows mercy." Yusuf Ali renders the phrase in the following way: "In the name of God, Most Gracious, Most Merciful."[8] There are many different ways of translating the *bismillāh*, but the meaning is clear. God has the attribute of compassion, which results in His being merciful to His creatures. The following words of Hammudah Abdalati would certainly sound a chord of agreement in the hearts of Abdulla and Amiha:

> The mercy of God gives us hope and peace, courage and confidence. It enables us to remedy our griefs and sorrows, to overcome our difficulties and obtain success and happiness. Indeed, the mercy of God relieves the distressed, cheers the afflicted, consoles the sick, strengthens the desperate, and comforts the needy. In short, the mercy of God is active everywhere all the time in every aspect of our lives ... It is real and we can feel it with our hearts and appreciate it with our minds.[9]

The contemporary interest in the attribute of God's mercy is an important development in the Muslim doctrine of God. The overwhelming appreciation of God's power is being coupled with and conditioned by a deeper appreciation of God's mercy. As the same writer puts it: "The love of God for His creatures is immense and beyond human imagination. We cannot measure or count His favours." [10]

As we have already suggested, Muslim thinkers have struggled greatly, sometimes abstrusely, over the question of the relation of the attributes of God to the being of God. They have put questions and given answers such as the following:

1. Question: If God is one, how can He have parts? For example, if you say that God has the eternal quality of speech, does it not imply that there are two eternities, God Himself and God's Speech? This would result in two deities, which is impossible.

   Answer: The orthodox "answer" to the problem is set forth in the following phrase: The attributes of God "are not He, and they are not other than He."[11] They are in the essence of God, but distinct from it.

2. Question: If God is unique, how can He be described? For example, if you literally interpret the saying of the

Qurʾān that God sits on a throne, does it not mean that He has a kind of describable human form, which is impossible?

Answer: The orthodox "answer" to this problem is the following: The descriptions of God in human terms, as they appear in the Qurʾān must be accepted without explaining how (bi lā kaifa) and without attempting or extending human comparisons.[12]

3. Question: If God is all-powerful, how can He be assigned apparently limiting characteristics? For example, if you say that He is merciful, does it not mean that He cannot be unmerciful? The definition limits the freedom of God, which is impossible.

Answer: The orthodox "answer" to the problem is this: God cannot be limited. The attributes of God describe God, but they do not bind the will of God. God is powerful over everything, and it may even be said that "it is not incumbent upon God to do that which is best for His creatures."[13]

Abdulla and Amina have never discussed such questions. Such problems have never come up for consideration in their family circle. They are part of the theological heritage of Islām, but they are not a part that has reached them personally. In fact, they are not interested in those complicated issues. They are more interested in the practical dimensions of their daily lives, and how God relates to those dimensions. Their view of things is therefore basically simple. God is Real, and there is no God but Allāh. He is *for real*. Therefore He must be worshipped and glorified, surrendered to and obeyed, trusted in and followed.

There is no god but God!	*Lā ilāha illā Allāh!*
God is very great!	*Allāhu akbar!*
Glory be to God!	*Subhāna ʾllāhi!*
Praise be to God!	*Al-ḥamdu lillāhi*
If God wills!	*In shāʾ Allāh*
In the name of God,	*Bismillāhi raḥmāni raḥīmi!*
the Merciful, the Compassionate!	

It is with and through these words that Abdulla and Amina prefer to think about God. Starting with praise, they then direct their attention to what the Reality of God implies for life in this world. God is a Mystery, but there is no mystery about what they should be doing as the servants of God. They should be alive to God and His will.

> O ye who believe! Observe your duty to Allāh. And let every soul look to that which it sendeth on before for the morrow. And observe your duty to Allāh! Allāh is Informed what ye do (59, 18f.)

This leads us to consider in greater detail the question of God's relation to the world and humanity. How does the Lord of the Worlds connect with the world?

Notes

[1] Kenneth Cragg, *Alive to God. Muslim and Christian Prayer* (London: Oxford University Press, 1970).

[2] ʿAlī ibn Abī Tālib, *al-Hizbu s-saifī*, in Constance Padwick, *Muslim Devotions* (London: S.P.C.K., 1961).

[3] A. J. Arberry, *The Koran Interpreted* (New York: MacMillan, 1944).

[4] *Lessons in Islām Series. Book No. I* (Lahore: Sh. Muhammad Ashraf, 1975), p.18.

[5] Arberry, op.cit.

[6] Hizbuʾt-tarīkatiʾl-ʾashshāqiyya, in Padwick, p. 73.

[7] For an excellent summary of the beautiful names see L. Gardet's article on "*al-asmāʾ al-husnā*," in *Encyclopaedia of Islām*, Vol. I, pp. 714-17. R. Stade, *Ninety-Nine Names of God in Islām* (Ibadan: Daystar Press, 1970), deals with the version of Al-Ghazālī, the premier Muslim theologian, while S. Friedlander, *Ninety-Nine Names of Allāh* (New York: Harper & Row, 1978), presents a Sūfī version. Two additional names that appear in some lists are *Al-Rabb*, Lord, and *Al-Sadīq*, Righteous One.

[8] Abdulla Yusuf Ali, *The Holy Qurʾān. Text, Translation and Commentary* (Washington: Islāmic Center, 1976 repr. of 1946).

[9] Hammudah Abdalati, *Islām in Focus* (Aligarh: Crescent: Publishing Co., 1973), pp. 5f.

[10] Ibid., p. 5.

[11] E. E. Elder, tr. *A Commentary on the Creed of Islām. Saʿd al-Dīn al-Taftāzānī on the Creed of Najm al-Dīn al-Nasafī* (New York: Columbia University Press, 1950), p. 51. See also H. A. Wolfson, *The Philosophy of the Kalam* (Cambridge: Harvard University Press, 1976), Ch. II.

[12]I. Goldziher, *Introduction to Islāmic Theology and Law*, tr. by A. and R. Hamori (Princeton: Princeton University Press, 1981 from 1910 version), pp. 92ff.

[13]Elder, p. 97.

4

The World and Humanity Belong to God

The story of Muslim faith in God has another chapter. For we must now ask the question: what does Allāh, the Almighty God, have to do with us? How do Abdulla and Amina answer this primary religious question?

Their answer comes from an affirmation. My Muslim friends declare that God is "the Lord of the Worlds." This powerful phrase is taken from the first verse of the Qurʾān, where God is called *rabb al-ᶜālamīn*, "the Lord of the Worlds." God has a lot to do with us because He is the Lord. In their prayers Abdulla and Amina daily declare that *the world and humanity really belong to God*. From the side of God this means that He exercises His Lordship over the world. From the side of creation, it means that both the stars in the heavens and the insects on the earth, and certainly all human beings must surrender to the Almighty.

In considering this testimony to faith, "Lord of the Worlds," both words are equally important. The term "Lord" points to mastery, direction, command. The term "worlds" encompasses all of life. Muslims are deeply concerned about God's will for their life in this world. On the whole, when they talk about God, they do not spend much time in speculating about the nature of God. The nature of God is, after all, a mystery, but there is no mystery in what God wants us to do. As a result, the religion of Islām places considerably more emphasis on right thinking about pious behavior (orthopraxy) than it does on right thinking about God's being (orthodoxy). Muslims want to apply their faith in God to life in this world.

The Muslim trend to practicality in religion is very strong. It marked Islām from the beginning, and it has become even stronger in contemporary Islām. Although Muslim thinkers continue to deal with theological issues from time to time, the emphasis is on pragmatic issues. Thus, if you would make a list of the various matters that Muslims discuss in their societies, the highest places would be given to such questions as how should Muslims carry on their lives in this world, what is the Muslim answer to pressing social and economic issues, and how should they overcome their down-to-earth problems?

As an example of this reality, we may consider a listing of the current concerns of Muslims in India, as noted by Haneef Juwaid, a Bangalore advocate. He first includes some of the various aspects of the problem of communalism and inter-religious relations, and Muslim worries in that connection. Then he highlights such problems as the following:[1]

—the stepmotherly treatment of the Urdu language;

—the refusal to allow Aligarh University to exercise its Muslim character;

—the threat to Muslim personal law by the pressure toward a uniform civil code;

—the inadequate Muslim representation in government positions.

Other observers would throw in employment and education issues. Juwaid closes by suggesting that the cumulative effect of all these problems is the unfortunate development of a "fear psychosis." These are all very practical matters, related to a particular local situation. Their gravity can barely be understood or appreciated by outsiders, but they are intensely meaningful for those involved. Theological issues do not appear on this agenda, in a direct manner.

A similar kind of listing could be made for almost every Muslim society, differing according to the local situation, but common in their basically practical orientation. Thus, for example, Muslims in the United States would include such issues as the following among their important concerns:

—how shall we keep our faith alive in a non-Muslim environment; especially, how shall we transmit our faith effectively to our children;

—how shall we relate to Christian festivals such as Christmas and Easter, and their public celebrations;

—how shall we obtain the necessary convenience for five daily prayers, when society is not geared for such a custom;

—how shall we get hold of land and property for mosques and cemeteries;

—how shall we obtain properly butchered meat; that is, meat that has been butchered with the use of the name of God;

—what should be done about the mixing of sexes, which is an alien custom to many;

—what should be done about the various problems associated with inter-marriage;

—what should be done in relation to the taking of interest, which is forbidden in classical Islām; and

—what steps, if any, should be taken to deal with media- and print-caricatures of Muslims?

Once again, theology in the narrow sense does not appear on the list. Indonesians and Saudi Arabians, Nigerians and Bangladeshis would each list their own problems, many of them distinct from each other. What would bind them all together would be the common concern to make sense out of individual and community living in this world.

Having said all this, however, we must add that Muslim life in this world is God-referenced. The practical issues are not dealt with as though God has nothing to do with them. That cannot be imagined! On the contrary, Muslim life is lived in the shadow of the affirmation that God is the Lord of the Worlds. Muslims want to do what God wants them to do. They therefore seek to know the will of God, and Muslim pragmatism is very much a religious pragmatism, and not a secular orientation. Their solution to the human problems that they encounter is located in the principles and the law of God. That raises the fundamental question of how Allāh is connected to the world, and we turn to that question now.

A. God is Connected with the World

An English novelist, Rudyard Kipling, penned the immortal words: "East is east, and west is west, and never the twain shall meet." He was wrong, as it turned out, but I want to apply his image to the Muslim idea of God. In regard to that could one say: "God is God, and man is man, and never the twain shall meet"? This phrase would communicate the thought that for Muslims God is so great and so majestic that there is little room left for a connection between God and humanity. A noted scholar of Islām, Sir Hamilton Gibb, in fact, pointed to the primary tension that marks all religious experience, that is, the tension between God's transcendence and God's immanence, God's otherness from us and God's presence among us.[2] The phrase "God is God, and man is man, and never the twain shall meet" might well express the strong Muslim emphasis on the transcendence, the beyond-ness of God. It would, however, be as misleading as Kipling's phrase if it created the idea that Allāh is not connected with the world.

Muslim faith declares that He, the Majestic One, is also the connectional Lord of the Worlds, and it testifies that there actually is a strong linkage from God's side with the world and with human beings. In what does that linkage consist? It consists in the idea that the Absolute God is also the Beneficent Creator and Ruling Lord, who has a claim on the world and on humanity, and who exercises that claim. When Abdulla testifies, *Allāhu Akbar!* and *Lā ilāha illa Allāh!*, he also witnesses that the world and humanity belong to God. God has made them, has sovereignty over them, and will judge them in the end. The Qurʾān does not present a disinterested deity. It rather portrays a very interested God, who is concerned about the fate of His creation and the people that He has brought into being. He is not only the Source of the universe, but the Lord of its worlds. Abdulla and Amina firmly believe that Allāh is the Lord of *their* worlds also. From the early-dawn prayer when the voice cries out that "devotion is better than sleep," to the late night prayers when the day's activities are over, and through all the hours and events of life in between, they believe that their individual and social affairs are to be conducted as though Allāh is observing them. And as the ancients said, can He not see a black ant crawling on a black rock in the middle of the night?

B. God Creates the Worlds

In every religion people must think about the relation of their traditional faith to modern discoveries. No issue has drawn greater attention than the beginning of the world. In his everyday life Abdulla meets may people who think that the world has always been there, or that it came into being of itself. On his part, Abdulla cannot accept that. He does not reject science. But He and the majority of his fellow Muslims believe firmly that God is at the beginning of things, and they accept in faith the traditional creation account as it is found in the Qurʾān.

The Qurānic account of creation is plain and clearcut. God created the world out of nothing with His all-powerful command, "Be!" (*kun!*), and it was. He made the heavens and the earth without wearying, in six days [note: no seventh day is mentioned], placing them into seven levels each. Therein He set the sun as a lamp and the moon as a light, fixed the zodiac, and spread the earth out as a carpet. With divine wisdom He added the various elements of nature in their proper proportion, with a fixed term and quantity for each. Eloquently the Qurʾān expresses the grandeur of God's creation and the wonder that its consideration should inspire in us. We should understand its marvels as portents and signs that we should read and understand. How is it possible to give glory and allegiance to anyone beside God? "This is God's creation! Show me what others beside Him have created!" (31:10).[3] Even if humans sometimes do not do so, the creation itself knows its Author.

> All that is in the heavens and all that is in the earth glorifieth Allāh; unto Him belongeth sovereignty and unto Him belongeth praise, and He is able to do all things. He it is who created you ... ! (64:1)

So Abdulla and Amina look at the palm trees and the rice fields, and the forest-covered hills, and the waters of the sea, and the living creatures that are in them, and they see all this as God's handiwork and the sign of God's mercy. They see the same when they look at human beings. For God creates humanity also, and we too belong to Him.

God used material in creating human beings, and the Qurʾān mentions these substances: earth, water, fluid, clots of blood. Using them God made humans with a perfect symmetry, employing a process:

> Verily We created man from a product of wet earth; Then placed him as
> a drop (of seed) in a safe lodging; Then fashioned We the drop a clot,
> then fashioned We the clot a little lump, then fashioned We the little
> lump bones, then clothed the bones with flesh, and then produced it as
> another creation. So blessed be Allāh, the Best of creators! (23:12–16)

It is not surprising that some modern Muslims interpret this
Qurānic process as a *prediction* of the idea of evolution. More
important, however, are the moral teachings it is said to convey.
The fact that humans are of humble origin, earthy, is an indicator
that they must always remember their true status as the creatures
of God. And the process of creation teaches that the existence and
the life of human beings are totally dependent on God.

Even though humanity is created from potter's clay, God has
also given to human beings a special quality. The nature of that
special quality becomes clear from 32:9, where the Qurān
declares: "He [God] breathed into him of His Spirit." Thus human
beings are constituted with a spiritual nature. Elsewhere this is
referred to by the term *fitra*, which has been defined as "a kind of
way of creating or being created."[4] The key passage is 30:29.

> Set thy face steadfast towards the religion as an Hanif, according to the
> constitution [fitra], whereon God has constituted man; there is no
> altering the creation of God, that is the standard religion, though most
> men do not know.[5]

Human beings have been constituted for God, and this spiritual
constitution is the basis of their life of obedience.

The Qurān goes on to say that God created a mate for the first
man, who is called Adam, from this essential soul.

> O mankind! Be careful of your duty to your Lord Who created you
> from a single soul, and from it created its mate, and from them twain
> hath spread abroad the multitudes of men and women (4:1).

(It is only later Muslim tradition that identifies the mate as Eve.)
After completing the task of creating the first human beings God
placed them into a garden, where humans could freely share its
fruits and its pleasures.

God gave to human beings a high calling to go with their
special constitution. The Lord of creation said to the angels: "I am
about to place a vice-regent on earth" (2:30). We read that the
angels objected to this decision because they believed that

humanity would produce a great deal of harm and bloodshed. The Creator continued with His plan saying: "Surely I know what you do not know." The term "vice-regent" is highly significant for many contemporary Muslims. They see in it a divine mandate for responsible and creative human action in developing a socially and environmentally just world. God went farther then, and "He taught Adam all the names" (2:155), which is usually interpreted to mean the animals, thus reinforcing humanity's high calling. God then, as it were, taught the angels a little lesson, when He ordered Adam to inform them of the names!

There is another side, however, to the creation of human beings, and that is the element of human frailty and mortality. In the Qurānic picture of the creation of humans, immortality is not a natural endowment. The Qurʾān affirms that "every soul shall taste of death" (21:34–35). Neither is moral perfection or holiness considered to be a natural endowment. For the Qurʾān says that humans are created "weak" (4:28), "prone to evil" (12:53), and "destined for trouble" (91:4). In fact, both the sin and the piety of a human soul are in some sense "taught" by God Himself (91:7). Thus humans are created with the potential for both good and evil. It is on this basis that great modern Muslim thinkers such as Sir Muhammad Iqbāl (d. 1938) and ʿAlī Shariati (d. 1977) have written of the great and continual human struggle between mud and spirit (Shariati) and the acceptance of error and moral failure as the price of human advance in a co-creation of the developing universe (Iqbāl).[6] What happened to human beings as the result of this blend of natural potentiality we shall take up later when we deal with sin and salvation.

God, the Creator of the universe, also made the angels, the creatures of light, to be His servants, and out of fire He made the lesser spirits called *jinn*.

Let us look next at God's continuing relation to this world that He made and that belongs to Him.

B. God's Relation to the World and Humanity

God maintains His sovereignty or "ownership" of the world by an ongoing relationship. How may we describe the relation of God to humans? We may do so through four themes:

1. Distance and nearness
2. Providence and guidance
3. Predetermination and control
4. Judgment and decision

1. Distance and Nearness:

On the one hand, Abdulla and Amina believe, God is very distant from humans. He is far above His creation and totally separate from people. Humans cannot reach God any more than they can touch a star with their fingertips. He is beyond human comprehension and beyond human influence. Nothing people do can compel God to act in a certain way. He is the Absolute Lord and Master of His creation. He is the High and Lofty One, the Utterly Beyond. Because He is so far from human beings it is not possible for them to think of having a personal association with God that is similar to human relationships.

At the same timer Abdulla and Amina know that God is very near to humanity. The Qurʾān, in fact, says that God is nearer to humans than a person's own jugular vein! His Presence is everywhere, and His mercy is in every good thing. A true human being therefore will respond gratefully to that nearness. Sūfi Muslims place great stress on the element of God's nearness, and they use it as a basis to seek a kind of spiritual oneness with God. They argue that the souls of men and women thirst for God, and God answers that need. On the other hand, orthodox Sunnī Muslims are very wary of this argument. They are urgent to preserve God's transcendence, and they argue that human beings must be content with their created role as the servants of God. They insist that the constant human tendency toward *shirk*, associating partners with God, including one's own self, must be strictly avoided!

God is very far from humanity, and yet very near to humanity. In philosophic language, could we say that God is ontologically distant, but existentially near? Because He is a dimensional other, no intimacy is possible with God. On the other hand, because God is close to humanity as its Watchful Lord obedience to Him is essential. Distance and nearness converge in the religious attitude of surrender:

I am commanded to surrender to the Lord of the Worlds (40:66).

O mankind! Ye are the poor in your relation to Allāh. And Allāh! He is the Absolute, the Owner of Praise. If He will, He can be rid of you and bring a new creation. That is not a hard thing for Allāh (35:15).

2. Providence and Guidance

The second aspect of God's relation to the world that He created may be described under the heading: providence and guidance.

a. Providence. We begin with providence. At this point we are reminded of God's "Beautiful Names." Many of them have to do with God's kindness and beneficence. We have already seen how the attribute of God's mercy is emphasized by Muslims today. God's power, prompted by mercy, takes the form of providence, that is, a caring concern for both the physical aspects of creation and for human welfare.

In this light, the Qurʾān is seen to emphasize two important things: the creation itself is good, and the Creator continues to be involved in its goodness. The Creator, Who once created, goes on creating. He is involved with nature and directs its activities. The idea is summed up in 10:4 and 13:2.

Lo! your Lord is Allāh who created the heavens and the earth in six days, then He established Himself upon the Throne, directing all things (10:4).

Allāh it is who raised up the heavens without visible support, then mounted the Throne, and compelled the sun and the moon to be of service, each runneth unto an appointed term; He ordereth the course ... Lo! herein verily are portents for people who take thought (13, 2–3).

This divine involvement in the flow of nature is linked with the words "for you." The creation is intended for humanity's good:[7]

The cattle too have we created for you; in them is warmth and profit, and from them do you eat .... And horses too, and mules, and asses, for you to ride upon and for an ornament—He created also what you know not of ... He it is who sends down water from the sky, whence you have drink, and whence the trees grow, whereby you feed your flocks. He makes corn to grow, and the olives, and the palms, and the grapes, and some of every fruit;—verily in that is a sign unto a people who reflect. And he subjected to you the night and the day, and the sun and the moon and the stars are subject to His bidding. Verily in that are signs for a people who are mindful. He it is who has subjected the sea, that ye may eat fresh flesh therefrom; and ye bring forth from it ornaments which ye wear—and that ye may search after His grace—and haply ye may give thanks. And he has cast firm mountains on the earth lest it move with you; and rivers and roads; haply ye may be guided ... But if ye would number the favours of God, yet cannot count them ... (16,5–19).

Abdulla and Amina accept these assurances reverently. They do not only believe in the powerful God of creation. They feel that the same God is powerfully and helpfully at work in their personal affairs, and they firmly believe that their daily existence, in the end, is dependent on the gracious care of God.

Like all human beings Abdulla and Amina contend with the mystery of evil, the problem of nature that often seems out of control. In April 1993, a fierce cyclone submerged thousands of Muslim children in southern Bangladesh. In March 1994, a tornado killed a number of Christian children in Georgia, U.S.A., when the walls of a church collapsed on them as they were conducting a little drama. Abdulla and Amina cannot fathom these mysteries. They believe that the entire creation is God's and that ultimately all things must come from God, even those things we call evil. But they also believe that these things cannot happen with God's desire and pleasure, and they weep over the death of the children and share the suffering of the parents. They cannot solve these apparent contradictions. When good things happen, they humbly say, al-ḥamdu lillāhi, "praise to God!" When bad things happen, they commend themselves to the will of God, and they continue to believe "that Allāh enlargeth providence for whom He wills" (39:52).

b. Guidance. God's providential care is not limited to the physical and bodily realm. It also extends to the human spirit. In current language, Allāh is wholistic in His concerns. He is the Guide for humanity's spiritual pilgrimage, as well as the Preserver of the world's physical welfare.

Humanity needs divine guidance (*hidāyat*) because of the reality of human limitation. From the story of creation we have seen the nature of those limitations. They include intellectual finiteness and moral frailty. Where then can guidance come from? Its only possible Source is God, and the Qurʾān testifies that God does provide it:

Say, verily guidance is from God. That is the true guidance (6:71).

Lo, the Guidance of Allāh *is* the Guidance (2:120).

How does God provide His guidance to humanity? He gives it first of all through instinct and reason, which God has given humans in their creation. By their means people should be able to read the signs of God in creation, and they should be able to heed the inner light of the spirit:

> Did we not assign unto him two eyes and a tongue, and two lips, and guide him to the parting of the mountain ways? But he hath not attempted the Ascent—Ah, what will convey unto thee what the Ascent is! It is to free a slave, and to feed in the day of hunger an orphan near of kin, or some poor wretch in misery, and to be of those who believe and exhort one another to perseverance, and exhort one another to pity (90:8).

Human beings, however, do not heed the external testimony of nature or the inner voice of reason and conscience, and they go continually astray. God therefore, in His mercy, has provided special guides to human beings so that their spirits may become aware of the Creator God and respond to Him in faith and obedience. He has, as it were, instituted a history of divine guidance. From time to time He sends prophets, messengers, and sacred revelations to give *hidāyat* to human beings. "Indeed, We sent forth among every nation a messenger saying, 'Serve your God and eschew idols!'" (16:38). This spiritual guidance is God's greatest gift to humanity. The concept of guidance is crucial in Islāmic thought. To understand it is to understand the faith and feeling of Abdulla and Amina. Because of its critical importance, we will deal more fully with this theme in the section on the Qurʾān, and in the section on sin and salvation.

Thus, in a variety of ways, broadly covered by the terms providence and guidance, God the Merciful and the Compassionate One reaches out to His creation, in order to preserve what belongs to Him.

3. Predetermination and Control

The world and humanity belong to God. The third aspect that expresses that principle, and the one that expresses it most strikingly, is the well-known Muslim doctrine of predestination.

The teaching basically signifies that God is in real control of His creation. How does He control it? Does His in-charge-ness imply that He has decided everything in advance, including all human actions? That is what we call predestination. Or does His in-charge-ness mean something less than total control? That implies that there is an area of human freedom. Muslims have debated the question over the centuries. Those who argue that the reality of God's rule implies absolute control have included predestination as an article of faith. Those who argue that divine control and human responsibility are both necessary for true religion have agreed that predetermination refers to the context of a human being's life, which is given to him or to her, and not to the actions themselves. In classical times Muslim opted for a strict doctrine of predestination. In modern times Muslims are choosing a combination of divine control and human responsibility.

The tension between these two positions is found in the Qurʾān itself. It teaches both divine responsibility and human responsibility. Classical theologians said that the primary emphasis is on the former; contemporary Muslims suggest that the latter is the proper reading. Sometimes the tension is found in the same verse. The famous passage, 13:11, is an example. The first part of the verse states: "Lo, Allāh changeth not the condition of a folk until they [first] change that which is in their hearts." This saying has become the Magna Carta of those who wish to arouse Muslims to a life of active dynamism and positive change. The second part of the verse, however, reads: "And if Allāh willeth misfortune for a folk, there is none that can repel it." This part suggests that God wills human destinies, and human issues are fundamentally in the hands of God.

Let us probe a little further into this most difficult of issues. On the one hand, Allāh deals with humans as though they were free. He reveals His signs and gives His guidance to humans precisely so that they can choose to do good and to reject evil. Through His messengers He calls on humans to repent and to obey, and he warns them of the wrath to come, should they resist His grace. "The truth is from your Lord; let him who will believe, and let him who will be an unbeliever" (18:30). The choice is theirs. So Abdulla and Amina, in their normal and everyday life, act as though they were in control of the situation and fully responsible.

Abdulla and Amina, however, also believe that God is in ultimate control, the Lord of nature and the Director of human affairs. There are many passages of the Qurʾān[8] that assert not only that God is in charge but that He predetermines events, and that He brings them to pass according to His knowledge and power. "Verily this (Qurʾān) is a reminder, and whoso willeth, taketh the way to his Lord; but will it ye shall not, unless God wills it" (76:29–30). This seems to put it very plainly: unless God wills something, it cannot happen. On the basis of such passages as this one, and reflecting the view that surrender implies submission to the dominant will of God, Muslim theologians in classical times developed the famous doctrine of predestination.

The main points of the traditional doctrine are these:

—God alone is Creator, and therefore all that is and all that happens is His creation; there cannot be more than one Creator;

—God, the eternal Creator, has foreordained all that is and all that happens; everything is recorded in advance in God's eternal decrees (*taqdīr*);

—What God has eternally decreed He commands and brings to pass in human history;

—Both good and evil take place by the predetermination and predestination of God;

—The faith and piety of the believer, and the unbelief and impiety of the unbeliever are equally produced by God, although the latter is not by God's pleasure;

—What reaches someone could not possibly have missed that person, and what misses persons could not possibly have reached them.

This teaching, as summed up by the classical theologian, Al-Taftāzānī, suggests that there is no way a person can interfere with or change what has been decreed by God; in fact, a person cannot will what God has not already willed. His logic is expressed in the words: "Allāh leads astray whom He wills and guides aright whom He wills, and it is not incumbent on Allāh to do that which is best for the creatures."9

This interpretation of God's predestinating relationship with human beings resulted in attitudes of fatalism and passivism that are part of the psychological heritage of many Muslims. The attitude is summed up in the famous quatrain of the Persian poet, Umar Khayyām (d.1123):[10]

> A stark and solemn truth I say
> Not as in parables to preach:
> We are but counters, all and each
> That Heaven moveth at its play.
>
> We stir awhile, as if at will,
> About the chessboards of the days
> Till in the box of death Time lays
> Our pawns, to be forever still.

Modern Muslims have taken up their cudgels against this view, partly because they are convinced that it represents an incorrect interpretation of the Qurʾān, partly to overcome the passivism that is impeding Muslim development. Mawlāna Abūl Kalām Āzād (d. 1958), the great Indian Muslim theologian, chooses to view God as the heavenly Gardener, rather than as an arbitrary Ruler. That metaphor is the better picture of God's Lordship over the worlds, in Āzād's perspective. As the heavenly Gardener God gives each created object an appropriate mold, a role in life, and guidance in that role, but He does not predestinate human actions or human destinies. A creature's life is to be worked out freely, in conformity with the capacities and imitations that it naturally has, and in response to the impulse and need for growth. Āzād therefore declares: "The meaning of taqdīr is 'to assign' a particular role to everything, whether quantitatively or qualitatively."[11] The individual is to responsibly exercise his or her role under the benevolent guidance of the Gardener-Lord. As do other modern Muslims, Āzād believes that such an interpretation of God's will is necessary both to preserve the justice and mercy of God, and to enable human morality and progress.

Nevertheless, the great tradition of predestinarian doctrine influences Abdulla and Amina, and colors their reactions. That is why Abdulla so often adds the phrase *in shāʾ Allāh*, "if God wills," to what he says. "*In shāʾ Allāh*, my child will get well." Or," *in shāʾ Allāh* we will meet again." It is true that the repetition of the *in shāʾ Allāh* has become a kind of habit for Abdulla. He does not consciously think about its meaning when he says it. If he knew about the saying reported by Imām Jaʿfar al-Sādiq, he would be taken by its wisdom: "When the Commander of the Faithful was asked about the decree [of predestination], he replied: 'It is a deep sea, venture not into it.'"[12] Abdulla and Amina are certainly not theologians, and they are not at all knowledgeable about the great debates in Islāmic thought over the tension between divine creative power and human freedom. They will not venture into this sea! They simply accept both sides of the equation without trying to solve the paradox. It is when some great joy or terrible suffering comes that the puzzle surfaces. Their answer is summed up in 9:51.

> Say: Naught befalleth us save that which Allāh hath decreed for us. He is our Protecting Friend. In Allāh let believers put their trust!

4. Judgment and Decision

Muslims believe that there is an ending as well as a beginning. What God has begun in creation, what He controls through His direction, He brings to a conclusion in judgment. This is the final aspect of God's relation to the world. At the appropriate time, God will raise up all human beings on the Day of Resurrection, will call them all to the Judgment seat, and then finally He will bring the creation process to a dramatic conclusion. It is then that the whole world, believers and unbelievers, will fully understand that they belong to God. For the unbelievers on that day, "fire will be an awning over them," but for the blessed faithful the word will be "Enter thou my Garden." Heaven and hell are articles of faith for Muslims, and both are pictured in graphic language and vivid metaphor.

We will later take up the Judgment Day in detail when we deal with the beliefs of Muslims. For the moment it is sufficient to say that Abdulla and Amina pass through this life with the realization that they must some day stand before God on a day when every soul must give account. This world must therefore be regarded as a portico and preparation ground for the next world. *The Day is coming!* Abdulla and Amina do not know what the issue on that day will be. But the fact that God will call them to account presses hard on them and compels them to deal seriously with their *islām*.

> But man would fain deny what is before him.
> He asketh: When will be this Day of Resurrection?
> But when sight is confounded
> And the moon is eclipsed

And sun and moon are united,
On that day man will cry: Whither to flee!
Alas! No refuge!
Unto thy Lord is the recourse of that day.
On that day man is told the tale of that which he hath sent before and left
    behind ...
Nearer unto thee and nearer,
Again nearer unto thee and nearer [is the doom].
Thinketh man that he is to be left aimless?

(75:5–13; 34–36)

E. H. Palmer translates the last verse: "Thinketh man that he shall be left to himself?"

C. Our Response to God

Since God does not leave us to ourselves, we must respond to Him.

"Allāh! There is no God save Him, the Alive, the Eternal" (3:2). "Praise be to Allāh, unto Whom belongeth whatsoever is in the heavens and whatsoever is in the earth. His is the praise in the Hereafter, and He is the Wise, the Aware" (4:1). "Say, O Allāh! Owner of Sovereignty ... Allāh biddeth you beware (only) of Himself. Unto Allāh is the journeying" (3:26.28). Since our journeying is to God, our life is to be inwardly a life of awareness, and outwardly a life of praise. The two words that capture the inward and the outward response are *islām*, surrender, and *ibādat*, worshipful service. But we can identify six other elements of Muslim feeling toward the Lord Who creates the world and humanity, Who is both far from us and near to us, Who rules guides the world, who predetermines it and controls it, and Who brings it to resurrection and judgment.

The first of these elements is gratitude (*shukr*). Again and again the Qurʾān calls on the believer to be thankful for God's merciful creation. Humanity's thanklessness cannot hurt God, but He is not pleased with ingratitude. Moreover, it is the root of unbelief. The term for unbelief is *kufr* and the unbeliever is a *kāfir*. The root meaning of the Arabic term is ingratitude. To be an unbeliever is to be ungrateful. Conversely, gratitude for God's signs is the essence of true faith. "If ye give thanks, He is pleased therewith" (39:7). Abdulla and Amina express their thanks to God more through language than through ritual, and the words *al-ḥamdu lillāhi,* "Praise to God," are frequently on their lips.

The second element is faith *(imān),* the other side of the coin of gratitude. Gratitude and faith are interactive. Especially when they see the birth of one new baby after another, "creation upon creation," they are to join in saying: "Such is Allāh, your Lord ... There is no God save Him" (39:6). Al-Ghazālī, the great theologian of Islām, quotes two invocations which he assigns to Adam and Abraham. They illustrate the elements of submission, penitence, trust and commitment, which constitute the religious attitude of faith, as contrasted with the formal acceptance of a set of beliefs and practices:[13]

Adam's Invocation

Allāhumma! ... Thou knowest my need, so grant me what I ask. Thou knowest what is in my soul, so forgive me my sins. Allāhumma! I ask Thee for a faith that will enliven my heart, and a perfect assurance so that I may know for sure that nothing will ever befall me save what has been written for me, O Thou possessor of majesty and honor.

Abraham's Invocation

When Abraham arose in the morning he used to say: "Allāhumma! This is a new creation, so may it open with my being obedient to Thee, and may it close with Thy pardoning me and being well pleased with me. Provide for me in it some good Thou wilt accept from me, increasing it and multiplying it for me, and forgive me for whatever evil I do therein. Thou art the Forgiving, the Merciful, the Beloved, the Generous."

The third element is remembrance and worship, which are virtually identical. The spiritual concept of remembering (*dhikr*) is highly emphasized in Islām. There is an interactive relationship between God's remembering of us, God's reminding us, our remembering of God, and our reminding of each other. "And do thou ... remember thy Lord within thyself humbly and with awe, below thy breath, at morn and evening. And be thou not of the neglectful" (7:205). Remembrance leads to worship and is part of worship. Worship, in turn, is really the reason that God created the *jinn* and humans—"that they might worship me" (51:56). Remembering has become a key element in Muslim devotion, and the five daily prayers are only one expression of it. Sūfi Muslims particularly treasure the concept and practice.

The fourth element is the fear of God, which is an inclusive idea. Since Muslims cherish an overwhelming sense of God, it is natural to speak of the fear of God. This does not imply fear in the sense of being afraid, although that emotion cannot be eliminated. It means rather a holy fear, a combination of profound awe and overwhelming respect that maintains the awareness of God in a seemingly godless world. "They only are the (true) believers whose hearts feel fear when Allāh is mentioned..." (8:2). Perhaps at no time do Muslims feel this emotion more deeply than when they attend the pilgrimage to Mecca.

The fifth element is the attitude of piety (*taqwā*) that flows from the fear of God. In Arabic the words fear and piety stem from the same root term which means to keep, to preserve. It is up to faithful humans to keep and to preserve the honor of God, and they do so by leading a pious life. There are important ritual expressions of Muslim piety, which we will discuss later, but *taqwā* is an ethical idea rather than a ritual idea. It is therefore coupled with the word *birr*, righteousness, and a classic passage in the Qurʾān puts the two together in a powerful manner (2:177):

It is not righteousness [*birr*] that ye turn your faces to the East and the West; but righteous is he that believeth in Allāh and the Last Day and the angels and the Scriptures and the Prophets: and giveth his wealth for love of Him, to kinsfolk and to orphans and the needy and the wayfarer and to those who ask, and to set slaves free; and observeth proper worship and payeth the poor-due. And to those who keep their treaty when they make one, and the patient in tribulation and adversity and time of stress. Such are they who are sincere. Such are the God-fearing [*taqwā*].

The sixth and final element is obedient service. The glory of humanity is to be the servants of God. Do not aspire to more than that, for in being a servant of God you have achieved the highest thing. Amina, we have seen, means faithful one. Abdulla means servant of God. Amina and Abdulla are the faithful servants of God. They do not wish to be less than that, nor more than that. The frame of reference for their obedience is the law of God, for God the Master has prescribed a way of life, the path, the clear road that believers should tread (*sharīʿa*). In the first chapter of the Qurʾān Muslims pray: "Lead us in the straight path, not the path of those who go astray." It is in following the straight path that one becomes a vice-regent of God. And the straight path that Muslims regard as congruent with the will of God for life in this world is the *sharīʿa*, the law of Islām. With that final thought, we leave our discussion of the Muslim doctrine of God.

I have said that my Muslim friends believe in God, and I have further said that they believe that we and the world belong to God. This is the substance of the Muslim confession *lā ilāha illā Allāh*. Professor Louis Gardet has well summarized Muslim faith and feeling in regard to God, and in concluding I cannot do better than to repeat his compelling words:[14]

> What remains affirmed is the faith in God most High Who speaks to men by His prophets and apostles, revealing no more of Himself than the "most beautiful Names," whereby He indicates and conceals Himself... A faith which does not require God to be explicit about Himself, while it holds fast [to His Word] and resigns itself [to Him]—in a unique act which bears witness both to the divine omnipotence and to the responsibility of the "slaves." The inner attitude of the believer is rightly then a total and confident surrender of the self ... to God to Whom one puts no questions, but Whom one knows according to His Word, to be the just Judge and supreme Help ... This, first and foremost, is what the Muslim has in his heart when he pronounces the name Allāh.

We may find another summary of the Muslim emotion regarding Allāh in the Qurʾān itself:

> "... But only as seeking the face of his Lord Most High. And surely in the end he shall be well content" (92:20).[15]

Let us now turn to the second part of the Muslim confession: *wa muhammadu rasūl Allāh*, which means "and Muhammad is the messenger of Allāh." As we do so, we will not only discover where the Muslim faith in Allāh originated, but we will also meet the Founder of historical Islām in the person of the Man of Mecca.

Notes

[1]Muslims and the Uniform Civil Code," *Religion and Society*, Vol. XXVI, No 4, December 1979, pp. 90f.

[2]Gibb develops this theme in his seminal study, "The Structure of Religious Thought in Islām," *Studies on the Civilization of Islām*, ed. by S. Shaw and W. R. Polk (Princeton: Princeton University Press, 1962), pp. 176–218, first published in *Muslim World*, Vol.38 (1948). He says, p.207, that "by eliminating any relation

between God and man, it [Muslim theology] dammed up the springs of religious experience."

[3]Translated by E. H. Palmer, *The Koran (Qurʾān)*, (London: Oxford, 1900).

[4]D. B. MacDonald, *EI²* , II, p.932.

[5]Palmer, op. cit.

[6]Cf. Ali Shariati, "Anthropology: The Creation of Man and the Contradiction of God and Iblis, or Spirit and Clay," *On the Sociology of Islām*, tr. by H. Algar (Berkeley: Mizan Press, 1979), pp. 88–96; Sir Muhammad Iqbal, *The Reconstruction of Religious Thought in Islām* (Lahore: Sh.Muhammad Ashraf, 1962), pp. 82–88. Iqbal says that "Man's first act of disobedience was also his first act of free choice" (p. 85).

[7]Palmer, op. cit.

[8]Qurānic passages cited in support of the doctrine of predestination include: 6:39,126,150; 11:118–19; 16:38; 37:94; 58:22; 76:29–30. Those cited in support of human free will include: 6:149; 18:11; 18:28 40:43; 53:32.

[9]E. E. Elder, tr., *A Commentary on the Creed of Islam*, p. 89. Cf. pp. 80–98 on "The Creator and the Actions of His Creatures."

[10]John A. Williams, "The Will of God," *Themes of Islāmic Civilization* (Berkeley: University of California Press, 1971) pp. 184f. Williams gives a broad selection of classical passages on the issue of predestination (pp. 133–90). For an opposing, modern view, cf. Daud Rahbar, *God of Justice* (Leiden: E. J. Brill, 1960), especially pp. 141–79, where he argues against the theory that God's mercy and love are capricious.

[11]Mawlana Abul Kalam Azad, *The Tariuman al-Qurʾān*, Vol.I, *Sūrat-ul-Fātihā*, tr. by Syed Abdul Latif (Bombay: Asia Publishing House), p. 27. Cf. especially his stimulating section on Divine Providence: Rubūbiyāt (pp. 17–44).

[12]A. J. Arberry, ed., *Islām. Muhammad and His Religion* (New York: The Liberal Arts Press, 1958), pp. 153f. The quotation is from a Shīʿite tractate, Ibn Bābawaih's *Risālat al-Iʿtiqādāt*, pp. 100–102.

[13]Ibid., pp. 237f. The quotation is from al-Ghazāliī's *Ihyā ʿUlūm ad-Dīn* (Halabi edition: Cairo, 1929, pp. 284ff.)

[14]*EI²*, I. p. 417.

[15]Palmer, op. cit.

5

My Muslim Friend Honors the Prophet

Muhammad! The name stands in the most honored place in Islām. It stands beside the name of God Himself. "There is no deity except Allāh, and Muhammad is the messenger of Allāh." As I introduce you to my Muslim friends, I would like you to consider the fact that they honor Muhammad above all other human beings. The admiration is overwhelming. It is so strong that it cannot be expressed. Yet it is expressed in countless ways and in numberless forms. It is true that Muhammad was only a human being, yet what a human he was! One Indian Muslim poet summed it up when he said:[1]

> Certainly Adam is God's special friend, Moses the one with whom God spake, Jesus is even the spirit of God—but you are something different!

What is that difference that separates Muhammad from all other humans, in the Muslim view? It comes down to two things: a quality of personality and a specialty of function. We will begin our consideration with the aspect of Muhammad's function.

"Guide us on the straight path" is the fifth verse in the famous opening prayer of the Qurʾān, the first sūra, which is repeated regularly by Muslims. In those words the Muslim believer asks God for what he/she considers to be the greatest of all human needs—clear direction for the path of life. The promise of a divine answer to that prayer also comes from within the Qurʾān, where God declares that He Himself will be the Guide [al-Hādī] for humanity. "Allāh sufficeth for a Guide and Helper" (25:31). "Say: Lo! the guidance of Allāh (Himself) is Guidance!" (2:120). "Our Lord is He Who gave everything its creation, then guided it aright" (20:50). God's guidance, that is, His reminder of who He is and what He desires, is His gift to His creation. In fact, it is His greatest gift and the ultimate token of His mercy. In this way, divine mercy and divine guidance are intimately linked in Islām. But how does guidance come?

It comes through *prophets* whom God sends with His message, and has graciously sent from the time of Adam. "We gave them of our mercy" (20:50), says the Qurʾān, speaking of prophets. The greatest of them, and the last of them, is Muhammad of whom God says: "We have sent thee not save as a mercy for the people" (21:107). Muslims believe that God has chosen and called Muhammad to be the final and universal guide for humanity. He has not only given him the command: "Call them to guidance!" (18:58), but He has also given to Muhammad the divine message that provides the content of the guidance. Thus, through Muhammad God has revealed both His will and His compassion for humanity, by granting the spiritual instruction that all humans require. Muhammad is only the channel for that final revelation of God, but that position gives him a crucial role in Islām and in the respect of all Muslims. In understanding Abdulla's faith and feeling, and that of the host of other Muslims, it is clearly necessary to give special consideration to that person of whom it is said:

> And those who believe and do good works, and believe in that which is revealed unto Muhammad ... He riddeth them of their ill-deeds and improveth their state (47:2).

> He [Allāh] it is Who hath sent His messenger with the guidance and the religion of truth, that He may cause it to prevail over all religion ... Muhammad is the messenger of Allāh! (48:29)

Abdulla loves Muhammad not only because of his special function, but also because of the quality of his character and personality. The name *muhammad*, like its shortened form *ahmad*, means "the praised one." Muhammad is the praised one, praised not only for his vocation, but also for his character. The Qurʾān calls him—and Abdulla reverently agrees—"a noble pattern ... for all who hope in God" (33:21). To follow him, and to imitate him, is to be authentically on the path of God, and it is every devout Muslim's personal goal.

The affection for Muhammad is expressed in various ways—by the remembering of whatever he said and did (*Hadīth*), by the celebration of his birthday (*mīlād al-nabī*), by the stories of his exploits that are recited in public and in homes (*mawlūds*), but above all by the calling down of blessing upon the Prophet and his family (*tasliya*). You may have noticed an unusual phenomenon that takes place in Muslim groups whenever the

77

name of Muhammad is mentioned. A sound ripples through the audience, the recitation of the Arabic phrase *sallā ᵓllāhu ᶜalā ᵓn-nabī*, that is, "May God bless the Prophet!" When Muhammad's name appears in print in English-language publications, four letters, *pbuh*, are added in parentheses behind his name. The letters stand for "Peace be upon him!" The calling down of God's blessing upon the Prophet is not only an act of due reverence, but it is also an action that brings great personal merit:[2]

> And make our calling down of blessing on him a key, and by it open to us, O Lord, the veil of acceptance, and accept, by the blessing of my Beloved ... the litanies and vocations which I now recite, and my love and magnifying of Thyself.

The respect for Muhammad's role and character is so pronounced that it makes possible the saying: "To understand Islām is to understand Muhammad." The saying must be guarded by adding that Muslims do not believe that the Prophet Muhammad originated Islām. Of course, the historical religion that the world calls Islām can be traced to the advent of Muhammad on the global scene. But Muslims believe that God is the founder of Islām, and the religion of Islām began at the beginning of creation, with the first human beings. Since that time, God instils true religion into the heart of every human being at birth. The Creator God is properly the originator of *islām*. But, alas! human beings go astray, some as erring Muslims, some as members of other religions, some as secularists or even atheists. So God, through His prophets, calls humanity back to true surrender and obedience. He has done this preeminently through Muhammad who restored true religion to the world, gave it new life, formed and exemplified it, and provided the necessary leadership for its revitalized existence. In a sense, therefore, we can say that to understand Islām is to understand Muhammad. Abdulla would not put it quite that way. He would find the phrase slightly off the mark. He would prefer to say: "Muhammad proclaimed *islām* truly and practiced it purely."

Orthodox Muslims resist the trend to turn respect for Muhammad into the veneration of Muhammad. The followers of one noted reformer, ᶜAbd al-Wahhāb, even destroyed the shrine of the prophet Muhammad in Medina to negate such veneration (1804). Yet the respect continues at profound levels of

78

appreciation. When my family and I left South India after 23 years of living in a Muslim village, the Muslim youth society of the area sponsored a farewell and asked me to give an address. They assigned the topic, "What do you think of Muhammad?" The highest tribute that they could pay a friend was to ask him to speak about Muhammad. After I arrived at my new place of residence in Canada, the Muslim Association of the area asked me to speak at its annual celebration of the birthday of the Prophet. They selected the topic. Once again it was, "What do you think of Muhammad?" For Muslims that is the happiest of themes, and the natural and simplest answer that they themselves will give to that question is: "Muhammad is the Messenger of Allāh!"

A. Prophets and Books Before Muhammad

When God created the world, as we have already noted, the truth of Islām was present. But because of human weakness and Satanic influence, the world from time to time neglected or turned away from true religion. God mercifully sent prophets and apostles whose task was to preach the Unity of God and to warn people of His impending judgment. While these prophets were frequently rejected by the people, God vindicated them by punishing the rebellious and unbelievers. Through some of these chosen ones, though not all, God revealed sacred scriptures to confirm the oral preaching.

The names of these prophets and apostles, as many as are known, are revered by Muslims. In the Qurʾān, 28 such prophets are mentioned, of which 21 are also found in the Bible (18 in the Old Testament; three in the New Testament). Some of them have particularly high standing among Muslims, including Adam; Noah; Abraham and his sons, Ishmael and Isaac; Moses; Jesus; and, of course, Muhammad. The word *nabī* (prophet) is added to the end of a name when it is spoken; sometimes the word *rasūl* (messenger) is added. Since the subject of the prophets is taken up in detail in chapter 10, we will not say more than this. A preliminary word, however, must be added in regard to the sacred books of Islām.

Four of the known prophets of Islām were given sacred books that are now in existence, namely, Moses, David, Jesus, and

Muhammad. The names of the books revealed to them are:

    a. The *Tawrāt* (Torah) - the book given to the Jews through Moses; the Pentateuch.

    b. The *Zabūr* (Psalms) - the book given to the Jews through David.

    c. The *Injīl* (Gospel) - the book given to the Jews through Jesus; the Evangel.

    d. The *Qurʾān* - the book given to the Arabs and to the world through Muhammad; the "Recital."

In Muslim opinion, there may have been other prophets and other sacred books than those noted above. In fact, in the madrasa where Abdulla attended religious school, he was taught that there were thousands of prophets and as many as 104 sacred scriptures. But the ones that Abdulla recognizes and respects today are those we have listed. In that listing, as we have already indicated, the final prophet and the final revelation are Muhammad and the Qurʾān respectively. Let us now turn to the background of Muhammad's appearance on the world scene.

B. Pre-Islāmic Arabia

Arabia! The word conjures many images. Only in modern times has it received the adjective "Saudi". The term "Saudi" refers to the current ruling family. The ancient name of this great peninsula that bridges Europe, Africa, and Asia is simply Arabia. A huge area (820,000 sq. miles), it nevertheless has a relatively small population (16,500,000). In modern times, the country has leaped from a "camel economy" to an "oil economy" in less than 50 years, from a relatively sleepy and poverty-stricken condition to the status of a bustling modern nation. Yet even now the old traditions continue, especially among the nomadic section of the populace called *badwā*, or bedouin.

Many people are accustomed to think of Arabia as one large sand dune, but the country has distinct topographical areas with differing features. The well-known regions of sandy desert, the "empty quarters," do exist. But there are also the rich oases, noted for the production of dates. In addition, the higher valleys along the Red Sea provide farming areas that produce millet, wheat, and vegetables. The southern part of the peninsula, known as Yemen, receives almost tropical rains. Finally there are the cities—the holy cities of Mecca where Muhammad was born, Medina where Muhammad is buried, the modern capital city of Riyadh that was only a village at the time of Muhammad, and Jidda, the thriving port city of Mecca.

As we look back to the time of Muhammad, we see the same scene, with the addition that caravan routes crisscrossed Arabia. At that time, an important route passed from the south of Arabia through Mecca and Medina to the trade centers of the Middle East in Egypt, Palestine, and Syria. We cannot say, therefore, that the Arabian peninsula was unknown to the rest of the world, but it was relatively isolated. At the southern end was the ancient, settled culture of Yemen. The northern areas bordered on the centers of civilization in the Middle East, all more or less under jurisdiction of the Eastern Roman Empire, centered at Constantinople (now Istanbul in Turkey). To the immediate East lay Persia, and its rich heritage. Thus the edges of Arabia were better known, while the interior had something of a hidden quality. No one could have guessed that from that region Arab energy was ready to explode.

Muhammad's dates are A.D. 570–632. At the time of his birth a great power conflict swirled around the edges of Arabia. The two great powers of the day were Persia and Byzantium. Persia (Iran) had been a dominant world force for more than a thousand years. Its Zoroastrian religion was based on a theory of eternal cosmic struggle between good and evil, light and darkness. It had effectively resisted the new religion of Christianity that had swept across the Mediterranean world. The other great power was Byzantium, or the Eastern Roman Empire, a Christian Empire founded by Constantine the Great after his conversion, in A.D. 325. While western Rome collapsed, eastern Rome or Byzantium flourished. These two—Persia and Byzantium—were locked in a furious struggle for ascendancy. First one, then the other won out as their armies periodically engaged with each other and fell back exhausted. As they fought, the Arabs were caught between these great events. On the northern borders, Arab tribes (Ghassanids) lined up with Byzantium, but in the East the border tribes (Lakhimids) favored Persia. In the interior of Arabia, however, life went on in traditional patterns. What was the shape of pre-Islāmic Arab culture?

Later Muslims have called the period before Muhammad the *jāhiliyya*, that is, the time of darkness when the light of Islām was not yet present, and there was great cultural backwardness. It was,

81

to be sure, a somewhat primitive age, but the existing Arab culture provided the matrix for the birth of historic Islām, and its cultural patterns inevitably influenced later developments. Some of the Arabs lived in permanent homes in valleys, where they carried on farming; some lived in towns and villages, and were active in commerce; and some were nomads who moved from oasis to oasis with their herds of animals. Their social organization was tribal, and there was the highest respect for blood ties. Much rivalry existed between the different tribes and clans, which was controlled by customs such as a sacred month in which no warfare was permitted. In fact, the people were marked by an interesting combination of individual freedom and regard for the established custom that ensured their survival in a testing environment. Above all, they were realists and pragmatists. Love of combat, respect for courage, an appreciation of poetry, and generous hospitality were other characteristics of Muhammad's people.

Religiously most of the people were polytheists and nature worshippers. They worshipped sun, moon, and star gods; wood and stone gods; and three female goddesses (al-Lāt, al-ᵓUzzā, and Manāt) whom they regarded as the daughters of a superior deity that some identified with Allāh. The use of sacred objects and magic was common, and the activity of lesser spirits called *jinn* (cf. genie) was accepted. The city of Mecca was a religious center. It was the home of the Kaᶜba, a cube structure that housed many idols, including the stone statue of the god Hubal. During the annual festival month many pilgrims from all parts of Arabia visited the city and the shrine, walking around the Kaᶜba and its famous black stone. The sense of the afterlife was rather hazy. Morality was a customary matter rather than being connected with religion. Male-female relationships were rather easygoing, baby daughters were occasionally buried in the sand when there were too many mouths to feed, and at Muhammad's time there was a growing division between the wealthy few and the many poor. However, as noted earlier, a few people of a higher spiritual standard had also arisen. They were called *hanīfs*, a term which means "those who turn away." They had begun to turn away from the prevalent polytheism to the worship of the Most High God, whom they called Allāh. The Qurᵓān commends *hanīf* religion as the true, natural monotheism, and it associates the term very closely with Abraham and his faith.

The latter point brings us to a consideration of the Jewish and

Christian presence in Arabia at the time of Muhammad. The Jewish population was considerable as the result of repeated emigrations from Palestine. The city of Yathrib or Medina had three large Jewish tribes who represented a major section of the populace, and there were settlements in other areas as well. In the earlier part of the century (510) a short-lived Jewish kingdom had even been established in the Yemeni area of the peninsula, which had allied itself with Persia. The Jews were engaged in both agriculture and commerce. Jewish ideas—the unity of God, law, prophets, sacred books, festivals and ritual practices—were well-known in Arabia, and the engagement with the Jews was to be an important element in Muhammad's career.

The nature of the Christian presence is less certain. There do not appear to have been many Christians within interior Arabia, although some individuals may have filtered in from the edges. In the southern part of Arabia, at Najran, a Christian governor named Abraha, supported by Ethiopia, set up a Christian center (525), replacing the Jewish kingdom, and later Muhammad had relations with this group. Christian ideas, however, were not well-known, and the New Testament was not yet translated into Arabic.

At Muhammad's time the life of the Christian church in general was characterized by controversies over the personality of Jesus Christ, which had resulted in major divisions: Orthodox (Byzantium); Monophysite (Ethiopia, Egypt, parts of Palestine); and Nestorian (parts of Syria, Persia).[3] These disputes had great political impact, as well as religious, and they seriously weakened the church. The partially Christianized Ghassanid Arab tribes in the north and the Lakhimids in the East had been drawn into both the religious and political aspects of the controversies. In addition to these major groups, there were minor sectarian and apocalyptic groups. Finally, the church also faced the problem of moral corruption at the court and superficial popular piety at grassroots levels. The form of Christianity that Muhammad seems to have personally observed was the monastic type, and the Qurʾān speaks positively about the character of monks. In sum, the number of Christians in Arabia was few, and the Christian message around Arabia was confused.

Abdulla and Amina have only a limited interest in the condition of pre-Islāmic Arabia. Like other Muslims they do not believe that the cultural and religious context of Arabia had a causative or molding effect upon the revelations that Muhammad received.

Those revelations represent the eternal Word of God, and Muslims reject the notion that God's unchanging Word was formed by or influenced by human history. It was rather delivered within history, and the cultural and religious environment provided only the *occasions* for the revelation of God. Muslims, however, do recognize that the nonrevelatory development of the early Muslim community was shaped by its living experience with its environment. On the whole, Abdulla and Amina simply look at the pre-Islāmic period as the time of *jāhilīyyat*, which was successfully overcome, and now they and all Muslims must unite to dispel the equally distressing "jāhilīyyats" of the present age.

There is one critical element in the pre-Islāmic period, however, that is of vital importance for Abdulla and Amina. That is the tradition of Abraham-Hagar-Ishmael that lives in pious memory and that is part of the religious story-telling of Islām. Muslims view the Arab people as the descendants of the family of Abraham through his son Ishmael. Tradition has it that after the dispute with Sara, Abraham, "the friend of God," came down to Arabia with Hagar and their son, Ishmael. There father and son together built the foundations of the Kaᶜba.[4] Abraham's footprint is still to be seen there, and Ishmael's burial place is beside the Kaᶜba! Then, after Abraham abandoned Hagar and Ishmael, God delivered them in a special way. As Hagar in her distress ran back and forth between two hills, God's angel struck the well of Zem Zem that continues to flow in the holy shrine at Mecca, and her running back and forth is emulated by every pilgrim to the Kaᶜba. Ishmael then settled in Arabia where he intermarried and went on to become one of the forefathers of the Arab peoples. Although the form of the tradition varies, all Muslims feel a special kinship with Abraham, Hagar, and Ishmael. In the Qurʾān Abraham holds a prominent place as an authentic *muslim*, whose pure monotheism represents the true pattern to which all later religionists should return. In the case of Arab Muslims, the felt kinship is ethnic as well as religious, and Ishmael is regarded as a physical as well as a spiritual ancestor.

And so now we come to Mecca, the birthplace of the Prophet Muhammad. Imagine any busy city that combines both business and religious activities, and it summarizes Mecca. It was an influential center for that time and place. There a tribe named Quraysh held the most prominent position in the city. Its members were political and commercial leaders, and they also held the privilege of caring for the important functions at the Kaᶜba shrine.

It was from that tribe that Muhammad was born around the year A.D. 570.

C. Muhammad and His Early Life

Although there are many stories about Muhammad's family, his birth and his early life, we cannot discover much information from the Qurʾān itself. The information was stored up in the memory of his companions and followers. Some of it was expressed in Ḥadīth, the traditions of Islām. More of it was gathered in *sīra*, that is, biographies of the Prophet. The earliest major biography (Ibn Isḥāq) comes from a period at least a century after the death of the Prophet.[5]

Family relationships are very important for Muslims, and they affect both public and private life. Genealogies are therefore cherished information, and this is true also of the genealogy of Muhammad. It is elaborated extensively, and the information that it contains is a door to the understanding of many of the events that took place in early Islām. Muhammad's immediate relatives were the following:

> Great-grandfather—Hāshim [Clan head; the clan had a rivalry with the cousin clan of Ummaya]

> Grandfather—ʿAbd al-Muttalib [wife Fatima; guardian of Muhammad when his father died]

> Father—ʿAbdulla [died before Muhammad was born; Muhammad was called Ibn Abdulla, son of Abdulla]

> Mother—ʿAmina [died when Muhammad was six years old]

> Uncle—Abū Tālib [one of several of Abdulla's brothers; became Muhammad's guardian after his grandfather died][6]

It is clear from the above that Muhammad had a troubled youth. His father died on a trading trip, and Muhammad never saw him. His widowed mother had only modest means and depended on the help of Muhammad's grandfather, ʿAbd al-Muttalib. Until about the age of five he was given into the care of a bedouin family outside the perimeters of Mecca, where he breathed the healthier air of the countryside and where he learned its pure Arabic. In his sixth year his mother and he went to Medina to visit relatives. There his mother sickened and died, and Muhammad was brought back by a servant. His grandfather took charge of the orphaned and poverty-stricken child, but two years later tragedy struck again when ʿAbd al-Muttalib died. Finally, it was his uncle Abū Tālib, who came to the rescue and—without ever becoming a Muslim himself—remained as Muhammad's firm protector to the end of his life. Muhammad never forgot his childhood experience as a poor orphan, and later he constantly called his followers to compassionate concern for the orphans and the poor.

There are many pious traditions and legends associated with the birth of the Prophet Muhammad. In one way or another they all make the point that Muhammad was specially chosen by God and that his character developed in a special way. Most Muslims agree that his birth was the fulfillment of a prophecy of the Qurʾān, where Jesus announces: "O Children of Israel! Lo! I am the messenger of Allāh unto you, confirming that which was (revealed) before me in the Torah, and bringing good tidings of a messenger who cometh after me, whose name is the Praised One [ahmad]" (61:6). "Praised one," it may be recalled, is the meaning of the name Muhammad, of which Ahmad is an abbreviated form.

As Muhammad grew up he became involved in his family's trading activities. He may have made some journeys to Syria and Palestine, although there is no positive evidence that he did so. The extent of his formal education is a disputed question. There is a phrase in the Qurʾān (7:157) that refers to Muhammad that may be translated either as "the Prophet who can neither read nor write," or as "the Prophet who is not of those who read the scriptures." Most Muslims prefer the rendering "illiterate" for the key word ummī, rather than the possibility of "untutored."[7] In any event, there was no doubt about Muhammad's sagacity, and this issue did not affect his standing in the community, which was high. He was known for his efficiency and reliability. A story that circulates the Muslim world underlines his reputation. It relates to the rebuilding of the Kaʿba that was taking place at the time. The question was: who would replace the sacred Black Stone into its position in the corner of the building? It was a political as well as a religious question, for there was a dispute among four leading clans as to who would have the honor and privilege. When Muhammad came by, his advice was sought. He called for a blanket, placed the stone in its center, asked each of the clan heads to lift one of the corners, had the stone carried to the Kaᶜba, and then he himself placed it into position. He was Al-Amīn, the "trustworthy one."

Muhammad's whole personal life, including his economic condition, experienced a considerable change for the better when he married a senior merchant-lady named Khadīja, for whom he had been working. This twice-married, well-to-do widow was 15 years older than Muhammad, but the age differential was not a factor in the happy marriage. Khadīja presented Muhammad with several children, of whom four daughters survived to bring joy to his life. Moreover, she provided him with steady employment and financial security. For the next 15 years Muhammad conducted commercial activities in her business and generally led a normal life. Khadīja was later to become Muhammad's first convert, and she supported him with strong conviction in the events that were soon to take place. During her lifetime Muhammad never took another wife.

Two other individuals that were to be important for Muhammad also became part of the family scene. Khadīja and Muhammad had two sons, Qasim and ᶜAbdulla, but they both died in infancy. The lack of a son was to be a great personal grief for Muhammad throughout his life, but it was offset by the adoption of two young men. The first was ᶜAlī, the son of Abū Tālib, and therefore Muhammad's cousin. He not only adopted him as a son, but he also gave his daughter, Fāṭima, in marriage to ᶜAlī. Their two sons, Ḥasan and Ḥusain, provided Muhammad with male grandchildren. ᶜAlī himself became one of the great leaders of Islām. The second young man was Zayd ibn Ḥārith, who was a slave of Khadīja from the partly Christianized tribe of Kalb in Syria. Khadīja presented him to Muhammad as a gift, and Muhammad gave him his freedom and adopted him as a son.

Everything was in place for Muhammad to lead a comfortable and settled life—a family, employment, security, community respect. But that life was not to remain an ordinary one. There was something pressing and disturbing in Muhammad's heart. His restlessness took him frequently to solitary places around Mecca where he spent long hours in meditation. We cannot tell what all the reasons were for that feeling. Was it simply his natural tendency? Was it personal dissatisfaction with the course of his life? Was it unhappiness over the religious standards of the Arabs? Was it anger over the deteriorating social conditions? Was it influenced by his experience with Ḥanīfs, Jews, or Christians? What was it? Something drove him to a barren cave on Mt. Hira, outside of Mecca.[8]

Abdulla is quite sure of what was happening—he believes that God was at work in this process. God was preparing to give His greatest gift of guidance to humanity, and Muhammad was his chosen servant for that purpose. Then came the moment that changed the course of human history.

D. The Call of Muhammad

Muhammad's biographer, Ibn Ishāq, tells how the moment came. Muhammad, then about 40 years of age (610), was asleep at Mt. Hira in the sacred month of Ramadān. His wife also was in the general area. It was night. Suddenly the angel Gabriel (Jibrīl) appeared to him. The angel showed him a cloth upon which was some writing, and commanded Muhammad to recite the words:

> Recite!: In the Name of thy Lord who created, created man of a
> blood-clot;
> Recite!: And thy Lord is the Most Generous,
>   Who taught by the pen,
>   taught men that he knew not. (96:1–5)

Then Gabriel left, and Muhammad awoke from his vision. He was deeply troubled. He feared that he would be classified as some sort of a soothsayer, or worse, as a man possessed by an evil spirit. He even contemplated self-destruction:[9]

> Woe is me, poet or possessed—Never shall the Quraysh say this of me!
> I will go to the top of the mountain and throw myself down that I may
> kill myself and gain rest.

As he walked up the mountainside, Muhammad heard a voice from heaven saying: "O Muhammad, you are the Apostle of God, and I am Gabriel!" Muhammad looked up and saw the angel, this time as a man standing on the horizon. No matter in which direction he turned, he kept on seeing him. Muhammad stood transfixed until the vision left him. Then he returned to Khadīja, even more troubled than before.

After the first shock of the story, Khadīja comforted Muhammad, declaring that he was surely chosen to be a prophet for their people. Quickly she hurried to a cousin named Waraqa, a Hanīf with possible Christian leanings, and a person in whom she had confidence. He confirmed her hope and commanded her, "Bid him be of good heart!" Later Waraqa is reported to have met Muhammad personally and encouraged him. He suggested that Muhammad was having the same experience as Moses and that, like Moses, he too would experience much difficulty in his career.

After the mountain experience Muhammad returned to Khadīja. From this point the precise sequence of events is uncertain. At some point Muhammad sat trembling and in a state of exhaustion, and he asked Khadīja to wrap him in a cloak. Then came the words:

> O thou who are covered! rise and warn! thy Lord magnify! and thy garments purify! and abomination shun! and grant not favors to gain increase! and for thy Lord await! (74:1–7).

Thus at the beginning of his prophetic career Muhammad received two fundamental commands that were now to determine his life: to recite that which was revealed to him, and to warn humanity of the reality of God.

Once a year, all over the world Muslims gather on the 27th day of Ramadān to celebrate that first "night of power," or "night of destiny" (*lailat al-qadr*). The Qurʾān itself speaks of that historic night:

> Behold, We sent it down on the Night of Power;
> And what shall teach thee what is the Night of Power?
> The Night of Power is better than a thousand months;
>> in it the angels and the Spirit descend,
>> by the leave of their Lord, upon every command.
> Peace it is, till the rising of the dawn (97:1–5).

And to that Abdulla and his friends say, Amen! and Amen!, as they sit outside and look up at the dark sky and twinkling stars.

The Night of Power now became the Night of Destiny as Muhammad took his message into Mecca.

Notes

[1]Alam Muzaffarnagari, in Annemarie Schimmel, *And Muhammad is His Messenger* (Chapel Hill: University of North Carolina Press, 1985), p. 64.

[2]Padwick, Muslim *Devotions*, p. 162.

[3]The complex question that the Christian church faced in its teaching about Jesus was how the divine and human natures of Jesus were related to each other. The answer was considered important because of its connection with the doctrine of salvation. Monophysites emphasized a fusion into one nature, in which the divine aspect dominated. Nestorians stood for a union of the two natures which kept them distinct, upholding the human aspect. Orthodox held to the middle ground of one personality with "two natures, without confusion, without change, without division, without separation." The Council of Chalcedon (431) upheld the Orthodox view. The problem was that Orthodox Byzantium attempted to impose the decision on the other parties, causing deep resentments that lie behind many of the conflicts of this period. Cf. A. C. McGiffert, *A History of Christian Thought*, Vol. I (New York: Charles Scribner's, 1932), pp. 276–90, for a full discussion of the issues.

[4]An alternative legend says that Adam established the foundations of the Ka'ba, and Abraham rebuilt them. Cf. A. J. Wensinck,"Ka'ba," *Encyclopaedia of Islam*, First edition, IV (London: E. J. Brill, 1938), pp. 191–95.

[5]In Addition to Ibn Ishāq (d. A.D. 767), Al-Wākidī (d. A.D. 874) and al-Tabarī (d. A.D.923), constitute standard *sira*. The modern Muslim biography of widest circulation is Muhammad Haykal, *The Life of Muhammad* (North American Trust Publications, 1976). W. M. Watt, *Muhammad, Prophet and Statesman* (London: Oxford Press, 1961), an abridgement of the author's *Muhammad at Mecca* and *Muhammad at Medina*, provides easy access to the life of the Prophet.

[6]Maxime Rodinson, *Mohammed*, tr. by A. Carter (London: Penguin, 1971), p. 325, gives a full genealogy of Muhammad, together with much other valuable information on the background to Muhammad's life.

[7]Pickthall, *Koran*, p. 133, fn.l.

[8]For a psychological study of Muhammad's religious experience, cf. Tor Andrae, *Mohammed, the Man and His Faith* (London: George Allen & Unwin, 1936).

[9]A. Guillaume, tr. *The Life of Muhammad. A Translation of Ibn Ishāq's Sīrat Rasūl Allāh* (Lahore: Oxford University Press, 1967), p. 106.

6

The Prophet in Mecca: Struggle and Trial

A. The Message is Proclaimed

It is fair time in Mecca! Imagine the sight! The market is jammed with people, many from distant places. There is hustle and bustle as business flourishes and conversation goes on everywhere. Here are the vegetables: cucumbers, pumpkins, onions, and garlic. Nearby are the sweetmeats. There is the place to buy milk, and over there is the mutton shed. Yonder are the aromatics from Yemen and the spices from Hadramaut. The leather salesman is busy. So is the gold vendor with his wares from the ancient mines of Mecca. Farther out you can see the place to buy fresh young date palms. Dates are everywhere! In the distance you can hear the bawling of the animals that are for sale. An enterprising man is selling pots of fresh water from Zem Zem. The lanes to the sanctuary of the Ka^{c}ba are jammed. The statues of the gods and goddesses fill and surround the shrine, and people are busy with their rituals. The pressure for food and lodging is great. In the better buildings nearby, some multi-storied, leading businessmen and town leaders carry on their transactions. The people of Mecca seem happy at the moment, despite some real problems. The annual fair is going well. Into that busy scene walks Muhammad, burdened with a message that he claims is from God.

Those who have made public speeches or homilies have little trouble recalling their first experience. What a feeling it was!—a combination of dread and anticipation. Would I forget my thoughts? Would the audience appreciate what I say? Would they be upset? Or would they go asleep? What would happen? Would I make a fool of myself, or would I do my job well? Who can imagine the feelings of Muhammad as he came into Mecca from his experience at Mt. Hira? He was not an orator or educator, used to giving public lectures. Nor was he a religious leader, a politician, or a poet. Rather he was a businessman, for whom ability in public speaking is not a special requirement. It is true that Arabs are naturally gifted in rhetoric, and it is also true that Muhammad himself had great natural talents. Yet, now Muhammad had to take on what was for him a new role, and find ways of proclaiming a new message to an unsympathetic audience. Was he worried or nervous? Abdulla and Amina would not care to probe deeply into that question. They are convinced that Muhammad was faithful to the divine command, Recite!, and carried out the task effectively.

It did not happen overnight. The first three to four years of Muhammad's prophetic activity were essentially low key. There was a carefulness in his approach. The revelations, after all, were initially new and few. Moreover, he was quite aware of the implications of those that he had received. It seems that Muhammad sometimes utilized prayer as an approach, reciting the revelations in connection with his prayer. People drew near to him and listened, and when they asked him what he was saying, he made his witness to them. Other times he spoke with individuals, for example, with ʿAli; whom he advised: "Bear witness that there is no god but Allāh alone, without associate ... and disavow Al-Lāt and al-ʿUzza; and renounce rivals."[1] Sometimes he met over food with a circle of clan leaders, and sometimes he published the message openly.

The first reaction of Meccans to Muhammad's proclamation of *islām* was generally negative. They responded with a mix of curiosity and puzzlement, laughter and disdain, annoyance and outright anger. To understand this reaction we must look at the basic elements of the first messages that Muhammad gave to the wondering citizens of his city.

Some of the features of Muslim faith, including the doctrine of God, have been dealt with above.[2] Here we will step back to underline the content of Muhammad's *first* teaching. The Qurānic revelations occurred over the space of 23 years, and Islāmic ideology developed as the Muslim community developed. Although all the revelations have equal authority for Muslims, those that were proclaimed first have a natural primacy and significance because they reveal what God regards as the core of religious knowledge and life. In addition, the content of these revelations help us to understand the initial response of the Meccan community. We can identify six major points in Muhammad's early preaching.

1. The Powerful Goodness of the Creator Lord

Dominating the earliest revelations is the proclamation of the power and goodness of the Creator. They declare: All around you can see God's powerful and merciful handiwork in nature. Why not therefore recognize it and acknowledge its Author? The point is made clearly in an early Meccan sura [55], which is named "The Beneficent." Thirty times come the powerful words: "Which of the favours of your Lord would you deny?" They beat on the consciousness of the hearer like a drum. There are other representative passages:

87:1-5   Praise the name of thy Lord the Most High,
Who createth, then disposeth
Who measureth, then guideth,
Who bringeth forth the pasturage,
Then turneth it to stubble.

80:24-32   Let man consider his food:
How we pour water in showers
Then split the earth in clefts and
    cause the grain to grow therein,
And grapes and green fodder,
And olive trees and palm trees ...
And fruits and grasses:
Provision for you and your cattle.

88:17-21   Will they not regard the camels, how they are created?
And the heaven, how is it raised?
And the hills, how they are set up?
And the earth, how it is spread?
Remind them ...!

2. The Reality of the Day of Judgment

Twinned with the proclamation of the power and goodness of God was the announcement of the Day of Judgment, preceded by the resurrection of all humanity. Nowhere in literature is the Day of Judgment depicted more vividly than in the early revelations of Muhammad. On the other side of that awful Hour lie the gardens of Paradise and the jaws of Hell. So humanity, alert! and make your choice now for God. The following is a representative passage:

82:1-7, 10-18   When the heaven is cleft asunder,
When the planets are disbursed,
When the seas are poured forth,
And the sepulchers overturned,
O man! What hath made thee careless concerning the Lord, the Bountiful,
Who created thee, then fashioned thee, then proportioned thee? ...
Lo! there are above you guardians,
Generous and recording,
Who know (all) that you do.
Lo! the righteous verily will be in delight,
And lo! the wicked verily in hell;
They will burn therein on the Day of Judgment,
And will not be absent thence.
Ah! What will convey unto thee what the Day of Judgment is
Again, what will convey unto thee what the Day of Judgment is! ...

3. The Duty of Grateful Worship

Muhammad's first message was a call to gratitude and worship. The mercy of God produces a sense of gratitude. Reflect!, remember! give thanks! are words that appear again and again. The first outlet for gratitude is the sincere worship of God alone. The remembrance of the coming judgment, in turn, produces an urgency for the wider service of God in daily life. The two are summed up in the refrain that runs through the early revelations: "Believe and do good works." Representative passages follow:

1,1-4   Praise be to Allāh, Lord of the Worlds,
The Beneficent, the Merciful
Owner of the Day of Judgment,
Thee (alone) we worship; Thee (alone) we ask for help.
Show us the straight path.

16:3ff.   He hath created the heavens and the earth with truth ...
And he hath created the night and the day, and the sun and the moon to be of service to you ... Lo! herein indeed are portents for people who have sense ... That haply ye may give thanks ... Will ye not then remember?

96,3-5   So let them worship the Lord of this House
Who hath fed them against hunger,
And hath made them safe from fear.

84:6   Thou, verily, O man, art working toward thy Lord a work which thou wilt meet (in His presence).

4. The Duty of Generosity

The first proclamations of Muhammad included powerful attacks on greed and the neglect of the helpless. Human beings should strive to emulate the generosity of God. The poor, widows, and orphans are singled out for attention, and Muhammad's voice may have shook with the emotion of his own memories as he spoke. In an increasingly materialistic society he called people to a liberality of spirit and concern for the downtrodden. Here are representative passages.

94:1-5   Woe unto every slandering traducer,
Who hath gathered wealth (of this world) and arranged it.
He thinketh that his wealth will render him immortal.
Nay, but verily he will be flung to the Consuming One.
Ah, what will convey unto thee what the Consuming one is!
(It is) the fire of Allāh, kindled ...

89:17-24   Nay, but ye (for your part) honour not the orphan
And urge not on the feeding of the poor,
And ye devour heritages with devouring greed
And love wealth with abounding love.
Nay, but when the earth is ground to atoms, grinding, grinding,
And thy Lord will come with angels, rank on rank,
And hell is brought near on that day; on that day man will remember,
But how will the remembrance (then avail him)?

90:12-16   Ah, what will convey unto thee what the Ascent is!—
(It is) to free a slave,
And to feed in the day of hunger
An orphan near of kin,
Or some poor wretch in misery ...

The four emphases outlined above represent the central foci of the first revelations and Muhammad's early preaching. However, in addition there are two other themes that also appear, although in a more subdued manner, and they are gathered up in the *shahāda*, the confession of faith in Islām.

5. The Soleness of God

The earliest revelations lifted up the Lordship of God and, by implication, the soleness of God. In the first sūras we do not see many direct attacks on idolatry. They do not contain the outright denunciations of polytheism that the later Meccan sūras do. The problem of the gods and goddesses is dealt with indirectly by focussing on the supremacy of Allāh. The Prophet Muhammad made the implication clear to his intimates—if Allāh is Lord, then there is no other god. Allāh alone is real, and He only is deserving of recognition and worship. As time passed the proclamation became explicit:

72:18-20   And the places of worship are only for Allāh, so pray not unto anyone along with Allāh... Say (unto them O Muhammad): I pray unto Allāh only, and ascribe unto Him no partner.

109:    Say: O disbelievers!
I worship not that which ye worship;
Nor worship ye that which I worship.
And I shall not worship that which ye worship.
Nor will ye worship that which I worship.
Unto you your religion, and unto me my religion.

6. The Authenticity of Muhammad's Vocation

As the turmoil in Mecca increased and as Muhammad began to come under attack, it was important that he be reassured about his vocation. Revelations came that assured him that his vocation was a genuine one and that he was an authentic messenger of God. Representative passages include the following.

73:1-10   O thou wrapped in thy raiment! Keep vigil ...
and chant the Qurʾān in measure,
For We shall charge thee with a word of weight ...
So remember the name of thy Lord and devote thyself with a
complete devotion—
Lord of the East and the West: there is no god save Him;
So choose thou Him alone for thy defender—
And bear with patience what they utter ...
Leave Me to deal with the deniers ...!

86:13-17   Lo! this (Qurʾān) is a conclusive word,

96

It is not pleasantry.
Lo! they plot (against thee, O Muhammad)
And I plot a plot (against them).
So give a respite to the disbelievers,
Deal thou gently with them for a while.

93:3-5   Thy Lord hath not forsaken thee nor doth He hate thee,
And verily the latter portion will be better for thee than the
former,
And verily thy Lord will give unto thee so that thou wilt be
content.

B. The Response of the Meccans

In these words, and others like them, Muhammad proclaimed the message. What happened? At first, not much. In fact, it was tough going for the next ten years. There were a few bright spots for some people were attracted by the message and by the fervor of Muhammad's preaching. Among these were a number of relatives and friends. The first was Khadīja, his wife, whose supporting role we have already noted. We have also mentioned ʿAlī, his young nephew who, in Sunnī Islām, became the fourth caliph (successor) of the Prophet; in Shīʿa Islām he is regarded as the first legitimate successor. There were other important accessions, individuals who later assumed a leading role in the development of Islām. As a group they are known as "the Companions" of the Prophet, and they occupy a position of great honor in Islām.

Prominent in this group of future leaders was Abū Bakr, a leading merchant, a popular man, and a person admired for his integrity. When this respected person chose to accept the message of islām, it raised the level of awareness in Mecca. He later became the first Successor to Muhammad. ʿUthmān, a wealthy young relative, who was leading a life of ease, paid the price involved in following Muhammad. He was to become the third Successor to the Prophet. Muhammad's uncle, Hamza, became a Muslim and thereby offset the opposition of other uncles. The conversion of ʿUmar ibn al-Khattāb was one of the most important events in early Islām, and his is a special story.

ʿUmar was a fiery Meccan leader who had opposed Muhammad all the way. Enraged at Muhammad's activity, he had set out to disperse a gathering of Muslims. On the way he was intercepted by a member of his clan, who advised him to take care of his own household first. It seemed that his sister and her husband had become Muslims. ʿUmar hurried to their home, and from outside he heard a slave reading the latest revelation, the 20th sūra. He rushed in, attacked his brother-in-law with a sword, but inadvertently struck the face of his sister and drew blood. The sight cooled him down, and he asked what they had been reading. His sister refused to show him, since as a polytheist he was ritually unclean. ʿUmar went elsewhere and found the sūra:

> A revelation from Him Who created the earth and the high heavens,
> The Beneficent One Who is established on the Throne
> Unto Him belongeth whatsoever is in the heavens and whatsoever is
>   in the earth, and whatsoever is between them, and whatsoever is
>   beneath the sod ...
> Allāh! There is no God save Him. His are the most beautiful names.
>
> (20:4-8).

The impetuous ʿUmar rushed to the place where Muhammad and his followers were gathered and offered his allegiance.[3] Later he became the second caliph, and the man most instrumental for the rapid spread of Islām.

These were bright spots indeed, but the general picture was not bright. There were not many converts, and most of them were from the lower class, economically and socially. When the persecution came—as it inevitably did—they did not fare well at all.

After tolerating Muhammad for a while, most of the leaders of the city, including the chief men of his own tribe, began to oppose him. Prominent among his opponents were his own uncle, Abū Lahab, and Abū Jahl, a Qurayshite leader. The reasons for the opposition were mixed. It is always hard to be preached at by one of your acquaintances or by a member of your own family. Some of the Meccans really felt loyalty to their gods, and they resented Muhammad's criticisms. Certainly they did not want their tribal customs changed! Others may have had the feeling that this new movement would upset their traditional political setup, and socially they could feel a division coming. A delegation came in protest to Abū Talib, saying:

> O Abū Talib, your nephew has cursed our gods, insulted our religion, mocked our way of life and accused our forefathers of error; either you must stop him or you must let us get at him ...[4]

But perhaps the main concern was economic. If one god named Allāh would rule Mecca, what would happen to the shrine and to the income it produced from the pilgrims? Mecca might be ruined!

Thus the leaders of Mecca did everything they could to discourage Muhammad. They made fun of him and his message in various ways, and he was physically threatened. His uncle, Abū Talib, prevented any serious harm from befalling Muhammad. His few followers, however, were not so fortunate. Some of them gave way under the persecution, but the majority remained loyal. An example of suffering loyalty was Bilāl. He was an Ethiopian slave who had accepted Islām. He was brought out into the heat of the sun, thrown on his back, with a heavy rock placed on his chest. His master ordered, "You will stay here till you die or deny Muhammad and worship al-Lāt and al-ʿUzzā." Bilāl endured, saying simply: "One! one!" Abū Bakr finally bought him and freed him to release him from his torture.[5] Bilāl was honored by the Prophet by being given the appointment as the first *muezzin*, that is, the one who gave the call to prayer. Later in history, especially in North America, Bilāl became the symbol of Islāmic racial equality.

The situation became so desperate that Muhammad felt constrained to ask the most vulnerable of his followers to emigrate to Abyssinia (Ethiopia), across the Red Sea. Up to 70 of them did so. In Ethiopia they were given a friendly reception by the Christian monarch who interviewed them, was pleased with what they said, and gave them refuge. Later most of these emigrants returned to Mecca, but they never forgot, and Muslims as a whole have never forgotten, that it was a Christian ruler who harbored the first Muslim refugees.

In Mecca, Muhammad and his friends were deeply troubled. The Prophet himself went through a series of testing experiences. He was physically maltreated. His clan was boycotted. Every emotional pressure was brought against him, including loyalty to the tribe and to the Kaʿba. He was asked to compromise his message and to admit to the existence of the goddesses, Al-Lāt, al-ʿUzzā and Manāt, of whom the Qurʾan finally said: "They are but names which ye have named" (53:23). The greatest trial, however, occurred when he went to Taif on a preaching mission.

Taif was a city about 60 miles from Mecca. In some despair regarding the attitude of the Meccans, Muhammad went to Taif with his message, hoping for a better reception. It did not turn out that way. The people of Taif had a deep commitment to their deities, and they rejected Muhammad and his companion, Zayd, and pelted stones at them. Bruised and bleeding, they retreated from Taif and sought refuge in a garden, where he was ministered to by a Christian slave named ʿAddās.6 At this time comforting revelations came to him. The most famous is 17:1:

> Glorified be He who carried His servant by night from the Inviolable Place of Worship to the Far Distant Place of Worship, the neighborhood whereof We have blessed, that We might show him of our tokens!

Another translation goes like this:

> Celebrated be the praises of Him who took His servant a journey by night from the Sacred Mosque to the Remote Mosque, the precinct of which we have blessed, to show him of our signs.7

This mysterious and much-loved passage has been greatly elaborated by later Muslims, especially by the mystics of Islām, the Sūfis. The Sacred Mosque is identified as Mecca. The Remote Mosque is Jerusalem. In a timeless moment Muhammad was carried to Jerusalem, and from there he was transported to the heavenly places. In the various levels of heaven, he met the great prophets, and finally experienced the vision of God. Thus comforted and encouraged, he was taken back to Taif. His bed was still warm, and the water jar that had been knocked over at his departure was still running! Nothing of this is in the Qurʾān, but for the Sūfi mystics the miʿrāj (ladder; ascent) of Muhammad becomes an allegory for every human being's spiritual ascent to the divine.8 From Taif, the struggling and suffering Muhammad returns to Mecca.

One Muslim author calls these the "Darkest Days."9 It was now the year 620, ten years after Muhammad's first revelation experience. Khadīja had died. Abū Tālib had died. Comforter and protector were gone. An enemy uncle has become the clan head. Personal indignities are heaped on Muhammad. He still has the protection of a community leader, but the situation is precarious. Is this the end of Islām? Perhaps the question was in the air, and Muhammad himself may have wondered. Then came a ray of hope from the north that completely changed the Muslim situation.

In the north lay the city of Medina (Yathrib), 250 miles from Mecca. Muhammad had family connections there. More significant than that was the fact that Medina had a quite different social mix than Mecca. It was dominated by two major Arab tribes (Aws and Khazraj), both polytheistic, who were at odds with each other. In addition, there were three distinct Jewish tribes, who had considerable economic strength. The city lacked unity and had no single leader who could make it pull together. By this time Muhammad's fame had reached the people of Medina. His message, as far as they understood it, may not have seemed so threatening to them, as it did to the people of Mecca. Because of Jewish and *hanīf* influence the concept of monotheism was known, and Medina was not a pilgrimage town. In 620 six Medinans met Muhammad at the pilgrimage; they were impressed, and their reports must have sparked the interest of Medina. In 621, twelve men came and made a pact with Muhammad known as the Pledge of ʿAqabah, in which they agreed to cease idolatry, theft, adultery and infanticide, promising to follow Muhammad in all good things. A year later, 73 men and two women from Medina came to Mecca and joined in the Second Pledge of ʿAqabah. They invited Muhammad to come to Medina, and vowed to defend him. The die, as it were, was now cast, and Muhammad crossed the Rubicon!

In 622 came the Hijra. The term *hijra* means emigration. The invitation to Medina provided an opportunity for safety and freedom, and a better context for the proclamation of Islām. Although some had to remain behind, many of Muhammad's companions began to migrate. Finally Muhammad and Abū Bakr did likewise. The Quraysh attempted to stop his departure, but Muhammad succeeded in evading them by hiding in a cave for three days. He arrived safely in Medina where he quickly established his power and founded a state.

The Hijra is important because it marks the beginning date of the Muslim calendar. It is more important because it marks the beginning of Islāmic success. In Medina Muhammad began his task of forming a new society dedicated to Allāh and ruled by Him. It was not easy. The task required great leadership, hard decisions, courageous struggle, and broad vision. By the end of Muhammad's life, only 10 years later, all opposition was overcome, and Islām had become the religion of most of the inhabitants of Arabia. It was a remarkable achievement. Let us examine that achievement next.

Notes

[1] Ibn Ishaq, *Muhammad*, p. 115.

[2] Cf. Chapters 3, 4. For the content of Muhammad's first preaching I have utilized but adapted the analysis of W. Montgomery Watt, *Muhammad, Prophet and Statesman* (London: Oxford University Press, 1961), pp. 22–34.

[3] Ibn Isḥāq, *Muhammad*, pp. 155–158.

[4] Ibid., p. 119.

[5] Ibid., p. 144.

[6] Ibid., p. 193.

[7] E. H. Palmer, tr. *The Koran (Qurʾān)*, (London: Oxford, 1960), p. 235.

[8] The best study of the *miʿrāj*, the heavenly journey of the Prophet, is Anne-Marie Schimmel's chapter on the topic in *And Muhammad is His Messenger*, op.cit., pp. 159–75.

[9] H. M. Balyuzi, *Muhammad and the Course of Islām* (Oxford: George Ronald, 1976), p. 38.

The Prophet in Medina: Triumph and Advance

There are three primary reasons why Abdulla and Amina accept and honor Muhammad as the Prophet of God: his revelation, his success, and his character. For these reasons they place his name beside the name of God in the confession of Islām:

Lā ilāha illa Allāh, wa Muhammadu rasūl Allāh

There is no god but God, and Muhammad is the messenger of God

In this chapter we will consider the element of *success* in terms of six problems that Muhammad was able to solve as he moved from the struggle and trials of Mecca to the mounting progress of Medina. As a preamble to the story of the solution of those six problems we will briefly consider the famous Agreement of Medina.

A. From Preacher to Statesman: The "Constitution" of Medina

There is a revealing story told by Ibn Ishāq regarding Muhammad's arrival in Medina.[1] After a stop to recover from the hard journey, he had to take a decision as to his permanent headquarters. From every side came the cries, "Stop here! Alight here! Stay at our house!" Muhammad well understood the rivalries in Medina. So he said, "Let the camel go her way!" Where the camel stopped, he stopped. It was by a plot of land owned by two orphans. The arrangements were quickly made, and this property became the location of Muhammad's first home, as well as the first mosque in Medina. Right at the beginning of his Medinan career Muhammad revealed the sagacity of a born statesman.

In Mecca Muhammad was a suffering preacher. In Medina he

became a victorious administrator. Muhammad's life and the revelations of the Qurʾān reflect the dramatic difference in context. Abdulla and Amina, however, do not believe that there was any essential difference in Muhammad's calling, nor any fundamental alteration in his behavior in Mecca and Medina. The variations in style in Medina resulted from the change in context. While Muhammad was at Mecca, he had to proclaim the Unity of God and the Day of Judgment to an unbelieving people, so there was much preaching to do and little to administrate. At Medina, however, the majority of people accepted his message, and along with that success came the problems of organizing the new believers. This meant legislating and administrating. Whether he was in Mecca or Medina, however, in Muslim faith and emotion Muhammad was steadily and consistently guided by God throughout his prophetic career in all that he said and did. Abdulla and Amina are not really attracted to discussions of the possible personality development of the Prophet. They are much more interested in unreservedly thanking God for granting success to him and to the first Muslims in Medina.

The transition of Muhammad from the role of preacher to that of preacher plus social manager, and his ability to deal with that change, are both illustrated by the major agreement that Muhammad put into effect within the first year of his arrival in Medina. The treaty, which has sometimes been called "the constitution" of the city, played an important part in the problem-solving that followed, and because of its significance for interreligious relations and contemporary peace-making efforts, it is as important now as when first implemented.[2]

It is not clear to what extent everyone mentioned in the Medinan Agreement was actually involved in its creation. Despite the assertion that the agreement "obviously was written after consultation with the people concerned,"[3] it is evident that some of Muhammad's opponents would not have assented to it, and there is also no record that the Jewish tribes actually signed it. What is clear is that Muhammad took the provisions of the treaty seriously, and later presumed violations caused major repercussions.

The first part of the Agreement, which contains 47 clauses, deals with the relationships between the new settlers from Mecca and their believing helpers in Medina. The second part concerns the relations of Muslim believers with the unbelievers and the Jews in Medina, and it reveals Muhammad's willingness to set up accommodating arrangements with other communities of faith. The 20th clause, for example, states:

> And no Polytheist (*mushrik*) ... gives any protection to property and to life of any Quraishite, nor he comes in the way of any Believer in this matter.[4]

In the 25th clause the Jews are addressed similarly, as a recognizable and acceptable group:

> And verily the Jews ... shall be considered as a community (*umma*) along with the Believers, for the Jews being their religion and for the Muslims their religion ...[5]

Thus the document viewed all the citizens of the city—Muslims, non-Muslims and Jews—as one society bound together by common interests, but composed of distinct communities. There was in a sense a wider general *umma* that included everyone, and then particular individual *ummas* with their own concerns and with the authority to conduct their own community affairs.[6] The relationship between the distinct communities was spelled out, concentrating on the need for mutual defense against the enemies of the city, and in particular the Qurayshite enemies of Islām. The provisions, in effect, established mutual toleration and mutual support as principles, illustrated by a few specifics. From his perspective Muhammad's special role was to be the arbitrator of disputes on behalf of God, and disagreements were to be referred to him for decision.

B. Problems Met and Solved

We now turn to Muhammad's experience of rising success in Medina and deal with it in terms of a series of problems that he met and solved. They include the following:

1. Establishing a unified community;
2. Overseeing pressing physical needs;
3. Deepening the knowledge of Islām;
4. Relating to "Hypocrites" and to the Jews;
5. Overcoming the Meccans; and
6. Consolidating and expanding Islām.

In the process of handling these difficult issues, Muhammad's personal powers of leadership reached their fruition, and the faith of Islām became firmly established in the Arabian peninsula.

1. The Problem of Establishing a Unified Community of Believers

While the entry into Medina was a triumphant moment, the victory of Islām was far from assured. An immediate issue that presented itself was the unity of the Muslim believers themselves. They were relatively few in number and socially weak. If they did not hold together, Islām could not become an effective force in Medina. It might not even survive! Yet, in Muhammad's mind, there were more than merely pragmatic reasons for striving to create a unified community. At stake was an important principle—the principle that a new solidarity was being born that transcended all previous loyalties. The oneness of God must be translated into the oneness of believers (*tawhīd*). There were, however, two sets of loyalties that threatened this ideal just as it was being born. They were kinship feeling and party allegiance.

The first traditional loyalty was to the tribe. Tribal faithfulness was the living social creed of the Arabs. Even modern experience shows how persistent tribal loyalty is, and it was certainly not less so at the time of Muhammad. The new Muslim believers came from differing backgrounds. Would Islām, as it grew, become a series of Muslim tribes? The second threat was as much a psychological one as a practical one. It had to do with relations between the emigrants from Mecca (*muhājirūn*) and the believing Medinans who had helped them (*ansār*). In both groups there were some who felt that the Prophet should give them the priority place in the Muslim family. Would Islām divide over this issue?

Against both forms of division—blood-ties and groupism—the Qurʾān introduces the principle of the family of believers, the *umma*. Muslim believers represent a distinct and separate entity. Islām is to be a brotherhood as well as a faith, a lateral relationship with fellow believers as well as a horizontal relationship with God. "The believers are naught else than brothers ... make peace between your brethren" (49:10). The loyalty of believers toward each other is to take precedence over other relationships, natural or developed.

New laws were needed to express this daring concept, and the

Qurʾān provided them. These new laws did not represent a wholesale break with Arab culture but addressed the customs that had to be changed. For example, if there was a disagreement among believers, they were to bring them to the Prophet for settling. The Prophet was the Voice of God, and therefore God Himself would guide the family through its problems. This arrangement established the theocratic ideal [*theos*=God; *kratia*=rule], the principle that God is the Head and Ruler of the Muslim state.

Various other laws dealt with important areas of mutual relations. For example, a believer might not support an unbeliever against another believer, even if the unbeliever was from one's own tribe. Regulations were put in place governing marriage, inheritance, the sharing of alms, and so on. Usually the laws came into existence in relation to particular problems that arose from time to time.

Within the family unity the *muhājirūn* and the *ansar* were to respect each other's rights. Moreover they were to help each other. Muhammad devised a clever technique for overcoming the rivalry between the two groups. Among the Medinan helpers there was to be a special friend for each of the emigrants. The pairing was arbitrary and clearly made the fundamental point. Muslims were to be joined together in common allegiance and in common obedience to Allāh. "Ye have instead of Allāh no protecting friend or helper ... Allah hath turned in mercy to the Prophet, and to the Muhājirūn and the Ansār who followed him, in the hour of hardship" (9:116f.). The *umma* had come into being!

2. The Task of Overseeing Physical Needs

One of the first problems that Muhammad had to deal with after the Hijra was the economic disability of the Emigrants. Although they were still within their ethnic homeland, the Muslims experienced almost everything else that refugees commonly do. In modern times Islām has had much experience with that problem; for in the 1990s, the majority of the world's refugees have been Muslims. The Muslim encounter with suffering, however, began very early. It started as physical persecution in Mecca and continued as economic hardship in Medina.

Muhammad himself fully shared the experience. Dates and water were common fare for the Emigrants for days on end, and there was often no light in the crude homes. The land in Medina was occupied, and in any event the majority of the incoming Emigrants were not farmers. Apparently a few were able to start small businesses, but the majority had to eke out their existence as day laborers, more or less dependent on the charity of the Ansār. Health problems in the new and unfamiliar humid climate of Medina aggravated the situation. It is not surprising that the first mosque resembled a kind of refugee camp.

The memory of the early poverty and the strong Qurānic passages commending compassion on the poor have informed the Muslim attitude toward fellow Muslims who are hard up and needy. When Abdulla, who does the shopping for the family, enters the market, he usually passes a row of handicapped beggars asking for alms. He never passes by without making a gift to someone in the group.

The economic problems of the Emigrants were alleviated after some of the early Muslim raids on the Meccan trading caravans, and after some of the Jewish property was seized. Surprisingly soon, there was an actual turnabout in problems. Following the advance of Islām, considerable booty was taken. It became the custom for one-fifth of the amount to be placed at the disposal of the Prophet Muhammad for distribution to the needy (*bait al-māl*), and the remainder could be divided. Since huge amounts were involved, this resulted in occasional tension. Thus, the problem of poverty had become a problem of rapid wealth! Although many Muslims did become wealthy, Muhammad himself remained frugal in his habits and generous in his ways.

3. The Task of Deepening the Knowledge of Islām

The development of religious knowledge was a gradual one in early Islām. Muhammad himself participated in that development as each new revelation came. In the case of his followers, the religious knowledge of many must have been at a very superficial level. We know from the requirements that Muhammad gave to the Medinans at the Pledge of ʿAqabah that they were very simple and basic ones. In fact, one of the points of pride that Abdulla and Amina cherish in regard to Islām is its simplicity. However, simplicity and superficiality are two different things. Muhammad knew that he would have to engage in a program of religious education. He did so, using both symbolism and direct teaching.

The primary symbol was established right after Muhammad's entry into Medina. We have seen that the first thing that Muhammad did after the camel stopped was to buy the land and build a mosque. All the believers, Muhammad included, labored together to put up the basic structure—a series of huts around a central courtyard, and a raised platform. That structure became the center for the whole life of the small Muslim community in its social, religious, political, and economic activities. It said, in effect, "God is at the center of all things." In their history, Muslims constantly have been calling themselves back to this basic principle.

Muhammad also continued to give direct instruction regarding the will of God, especially through the revelations that came to him. Those revelations were somewhat different now, in style and content, from what they were in Mecca. They were longer rather than shorter, more sedate rather than impassioned, more instructional than exclamatory, more this-worldly than next-worldly, more issue-oriented than strictly theological. They seemed to be more concentrated on the task of deepening faith than arousing faith. In content too there were many new emphases, such as a stress on the role of the prophet Abraham. Muslim commentators point to the new circumstances in Medina that required this development in style and content, a situation summed up by Fazlur Rahman's phrase, "the community-state building process at Medina."[7]

Muhammad did not depend only on his own teaching to develop the religious knowledge of the first Muslims. He appointed a group of Qurʾān readers, whose task was to repeat the revelations. How successful was their work? Did the Muslim believers really grasp the meaning of Islām? It is impossible to answer that question. Surely the understanding of the faith must have varied greatly from person to person. The point was made, however, that the faith must be taught. It must be handed on. Muslims caught that idea and ever since they have been very concerned about transmitting the truths of Islām. They have tried to do this through a major system of religious education called the *madrasas*. (Lower schools are sometimes called *kuttab*, and schools of higher study *dar al- ulum*). Parents like Abdulla and Amina are committed to the training of their children in the recitation of the Qurʾān, and in general religious knowledge. The *madrasas* vary greatly in style and quality, but they represent the same interest that Muhammad had at Medina, the deepening of the faith.

4. The Task of Relating to the Hypocrites and the Jews

The first three problems—creating unity among Muslims, taking care of physical needs, deepening spiritual knowledge—were internal ones. The believers could work at the solutions directly. The other three problems, however, were external ones. They involved people who did not agree with Islām or did not cooperate with Muslims. They were therefore more difficult to deal with, and the dealing required all of Muhammad's ability. As Muhammad Haykal put it:

> The fact that the presence of Muslims, Jews, associationists [=polytheists, ed.] and *munafigun* [=hypocrites] in one city with all their disparate ideals and customs, made that city a political volcano replete with explosive power.[8]

a. The Unbelievers and Hypocrites

There were some Arabs in Medina who maintained their traditional polytheistic faith. The rapid spread of Islām in the city gradually isolated this group until they disappeared. Another group presented much more difficulty. They were called the *munāfiqūn*, a word that has been translated by such terms as "hypocrites," "doubters," "dissemblers." They were monotheists and adhered to Islām, but only halfheartedly. They could not be counted on. They did not appear to like Muhammad's authority, and some of them even set up a parallel mosque. Their leader, and Muhammad's chief opponent in Medina, was ʿAbdulla ibn Ubayy. He was a senior and powerful leader, and Muhammad never attacked him directly. In effect, he said, "Let God take care of this matter." Throughout the decade Ibn Ubayy attempted to undermine the Muslim movement and Muhammad's leadership, but the Prophet's indirect approach proved successful. By the time Ibn Ubayy died, his support had thinned out. Muhammad granted his request to use one of the Prophet's shirts as a funeral shroud and even conducted his funeral rites, much to the chagrin of some of Muhammad's followers. The story of the unbelievers and the

Hypocrites illustrates the Prophet's capacity for patience and restraint, in the interest of long-term goals.

b. The Jews of Medina

The issue of Jewish opposition was much more contentious, and the solving of this problem arouses mixed emotions. In the end, two of the three Jewish tribes were exiled, and the male members of the third tribe were executed.

Muhammad had anticipated a hopeful and positive relationship with the Jews, and we can sense his reaching out toward them. He believed that the Jews would recognize his prophetic vocation as a legitimate succession in the line of the great Jewish prophets of old. He felt that his message of surrender to one God would strike a chord with the Jews and that they would happily regard it as divinely given. The positive relation he desired was expressed by the choice of rites and ceremonies. For example, Muhammad and his followers prayed toward Jerusalem and fasted on the same days as the Jews. The Qurɔān itself was studded with references to the Jewish prophets and scriptures.

Apparently these overtures were not welcomed by the Jews, who rather scornfully rejected Muhammad's claims. Ibn Ishaq records the response in these words:

> About this time the Jewish rabbis showed hostility to the apostle in envy, hatred, and malice, because God had chosen His apostle from the Arabs. They were joined by men from al-Aus and al-Khazraj who had obstinately clung to their heathen religion ... It was the Jewish rabbis who used to annoy the apostle and introduce confusion ...[9]

The Muslim disappointment was extreme, and it was reflected in a number of ways.

The Qurɔān itself testifies to the Muslim disappointment, and it gives progressively greater attention to the role of Abraham in the development of Islām. Moses, to whom there are many references in the Meccan sras, stands out now as the prophet of the Jews, but Abraham predates particular religious developments such as Judaism and Christianity, and he is the spiritual father of all true believers, with a special relation to Arab Muslims through Ishmael. It is therefore to him and to his Islām that Muslims must look for guidance.

Muslim disappointment was also expressed by the rejection of

Jewish custom. The most symbolic and dramatic moment came when the Qurʾān altered the *qibla*, the direction of prayer. One day as he was praying Muhammad wheeled in his tracks and turned toward Mecca and its familiar shrine, the Kaʿba. The Qurʾān declared:

> We appointed the *qiblah* [Jerusalem] which ye formerly observed only that We might know him who followeth the messenger from him who turneth on his heels ... And now verily We shall make thee turn (in prayer) toward a *qiblah* which is dear to thee. So turn thy face toward the Inviolable Place of Worship... (2:142f.).

This event supported Muhammad's sympathy for his own culture and his tender feelings for his traditional home.

While the problem of the religious relationship with the Jews was being clarified, the political problem was not solved. The Jews represented a dominant and uncontrolled force in the city. Moreover, they were being incited by Ibn Ubayy and other opponents to lessen their support of Muhammad, and even to lend quiet aid to the Qurayshites. Although the constitution of Mecca implied mutual defense, there was a great deal of suspicion in the air. The relationships gradually went downhill and finally resulted in tragedy. The first Jewish tribe, the Banu Qaynuka, did not apply the problem-solving arrangements established in the Medinan Agreement in the case of a personal dispute between a Jew and a Muslim, to the satisfaction of the Prophet, and they were expelled from the city with their possessions, moving to the oasis of Khaybar. A member of a second Jewish tribe, the Banu Nadir, was suspected of attempting to assassinate the Prophet as he was awaiting a decision outside a meeting of the Jewish Council. The Banu Nadir were required to abandon the city with what they could carry on their camels.

In the opinion of Muslims, the third Jewish tribe in Medina, the Banu Qurayzah, failed to hold true to important treaty requirements for the mutual defence of the city. Affairs came to a head at the Meccan invasion of Medina in 627. There was extreme suspicion and some evidence that the Banu Qurayzah had supported the enemy, and certainly they had only participated halfheartedly in the defense of Medina. Thus they seemed to represent a very serious danger, the enemy within.

After the battle was over, the Prophet Muhammad decreed that the matter would have to be judged by an arbitrator. The selected arbitrator was from a tribe that had traditionally supported the Banu Qurayzah, so they emerged hopefully from their fortified area. The arbitrator, who had been heavily wounded in the battle and was soon to expire, chose to render a stern judgment—the male members of the Jewish tribe were to be beheaded, and females and children were to be enslaved. Committed to the arbitration process, Muhammad assented to the decree, saying, "God is pleased with your judgment, O Sad, and so are the believers. You have surely done your duty." Muhammad Haykal sums up the majority opinion of Muslim commentators, regarding the massacre as a necessary evil in a struggle for survival:

> However harsh the verdict which the arbitrator had reached in this regard, it was dictated by self-defense, as the arbitrator had become convinced that the presence or destruction of the Jews was a question of life and death for the Muslims.[10]

It was a violent end to a promising beginning, however, and only a few Jews remained in Medina. Jewish opposition in Arabia was fully and finally overcome in 628 when Muslim forces captured the oasis of Khaybar.

This is the historical background to the *paradoxical* feelings that Abdulla and Amina have toward Jews. On the one hand, there is positive appreciation for their prophetic heritage, common views, and shared values. Thus Jews (together with Christians) are called people of the book (*ahl-kitāb*), that is, people who have received the legitimate scriptural guidance of God. They therefore enjoy a special status. It is also a fact of history that Jews often lived more comfortably within various Muslim empires than in Western nations, and especially at the time of the Inquisition in the West they sought refuge in large numbers in Muslim lands. On the other hand, there are residual feelings of bitterness related to the Jewish rejection of the Prophet and Jewish opposition to his authority. In contemporary times, the question of Israel and Palestine has further troubled the relationship, since the Muslims of the world have deep empathy with the sufferings of their Palestinian brothers and sisters. An increasing number of modern Muslims, anxious for peace and for a renewal of positive relations, look to the Agreement of Mecca as the true guide of Muhammad's intention and hopes, and the basis for fresh and creative Muslim approaches to current problems. Abdulla and Amina now share that hope.

5. The Task of Overcoming the Meccans

The major problem that Muhammad had to work out was the problem of Mecca. Muhammad, it is clear, loved his home town, and he had a deeply affectionate relationship with most of its citizens, who included members of his family and many friends. He also well understood the symbolic significance of Mecca. Islām could not become the religion of Arabia if it did not become the religion of Mecca. This helps account for his determination to pursue matters with the Meccans. It also explains the painfulness of what followed. The task of dealing with Mecca involved military action, which Muhammad now undertook in the face of the continuing Meccan threat, and the conflict that ensued had more than the usual tragedy that accompanies war because many of those involved were old friends, and even blood relatives. Civil wars are always the most sorrowful! Within eight years, however, Muhammad and his devoted Muslims had succeeded in overcoming the Meccans.

The key dates are the following:

> 624—Initiation of action at Nakhla, and the Battle of Badr: the exhilarating experience of success;
> 625—The Battle of Uhud: the answer to failure;
> 628—The Treaty of Hudaibiyat: the pragmatic wisdom of Muhammad;
> 629—A pilgrimage to Mecca: cultural identification; and
> 630—The capture of Mecca: the magnanimity of the Prophet.

The outstanding leadership of the Prophet was the main factor in this major accomplishment. It had several components. The first was his determination. It was illustrated by the fact that the action began with a Muslim raid on a Meccan caravan at Nakhla during the sacred truce month when warfare was forbidden under Arab culture. It was evident that traditional custom would not be permitted to stand in the way of God's truth! Another element was his personal courage. He risked battle against heavy odds, and when necessary he personally entered the fray. His military skill was another factor in the achievement. He introduced new methods of fighting that startled the enemy. Of all the elements in his leadership, the most important one was his great inspirational quality. He aroused and animated his followers. They, in turn, were intensely loyal to him. The Qurʾān was a major factor in encouraging the Muslims to fight for God and for Islām, promising great and immediate rewards to those who would die in battle:

> Fight them, till there is no persecution and the religion is God's entirely; then, if they give over, surely God sees the things they do ... (8:40).

> If you are slain or die in God's way, forgiveness and mercy from God are a better thing than you amass; surely if you die or are slain, it is unto God you shall return ... Count not those who were slain in God's way as dead, but rather living with their Lord, by Him provided, rejoicing in the bounty that God has given them ... (3:153.164).

To this rousing call the first Muslims responded, with both fervor and sacrifice.

The most important encounter was the first major one, the battle of Badr, in 624. Its genesis was simple. Muhammad and the Muslims attempted to intercept a caravan of Abū Sufyān, longtime leader in Mecca and enemy of Muhammad. The Meccans sent an army to relieve the caravan, which escaped. The army of Mecca pressed forward, intent to overcome Muhammad once and for all. The two groups met at Badr, near Medina. There an outnumbered band of 300 Muslims defeated a superior force of 900 Meccans. As battles go, the numbers involved were small, but the Battle of Badr must nevertheless rank as one of the most significant in history. It is impossible to overstate the impact of the victory on the psychology of Muslims and on the course of later events.

Those who are familiar with Muslim family life in different parts of the world may have witnessed a scene similar to this—Abdulla and Amina with their family and friends are gathered in their home listening to the singing of Muslim ballads. Among the most loved songs are the songs of Badr. As they recall the victory of God, they echo the joy of Muhammad himself and the first Muslims, as expressed in the Qurʾān (8:10.17f.):

> Victory cometh only by the help of Allāh. Lo! Allāh is mighty, Wise ... Ye (Muslims) slew them not, but Allāh slew them ... Now hath judgment come unto you (Quraysh)!

Not only is Badr celebrated in the songs of the home, but also in the meditations of the mosque. It is a persistent sermon theme. In a sense, what the crossing of the Red Sea was for the Jews, what the ascension of Jesus was for the Christians, the battle of Badr is for the Muslims. The "Lion of Islām," ʿAlī b. Abū Talib, who participated in the Badr victory at the side of his father-in-law, Muhammad, voiced the universal Muslim emotion:

> Have you not seen how God favoured his apostle
> With the favour of a strong, powerful and gracious one;
> How he brought humiliation on the unbelievers
> Who were put to shame in captivity and death,
> While the apostle of God's victory was glorious,
> He being sent by God in righteousness ...
> At Badr He gave them into the power of His apostle
> And an angry army who did valiantly ...
> Now they are in Hell,
> Too occupied to rage furiously against us.[11]

K. K. Muhammad Abdulkarim sums up the Muslim view: "In the history of Islām a singularly important event is Badr. It is with the victory of Badr that the ascendancy of Islām and Muslims began."[12]

Victory has its own testing quality, but it is defeat that holds the greater challenge for a leader. That challenge came next. The Meccans were not content to sit back and accept the stunning defeat of Badr. In the next year (625) they therefore launched a punishing attack on Medina in the Battle of Uhud. Muhammad and the Muslims were overcome, and the Prophet himself almost lost his life in the fighting. The Meccans chose not to press their advantage and withdrew in triumph. They may have thought that this would put an end to the Muslim movement. With startling rapidity, however, Muhammad rallied the survivors, managed to control the dissidents in Medina, and recovered strength again. The Qurʾān dealt with the setback of Uhud as a test. It was God's way of discriminating between the true and the false believers. The Qurʾān declared:

> If ye have received a blow, the (disbelieving) people have received a blow the like thereof. These are (only) the vicissitudes which we cause to follow one another for mankind, to the end that Allāh may know those who believe and may choose witnesses from among you; and Allāh loveth not the wrong-doers. And that Allāh may prove those who believe, and may blight the disbelievers (3:140f.).

Muhammad's inspirational and aggressive leadership won the day, and the faith of the Muslim believers was proven. The Prophet, as Haykal[13] puts it, "prepared himself for recapturing and reestablishing Muslim power and reputation." The believers stayed with him. The personality of the Prophet and the message of Islām combined to produce an almost total dedication and willingness to sacrifice for the cause of Islām. Military energy and prowess carried the movement forward, almost irresistibly. One more siege of Medina took place, the "Battle of the Ditch," in 627. Up to 10,000 Meccan warriors, allies, and camp followers surrounded Medina again, but this time cold weather, short supplies, and Muhammad's defense tactics caused them to withdraw. The result was inconclusive, but the withdrawal had the effect of another triumph. As Muhammad's fame spread wider and wider, various Arab tribes in the peninsula began to consider the advantages of associating with the Prophet of Medina. Meccans themselves started to reevaluate their situation. Were we wrong about this man? Should we make an accommodation of some kind? While they were thinking about it, the strength of Muhammad's opposition was dwindling away.

Emboldened by these developments and showing a remarkable self-confidence, Muhammad next resolved to undertake the minor pilgrimage (ʿumra) to Mecca, in the year A.D. 628. The fact that a supposed enemy could go to the very center of his opponents to carry out a religious duty says worlds about the power of Arab custom! Moreover, the fact that Muhammad would make the pilgrimage to Mecca with all its idols still intact reveals both his commitment to that shrine and his willingness to make short-term accommodations for the sake of an ultimate goal. That willingness was now illustrated in another way.

The Meccans were not inclined to yield to this remarkable plan! This was too much! However, they decided not to attack the pilgrim Muhammad. They met him outside Mecca at a place named Hudaibiyat, refused him and his followers entry into the city, and negotiated a treaty instead. The Treaty of Hudaibiyat was not entirely favorable to the Muslims. Consider its provisions. Muhammad had to postpone the pilgrimage for one year, to agree to send back Meccan minors who had gone to Medina to join Islām, and to sign with the name Muhammad Ibn Abdulla (son of Abdulla) rather than the designation Muhammad the Prophet. On the other hand, the Meccans agreed to permit Arab tribes to align themselves with Muhammad, to abandon hostility for 10 years, and to allow Muhammad to enter Mecca the following year to perform the lesser pilgrimage. Some of Muhammad's followers, including ʿUmar, were aghast. They viewed the treaty requirements as negative to the interests of Islām and virtually rebelled. The Prophet had to chide them and call for a fresh pledge of loyalty. His view was a longer one than theirs. He believed that the positive elements of the treaty outweighed the negative ones, and once again he proved to be right.

Events moved quickly now to a culmination. In A.D. 629, Muhammad and 2,000 of his followers performed the three-day pilgrimage in Mecca. What a feeling they must have had as they visited their old home! What astonishment the Meccans must have felt as they watched them! Their leaders moved quickly now to align themselves with this dominant figure. Later "old" Muslims became rather irritated when some of these opportunistic, last-second converts assumed leadership positions in the Muslim family! In A.D. 630 Muhammad returned with 10,000 men and captured Mecca. As they came in sight of the city boundary Abū Sufyān, the leader of the opposition, made his decision and "chose Islām." Muhammad, in turn, showed unusual leniency toward the people of Mecca. Only a few were punished, mainly poets and singers who had mocked the Prophet.

The end came when Muhammad reached the Kaʿba shrine and destroyed its idols. As the cornelian stone statue of Hubal fell with a crash, it is believed, verse 17:81 of the Qurʾān was revealed: "Truth has come and falsehood has vanished away. Lo! falsehood is ever bound to vanish." The problem of Mecca had vanished too, but Muhammad chose to return to Medina, which remained his headquarters for the last two years of his life.

6. The Problem of Consolidating and Expanding Islām

We turn now to the last of the six problems that Muhammad dealt with in the process of his forward progress at Medina. In the final two years of his life, 630–632, Muhammad continued and completed his work of rallying the whole population of the Arabian peninsula to the cause of Islām. Although there were certainly varying shades of loyalty and some remaining pockets of opposition, he did reach the objective. In the achievement of this goal, Muhammad showed great wisdom in handling the complex treaty arrangements that the different tribes required. Moreover, he displayed considerable generosity, even to former bitter enemies who accepted Islām and joined their political allegiance to Allāh's cause. At this stage many of Muhammad's followers had trouble identifying with this generosity, which even included the liberal sharing of booty, but they remembered it later. The term "triumphal advance" properly describes this peaking of Muhammad's career.

The final period is important not only as the fulfillment of a dream, the dream of the Arab people committed to Islām. It is also important because some significant Muslim principles were established in the process. These principles were controlling factors in later Muslim development. We will take them up under two headings: principles related to Muslim expansion, and principles related to the people of the book—Jews and Christians.

a. Principles related to Muslim Expansion

(i)   The principle that polytheism and idolatry would not be tolerated in Arabia.

In the year 630, at the Battle of Hunayn, Muslim forces under Khālid, the "Sword of Islām," defeated the city of Taif, the last bastion of Arabian polytheism. In the following year, Abū Bakr sent notice to Mecca that no polytheists would henceforth be admitted to the city for pilgrimage.

(ii)   The principle of moderation in religious requirements.

The requirements that were laid upon new Arab tribes joining Islām were simple ones: the acceptance of Islām; instruction in the knowledge of the Qurʾān and in the method of prayer; the ceasing of certain pagan practices, including ancestor worship; the covering of women; and a commitment to payment of alms. Later Muslims have taken pride in the belief that Islām is geared to the natural capacities of humans and does not require more than is achievable. This point was made by the Prophet in his dealing with the rough and ready Bedouin tribes.

(iii) The principle of full Muslim participation in the expansion of Islām.

Muhammad had attempted to instill the principle that all Muslims are equal before God, and all have a common responsibility for the work of God. The principle was underlined in A.D. 631, when the Prophet sent an army north to Tabuq. He insisted that every able-bodied male, with essential exceptions, participate in the expansion of Islām. Although some grumbled and held back, the wide participation in that effort made an important point that has carried through in the history of Islām.

(iv) The principle that Islām should expand beyond Arabia.

Should or could Islām expand beyond the borders of Arabia? There could have been some doubt about the answer. After all, the Qurʾān was in the language of Arabia, "a decisive utterance in Arabic" (13:37). "Lo, We have revealed it, a Lecture in Arabic, that ye may understand" (12:2). "We have inspired in thee a Lecture in Arabic, that thou mayest warn the mother-town and those around it ..." (42:7). It would not have been surprising if the Muslims had thought of Islām as an Arabic ethnic religion, meant for the motherland. The idea that it might be a world religion was certainly far from their minds.

The Prophet Muhammad, however, gave symbolic hints of his wider vision. On two occasions (Muʾta and Tabuq) he sent large forces to probe the northern boundaries of Byzantium-controlled territory. Muslim historians give strong credence to the traditions that Muhammad sent a series of letters to surrounding world leaders, calling upon them to accept Islām. There certainly is evidence that such a letter went to the Christian ruler of Egypt. The latter sent two Coptic Christian slave girls as gifts for Muhammad; one of these named Mariya became Muhammad's wife and bore his only son, Ibrahim, who died in infancy.

The idea that Islām has a global mission has been held by Muslims in the past, but is very firmly believed by Muslims today. The term *daʿwa*, or call, which is the equivalent of mission, is now widely used by Muslims to express the religious duty of commending Islām to the world.

b. Principles Related to the People of the Book

The Qur'ān created a special status for those religious communities considered to be "people of the book" (*ahl al-kitāb*). The "people of the book" are human communities who have received a legitimate prophetic revelation from God in book form. They are clearly identified in the Qur'ān (5:69):

> Lo! those who believe, and those who are Jews, and Sabaeans, and Christians whosoever believeth in Allāh and the Last Day and doeth right—there shall no fear come upon them, neither shall they grieve.

Another passage indicates that those who are people of the book must yield to Muslim authority and provide a payment of tribute (*jizya*). Later Muslims interpreted this requirement to mean that in return for the payment of this special tax Jews and Christians would have the right to live in Muslim lands, to practice their religion, to enjoy other rights, and above all, to have the protection of the Muslim ruler. They would also be people of the covenant, *ahl al-dhimma*, whom the Muslim state would be "obligated" to protect. In Muhammad's lifetime, the application of this basic principle came as the result of his dealing with the Jews of Khaybar and the Christians of Najran.

(i) The Jews of Khaybar

When Muhammad's forces captured the oasis of Khaybar (629), it was occupied by large Jewish settlements. The Jews were allowed to remain on condition that they would pay 50 percent of their crop income as a land tax (*kharāj*) to the Muslim treasury. This principle later applied to Muslim landowners in occupied territories, although the percentage of tax varied. The income thus obtained was used in the same way as the *bait al-māl*, the 20 percent of booty assigned to the central Muslim treasury and administered by the Prophet. It was intended primarily for the care of the poor and needy.

(ii) The Christians of Najran

We have already noted the existence of an Arab Christian community at Najran, in north Yemen. Around 630, the Christians of Najran sent an embassy to Medina to meet Muhammad. They felt it prudent to establish a relationship with the new power. However, they were also interested in engaging the Prophet in religious discussion. They too called God *Rahmān*, the Merciful, and they were interested in the man who began the messages he proclaimed with the words: "In the Name of God, the Merciful, the Compassionate." The religious discussion was inconclusive, but a treaty was struck between the Christians and the Muslims, which provided a pattern for later relationships.[14]

Muhammad agreed to place the Christians of Najran under his protection. No attack on Christians or their property would be permitted. The Christian practice of religion could proceed under the guidance of existing bishops, priests, and monks. The Christians on their part would have to recognize the supremacy of Muslim rule and, as the required tribute, provide 2,000 garments annually. Perhaps the dazzling clothes that the Christians wore to the conference provoked this provision! In the case of war, Christians would have to provide 30 coats of mail, 30 camels, and 30 horses to the Muslim army. The primary change required of Christians was that they would have to give up the practice of usury.

The people of the book principle means that Abdulla and Amina have generally positive feelings toward Christians. They do believe that Christian teaching has strayed from the true revelation of God in a number of ways, as the Qurʾān testifies. Further, they feel that Christians in the course of history have done harm to Muslim societies through physical and economic oppression. They also believe that Christians have often failed to appreciate the true spirit of Islām and have even allowed the creation and spread of caricatures about Muslims. So they harbor mixed feelings. In general, however, they understand and accept the special relationship that the Qurʾān has established between Muslims and Christians.

Next to Abdulla's and Amina's house is a Christian home. They have lived side-by-side for years, and they have a good relationship with their neighbors. They greet each other on their mutual festival days. They attend each other's wedding feasts. They worry together about sickness and unemployment. They inquire about the condition of the children. They help each other in a variety of normal ways. Abdulla and Amina have long forgotten about the treaty that the Prophet made with the Christians of Najran, if they ever knew it; but they do know that their neighbors are people of the book, and that the direction (*qibla*) of their lives is toward God. They respect their neighbors for that and feel an affinity with them.

C. The Death of Muhammad

To the end of his life Muhammad held tightly to the reins of control in the Muslim *umma*. Sunnī Muslims do not believe that he appointed a successor to himself, although Shīʿia tradition maintains that he designated ʿAlī for that role. The Qurʾān was silent on the issue, and we do not know why Muhammad did not make a formal statement on the matter. Perhaps he did not wish to disturb the harmony of the group that he had masterfully pulled together. He was sensitive to the strengths and failings of the many strong men and women who were attracted to his banner, and he kept them working together and used their abilities wisely. Some like Abū Bakr and ʿUmar were noted for being faithful and true. Others like ʿAlī were strong in piety and were critical of moral laxity. Some like Khalid were quick with the sword and needed some restraint. There were opportunists who needed watching, others who did not really understand the principles of the new faith, and a few who even turned against it. It was Muhammad the Prophet who held them all together, and when his death came, the trauma was overwhelming.

In 632, Muhammad engaged in his "farewell" pilgrimage. With his full family he spent ten final days at Mecca, and the manner in which he conducted himself is the pattern for the pilgrimage to this day. He eliminated the pagan associations, but kept the traditional rites and ceremonies. He also presented some final teachings on various aspects of Muslim social life that have been traditionally passed on as a single sermon preached from the back of his camel. It is believed that this verse of the Qurʾān was revealed then:

> This day have I perfected your religion for you and completed My favour unto you, and have chosen for you as religion AL-ISLĀM (5:4).

Thus the official name of the religion was established. Finally, the close interrelationship of unity, piety, and leadership was proclaimed and many regard this passage as having been uttered then:

> O mankind! Lo! We have created you male and female, and have made you nations and tribes that ye may know one another. Lo! the

noblest of you, in the sight of Allāh, is the best in conduct. Lo! Allāh is Knower, Aware (49:13).

About two months after his return to Medina the Prophet Muhammad sickened and died. He had experienced two weeks of increasing illness and finally expired with his head in the lap of ʿĀʾisha, his favorite living wife. According to some, the last words that he spoke were, "No, the friend, the highest in Paradise." Terrible shock and panic followed his unexpected death. ʿUmar stood in the middle of the street and with his sword dared anyone to say that Muhammad had died. It was Abū Bakr who finally stilled the clamor when he addressed the throng of Muslims, saying, "O men, if anyone worships Muhammad, Muhammad is dead; if anyone worships God, God is alive, immortal."[15] Then he reminded them of the Qurānic passage 3:144:

Muhammad is but a messenger, messengers (the like of whom) have passed away before him. Will it be that, when he dieth or is slain, ye will turn back on your heals? He who turneth back doth no hurt to Allāh, and Allāh will reward the faithful.

Muhammad was buried at Medina, and by consent of the believers, Abū Bakr was chosen as his first successor.

D. Abdulla and Amina Love Muhammad

Muslim biographers tell us much about Muhammad's personality and habits. Abdulla, Amina and their friends are anxious to know every detail, since their life goal is to follow the path (*sunna*) of the Prophet. We will mention only a few of the things that various traditions report about him.

It is said that he had a pleasant personality. When his wife, ʿĀʾisha, was questioned about him, she used to say, "He was a man such as yourselves, he laughed often and smiled much." Yet he frequently remained silent for a long time when seated in the company of his followers. He spoke very distinctly and effectively and commanded the attention of his hearers. He walked very rapidly. He gave the impression that he had much to do and was determined to do it. At times, he felt doubt and depression, and several passages of the Qurʾān are intended to comfort him.

His humility and simplicity were notable. Even at the height of his power, ordinary people could approach him with their simple requests. He, in turn, visited the homes of others, including slaves. He was not ostentatious in his manner of living. Clearly he remembered his days of poverty as an orphan and his difficult times in Mecca. In his early days in Medina, as we have noted, he did not have much to eat at times, and meals were often taken in darkness because of the lack of oil. When prosperity came, it did not spoil him. Of the income from his properties in Medina, he used a considerable part for the benefit of Muslims and travelers. At the same time, he did not encourage asceticism. He personally enjoyed food. ʿĀʾisha used to say, "The prophet loveth three things—women, scents, and food. He has his heart's desire of the two first, but not of the last." He liked especially milk, cucumber, pumpkin, dates, sweetmeats, and honey, but he disliked onions and garlic. Like all Arabs, he was fond of cool, clear water.

He liked to do things around the house, especially cobbling shoes and mending clothes. He used toothpicks from a palm tree. He enjoyed riding his speedy horse "Subaha" and camel "Adhba." He did not appreciate poetry as many other Arabs did. He resented any suggestion that he had a kind of familiar spirit like a poet or a seer, and poets who lampooned him felt his wrath. He was a busy man and had little time for personal pleasures in the bustle of his many activities. Some of these had to do with family affairs.

He did have a large family. The number of wives was 11 or 12, depending on the status of Mariya. Factors in the marriages include affection, compassion for widows, family alliances, and hope for a son. Muhammad felt sorry that he never had a son. We have mentioned that Mariya, gave him a son, but little Ibrahim died in his second year. His remaining children were all daughters by Khadīja. As we have seen ʿAlī, his cousin, married Fāṭima, his daughter, and their two sons, Ḥasan and Ḥusain, were the only direct hale descendants of the Prophet. Muhammad did not marry a second time until his beloved Khadīja had died. Most of his other wives were older widows and divorcees. ʿĀʾisha provided the leadership in the group, of whom nine remained living at the time of the Prophet's death.

As to Muhammad's personal appearance, Muslims do not greatly concern themselves with that question. There is a tradition that he had curly hair, a reddish beard and a broad smile. Because of that tradition, some Muslim men dye their hair and beards a reddish hue. But Muslims very much hesitate to try to reproduce his appearance or portray him through the visual arts. To believers there is something disrespectful in that attempt, or even dangerous, since it may invite more veneration than appropriate. For believers it is not what Muhammad looked like but what he conveyed and what he represents that matters.

As we close this section on Muhammad the Prophet we should remember that Muslim love for Muhammad is expressed in many different ways and words. He is called "the Best of Humanity," "the Noblest of Creation," "the Ideal Prophet," "the Mercy to all Nations," and many other laudatory titles—far too many to repeat.[16] He is believed to have possessed the highest excellences that a human being can have. Although he himself claimed to do no miracle except the Qur'ān, many Muslims believe that he performed wonders. A host of legends have gathered around his personality and achievements, which some Muslims accept and others reject. Many, for example, believe that he will be a Mediator on the Day of Judgment.

On this point, however, all Muslims agree—Muhammad is *the example* for all to follow. He patterns the life of a true believer in God. There is darkness and danger about us as we travel through this world, but there is no doubt about the road that we should follow. It is the path of Muhammad, the path that is straight and true. The Qur'ān reveals Islām, and Muhammad defines it. *Lā ilāha illā Allāh, wa Muhammadu rasūl Allāh.* "There is no god but Allāh, and Muhammad is the messenger of Allāh." Abdulla and Amina honor the Prophet and firmly believe that he richly deserves his high place beside God in the creed of Islām. They not only esteem him highly but also love him very dearly.

The Muslim respect and affection for Muhammad cannot be expressed better than the words of his poet laureate, Hassan b. Thabit, who uttered these words after the death and burial of the Prophet:

Be generous with your tears and cries
At the loss of him whose equal will ne'er be found.
Those gone by never lost one like Muhammad,
And one like him will not be mourned till Resurrection Day....

I say, and none can find fault with me
But one lost to all sense—
I shall never cease to praise him....

O best man that ever walked the earth,
Leave us not ...
He shed a light over all creatures,
He who is guided to the blessed light is
Rightly guided ...
God and those who surround His throne, and good men
Bless the blessed Ahmad![17]

One can argue that sometimes silence is more eloquent than speech. A great teacher of mine, Daud Rahbar,[18] told me of his experience with Sir Muhammad Iqbāl, the poet-philosopher-statesman-hero of Pakistan. Iqbāl would argue with God, saying, "Allāh, why are you doing this? Allāh, why are you doing that?" But when Muhammad's name was mentioned, the famous man would become silent, his eyes would close, and tears would roll down his cheeks.

"... And Muhammad is the Messenger of God."

Notes

[1]Ibn Isḥāq, *Muhammad*, pp. 227f.

[2]M. Hamidullah, *The First Written Constitution in the World* (Lahore: Sh. Muhammad Ashraf, 1975; 3rd rev. ed.), p. 13. In the text it is referred to as the *kitāb*, writing, and *saḥīfa*, leaves. In contemporary usage it is often referred to as the *mucahada*, or covenant of unity. It has been cited as a pattern for the solution of interreligious problems from the Middle East to South Asia. For an example of this interpretation of the Medinan contract, cf. Syed Barakat Ahmad, "Non-Muslims and the Umma," *Studies in Islām* (xviii, p. 2, April 1980), pp. 86ff. He argues that it reflects a commitment to a "multi-religious, multi-cultural, plural community."

[3]Ibid., p. 13.

[4]Ibid., p. 47.

[5]Ibid., p. 48.

[6]Hamidullah, ibid., fn. 33, p. 35, points out that Ibn Isḥāq's version of the Agreement describes the Jews as an *umma*, a community, "along with" (*maʾa*) believers, while Abū ʿUbaid's version calls them a community "of" (*min*) believers. Both pronouns have powerful implication.

[7]Fazlur Rahman, *Islām* (New York: Anchor Books, 1968), p. 35.

[8]Haykal, *Muhammad*, p. 247.

[9]Ibn Isḥāq, *Muhammad*, p. 239.

[10]Haykal, *Muhammad*, p. 315.

[11]Ibn Isḥāq, *Muhammad*, p. 341.

[12]Introduction to Moyinkutty Vaidyar, *Badar Pāda Pātt* (Parapanangadi: Bayaniyya Book Stall, 1971. Malayalam), p. 11. This is a Mappila Muslim song from southwest India. Translation by author from Malayala.

[13]Haykal, *Muhammad*, p. 271.

[14]Rodinson, *Mohammed*, pp. 270f.

[15]Ibn Isḥāq, *Muhammad*, p. 683.

[16]Schimmel, *Muhammad*, pp. 10–22, provides a study of the names of the Prophet, including a list (pp. 257–59) of his 99 "Most Noble Names."

[17]Ibn Isḥāq, *Muhammad*, pp. 796-98.

[18]Dr. Rahbar, scholar of the Qurʾan and Urdu literature, and author of *God of Justice*, taught at Lahore, Istanbul, Hartford, and Boston. The conversation alluded to took place in 1965, in Hartford, Connecticut, U.S.A.

8

My Muslim Friend Adheres to the Qur°ān

It has been said that there is no end to the making of books. The piles of volumes in libraries and bookstores confirm that saying. Most books have a temporal quality. They need renewing, or they are stored or discarded. There are a few books, however, that have an enduring quality, that are referred to for life's solutions, and that shape whole peoples. The number of such books can be counted on the fingers of one hand. One of them is the Qur°ān (sometimes spelled Koran). Abdulla and Amina adhere to the Qur°ān, but more than that, they love it. They accept it as God's final Word to humanity, and as the foundation of their faith and life.

The Holy Qur°ān is the sacred scripture for over one billion people. As a book it is not very large. It contains 114 chapters and 6226 verses. But for the Muslim believer it is the most important writing in the world. It is the guiding star for life in this world, and it is the compass for the Muslim's journey to the next world. The Qur°ān is the tangible symbol of God's Reality, the exposition of His eternal will, and the most precious religious possession of Muslims. It is held totally sacred and is revered and extolled by all Muslims. Because of its divine nature, it is unhesitatingly referred to as the ultimate and infallible authority in all human affairs. It can safely be said that nothing is more important to Islām than the Qur°ān. Every Muslim individual, every Muslim family, and the entire Muslim community in the world ideally adheres to it and lives by it.

A. The Place of the Qur°ān in the Life of a Muslim Family

Amina is a pious woman. Her husband, Abdulla, owns a beautiful, decorated copy of the Qur°ān, and she sees to it that it is always kept wrapped in an honored place. Some of her friends are rather superstitious, They will sometimes take a verse from the Qurʾān, place it in a little container, and then tie it to their upper forearm as a protection against sickness and evil. Amina, an educated woman, does not approve of that practice. Still she yields to none in her veneration of the Sacred Book, and she tries to instill that same sense of the holy in her children.

Abdulla and Amina have three children. The oldest, Ashraf, has already entered the first year of college. The two youngest, Rashid and Fatima, are still at home. Rashid is 12 years old and Fatima is eight. They attend the local government school, but early every morning you will see them hurrying along the street with their friends. They are on their way to the religious school at the mosque, the *madrasa*. Although Arabic is not their native language, there they will learn to memorize and recite passages from the Qurʾān in Arabic. In this way, from childhood itself, Muslims develop a deep faith in the sanctity of the Qurʾān and its sound. Rashid and Fatima often do not grasp the meaning of the passages that they are reciting. Yet they have the feeling that they are doing something very important, and the training has long-lasting effect.

On his way home from work Abdulla is passing through a book market. In one section Qurʾāns of many different types are being sold. Next to them are other books related to the teachings of the Qurʾān. Abdulla picks up a well-known work, *The Mind al-Qurʾān Builds*.[1] On the back cover are some titles of books about the Qurʾān that are available from the publisher. They include: *A Geographical History of the Qurʾān, An Approach to the Study of Qurʾān, Beauty and Wisdom of the Holy Qurʾān, Glimpses of the Holy Qurʾān, The Holy Qurʾān for Beginners, In the Shade of the Qurʾān, Lessons from the Stories of the Qurʾān, Message of the Qurʾān, Prophecies of the Holy Qurʾān, Qurʾān-Based Teachings, The Qurʾān for Children, Virtues of the Holy Qurʾān, Qurānic Reasoning*, and *The Qurʾān and You*. There are many more. Abdulla wishes that he had the money to buy them and the time to read them all.

Abdulla loves the sound of the Qurʾān, as do all the members of his family. Tomorrow is the anniversary of the death of a family member. Abdulla has commissioned special readings of the Qurʾān as a memorial. Someone who knows the art will come to the house and do the readings. Whatever the devotional moment is, the sound of the Qurʾān is the key element. At birth, at puberty, at marriage, in times of sickness and at death—at all important life occasions the accents of the Qur'ān are heard, and they become the sacralizing sound that makes holy the special moment.

The chant of the Qur'ān is the best-loved music of Islām. Muslims have a somewhat ambiguous approach to music. In some parts of the Muslim world, such as South Asia and Indonesia, the Islāmic musical heritage is very rich, reflecting the indigenous culture. Nevertheless, among many Muslims there has been a traditional suspicion of the emotional aspect of music. It is believed to foster creature love and to detract from the purity and concentration of the objective worship of God. The great theologian, Al-Ghazālī, who knew about these hesitations, took the opposite view. He said:

> The heart of man has been so constituted that like a flint, it contains a hidden fire which is evoked by music and harmony... These harmonies are echoes of the higher world of beauty which we call the world of spirits; they remind man of his relationship to that world.[2]

The hesitation remains for many Muslims, however, and it is the intonation of the Qur'ān that has become the true music of Islām. When the reciter begins his powerful chant, the Muslim heart sings. Through the almost hypnotic rhythm of the chant Muslims literally *feel* their faith.

What we have said about music may be said about art. The writing of the Qur'ān is the best-loved art of Islām. Despite the hesitation of Muslims in regard to the portrayal of figures there are also parts of the Muslim world where artistic achievement is very high. The delicate miniatures of Mughul art are justly famous. Nothing, however, can take the place of the writing of the Qur'ān in the Muslim artistic mind. When you walk into Abdulla's home, you do not see any pictures on the wall, apart from some calendars and family photographs. Instead you see decorative Arabic script, often hung in frames. The script is a passage or phrase from the Qur'ān. Drawn with almost endless variation and with the greatest use of the imagination, the calligraphy of the Qur'ān has become the supreme art form in Islām. Not only in frames and in books, but also in tapestry, ceramics, brassware, and stone carvings—using almost any medium the words of the Qur'ān are intricately traced in myriad and seemingly infinite forms. They are in fact the expression of divine infinity translated into creaturely form.

In summary we may say that the Qurʾān is woven into the very warp and woof of Muslim life.

B. The Name of the Qurʾān

The word Qurʾān is an Arabic term that can mean both reading" and "reciting." The first word revealed to Muhammad (96:1) was believed to be "Read!" or "Recite!" The term Qurʾān can refer to a single passage, to a group of passages, or to the entire collection of sacred revelations which God gave through the Prophet Muhammad. It is now usually used for the whole Book.

Another common term for the Qurʾān is *al-kitāb*, which simply means "The Book." Abdulla may ask Rashid, "Please bring me the Kitāb." Rashid knows immediately which book his father means. There are other words used for the Qurʾān. It is also called *al-tanzīl*, which means "The Revelation." The word comes from a root that means "send down." God sent down, that is, revealed the scripture. Another expressive term for the Qurʾān is *al-furqān*. Furqān means the "distinction" or "separation." The Qurʾān is not only the distinction between truth and falsehood, but it also separates the community of believers from unbelievers. A term for the Qurʾān that is commonly used is *al-dhikr*, a spiritually significant word. It can signify either "reminder," that is, a warning or admonition from God; or it can mean "remembrance," that is, the remembering of God. The former points to God's intention in the Qurʾān, while the latter suggests the use of the Qurʾān in worship and meditation. A word meaning "wisdom," *al-hikma*, is also applied to the Qurʾān. It refers to the source of wise conduct. Parallel to it is the term *al-ᶜilm*, the "knowledge." The Qurʾān brings humans God's wisdom and knowledge. Finally, *al-huda*, or the "guidance," suggests the crucial significance of the Qurʾān for Muslims. God has graciously given His guidance to humanity throughout history, but the Qurʾān is God's final Word, His ultimate Guidance.

It is common to add a descriptive adjective to the term Qurʾān. In recent years the word "holy" has come into common use, and the phrase Holy Qurʾān is frequently seen. In older usage other phrases were more common: the Glorious Qurʾān, the Noble Qurʾān, and the Mighty Qurʾān.

The various names of the Qurʾān give us helpful clues to its profound significance for Muslims.

C. The Origin of the Qur'ān

We will deal with this topic in two parts. The first is: What view do Muslims take regarding the origin of the Qur'ān? The second is, How did the present book called the Qur'ān come into being, from a historical point of view?

1. Muslim Belief Regarding the Origin of the Qur'ān

My Muslim friends believe that the Qur'ān is the Word of God and not the word of man. Although the Prophet Muhammad spoke the words, he did not originate them. They were already in existence, and he only recited them. They are not his words, but God's words. As a pipe carries water from the source to the user, and it arrives fresh and untainted, so Muhammad received the divine words and transmitted them. In order to receive them, he was given a special grace of inspiration (*wahy*) by God.

In the chapter on Muhammad's revelation experience, we have already noted the circumstances of that event. There are three explanatory possibilities that Muslims have considered in regard to the actual process of revelation. The first is that Allāh spoke the words audibly to Muhammad, who heard them and passed them on accurately. The second is that they were conveyed to Muhammad's inner spirit, and he communicated them exactly as received. The third is that they came to him through an intermediary, the angel Gabriel (Jibril), and Muhammad then proclaimed the message to the people. Sometimes these views are combined, as suggested by a passage of the Qur'ān itself (26,192-195):

> And lo! it is a revelation of the Lord of the Worlds, Which the True Spirit hath brought down Upon thy heart, that thou mayest be (one) of the warners ... in plain Arabic speech.

Since the words of the Qur'ān are the Word of God, it is believed that the Qur'ān is essentially eternal and uncreated. From one point of view it seems like a human word. As a book, it is made by humans—the paper is manufactured and the letters are printed—and such a book can become old and disappear. So also, in human speech, the words can be brought into being by the pronouncing of the tongue, and they can be either memorized or forgotten. But, Muslims believe, these are only phenomenal things, human analogies. In its true and primary sense, the original words that Muhammad proclaimed are eternal and uncreated, of divine origin. In fact, Muslim teachers hold that the Qurʾān in its essence is the very Speech of God, that was always with God. Thus the Word of God has its being in the eternal nature of God. It is revealed to humans, and not created by humans.

There is another element that must be added to make the picture complete. That element is the idea of an eternal book that God created and that contains all the words that God intended to reveal to human beings. This is called "the Mother of the Book." This concept of a heavenly Qurʾān must be combined with the concept of the Eternal Speech of God. The picture of a heavenly Qurʾān that existed before creation is drawn from the following passages of the Qurʾān:

> Nay, it is a glorious Qurʾān in a preserved tablet [*lawḥ maḥfūz*] (85:21f.)

> We have made it an Arabic Qurʾān that maybe you will understand. And it indeed is in the Mother of the Book [*umma al-kitāb*] in Our Presence (43, 2ff.)

> And recite that which hath been revealed unto thee of the Scripture [*al-kitāb*] of thy Lord (18:28).

The explanation is that God, in Whose essence is His eternal and uncreated Word, created a heavenly book that is the prototype of His revelations to humanity. Each prophet received his appropriate portion, through the agency of Gabriel, and revealed it to his nation. Muhammad in turn is commanded: "And recite that which hath been revealed unto thee of the Scripture of thy Lord."

We can see in these ideas some of the difficult problems that from time to time perplexed Muslim theologians as they thought about the origin of the Qurʾān, even producing divisions in the *umma*. One unsolved problem is the relation between the eternal God and the eternal Qurʾān. Are there two distinct eternals, then? But this cannot be because that would be the equivalent of *shirk*, associating a partner with God. Yet their separation must also be maintained. Theologians tried to deal with the problem by identifying the eternal Qurʾān with God's attribute of Speech. Another problem arose out of the relation of the eternal existence of the book to the temporal events that it records. If the words of the Qurʾān are eternal, how is it that they seem to arise out of the historical events in the Prophet's lifetime? Did those events, for example, the battles of Badr and Uhud, produce the revelations? But how could a temporal event be a cause of the eternal Word? Theologians attempted to deal with this question by introducing the concept of "occasions." Human events are the occasions for the descent of revelation, but they are not the cause of the eternal Word which long preceded these events.

While questions such as these perturbed Muslim thinkers in the course of Islāmic history as they reflected theologically on the origin of the Qurʾān, Abdulla and Amina are not bothered by such issues. In fact, they are not really aware of the discussions that went on. It is their faith in God's Word that matters to them. They firmly believe that the Qurʾān, and its every phrase, is the literal and inerrant Word of God. They wonder at times about its meaning, but they do not wonder about its origin. They believe that it comes from God and that it represents God's final and greatest gift to humanity. They are happy to accept it as their sure and infallible rule of faith and life. It is their link with God, and they firmly resist any attempt to weaken its authority. Abdulla would agree with Ibn Masʿūd who said, "Whoever loves and admires the Qurʾān, loves God and his Messenger; whoever abhors the Qurʾān, abhors God and his messenger."[3] He would also appreciate what Aḥmad Ibn Ḥanbal stated:[g]

> I saw God in my sleep and said to him: "Lord! What is the best way to draw near for those who wish to draw near to you?" God answered: "Through my words (in the Qurʾān), Ahmad." Then I asked: "Lord! With or without understanding?" and he said: "With and without understanding ..."[4]

2. The Historical Formation of the Book

The Qurʾān did not take its present form until 23 years after the death of Muhammad. The finalization of the text of the Qurʾān is a fascinating story.

According to traditional Muslim belief the Preserved Tablet was first sent down by God from the seventh heaven to the first heaven. From there, the angel Gabriel transmitted the message of the Qurʾān to Muhammad in a progressive manner between the years 610 and 632. It is believed that they were impressed on his mind in such a way that he could recite them accurately to the people at the appropriate moments. Muslim tradition agrees that the Prophet Muhammad himself did not write down what was revealed, but others did, at the time of the revelation and later.

Writing in the seventh century in Arabia was not so important as memory. The power of memory in the preprinting and pre-TV eras was so great that it defies modern comprehension. It would not be unexpected that many of the recitations of the Qurʾān were memorized by his followers. Some that were used in the prayers became common property. Others were written down on various types of material by designated individuals, for the Prophet seems to have maintained an unofficial system of secretaries and instructors. Still there was no complete Qurʾān available in writing when Muhammad died. Muslim tradition reports that community leaders were quite concerned about the matter. They commissioned a secretary of Muhammad, Zaid b. Thābit, to collect the various parts of the Qurʾān, and he did so from the scraps of written materials and from the memories of the faithful. It is further reported that Zaid then gave the leaves (*suḥuf*) of the Qurʾān to Hafsa, the daughter of Umar ibn Khattāb, for safekeeping. Some would say, why Hafsa? The answer, might be, why not? Someone had to keep this precious material in pre-safety deposit box times, and it could well be the household of one of the great Companions of the Prophet who could do that task best.

The Zaid edition, however, was not the only collection of the Qurʾān in existence. Evidently there were at least four other versions circulating in different areas of the Muslim world. The differences between them were rather minor.[5] The version of ʿAbdullah b. Masʿūd (d. ca. 653) in Kufa did not include the last two sūras. The version of Ubayy b Kaʿb (d. ca. 639) in Syria included two extra sūras. There were also smaller differences of vowels, punctuation, and the order of the sūras. Although the variations were minor, their existence made it clear that something must be done. Moreover, the number of the original "Qurʾān-readers" who had memorized its contents was becoming fewer, as natural death and warfare took their inevitable toll. It was the Caliph ʿUthmān, the third caliph of Islām (644-55), who stepped into the breach and resolved to prepare an official version of the Qur'ān. He once again commissioned the invaluable Zaid b. Thābit, together with other Meccans, who undertook the task of establishing an official edition. Their version was accepted and was sent to key centers of the Muslim world, and all other versions were destroyed.

'Uthmān's version of the text of the Qur'ān fixed the consonants as we now have them, as well as the number and order of the chapters. Since written Arabic had not yet finalized its vowel structure, there could still be different readings of certain words, but for all practical purposes the text of the Qur'ān was now complete. The last remaining difference relates to the numbering of the verses that varies in different versions. These differences become apparent in English translations. This matter too is reaching its conclusion as the Cairo edition of 1925, called "the Kufic version," gains wide circulation.[6]

Like all Muslims, Abdulla and Amina are proud of the fact that there is full agreement in Islām over the text of the Qur'ān. They believe that God has preserved His Message without error, and they are confident that as they read it and recite it, they are listening to the very words of God.

D. The Arrangement of the Qur'ān

Readers of the Qur'ān who are not familiar with its arrangement experience immediate difficulty. It is not arranged topically, under subject heads. Nor is it arranged chronologically, in order of revelation. Rather it is arranged according to the length of the chapters. The first chapter stands alone as a special case, honored with the name *al-Fātiha*, the opening. It is the most famous chapter in the book, and the chief prayer of Islām. After that, however, the chapters go according to size, chapter two being the longest and chapter 114 the shortest.

Another "problem" in reading the Qur'ān is the style. It must be remembered that the Qur'ān represents preaching and prophecy, delivered by an impassioned speaker to a live audience. The Book was not prepared as a textbook. So within individual chapters the subject under discussion may change suddenly and frequently. Furthermore, it is difficult at times to conclude who is speaking to whom. A helpful point to remember is that the term "We" is a common Semitic "we of majesty," and usually when it is used, it is God Who is speaking.

Each of the 114 chapters or sūras of the Qurʾān has a name, taken from the body of the text, by which it is commonly known. For example, there is the Chapter of the Bee, there is Noah, the Star, and so on. Muslims usually refer to the chapters by their names rather than by number. At the head of every sūra except the ninth are the well-known words *bismi llāhi rraḥmāni raḥīmi*, which mean "In the Name of God, the Merciful, the Compassionate." This is referred to as the *bismillāh* or the *basmala*. The phrase is regularly used to open meetings, to begin speeches, or to inaugurate solemn events. At the beginning of 29 sūras of the Qurʾān there are some mysterious individual letters, whose meaning can only be guessed at. Some verse numberings include the *bismillāh* and the mysterious letters as verses, which helps to account for the differences in numbering. Each of the 6226 verses of the Qurʾān is called an *āya* (pl. *āyāt*), a term whose basic meaning is "sign" or "miracle." This is significant because it points to the Muslim belief that every verse of the Qurʾān is in essence a sign of God's will and a miracle of God's grace.

E. The Language of the Qurʾān, Its Miraculousness, and Its Recitation

1. The Language of the Qurʾān

The Arabic of the Qurʾān has a unique quality. Muslims customarily regard this beauty of language as part of the miraculousness (*iʿjāz*) of the Qurʾān. The Arabic language, of course, developed before the time of Muhammad, and there were quite a few outstanding Arab poets prior to his advent. But the language of the Qurʾān ushered in a new era, and in a sense created literary Arabic. Its form of rhymed prose has a linguistic power that makes it particularly well suited to the gravity of the message. Its resonant and elegant beauty must have immediately attracted the approval of the first Arab listeners, and ever since, its language has been the standard against which classical Arabic is measured. Finally, however, it is not its linguistic beauty, but it is the fact that this language became the vehicle of God's final Word that gives it its special place in Muslim affection. That is why, even though only 16 percent of the world's Muslims are Arab, 100 percent of the world's Muslims esteem the language of the Qurʾān, and try as much as possible to learn it.

It is no wonder, then, that for centuries many Muslims believed that the Qurʾān could not be translated into another language. The message and the linguistic carrier of the message were regarded as inseparably bonded. If you took away the carrier language through translation, part of the miracle of the Qurʾān was removed. Even now the idea of translation is not universally appreciated by Muslims, although such translations have become commonplace. I well recall the difficulties experienced by one such trail-blazer, C. N. Ahmed Moulavi, an erudite scholar in India, when he published the first translation of the Qurʾān into the Malayalam language.[7] His dedicated efforts were not welcomed by many. Now, even though such translations are becoming frequent, all Muslim translators guard the faith in its miraculous language through such titles as "The *Meaning* of the Glorious Koran" (Marmaduke Pickthall). The title indicates the viewpoint that no translation of the Qurʾān is really the Qurʾān itself, but only its interpretation.

The concept of sacred sound led to the Arabicization of the Muslim world, and this phenomenon in turn represents one of the most important unifying factors in Islām. Wherever Muslims go, and wherever they meet, they observe the same religious terminology and feel an immediate affinity for each other. Behind the universal Muslim greeting, *salaam aleikum*, lies a world of commonality derived from the Arabic Qurʾān. At the same time, the strong emphasis on the sacrality of a particular cultural sound inevitably involves problems, as well, for a global faith. At best, we may speak of formidable difficulties in the field of religious communication in the mosque and religious education of youth. At worst, the emphasis on sound can result in parrot-like, rote religion, and the emphasis on sacred letters can result in superstitious practices, including forms of magic. Muslims today are struggling to relate in a new way their respect for the sacred language and their concern to set forth the spiritual meaning of the Qurʾān.

Abdulla and Amina, as we have seen, accept the special place of the Qurʾān in their religious life. Because Arabic is not their natural language, they have a problem in probing its meanings. They know that they can leave the Book wrapped in its place of honor, basically untouched, as many Muslims do. But they are really interested in unwrapping its meaning for their lives. Abdulla has not had the opportunity to study Arabic intensively as many learned religious leaders in his country have done. An intelligent and educated man, he is less and less interested in sacred sound for its own sake and is more and more interested in the meaning of the Qurānic injunctions for his life in the contemporary world. He believes that God Who sent prophets to many nations wants him to understand that significance. He wants his children to understand it too. He is particularly worried about Ashraf who, he fears, may be losing grip on his faith. Amina too is concerned, and they both wonder how they can pass on their faith effectively.

2. Muslim Faith in the Miraculousness of the Qurʾān

The miraculousness of the Qurʾān is not only a matter of language and sound. There are additional elements in Muslim teaching concerning the miracle of the Qurʾān. The first is that it attests to the prophetic validity of the Prophet Muhammad. One acknowledged theologian of Islām[8] made the point in these words: "... The prophetic office of the Prophet—upon whom be peace—is built upon this miracle." In popular Islām it is believed that Muhammad performed a broad range of miracles, as we have noted, but many modern Muslims believe that he was responsible for only one, and that itself was God's doing. The Qurʾān tells of how Muhammad was attacked by opponents who were pressing him to produce miracles. Derisively they challenged him: "Produce a spring of water or a garden! Cause the heaven to fall! Create a house of gold! Ascend to heaven!" And the reply came, "Am I nought but a mortal messenger?" (17:93). In another verse the real point is made directly (17:88): "Verily, though mankind and Jinn should assemble to produce the like of this Qurʾān, they could not!"

Muslim theologians add other elements to the miraculousness of the Qurʾān. It is miraculous in the benefits that it brings: good news, guidance, warning, and truth. Human beings should learn from the spirits. The *jinn* declare: "Lo! it is a marvelous Qurʾān, which guideth unto righteousness, and we ascribe it to our Lord" (72:1f.) Then there is the fact that the Qurʾān reveals essential information about the past and the lessons of human spiritual history. Furthermore, it inerrantly foretells the future, charting the course of human events to come, and in their light calling for a moral response in the here and now. The Qur'ān itself best summarizes the element of miraculousness in God's gift of His Word:

> Lo! those who disbelieve in the Reminder, when it cometh unto them (are guilty), for lo! it is an unassailable Scripture. Falsehood cannot come at it from before it or behind it. (It is) a revelation from the Wise, the Owner of Praise (41:41f.)

3. The Recitation of the Qur'ān

The recitation of the Qur'ān, whether it is in public or in private, is an important ritual. Its recital is part of the surrendering of the believer to God, and it demands concentrated and devout attention.

> And I am commanded to be of those who surrender (unto Him), and to recite the Qur'ān (27:91f.).

> And when the Qur'ān is recited, give ear to it and pay heed, that ye may obtain mercy (7:204).

Muslims take great pride in their ability to recite passages from the Qur'ān. There are professional Qur'ān readers, but in this matter Muslims do not yield to the professionals. Some ordinary Muslims are able to recite the entire Qur'ān from memory. A believer who is able to do that is called a *ḥāfiẓ* and is held in high respect by the Muslim community.

When they approach the Qur'ān for reading and recitation, Muslims are advised to be ritually pure, that is, to have performed the same ablutions that are required for the five-fold prayer. The reader/reciter should assume a devout attitude and turn the body in the direction of Mecca. A sample opening prayer for this exercise is the 114th sūra of the Qur'ān: "I seek refuge in the Lord of mankind from the evil of the sneaking Whisperer [Satan]." A typical closing prayer could be: "O God, make the Qur'ān a mercy for me, and set it as a model for me, a light, a guidance and a mercy."

Since the words of the Scripture are divinely given, the actual reading or recitation should always be done very correctly. At the same time, it should also be done reflectively. As one goes along in the reading, it is acceptable to insert such phrases as "God is very great!" or "Glory be to God!" We have already noted that the melodious chanting has a powerful effect on both reciter and hearer, often producing tears of emotion. Since some believers are more capable than others in this art, they are called upon when the readings are done in groups. The progressive reading or recital of the Qur'ān is commended as an important spiritual exercise, especially in the month of Ramadān, and the Book is divided into 30 equal portions to make that possible.

F. The Teaching of the Qur'ān

In this section we will take up only two questions: what does the Qur'ān say about the Qur'ān, and what is the central thrust of the Qur'ān?

It should be remembered that the teaching of *Islām* is a wider idea than the teaching of the *Qur'ān*. This is so because in addition to the Qur'ān Islām drew on other secondary sources for the development of its teaching, and we will be dealing with them in the following chapter. An example will illustrate the point. Muslims agree that they should pray five times daily, but this number is not actually found in the Qur'ān itself—it stems from the tradition of Islām. Many similar examples could be cited.

1. What the Qur'ān Says About the Qur'ān

In his excellent survey, *The Teaching of the Qur'ān*, H. U. Weitbrecht Stanton neatly summarizes what the Qur'ān says about itself.[9] It descended on the Night of Power (97:1), that blessed night (44:2), in the month of Ramadān (2:185). The Word of God, recorded in the Original Book (43:4), has been revealed in portions (17:106). Its verses stem from the Wise One (11:1) and constitute a perfect revelation that clarifies difficult issues (5:101). It does not only represent sure knowledge but also a warning (69:51) and a reminder to the world (68:62). Its verses are both figurative and explicit (3:17), but essentially it is a plain sign (18:1) and a clear indicator to the heart of the believer (3:49). It is a revelation that has a conclusive message (86:13).

The Qur'ān is a glorious scripture (50:1) that comprises all the secrets of heaven and earth (27:75). Its coming was foretold by earlier scriptures which it confirms and whose truth it safeguards (3:3). Its lucid good news (17:9) brings healing to the faithful and ruin to the wicked (17:82). The faithful accept it as all from God, but its revelation increases the unbelief and rebellion of many who treat it as a lie (74:33–34). It is absolutely free from error (41:42), and whoso rejects it will be lost (3:4). It is above all the guarantee of the friendship of God: "Lo, my Protecting Friend is Allāh, who revealeth the Scripture. He befriendeth the righteous" (7:196).

2. The Central Theme of Guidance

There are many important themes in the teaching of the Qur'ān, and there could be many opinions about its central thrust. From the divine side, the unity of God is a dominant concept. From the human side, the idea of surrender to God controls the field. What combines the God-human relationship is the theme of guidance.

There is a development of ideas in the Qur'ān, which was revealed over the course of 22 years in relation to a variety of situations. We note especially that in the earlier Meccan period there is a heavy concentration on such ideas as the Greatness and the Beneficence of the One God, the Resurrection, and the Judgment, while in the Medinan period there is more emphasis on practical problems and legislation required for the establishment of Muslim society. Throughout the Qur'ān, however, there is a consistent emphasis on guidance, and the term in its various forms appears not less than 240 times.[10]

The Qur'ān declares that its basic purpose is to give guidance to the straight path:

> Ye were upon the brink of an abyss of fire, and He did save you from it. Thus Allāh maketh clear His revelation unto you that haply ye may be guided (3:103).

The guidance that the Qur'ān gives is to clearly define the nature of the straight path as a prohibiting of what is evil and enjoining what is good. The following of this guidance is what constitutes success.

> And there may spring from you a nation who invite to goodness and enjoin right conduct and forbid indecency. Such are they who are successful (3:104).

In sum the Qurʾān is the ultimate gift of God's grace, the granting of clear instruction regarding human behavior and human destiny. For that guidance men and women should be grateful, and in gratefulness they should be responsive to God's will.

The following quotation from Professor Fazlur Rahman is important for the clarity that it brings to this point:

> ... God's mercy reaches its logical zenith in "sending Messengers," "revealing Books," and showing man "the Way." This "guidance" (*hidāya*) is also kneaded into man's primordial nature insofar as the distinction between good and evil is "ingrained in his heart" (91:8) and insofar as men have made a covenant with God in pre-eternity to recognize him as their sovereign (7:172). Man often little heeds these and hence, particularly at times of moral crisis, God sends his messages, for it is the moral aspect of man's behavior which is most slippery and difficult to control and yet most crucial for his survival and success. Hence judgment is an imperative upon this whole process of mercy from creation through preservation to guidance, since it is through guidance that man is expected to develop that inner torch (called *taqwā* by the Qurʾān) whereby he can discern between right and wrong ... This entire chain—creation-preservation-guidance-judgment, all as manifestations of mercy—is so utterly reasonable that the Qurʾān states surprise and dismay that it is questioned at all.[11]

G. The Study of the Qurʾān

All Muslims respect the Qurʾān, but not all Muslims study it. For many believers the recitation of the sacred Book has priority over its study. This is a bone of contention among Muslims. Many educated people say that reciting without understanding has no value. The tradition of memorizing and reciting is very strong, however, and it is maintained throughout the Muslim world. In considering the study of the Qurʾān we will deal with adults, children and youth in turn.

Adult Muslims and the Qurʾān

Most adults do not study the Qurʾān in a very systematic way. Like Abdulla they are busy with the daily tasks of surviving and living in a demanding world. Many do not have the habit of reading. Moreover, the Qurʾān is not always available in their own language. Their religious instruction is gained primarily by listening to mosque sermons on Fridays, by attending special lecture classes during the month of Ramaḍān, by taking advantage of Qur'ān readings in the home, and by reading Muslim periodicals. Although most Muslim men know the basic teachings that come from the Qur'ān, in one sense it can be said that the "Furqān" is still a closed book for many.

Muslim women have a greater problem with Qur'ān studies. This is partly because their literacy rate is still low as compared to men in most Muslim societies. Furthermore, in many places they do not attend the mosque service. As a result they are dependent on what they have learned in the *madrasa*, on home readings of the Qur'ān, and especially in the night lectures given to both men and women on the nights of Ramaḍān. Their lack of study does not diminish the loyalty of Muslim women to the Qur'ān, and in fact modern Muslim women are looking to the reinterpretation of the Qur'ān as the basis for their progress and development.

Children and the Qur'ān

As we have noted, Muslim children attend the *madrasa*, which is frequently attached to a mosque, until the age of 12 or 13. The primary subject there is still the rote memorization and recitation of the Qur'ān. Other subjects are touched upon, but not very deeply. These topics include an introduction to Muslim faith and practice, worship forms, the biography of the Prophet Muhammad, and stories of other heroes of the faith. The *madrasas*—frequently called *maktabs* at lower levels—are everywhere in the Muslim world. They are conducted in rooms attached to mosques, in separate buildings, in homes, and in open places, with teachers of varied qualifications, and with a tremendous variety of approach, standard, and teaching methodology. Their purpose is not so much to open the mind as to impress the spirit. They seek to set a tone and to provide some simple rules for being Muslim. Modern community leaders have severely criticized their heavy dependence on memorization and their restricted curriculum. As a result, new forms of *madrasa* education are developing. Nevertheless, whether traditional or modern, the overall impact of the *madrasa* experience on Muslim faith and feeling is a powerful one. Above all, what Muslim boys and girls learn is respect for the Sacred Word. Combined with that, they also gain a sense of their identity as Muslims. The effect of this early concentrated exposure to the Qurʾān is to leave a virtually indelible mark on Muslim spiritual consciousness.

Muslim Youth and the Qurʾān

In every religion youth are faced with many problems and temptations. This is also true for Muslims. Like Ashraf many young Muslims make no effort to study the Qurʾān, and they seldom attend the mosque or religious meetings. At a formal level they respect the Qurʾān, but practically they do not spend time with it. Their minds and hearts are elsewhere. From football to jobs their thoughts are occupied with other concerns.

While this is true of many youth, there is another group of young Muslims that is very concerned about the Holy Qurʾān. In recent times the membership of this group has been increasing, and young people have played leading roles in the revitalization of Islām. An example is the activity of the Muslim Students Association in North America. Its members form Muslim clubs for youth, conduct special lecture programs, disseminate information, and encourage attendance at the mosque. They are very anxious to understand the relation of Qurānic themes to their general studies at colleges and universities. They face a problem that frequently there is no one available to help them study the Qurʾān in a fresh and stimulating way. At times they may read out of the Qurʾān what they want it to say rather than its actual meaning.

Although contemporary Muslims universally appreciate the Qurʾān and recognize the necessity of its study, there is still much room for the provision of fresh and stimulating materials for its study by various age groups.

H. The Exposition of the Qurʾān: The Development and Training of Clergy

At this point we will look at the development of Muslim clergy and their training. Clergy in Islām developed out of the need for the exposition of the Qurʾān. How that exposition is done is a function of their training.

1. The Development of Clergy in Islām

In one sense the development of clergy in Islām is unexpected. Islām has no priestly principle; rather, it has a strong principle of the equality of all believers. There is no one that can stand between the individual believer and God. There is no one endowed with a special authority or responsibility to mediate God's graces to humanity. To use examples from another religion—there is no pope, church council, voting convention, or ordination ceremony for clergy. Clergy do not have powers that laity do not have. Any Muslim can serve as a prayer leader. Any Muslim can be a theologian. In fact, most of the outstanding Muslim religious writers of this century have been nonclergy. In the Sunnī tradition a clergyman is simply a specially qualified "lay" person. In Shīʿa Islām there is a significant difference in approach that increases the authority of clergy, but that is for later discussion.

In spite of this equality theory, clergy not only developed in Islām but in the end their influence became as powerful as that of clergy in religions that maintain a priestly principle. The reasons for this development are simple enough, and one might say that it was inevitable. The practice of worship and prayer required a group of skilled people who would take care of these functions. Someone had to preach the sermon in the mosque. Someone had to teach the faith. Above all, someone had to interpret the meaning of the Word of God. As long as the Prophet was alive there was no problem, because the revelations answered the questions as they arose. As soon as Muhammad died the problems of interpretation commenced. Who had the time to really study these problems and the linguistic training to do that study well? Who could apply learning and experience to the issues of religious law? It is not surprising that within 150 years of the death of Muhammad the clergy were fully in place and had become the semi-official interpreters of the Qurʾān.

The ordinary term for clergyman in Islām is "learned person" (ʿalīm), which is usually used in the plural form, ʿulamāʾ. In view of what has been said there is no simple English term that expresses the meaning of this word accurately. The term clergy—which we are compelled to use for lack of something

147

better—is too strong. The translations "learned doctors" or "religious scholars" are sometimes used, but they too are misleading. The *ʿulamāʾ* are religious functionaries who have had some training and who, by the consensus of the community, exercise some authority. That authority, however, varies considerably from place to place and time to time. In South Asia the term *ʿulamāʾ* becomes *maulavi*, and in West Africa it is *mallam*. Other terms express specific aspects of the clerical function. The word *imām*, for example, refers to a prayer leader; in the Shīʿa community, however, the *Imām* is the word for the religious leader of the community. The term *mufti* applies to a respected member of the *ʿulamāʾ* who may provide an opinion (*fatwā*) on some difficulty legal or theological issue. The word *mujtahid* is used especially in the Shiʿa community to designate a senior scholar who has the grace and the authority to interpret the Qurʾān.

2. The Training of the Clergy: Traditional and Progressive

The body of Muslim clergy can be very roughly divided into traditional clergy and progressive clergy. Each group has a somewhat different approach to the study and exposition of the Qurʾān.

By "traditional" clergy we signify those who view themselves primarily as the guardians and transmitters of Muslim tradition. Their approach to the Qurʾān reflects this function, and their training is geared to it. The education of such a clergyman, common in Muslim societies, is as follows. After about five years of general education, the aspiring candidates will move to a mosque school (*dars*) or to a separate Arabic "College." For this approximately five-year period the course of studies is almost entirely Arabic and Qurʾān memorization. This will be followed by about four years of further training at a major institution for clergy studies. There the curriculum is narrow and focussed. The matters studied include Arabic, Qurʾān, and Qurʾān commentary, Ḥadīth and theology, legal studies, and practical duties. The lecture method is dominant in the classroom. The teacher lectures, the student receives. The student is not expected to interpret the Qurʾān for himself. The point of his training is to learn the tradition and how to pass it on to others.

A traditional Muslim clergyman admires the Qurʾān above everything else and dedicates his life to it, even though more often than not he has to work for very low pay. In terms of its explanation, he has the deepest respect for past authorities. His study of the Qurʾān is therefore more related to what previous generations have believed about it, rather than to its fresh application to the present age. For him the Qurʾān is the solace of Islām and the source of all true knowledge, and he gives equal respect to the traditional doctrines of the faith.

The second group of clergy and scholars may be called progressive teachers. They are those who wish to stress the authority of the Qurʾān over human traditions, to go back to it, to make it a living Book, and to reinterpret it in the light of contemporary needs and conditions. Though these teachers are still in the minority, their number is increasing. The training that these clergy undertake reflects their approach. They go through high school training before professional studies, and many take university degrees in Arabic studies. These students do not study Arabic mechanically but as a literary language, and they will also take general subjects such as history and language. In addition to dealing with the traditional Muslim schools of thought, they will also read widely from other Muslim authors and commentators. Their institutions support a rational approach to the study of the Qurʾān.

A person in this group also gives the Qurʾān first place in all matters. In fact, he is probably involved in some "back to the Qurʾān!" movement, trying to restore the Word of God to a position above the tradition of humans. He argues that the meaning of the Qurʾān has precedence over its sound, and he uses vernacular communication to make the message of the Qurʾān a living possession of Muslims. He supports mosque sermons in the local language and translations of the Qurʾān. He maintains that the Qurʾān should be interpreted by devout use of the reasoning powers that God has given to humanity.

As we shall see in the next chapter, much of the current theological debate within Islām is related to the controversy between these two approaches: Retain the tradition of the past, or build a modern interpretation of the faith.

I. The Exposition of the Qurʾān: Some Aspects of Tafsīr

Muslim scholars have written innumerable commentaries on the Qurʾān. Not only that, they have also written commentaries on the commentaries. The interpretative enterprise is called *tafsīr*. Here we will mention only some of the principles that scholars use in setting forth the teaching of the Qurʾān, particularly in regard to allegory and abrogation.

Traditional Muslim scholars, not surprisingly, pay much attention to the literal meaning of the text. They are greatly concerned about the linguistic niceties of Arabic grammar and vocabulary. While they do not use the historical method, in the sense that they view the passages of the Qurʾān as the product of a historical process, they nevertheless do look for the historical occasions (*asbāb al-nuzūl*) of the events in order to understand the meaning better. In this connection Muslim scholars have placed the words "Revealed at Mecca" or "Revealed at Medina" at the head of every chapter of the Qurʾān. The interpreters also look for help from Ḥadīth, the traditions of the Prophet, to fill out details of when and how a certain verse was uttered.

The scholars recognize the existence of ambiguous or allegorical verses in the Qurʾān. Ambiguous refers to obscure meanings and allegorical refers to figurative or symbolic expressions. The Qurʾān (3:7) declares:

> He it is Who hath revealed unto thee (Muhammad) the Scripture wherein are clear revelations—They are the substance of the Book—and others (which are) allegorical [*mutashābihāt*]. But those in whose hearts is doubt pursue, forsooth, that which is allegorical, seeking to cause dissension by seeking to explain it. None knoweth its explanation save Allāh. And those who are of sound instruction say: We believe therein; the whole is from our Lord; but only men of understanding really heed.

There have been different Muslim attitudes about the allegorical verses. Classical Sunnī commentators stay away from them and concentrate on the clear sayings of the Qurʾān. Shīʿite and Sūfi Muslims have a much greater interest in these verses. Modern commentators have a leaning toward metaphor and view their exposition as a challenge to be met.

Finally, traditional Muslim scholars also accept the concept of abrogation, the idea that some later verses replaced earlier verses.

The Qur'ān says (2:106): "Such of Our revelations as We abrogate or cause to be forgotten, We bring (in place) one better or the like thereof. Knowest thou not that Allāh is able to do all things?" Muslim scholars have spent much time and effort discussing which passages have been abrogated by which later verses. Although the number ranges from 5–200, most commentators accept about 20 such passages. The most prominent of these is the change in the direction of prayer (*qibla*), which was altered from Jerusalem to Mecca (2:132f.). Another example is the abrogation of Jewish fasts in favor of fasting in the month of Ramaḍān (2:179ff.). Passages such as 43:89 and 7:179 that advocate toleration and forgiveness of polytheists are said by some commentators to have been abrogated by 2:187 which authorizes militant action against them. The abrogating passage is called *nāsikh* and the abrogated passage is called *mansūkh*.

Muslim exegesis has a long tradition of famous scholars who have lavished loving and careful attention on the meaning. of the Qur'ān. Many of their names are not known by ordinary Muslims, but within Muslim halls of learning they are paid profound respect. The relationship of the scholars to each other is interesting, for they have developed their own kind of chain relationship, later scholars commenting on the interpretations of previous scholars. Landmark *tafsīr* figures include the following: the "founder," ʿAbdullāh ibn ʿAbbās (d. 688); al-Bukhārī (d. 870); al-Tabarī (d. 923), the acknowledged master, whose works cover a vast range; al-Ghazālī (d. 1111); al-Zamakhsharī (d. 1144); Fakhr al-Dīn al-Rāzī (d. 1209); al-Baidāwī (d. 1286); and the two Jalāls, Jalāl al-Dīn al Mahallī (d. 1459), and Jalāl al-Dīn al-Suyūṭī (d. 1505). Their combined work, *Jalālainī,* together with al-Baidāwī stands first in contemporary Muslim authority. Legal scholars like a al-Nawāwī (d. 1277), made their own contribution and rank equally high.[12]

The Qur'ān, the divine Word of God, is the infallible authority of Islām. But how do Muslims take decisions on matters that are not covered by the Qur'ān, and how do Muslims interpret the meaning of the Qur'ān for today? We turn next to that burning issue.

Notes

[1]Syed Abdul Latif, *The Mind al-Qurʾān Builds* (Chicago: Kazi Publications, 1983; first published, 1952). The book titles are advertised by Kazi.

[2]*The Alchemy of Happiness*, tr. by Claud Field (London: The Octagon Press, 1980), p. 6.

[3]Helmut Gätje, *The Qurʾān and its Exegesis*: tr. and ed. by A. T. Welch (Berkeley: University of California Press, 1976), p. 66.

[4]Ibid.

[5]Richard Bell, *Introduction to the Qurʾān* (Edinburgh: University Press, 1953), pp. 40–42, records the variations.

[6]The Leipzig Edition of Gustavus Fliegel (1842) was commonly used by orientalist translators of the Qurʾān. The variation in text numbering causes some difficulty in comparing translations.

[7]C. N. Ahmed Moulavi, *Parisuddha Khurān—Paribhāshāyum Wyākhyānawum* ("The Holy Qurʾān, Translation and Commentary") 6 vols. (Perumbavoor; Abdulla Majeed Marikar, vols. I and II, Calicut: By the Author; vols. III to VI, 1951–1961.

[8]Al-Bāqillānī, *Iʿjāz al-Qurʾān* (Cairo: 1930), in Arthur Jeffery, Islām, Mohammed and His Religion (New York: The Liberal Arts Press, 1958), p. 54.

[9]H. U. Weitbrecht-Stanton, *The Teaching of the Qurʾān* (London: S.P.C.K., 1919), pp. 10f. For modern treatments by Muslims cf. Fazlur Rahman, *Major Themes of the Qurʾān* (Chicago: University of Chicago Press, 1980), who sets forth the moral implications of the Book, and S. Abdul Latif, op.cit., who seeks its spiritual values in contrast to medieval interpretations.

[10]Mark Nygard counted the terms in preparation for his unpublished M.A. thesis, "The Concept of Surrender in Islām," the University of Regina, 1994.

[11]Fazlur Rahman, *Major Themes*, p. 9.

[12]Arguably the most influential modern commentary on the Qurʾān is that of Shaikh Muhammad ʿAbduh of Egypt (d. 1908); it was a partial commentary revised, completed and published in *al-Manār* by his disciple, Rashīd Riḍā; from there ʿAbduh's ideas travelled throughout the Muslim world.

9

Interpreting the Qur'ān: Ḥadīth and Other Sources of Faith

Islām has four official sources of roots of faith. The first and ultimate authority is the Qur'ān. Alongside it and very close to it in standing is Ḥadīth, the stories of the custom of the Prophet Muhammad. Of lesser authority but still important is *qiyās*, the principle of analogy. The fourth is of great practical authority, namely *ijmāʿ* or consensus, the agreement of the community. In addition, there are two unofficial sources, namely cultural custom (*ʿurf* or *adat*) and administrative practice or *qānūn*. It is through the use of these sources that Islām has elaborated its faith and practice.

The necessity for supplementary sources of faith may be illustrated by a current "problem" experienced by Abdulla and Amina. They both came from large families. Abdulla was the sixth child in his family, and Amina was the seventh in hers. Now they must consider the size of their own family. The government of their country has instituted a policy of population control and family planning. The messages that they receive from every side is "two is enough!" They already have three children and so they face a pressing question. Is family planning Islāmically permitted or is it to be considered un-Islāmic? There seem to be many differences of opinion among their fellow Muslims on the subject.

This is not the first time that such issues have faced Muslims. In every such case the question arises, where can we find our answer to the problem? Obviously they must first seek the solution in the Qur'ān, but if it does not speak directly on the subject, what are they to do next? The thought arose that the answer could be found in the custom of the Prophet based on the Ḥadīth. What if the answer is not there in the Ḥadīth? Could a clue perhaps be found by using an analogy from some established precedent? Finally, if that does not produce a satisfactory solution, there is no alternative but to turn to the general agreement of the community. This kind of thinking led to the development of the supplementary sources of faith.

Muslim problems have reached a more pressing stage, however, because on many matters there is no visible consensus, and no clear way of reaching it. On the issue of family planning, for example, there are real differences among Muslims, and these became evident in the United Nations Conference on Population in Cairo in 1994. When none of the traditional ways of grasping God's intention produce clear answers, what is next for the individual Muslim believer? Simply to go along with the current trend, whatever it is, does not seem responsible, or simply to accept the decisions of governmental administrators, without questioning them, also seems irresponsible. Many Muslims believe that there is another way—that is for individual Muslims to make up their own minds on a subject, according to their personal understanding of the meaning of God's Word. That is what is happening everywhere now in the Muslim world as individual believers are thinking through God's will for themselves. Muslim reformers call this *ijtihād*, the right of private interpretation.

Abdulla and Amina may not have worked out their decision-making process in these terms, but they know instinctively that all these elements are somehow involved—the Qur²ān, the Ḥadīth, analogy, consensus, custom, administration, and personal judgment. Accepting the Qur²ān as God's Word is one thing, but capturing its meaning is another. Perhaps the crucial religious question that contemporary Muslims face is how to interpret the Qur²ān for today in the light of the many new issues that are constantly arising.

In dealing with the issue of Qurānic interpretation we will raise three questions that apply to any religion that has a sacred and authoritative scripture. The first question is who has the right to interpret the scripture? The Muslim answer must take into account the Islāmic conception of religious authority. The second question is how is the scripture to be interpreted? For the Muslim answer we must look at the supplementary sources of faith: Ḥadīth, analogy and consensus. The third question is what is the correct interpretation? In considering that controversial issue we must look at the powerful sway of Muslim tradition. We begin with the first problem, the right of interpretation.

A. The Right to Interpret

The Qur'ān is the believer's link between heaven and earth. The question of who has the *right* to interpret it is therefore an all-important one. In the last chapter we pointed to the Muslim principle of equality of believers. Based on that principle the answer to our question is clear: every Muslim has the privilege. This answer is theoretically sound, but in practice Muslim clergy have assumed that right, becoming "the norm-givers of the Muslim community."[1] In modern times lay Muslims, led by a series of magnificent scholars, have begun to reclaim the right to interpret the Qur'ān and to apply it freshly to contemporary conditions. Muslim faith and feeling are caught up in this struggle.

Modern news media have tended to give rather unflattering presentations of Muslim clergy. It is suggested that Muslims are dominated by a clerical class that is very authoritarian and quite uninformed. While there is truth in the criticism, the picture also needs correction. The Muslim world is full of quiet, dedicated clergy, who love their faith and who are intent on doing their tasks honestly and well. They do not only carry out their duties with great faithfulness, but frequently for a very low remuneration. These are the clergy that many Muslims know, and they tender them their respect.

At the same time there is also a general sense of Muslim uneasiness about the role of some religious scholars, teachers and leaders. Many educated lay Muslims have complained openly about the clergy's lack of modern education, their interest in power, and their tendency to enter into affairs outside their range of competence. One set of reformers characterized the traditional *ʿulamāʾ* as the

> retrogressive elements ... who have not made any contribution to the social reformation of the Muslim community, but on the other hand, they have been continually keeping the Muslim masses in the fetters of superstitious beliefs and resisting any wind of change blowing from the progressive forces of society.[2]

Many Muslims long for a new age of great Imāms. At the heart of their concern is the desire to enhance the progress and reputation of the Muslim community and to help Muslims in dealing with modernity.

We now turn to the second question: how is the Qurʾān to be interpreted? For the classical Muslim answer we must consider the supplementary sources of faith, namely, the traditions of the Prophet Muhammad, the principle of analogy, and the powerful doctrine of community agreement. We begin with *Ḥadīth* and *sunna*.

B. Ḥadīth and Sunna

The word *ḥadīth* (pl. *aḥadīth*) means communication or story. It refers primarily to the stories of what Muhammad said and did. The word *sunna* means the custom of the Prophet Muhammad that is drawn from these stories. Ḥadīth became the second source of faith in Islām. There are two main reasons why this happened.

The first relates to the Muslim respect for the Prophet Muhammad. After his death the veneration of the Prophet grew and grew. While the revelations of the Qurʾān were primary for believers, almost as important was the life of the Prophet himself. The words that he spoke, apart from inspired utterances, were also remembered. Everything that he did and the way he did it were called to mind by his faithful followers. After all, was he not the Messenger of God, the Leader of the *umma* and the Noble Pattern for believers?

We have already referred to the second reason for remembering what the Prophet said and did. The revelations of the Qurʾān did not *directly* cover every aspect of human life. Whenever a new problem arose, therefore, people were inclined to ask, how did the Prophet deal with this or that? The problems became more acute when Islām moved out of the relatively homogeneous cultural atmosphere of Arabia into the great worlds of Mediterranean and Persian cultures. The penetration into other civilizations brought with it a host of fresh situations and unanswered questions. Knowing the Prophet's custom, his *sunna*, was now even more important than in earlier years.

In brief, both out of a spirit of veneration and for practical reasons Muslims went about gathering the stories of what Muhammad said and did. The stories were called Ḥadīth. The story gatherers and reciters also developed a methodology for determining legitimate Ḥadīth. Every Ḥadīth had two parts. One was the text itself (*matn*). The other was the chain of narrators who had transmitted the text from the days of Muhammad forward (*isnād*). That chain was considered the crucial element of the Ḥadīth. The story had to be traced back to one of the companions of Muhammad who actually saw him do a certain act or utter a saying. If the transmission was sound, it was considered that the content of the story was trustworthy.

The content of the Ḥadīth cover a broad range of topics from the very important to the seemingly slight. There are stories related to the basic religious obligations of Muslims. Other narratives expand on aspects of religious dogma, especially as it relates to the day of judgment, heaven and hell. Some deal with legal provisions related to civil and criminal law, while others touch on social obligations and manners. There are comments on specific Qurānic passages and other edifying statements on moral issues. One scholarly summary[3] lists the following categories of Ḥadīth: faith, knowledge, purification, prayer, funerals, alms-giving, fasting, the excellent qualities of the Qur'ān, the remembrance of God, God's names, the rites of pilgrimage, business transactions, marriage, the emancipation of slaves, retaliation, prescribed punishments, the duties of a judge, *jihād*, animals that may be slaughtered, foods, clothing, medicine, spells, visions, general behavior, the last times, and the fine qualities of the Prophet and his companions.

Examples of substantial Ḥadīth include the following[4]:

Ibn ʿUmar reported God's Messenger as saying, "Islām is based on five things: the testimony that there is no god but God and that Muhammad is His servant and messenger, the observance of the prayer, the payment of *zakāt*, the pilgrimage, and the fast during Ramaḍān.

Al-ʿAbbāʿs b. Abd al-Muṭṭalib reported God's messenger as saying, "He who is well-pleased with God as Lord, with Islām as religion, and with Muhammad as messenger will experience the savour of faith.

ʿUbada b. aṣ-Sāmit said: I heard God's messenger say, "If anyone testifies that there is no god but God and that Muhammad is God's messenger, God will keep him from going to hell."[5]

ʿUbād b. aṣ-Sāmit reported God's messenger as saying, "Five times of prayer have been prescribed by God. If anyone performs the ablution for them well, observes them at their proper time, and perfectly performs the bowing and showing of submissiveness during them, he has a covenant from God to forgive him; but if anyone does not do so, he has no covenant. If he wills He may forgive him, but if He wills not, He may punish him.[6]

Abū Dharr reported God's messenger as saying, "When you make soup, put in a lot of water and be mindful of your neighbors."[7]

Examples of lighter Ḥadīth include the following:

Shuraih b. Hānī said that he asked ʿĀʾisha what God's messenger did first when he entered his house, and she replied that he used a toothpick.[8]

Abū Huraira reported God's messenger as saying, "It is part of the *sunna* that a man should accompany his guest to the door of the house.[9]

In the course of early Muslim times more and more Ḥadīth came into general circulation. Ordinary Muslims loved them for the richness they gave to the tapestry of the Prophet's life, while scholars appreciated them because they helped with their understanding of Islām and their interpretation of the Qurʾān. They filled in many gaps. But a problem soon surfaced, and that was the issue of authenticity. Could the Ḥadīth be trusted? Not infrequently when someone wanted to prove a point of some kind or support a particular position, a new Ḥadīth was conveniently discovered! It is not too strong to say that the manufacture of Ḥadīth became almost a kind of religious industry. Then, too, the principle of authoritative tradition was also being extended to the words and actions of the family and the most respected companions of the Prophet. It appeared that the story-making was getting out of control, and rather than the Ḥadīth being a helpful, supplementary source of faith for Muslims, Islām was being threatened by the dangers of deliberate falsification and mere legendary. Clearly, something needed to be done.

A great scholar named al-Bukhārī (810–70), from what is now Uzbekistan, determined to try to bring order out of the chaos. He traveled widely and studied the accumulated mass of Ḥadīth to discover how many were genuine and how many were false. He made his decisions mainly on the basis of whether or not he could trace a reliable chain of transmitters. If the chain of narrators was seriously incomplete or if it included impious Muslims, it could not be accepted. Furthermore, an approved Ḥadīth could not contradict a clear saying of the Qurʾān or other sound Ḥadīth. On this basis Ḥadīth stories were classified on a range from sound to weak. Al-Bukhārī dreamed that in so doing he was "driving" flies off the person of Muhammad.[10] Drive off he did! It is said that he reduced the number of reliable transmitters from about 40,000 persons to 2,000, and the number of acceptable Ḥadīth from about 600,000 to 4,000! While the pioneering work of al-Bukhārī is considered primary, other Muslim scholars also worked on Ḥadīth criticism around the same time and formed their collections. The following Ḥadīth collections are especially esteemed by Muslims: al-Bukhārī and Muslim (d. 875), which incorporate only traditions considered sound (ṣaḥīḥ); Abū Dāwūd (d. 888); al-Tirmidhī (d. 892), al-Nasā'ī (d. 915), and Ibn Mājā (d. 886). The earliest of the four canonical Shia collections is by al-Kulayni (d. 939); the Shī'a Ḥadīth differ in matters related to the community's leadership and the Prophet's family. A great Sunnī legal scholar named al-Shāfi'ī (767-819) stabilized the position of Ḥadīth in Islām by assigning them a fundamental position in Islāmic law.

Was the effort of these dedicated Muslim scholars successful? Was the trustworthiness of the approved Ḥadīth really assured? Scholars generally agree that Ḥadīth provide sound information on the everyday affairs of the life of the Prophet Muhammad, but there is disagreement about their reliability in doctrinal matters. Fazlur Rahman speaks of "the lack of strict historicity on the part of much of its contents." He suggests that we should be sensitive to what was taking place—Muslims were utilizing Ḥadīth to crystallize and fashion Muslim orthodoxy, so that the theological activity of later generations "was largely transferred, through the medium of Ḥadīth, to the Prophet himself." As many modern Muslims do, he calls for "a genuine criticism of Ḥadīth" to enable a rethinking and reformulating of contemporary Islām.[11] Traditional Muslims do not agree. Anwar Qadri, while accepting that there was a "fantasy in Ḥadīth narration," considers the negative judgments of Ḥadīth to be extreme. He says, "In their criticisms of the narrators and in their search for chains of authority, accuracy and trustworthiness, they [Muslim Ḥadīth scholars] established a scientific and truthful criterion ... worthy of considerable trust."[12]

However they may be viewed, the Ḥadīth are an integral part of Islām and the source of much of its traditional teaching. Ḥadīth stands very close to the Qur'ān in the respect of traditional Muslims. Abdulla and Amina simply love the stories. The tales of the Ḥadīth are in their memories and in their blood, and they happily pass them on to their children. They recognize that the Holy Qurʾān is supreme, but they also believe that the Prophet said these words:

> Mālik b. Anas ... reported God's messenger as saying, "As long as you hold fast to two things which I have left among you, you will not go astray: God's Book and His messenger's *sunna*.[13]

> Jābir reported God's messenger as saying, "To proceed: The best discourse is God's Book, the best guidance is that given by Muhammad, and the worst things are those which are novelties...."[14]

> Al-Miqdām b. Maʿdīkarib reported God's messenger as saying, I have indeed been brought the Qurʾān and something like it along with it; yet the time is coming when a man replete on his couch will say, "Keep to this Qurʾān; what you find in it to be permissible treat as permissible, and what you find in it to be prohibited treat as prohibited. But what God's messenger has prohibited is like what God has prohibited ..."[15]

It is not easy for Abdulla and Amina even to consider giving up the Ḥadīth.

C. The Principle of Analogy

We now move to the third source of faith in Islām, the principle of analogy (*qiyās*). The addition of Ḥadīth as a source of faith did not meet all the needs of the growing Muslim family, for the Ḥadīth stories themselves needed interpretation and amplifying. So the search went on for another principle. Some Muslims thought that the idea of individual preference or expediency should take over next. Others felt that probably the concept of community welfare should govern an interpretation. Other Muslims came up with the third source of faith that most Muslims accepted, the idea of reasoning by analogy. This principle was used especially by legal experts in working out the laws of Islām.

The development of *qiyās* introduces the difficult area of the relationship between revelation and reason, an issue that has produced many dilemmas for Muslims. What exactly is the place of human reason in the interpretation of the Qurʾān? Muslims used three words especially to cover the field of rational interpretation, and each has a slightly different meaning. We have met the first, *ijtihād,* which refers to the right of personal interpretation. The second was *raʾy*, which means personal opinion drawn from rational reflection and philosophical speculation. The third was *qiyās*, whose meaning shaded in the direction of deductive reasoning applied to specific problems.

In the early stages of Muslim thought these ideas overlapped. They expressed the free intellectual climate that marked Islām and produced its remarkable high civilization. Muslims were utilizing reason (*ʿaql*) in a variety of ways to work out problems, and *qiyās* became a means for drawing fresh conclusions. It allowed for the development of ideas and drew Ḥadīth support. For example, Muhammad had sent Muʿādh to Yemen as a judge, and before his departure the Prophet asked him,

> "How will you decide when a question arises?" He replied: "According to the Book of Allāh," "And if you do not find the answer in the Book of Allāh?" "Then according to the *sunna* of the Messenger of Allāh." "And if you do not find the answer neither in the *sunna* nor in the Book?" "Then I shall come to a decision according to my own opinion without hesitation." Then Muhammad slapped Muʿādh on the chest with his hand saying, "Praise be to Allāh Who has led the messenger of the Messenger of Allāh to an answer that pleased him."[16]

As time passed, however, free and independent reasoning seemed to many Muslims to be a source of confusion and even threatening. It is pious obedience, not rational argumentation, that is the Muslim way; after all, it was said, the sin of the devil was that he had argued with God instead of obeying him! As a result *raʿy* was more or less dismissed, and *qiyās* was narrowed down in its scope to a form of applied reasoning, the logical application of a clear precedent. An example reveals the way it works. In the Qurʾān the consumption of an alcoholic beverage named *khamr* is forbidden. By a logical extension of this prohibition, all alcoholic beverages are forbidden. By a further analogy, harmful substances of any kind are not allowed to be taken into the human body, and so tobacco and drugs are not to be consumed. In this way, *qiyās* became a method for dealing with the Muslim desire for specific regulations.

We now go to the fourth and final source of faith in Islām that Muslims have used in interpreting the Qurānic way of life.

D. The Principle of Consensus

Islām now had three sources of faith: Qurʾān, Ḥadīth, Qiyās. The Qurʾān and Ḥadīth were substantive and primary, while

Qiyās played an auxiliary role. But without a fourth source the system of interpretation would not have been complete. That fourth foundation or root of faith is the principle of consensus (*ijmāᶜ*), the crucial principle of the agreement of the Muslim community. Finally someone would have to say what Muslims as a whole stood for and believed. Who was to do it? Who else but the members of the community of believers? ᶜ*Ijmāʾ* means the consensus of the whole community. It is, as it were, the collective consciousness of the Muslim family. It was natural that Islām would develop such a concept to avoid the anarchy of individualism. A religious group either develops a conscious system of defining ideology—sacred leaders, assemblies, confessional statements, and the like—or it develops something that is less self-conscious, more subtle, and yet still works. Muslims took the latter course.

In relation to the interpretation of the Word of God, the community of Muslims felt under threat from several sides. Creative imagination and invention was going on in relation to the Ḥadīth. Free-thinking speculation leading to far-out philosophies was going on in relation to rational interpretation. And to add to it, at another level, ruthless political rulers were manipulating ideas and movements to their own advantage. So a protective trend developed to institutionalize the common opinion, the middle way, of the general community. The idea remained at a subtle level because no clear process was set up by which the common opinion of the Muslim faithful could be identified. You could really identify the result of the process only after it happened. Since all Muslims are equal, it was assumed that all should be involved in the process, and the Qurʾān itself was cited in support of the principle of *ijmāᶜ*:

And whoso opposeth the messenger after the guidance of Allāh... and followeth other than the believers' way ... (4:115).

Thus we have appointed you a middle nation that ye may be witnesses against mankind (4:143).

These passages imply that there is a power in the Muslim community to identify the middle way of Muslim life. A famous Ḥadīth supported the feeling: "My community reaches no agreement that is an error" (Abū Dāwūd).

A comparison may be drawn with the tradition of "town

meeting" by which citizens in New England in the U.S.A. made their common decisions. Everyone in the town attended the meeting and everyone had a vote. The custom more or less died out when the communities became too large for that process. Let us extend the analogy to the Muslim world. How could you have a "town meeting" of that far-flung world? At first the concept of an *ijma'* of the whole community was a dynamic and working principle, but in practice it was soon narrowed to the agreement of the learned doctors of Islām. Only they had the skills to deal with the Qur'ān, Ḥadīth, and Qiyās. Of course, *'ulamā'* too were spread across the expanse of Islām, and they differed in their views. So a full unanimous opinion was only a dream. Nevertheless, the general consensus of the learned ones could be known—especially in such important centers as Medina—and as a result *ijmā'* became another and the final source of faith in Islām. On these four foundations—the Word of God, Traditions, Analogy, and Consensus—Muslims worked out their understanding of what God intended and expressed it in developed doctrines and laws.

Consensus still works. It is still in practice the final authority in Islām. It is this source of faith that in the end is likely to provide Abdulla and Amina with their answer to the issue of family planning. The growing consensus of the Muslim community in this matter is coming down in favor of the idea of population control, and various expressions of support are heard in almost every area of the Muslim world. It is more the method of family planning rather than the idea itself that remains controversial.

With the development of supplementary sources of faith Islām has worked out a formidable methodology for dealing with the interpretation of the Qur'ān and the development of Muslim ideas. Let us now go on to the last of our three questions, namely, what is the correct interpretation of the Qur'ān?

E. What Is The Correct Interpretation?

Probably no one could ever have predicted what happened next! As the general pattern of Muslim thought and life became established and as the learned scholars of Islām gained ever more authority through their interpretation of the Qur'ān and their skillful use of the other sources of faith, the teaching of the community became firmly fixed and virtually fossilized. About four centuries after the death of Muhammad the ʿulamāʾ came to a remarkable conclusion. They decided, in effect, that everything was now decided! All the interpretative questions had been addressed and answered. Religious knowledge was complete. Utilizing their authority as the formulators of consensus, by their own agreement they came to the conclusion that all the important questions about the meaning of the Qurʾān and, yes, the meaning of Islām, were answered. So they declared that the door of private interpretation was now closed. It was a monumental decision, and one that had great impact on the future of Islām.

What was to be the main task of Muslims from this time forward? The answer was plain and straightforward. The obligation of Muslims, henceforth, was to carry forward the traditions and interpretations of the past and to hand them on intact to the next generation. That principle of handing on was called *taqlīd*, imitation. The *taqlīd* principle was to dominate Islām until the middle of the 19th century, and in some places in the Muslim world it continues to be the prevailing attitude. What could be more noble than to hand on the truth that had been received as a gift from the founders of the faith? In the modern musical, "Fiddler on the Roof," the main actor sings, "Tradition ... Tradition." That could be called the song of the ʿulamāʾ, and they sang it faithfully and well.

The emphasis on tradition and imitation gave the clergy of Islām, its guardians, immense power. It is noteworthy that the Muslim *umma* that had stressed equality and maintained a broad variety of approaches in its early years eventually became subject to a very authoritative structure and a customary faith. The formerly fluid doctrine of consensus declined to agreement to rule out opinion contrary to tradition! Thus free thought was stifled, and Islām went into an intellectual decline from which it is emerging today under the impact of powerful new movements of thought.

The present age! Tumultuous, demanding, exploding with knowledge, living by change, unending and rapid change! With the burgeoning of knowledge in the 20th century and with the advent of many new issues, questions and problems, the whole matter of Qurānic interpretation has come under review by Muslims. No issue is more debated by them, and more vital for the future of Islām. Some Muslims are rebelling against what they consider to be the imperialism of "medieval thought"[17] and are demanding—and taking—the freedom to interpret the Qur'ān in the light of modern needs. They say that *taqlīd* no longer represents the answer, but rather the dynamic Muslim principles of the past must be recovered and implemented. Mohammed Jamali declares, "I believe that *ijtihad* in Islām will make it a permanently living religion by adapting its teachings to each age and generation in accordance with the requirements of that age and generation."[18] Other Muslims, however, are just as strongly and vociferously maintaining the necessity of faithfulness to the tradition that Islām has always held. Many are in the middle, seeking a middle way.

How well I remember the crisis in a Muslim village in December 1968, when the Apollo 8 spaceship circled the moon. In traditional Muslim interpretation the sun, moon, and stars are fixed in the canopy of the seventh heaven, reflecting the picture of medieval cosmology. How could a spaceship pass through a fixed canopy and circle a heavenly body? People argued the question, and some denied its possibility. This is only a crude example of a fundamental issue of tradition and change. There are far more important questions that Muslims are struggling with, related to the interpretation of the Qur'ān. Two overall trends dominate the scene: frequent criticism of traditional clergy and a strong call to Muslims to return to the Qur'ān. More specifically, Muslims today are asking questions such as these:

— How can we make the Qur'ān a living Book for contemporary Muslims?
— How can we modernize the traditional training of the *'ulamā'*?
— What is the meaning of the Holy Qur'ān for today? Are there fresh meanings that can be discovered?
— Can the door of private interpretation be more widely re-opened?
— Is there not a need for a new updated consensus that deals with current questions, and how can it be obtained in a divided Muslim world?
— How can the interpretation of the Qur'ān be rationally related to modern scientific discovery and historical investigation?
— How can traditional folk, who dearly love the interpretation of the past, and progressive people, who are longing for a more relevant religion for today, be brought together?

— Who will decide what a Muslim must believe today?

No matter from what perspective a Muslim approaches these questions, every Muslim who does so will be moved by the profound words of the great Muslim divine, al-Ghazālī who said,

> I then wish to arouse you from your sleep. O you who recite the Qurʾān to a great length, who take its study as an occupation, and who imbibe some of its outward meanings and sentences: How long will you ramble on shore of the ocean, closing your eyes to the wonders of the meanings of the Qurʾān? Was it not your duty to sail to the midst of the fathomless ocean of these meanings in order to see their wonders, to travel to their islands in order to gather their best produce, and to dive into their depths, so that you might become rich by obtaining their jewels? Do you not feel ashamed of being deprived of their pearls and jewels by your persistence in looking at their shores and outward appearances?[19]

It is not surprising that ordinary Muslims like Abdulla and Amina face the modern world with some feelings of perplexity. They do not ask all these questions themselves, but they feel some dissatisfaction and bewilderment. They know that there is a problem somewhere, but they cannot quite pin it down. Amid the confusion they are certain of only one thing: In the end the answers must come from the Qurʾān. Ḥadīth have some value, and their memory is in the blood. Reason must be employed, and analogies have their place. Consensus is a good thing, and the community's experience must be respected. But the Word of God must control the situation, its intentions must become clear, and it must guide the community to answer the question: what is Islām for today's world?

In the meantime, the life of the Muslim family goes on. Abdulla is rather concerned about their financial situation. Also, his father, Ahmad, is becoming very weak, and his thoughts are on that matter. Amina is concerned about some of the practical household matters, especially preparations for the festival that is coming up. She is also wondering about arrangements for Ashraf's marriage. Ashraf himself is thinking about a lot of matters, and often seems upset. Rashid and Fatima are very young and quite unconcerned about these questions, but the future is theirs. Amid it all, Abdulla's and Amina's beautiful Qurʾān continues to occupy its honored place in the house.

We next consider the beliefs and practices of Islām to which

Muslims give their priority attention.

Notes

[1]Ernest Gellner, "Doctor and Saint" in Nikki Keddie, ed., *Scholars, Saints and Sūfis. Muslim Religious Institutions in the Middle East Since 1500* (Berkeley: University of California Press, 1972), p. 308. Keddie, "Introduction," p. 2, places the rise of the *ʿulamā'* in the early Abbasid period.

[2]Miller, *The Mappila Muslims*, p. 281, quoting the Nadvat-ul-Ulama in Kerala State, India.

[3]*Mishkat al-Masabih*, tr. by James Robson (Lahore: Sh. Muhammad Ashraf, 1963) 4 vols. The *Mishkat* is a compilation of Ḥadīth from major collections.

[4]Ibid., I, p. 6.

[5]Ibid., p. 13.

[6]Ibid., p. 115.

[7]Ibid., p. 411.

[8]Ibid., p. 79.

[9]Ibid., III, p. 902.

[10]L. Bevan Jones, *The People of the Mosque* (Calcutta; Baptist Mission Press, 1965), p. 81.

[11]Fazlur Rahman, *Islām*, pp. 73, 293,311.

[12]Anwar A. Qadri, *Islāmic Jurisprudence in the Modern World* (Lahore: Sh. Muhammad Ashraf, 1973; 2nd rev. ed.), pp. 57, 198.

[13]*Mishkat*, I, pp. 47f.

[14]Ibid., p. 39.

[15]Ibid., p. 43.

[16]A. J. Wensinck, "Kiyas," *EI¹* , IV, p. 1092.

[17]Latif, *The Mind Al-Qur'ān Builds*, p. 12. Latif states: "The medieval mind has persisted and lives on and in its several local variations [is] still operative in every nook and cranny of the Muslim world."

[18]Jamali, *Letters on Islām* (London: World of Islām Festival Trust, 1978), p. 107.

[19]*The Jewels of the Qur'ān*, tr. by M. A. Quasem (London: Kegan Paul, 1983), p. 19.

10

The Tapestry of Faith: Basic Muslim Beliefs and the Destiny of Believers

We have arrived at the core of Muslim piety, the basic beliefs and practices of the faithful. Like every other religion, Islām too has much in it that is not in the active interest of the average believer. It may be that nine out of every ten Muslims have never heard of _____. You could fill in the blanks with a number of words and issues, some of which we have discussed. They belong to the great tradition of Islām, but they are rather remote from the daily religious reality of the ordinary Muslim family. They need to be known and studied as part of the great tradition, but they do not touch the Muslim soul. When we deal with the basic beliefs and practices, however, we have to do with the things that my Muslim friends deal with regularly in their religious experience.

Let us begin with a sketch of this "practical" Islām.

ISLĀM

The Beliefs of Muslims (*imān*)   The Practices of Muslims (*dīn*)

1. God	1. Confession
2. Angels	2. Prayer
3. Prophets	3. Fasting
4. Books	4. Almsgiving
5. Day of Judgment	5. Pilgrimage

The above is a minimal listing. On the side of beliefs, the classical Muslim tradition includes a sixth item, namely predestination. There are, of course, many other things that Muslims believe. In this chapter we will also consider the Muslim teaching on human destiny, including sin and salvation, heaven and hell.

On the practices side, some Muslims add the element of *jihād* or struggle to the list. It should be added that *dīn* is also called *ʿibādat*, which means worship-service; *islām*, the surrendered life; or *arkān*, the pillars of Islām. We now turn to the beliefs of Muslims.

A. The Belief in God

The primary belief in Islām is the belief in God. Since we have discussed the Muslim view of God in chapters 3 and 4, we refer the reader to that material. Muslim faith in God is the fountainhead of all other beliefs and practices. As Abul Aʿlā Mawdūdī says,

> Belief in God makes practical obedience to Him incumbent, and it is obedience to God which constitutes the religion of Islām. By this belief you profess that Allāh, the One God, alone is your God, and this means that He is your Creator and you are His creature; that He is your Master, and you are His slave; that He is your Ruler and you are His subject.[1]

With that understanding, we proceed to the second Muslim belief, the belief in those "spiritual and splendid beings"[2] called the angels of God.

B. The Belief in Angels

An angel is called *malʾak*. Although Muslims like Abdulla and Amina do not think about angels as much as some of the other basic beliefs, in folk Islām the reality of angels and spirits is taken very seriously. Muslims believe that God created the angels from light and that they are endowed with life, reason, and speech. They possess subtle bodies and are not in need of eating and drinking. They are gender-neuter, although they are referred to as "he," and they do not give birth.

The overall task of the angels is the praise and service of God. Within that general mandate, we may identify three specific functions. The first is to glorify God, and in so doing they symbolize what should be the chief concern of human beings. The second function is to serve as God's messengers (35:1), and they are content with that role, "not too proud to do Him service" (7:205). Their third duty has received considerable attention because it introduces the concept of intercession into Islām. The Qurʾān says (40:7):

> Those who bear the Throne, and all who are around it, hymn the praises of their Lord and believe in Him and ask forgiveness for those who believe (saying): Our Lord! Thou comprehendest all things in mercy and knowledge, therefore forgive those who repent and follow Thy way. Ward off from them the punishment of hell.

Most noteworthy are the great individual angels, whom we may term the "archangels." Some of their names are mentioned in the Qurʾān, but others of them, and almost all the details, come from Ḥadīth. Most attention goes to Gabriel (Jibrīl), the angel of revelation (2:97). It is "he" who transmits God's messages to the prophets. He is associated with the revelation to Mary, and is identified, traditionally, with the holy Spirit who supported Jesus (2:87). The angel Michael (Mīkāʾīl) is regarded as the patron of the people of Israel. Isrāfīl will sound the trumpet on the last day, while Izraʿīl is the angel of death.

There are also a host of lesser angels, some doing general service, others carrying out specific functions. Among the latter are the recording angels. The Qurʾān says (2:80): "Or deem they that We cannot hear their secret thoughts and private confidences? Nay, but Our envoys, present with them, do record." Muslim tradition interprets this passage to mean that two recording angels accompany every human being, one on the right and one on the left, writing down the good and evil deeds of that person. The interrogating angels, named Munkar and Nakīr, in a fearsome event, visit the dead after they have been buried in the graves and question them about their faith. An angel named Sijill is in charge of the scrolls that register the fate of humans. Ridwān has charge over Paradise, and Malīk over hell. There are a number of guardian angels (6:61) who care for human beings in their lifetime.

We turn next to the Devil and the devils. A remarkable event takes place when Muslims go on the pilgrimage. At a certain point in the ceremonies they approach three pillars and throw seven stones at each of them with all their strength. The pillars symbolize the devils and the forces of evil. The pelted stones declare the believers' intention to resist those forces. Muslims do not take this matter lightly. They believe that there are real, malevolent, and active devils, as well as good angels, and a whole dangerous world of spirits.

The leader of the demonic forces, the Devil, is also called al-Shaitān (i.e., Satan), or Iblīs. Iblīs rebelled against God at creation.

> And when We said unto the angels: Prostrate yourselves before Adam, they fell prostrate, all save Iblis. He demurred through pride, and so became a disbeliever (2:34).

So pride before God is identified as one of the two fundamental attitudinal errors of the Devil. The other is ungratefulness. "The devil was ever an ingrate to his Lord" (17:27).

After the creation the Devil was reprieved by God until the Day of Judgment, and he became the sworn enemy of humanity. "I shall come upon them from before them and from behind them, and from their right hands and from their left hands ..." (7:17). He set himself to the task of misleading humanity. Thus he is called the deceiving Whisperer, who strives to tempt all humans as he tempted Adam in the Garden (15:39–42); his suggestive whispering brought humans into trouble at the beginning of time, and he continues to lead humans "down the garden path." The Devil said to God, after God conceded to him the freedom to tempt humanity: "Then, by my might, I will surely beguile them everyone, save Thy single-minded slaves among them" (38:83f.). In that hateful task Satan is supported by a host of other devils such as Hārūt and Mārūt (2:102), who attempt to bring division and discord to humanity.

The enmity of the Devil and his cohorts means that there is a kind of spiritual warfare in the world, in which all humans are involved. Muslim tradition attempted to express that reality, and the body of Ḥadīth is full of homely stories about the demons and their work. For example, they are said to covertly eavesdrop on the conversations going on between God and the angels, and they use their illicitly gained knowledge to bring harm to humans; when angels spot them, they throw shooting stars at them! This kind of tale may give the impression that devils can be taken lightly, but that is not what is intended. In fact, some modern Muslims have depersonalized the concept of evil in various ways. Most Muslims, however, maintain their belief in the Evil One and the fearfulness of his enmity. They hear the warning of the

Qurʾān: "Whoso chooseth Satan for a patron instead of Allāh is verily a loser and his loss is manifest ... Satan promiseth them only to beguile. For such their habitation will be hell, and they will find no refuge therefrom" (4:119–121). When men and women are tempted by Satan, they should take refuge in God: "And say: 'My Lord! I seek refuge in Thee from the suggestions of the evil one'!" (23:97). The 114th sura is used in popular Islām as a magically powerful talisman to ward off Satan:

Say: I seek refuge in the Lord of mankind,
The King of mankind,
The God of mankind,
From the evil of the sneaking whisperer,
Who whispereth in the hearts of mankind,
Of the jinn and of mankind.

The *jinn*! The word brings us to the final group of spiritual beings in Islām. The *jinn* are lesser spirits (cf. the English derived word "genie"). The concept of such lesser spirits was present in pre-Islāmic Arabia and was carried over into Islām. In the Qurʾān there are frequent references to them, especially in sūra 72; the Qurʾān accepts their existence as a reality in God's creation, but takes a firm stand against the human tendency to worship spirits, as well as the actual animistic worship of Arabia (37:158).

The *jinn*, in Muslim belief, have been created by God from smokeless fire, and like human beings they were made for the worship of God (51:56). In contrast to the angels, they eat, drink and propagate. They are invisible and can pass through solid walls. At the same time, they can inhabit or appear in the form of animals and humans. There are good and bad *jinn* among them, *jinn* that are *muslims*, and *jinn* that are not. Their functions are minor, compared to that of angels and devils, but they are basically similar in nature. For example, if evil, they have a kind of nuisance-creation role; ranging from the souring of milk to the deceiving of humans. If they are good, they testify to the truth of the Qurʾān. "Say (O Muhammad): It is revealed unto me that a company of the Jinn gave ear, and they said: 'Lo! it is a marvelous Qurʾān'!" (72:1). Such *jinn* give help to humans in certain affairs; for example, they gave solace to Muhammad after his disastrous experience at Taif. Like the angels and the devils the *jinn* operate under the sovereignty of God and, in the end, they will be judged by God along with the whole creation. These spirits are in no way to be worshipped, and the Qurʾān prophesies against that human tendency: "And they imagine kinship between him and the jinn, whereas the jinn know well that they will be brought before (Him)" (37:158).

Abdulla and Amina believe in the unseen world and the reality of angels, devils, and *jinn*. Some of their neighbors get a smile on their faces when the words are mentioned as though moderns cannot take these things seriously. Others of their neighbors go to quite opposite extremes. They allow their fear of the unseen world to lead them into a variety of magical and superstitious practices in order to control the spirits. Abdulla and Amina reject any superstition. They believe that the angels are God's agents for good, and they "seek refuge in God from the mysterious and unseen powers of evil,"

> From the evil of that which He created
> From the evil of the darkness when it is intense,
> And from the evil of malignant witchcraft,
> And from the evil of the envier when he envieth (113:2-4).

C. The Belief in Prophets

Muslims love the names of their heroes, and among them especially their prophets. It is not surprising that there are so many Ibrahims and Ismails and Muhammads in the world! This affection testifies to the importance of prophecy in Islām.

The spiritual idea of prophecy is laid down in the Qurʾān and rests on this basis—that God wants every human community to receive the revelation of His will.

> And for every nation there is a messenger. And when their messenger cometh (on the Day of Judgment) it will be judged between them fairly, and they will not be wronged (10:48).

> And verily We have raised in every nation a messenger (proclaiming): Serve Allāh and shun false gods (16:36).

With this in mind God graciously chooses certain individuals, guides them to the straight path, and gives them "the Scripture and command and prophethood" (6:90). With the gift of prophethood these messengers of God clarify what is needed for life in this world, and what is needed for eternal bliss. As Ibn Khaldūn, the great Muslim historian, put it:

> Be it known to you that Allāh—glory be to Him—has [at various times] chosen individuals from among mankind whom He has honored by Himself speaking to them to mold them according to His understanding, and to make them the mediators between Himself and His servants. As a result they teach men what things are for their betterment, urging them to take the right path and laboring to hold them back from Hell Fire by pointing out to them the way of escape.[3]

There are different opinions as to the number of such illustrious messengers. Some estimates—obviously mere guesses—go into the thousands, while others say that the actual number cannot be limited or known. Another disputed area is the difference between prophet (*nabī*) and apostle/messenger (*rasūl*). It is suggested that a *nabī* is an inspired teacher who guides the people orally but brings no book, while a *rasūl* is a prophet who is scripturally inspired. The words, in fact, are used interchangeably.

More significant is the question of a prophet's qualifications and functions. The first requirement is that such a person must have received a divine grace called *waḥy*. This is a special quality of inspiration, the capacity to receive an objective revelation from God. There is a lesser form of inspiration which should not be confused with *waḥy*. That is *ilhām*, which means illumination. Saints may have the gift of spiritual illumination, but only prophets are directly inspired with "the weighty discourse" of the Word of God.

A second prophetic qualification is the moral one. A prophet should have a noble character and be pious, faithful, and truthful. In later Islām it has been taught that a prophet is preserved from sinning, at least from serious sins. In the Qurʾān itself the prophets are portrayed as fully human beings, with many of the normal problems of ordinary people. There are many examples of prophets praying for forgiveness. After the first crisis of disobedience Adam said: "We have wronged ourselves. If thou forgive us not and have not mercy on us, surely we are of the lost" (7:23). Noah said: "My Lord! Forgive me and my two parents" (71:28). Abraham said: "... And Who, I ardently hope, will forgive me my sin on the Day of Judgment" (26:82). Moses prayed: "My Lord! Lo! I have wronged my soul, so forgive me" (28:16). And God declares to Muhammad, "Then have patience (O Muhammad). Lo! the promise of Allāh is true. And ask forgiveness of thy sin..." (40:55). Again, "Lo! We have given thee (O Muhammad) a signal victory, that Allāh may forgive thee of thy sin, that which is past and that which is to come... (48:12). While the passages are forthright, the emotion of Muslims is in the particular interpretation given to these passages.

The overall Muslim view is that the prophets of God were guarded from serious moral failure that would make them unfit vehicles for God's Word. As to lesser errors there is disagreement. Most Muslims, however, are not willing to accept that prophets are sinful except in the mildest sense. Al-Juwainī says: "As for those sins which are counted as venial ... reason does not deny them, and in my opinion there is no decisive proof that has come down to either deny such or to affirm them."[4] A contemporary Muslim puts it this way: "They were infallible in that they did not commit sins or violate the Law of God. But as mortals they made some unintentional mistakes in some human affairs and decisions."[5]

A third quality of a prophet is the ability to do miracles. Prophetic miracles are different and superior to miracles performed by saints in that they arise from a specific challenge and are proof that the prophet is engaged in God's activity. The Prophet Muhammad himself did not claim to be a miracle-doer; for him the Qurʾān itself was the miracle that testified to his vocation. The Qurʾān says, "And they say: Why are not portents sent down upon him from his Lord? Say: Portents are with Allāh only, and I am but a plain warner" (29:50). Later tradition, however, mentions many miracles of the Prophet. In the case of the other prophets, such as Moses and Jesus, miracles are frequently mentioned as the divine attestation to their message, and these are elaborated in legendary description.

The number of prophets mentioned in the Qurʾān is 25–29, the range indicating that there is some variation in listings. Nineteen of these are familiar to readers of the Hebrew Bible, three are in the New Testament tradition, and seven are not known outside the Qurʾān. Muhammad is the final messenger and is therefore called "the seal of the prophets." Other major prophets include Noah, Abraham, Moses, and Jesus. No matter how great they are, there is a consistent sense that the prophets "walk humbly" before the Almighty. That is typified by Noah who said: "I say not unto you, 'I have the treasures of Allāh,' nor 'I have knowledge of the unseen,' nor say I: 'Lo! I am an angel!' Nor say I unto those whom your eyes scorn that Allāh will not do them good." (11:31). In the following we will provide a few facts, drawn mainly from the Qurʾān, on each of the prophets.[6]

Ādām: Adam is the first prophet as well as the first human being. He was given a high status as God's vice-regent on earth. He erred, however, in yielding to the Tempter, but God restored him and gave him the good news of His guidance.

Nūh: Noah is called "the grateful servant of God." With Abraham, Moses, and Jesus, he is one of the "covenant prophets." The story of the flood and Ark is related in the Qurʾān. Tradition reports that the donkey was the last animal to board the ark. The devil entered by hanging on to its tail. Noah did not have time to get rid of him before he had to close the doors!

Ibrahīm: Abraham is a crucial figure in Islāmic history. Called "the friend of God," he forsook polytheism and turned to the worship of the Creator God. He is therefore the prototype of true Muslims. Since he predates the Jewish and Christian religions, he also shows that Islām is the primordial faith. He is the builder of the Kāʿba in Mecca.

Lūt: Lot was Abraham's emigrant colleague, and he is referred to as a person of judgment and knowledge. He is also a prophet of punishment, and the story is told of the evil of Sodom and its fall.

Ismāʿīl: Ishmael is a "keeper of his promise." The son of Abraham and Hagar (who holds a position of prominence in Islām), Ishmael carried forward their faith as *muslims*, and he is also regarded as a physical father of the Arab peoples. He helped his father in the building of the Kāʿba.

Ishāq: Isaac is the child of promise, born when Abraham and Sarah were old. The Qurʾān tells the story of how Abraham was tested by being called upon to sacrifice his son, who is not named. Most contemporary Muslims believe that the son was Ishmael.

Yaʿkūb: Jacob is regarded as a brother of Isaac. He became blind through sorrow, but regained his sight when Joseph's coat touched his eye.

Yūsuf: Joseph is a major figure in the Qurʾān, the entire 12th sūra being devoted to his story. He testifies to the kindness of God, and he himself is a model of generosity and virtue. Many stories about Joseph and his beauty are recorded in Muslim tradition.

Mūsā: A major prophet, Moses is granted illumination, instruction, and guidance by God. He was the recipient of the Torah (*tawrāt*), an inspired scripture. God's powerful messenger to the Pharaoh, he performed nine miracles in Egypt, as well as others in the wilderness. He led the Israelites to safety, brought them the instruction of God on tablets—which he destroyed because of their disobedience—and finally piloted them to the promised land. He alone saw God face to face.

Hārūn: Aaron was the eloquent spokesman for Moses. For fear of the Israelites he participated in the erection of the golden calf, but was forgiven.

Dāwūd: David is also called the vice-regent of God. He is a fashioner of armor and the slayer of Goliath. He possessed the gift of song and is the recipient of the Psalms (*zabūr*), one of the revealed scriptures. He sang (34:9), "O ye hills and birds, echo his songs of praise."

Sulaimān: Solomon is frequently mentioned in the Qurʾān. As a youth, he surpassed even David, his father, in administering justice. Possessing remarkable powers over nature and *jinn*, he knew the languages of birds and animals and could control the wind. His wisdom compelled Bilqis, the Queen of Saba, to submit to him. Many legendary stories further embellish the history of Solomon.

Idrīs: Identified by some with Enoch, Idrīs is an upright prophet, with a special capacity for patience, who was raised to a high place.

Aiyūb: Job was the enduring servant of God. He was tested by God and prayed for help: "Lo! ... Thou art Most Merciful of those who show mercy" (21:84). In answer to his prayer, God removed the adversity and restored him to prosperity.

Yūnus: Jonah, "he of the fish," gives his name to the tenth sūra. He symbolizes the human attempt to flee God and God's rescue of the erring. The story of his prayer from within the belly of the whale is told. Jonah is sometimes identified with the next prophet, Dhuʾ-Nūn.

Dhuʾl-Nūn: The story of this prophet is similar to Jonah's. His name signifies "Lord of the fish." Thinking that God had no power over him, he ran off in anger. When God punished him, he called out the *shahāda* from the darkness, and God delivered him.

Ilyās: Elijah called upon his people to fear God Who is the "Best of creators," and to turn from the worship of Baal. When he experienced reprisals, God gave him peace, as one of His servants who have believed and done well.

Al-Yasaʾ: Elisha was chosen by God and guided to the straight path. He warded off evil and had a happy journey's end in the Garden of Paradise.

ʿUzair: Possibly Ezra, there is only one reference to him in the Qurʾān, and he is not included in every list of prophets. The Qurʾān says that the Jews mistakenly took him for "the son of God."

Hūd: The eleventh sūra is named after Hud. He was sent to the people of ʿĀd, who are associated with the time period after Noah. He was courageous and proclaimed repentance and the abandonment of idolatry. "Have you no sense?" he cried. The people, however, flouted their kinsman, whereupon God imposed His curse upon ʿĀd as a punishment.

Ṣāliḥ: Salih was sent to the people of Thamūd in Eastern Arabia. He called on them to remember the bounties of God, to seek forgiveness, and to serve Him alone. When the people lampooned him, God sent a calamitous earthquake upon them. Ṣāliḥ had the last word. He said, "But ye love not good advisors" (7:79).

Shuʿaib: He proclaimed God's message to the people of Midian, especially emphasizing honesty in weights and measures. "Watch! Watch!," he cried. The people said, "We can do what we wish with our money." The judgment of God came against them, and they died in a natural calamity. Later Muslims thought that Shuʿaib might be the father-in-law of Moses.

Dhuʾl-Kifl: Perhaps the son of Job, little is told of Dhuʾl-Kifl. Like Idrīs and Job, he was one of the patient and righteous ones whom God entered into His mercy.

Dhuʾl-Qarnain: The name means "two-horned,' and the figure in the Qurʾān resembles a world conqueror. It is not surprising that some commentators see in him a variety of kingly figures. He was "strong in the land" and devised a successful barrier against Gog and Magog.

Luqmān: Luqman gives his name to sūra 31. He was granted the gift of wisdom, and is known as the master of wise sayings. The Qurʾān contains these proverbial words: "And if all the trees in the earth were pens and the sea, with seven more seas to help it (were ink), the words of Allāh could not be exhausted" (31:27).

Zakārīyā: Zakariah, the servant of God, prayed to Him for an heir. When God acceded, Zakariah felt doubt and, as a result, was not able to speak for three nights. He and his wife, however, were humble before God and vied in good works. He also became the guardian of the Virgin Mary.

Yahya (John the Baptist): John was a special gift to his parents in their old age. Even as a boy he had the gift of compassion, purity, and a sense of duty. When he grew up, he became a pious and authoritative prophet. Above all, he received the Book with steadfastness and with a desire to confirm the Word of God. "So peace upon him the day he was born, and the day he died, and the day he shall be raised alive!" (19:15).

ʿĪsā (Jesus): The usual name for Jesus is "son of Mary," but he has several other names and titles. They include Messiah, a word from Him, a spirit from Him, a slave to God, prophet, messenger, a revelation for mankind, a mercy from Us, one of the righteous, a pattern, illustrious in this world and the next. Jesus was born of a virgin. Like Adam, he was created with the powerful word "Be!" He brought clear proofs and wisdom about God, received the Gospel, taught clearly, and was strengthened by the holy Spirit. He witnessed to God and urged people to keep their duty to Him. "Allāh is my Lord and your Lord, so worship Him! That is the straight path." He did miracles including shaping a bird like clay, healing the blind and lepers, and raising the dead. He was not slain, but rather God took him to Himself. Eventually he will die (most Muslims assume after he has come again in the Last Days), but before he dies all the people of the scripture will believe in him, and he will be a witness of that. In sum, he is a "portent" and an "example" for humanity.

Muhammad: The life of Muhammad has been treated in chapters 4–6 of this work. In the Muslim view, Muhammad is the greatest of the prophets, and with him the stream of prophecy ends.

In the above listing the names of Dhuʾl-Nūn, Dhuʾl-Qarnain, Lukmān and ʿUzair are those most frequently omitted from current Muslim lists of the prophets. The remaining 25 names represent an impressive array of leaders. Abdulla and Amina, and their friends, not only believe in the prophets, but they also draw on their lives for inspiration, and they pass on the stories to their children. In addition, they revere the scriptures given through the prophets. We now turn to the Muslim belief in sacred scriptures.

D. The Belief in Books

Throughout this work we have emphasized the commitment that Muslims have to the Qurʾān. But my Muslim friends do not believe only in the Qurʾān. Often Jews and Christians are startled to discover that Muslims also pay great respect to the Torah and the Gospel. At the same time, many Muslims do not regard the current text of the Torah and the Gospel as accurate.

This is by way of introduction to the next Muslim belief—the belief in sacred books. Even a casual reading of the Qurʾān will reveal that God has not given a single revelation, but rather a series of revelations to humanity. The Qurʾān is, as it were, the Mt. Everest in the range of divine revelations, but other peaks precede it. God, the Ruler of the Worlds, will allow no human community to have the excuse that it had no chance to hear either His warnings or His good tidings. Therefore God says to Muhammad (4:163f.):

> We inspired thee as We inspired Noah and the prophets after him ... and messengers We have mentioned unto thee before and messengers we have not mentioned unto thee.

There is an interesting passage in the Qurʾān (3:81) that pictures God as making a covenant with prophets. God declares that He has given each one an appropriate scripture and, it is implied, that they should feel greatly honored by that distinction. But when a successor messenger appears who confirms the previous scripture, they should also esteem him and render him help. The proper attitude toward the various scriptures that God has previously revealed is then summed up (v.84):

> We believe in Allāh and that which is revealed unto us and that which was revealed unto Abraham and Ishmael and Isaac and Jacob and the tribes, and that which was vouchsafed unto Moses and Jesus and the Prophets from their Lord. We make no distinction between any of them....

What were these sacred scriptures that were "revealed aforetime"? Muslims traditionally believe that there were 104 such writings. Not all of these, however, were books in the ordinary sense. A hundred of them were really sets of "leaves" (*suhuf*). This reminds us that there were different kinds of writing materials in ancient times. Only the final four are really books in the modern sense. These final four are the *tawrāt* (Torah), which was given to Moses; the *zabūr* (Psalms), which was revealed to David; the *injīl* (Gospel), which was given Jesus; and the Qurʾān, which was revealed to Muhammad. (It now becomes very clear why the Qurʾān calls Jews and Christians *ahl al-kitāb*, "people of the book"). What happened to the leaves or scrolls of the older scriptures is not known, but the Qur'ān suggests that they contained "good things" and "plain warnings"; for example, they explained

> that no laden one shall bear another's load,
> And that man has only that for which he maketh effort,
> And that his effort will be seen And afterward he will be repaid for it with fullest payment!
> And that thy Lord—He is the goal (87:38–42).

It is not the earlier scrolls, however, that the Qur'ān emphasizes. It has much more to say about the three sacred books that immediately preceded it, namely the Torah, the Psalms, and the Gospel, and we will look at each of these in turn.

1. *Tawrāt*: Muslims use the word Torah to designate the Pentateuch that was given to Moses, and by extension it can also refer to the whole body of the Hebrew Bible/Old Testament.

In the Qur'ān it is stated that God gave the Torah to Moses as a gracious guidance for the people of Israel:

> And we verily gave Moses the guidance, and We caused the children of Israel to inherit the Scripture, a guide and a reminder for men of understanding (40:56f.).

The Torah provides the Israelites with sufficient direction to enable them to conduct their lives successfully and to meet their Lord.

> We gave the Scripture unto Moses ... an explanation of all things, a guidance and a mercy, that they might believe in the meeting with their Lord. And this is the blessed Scripture which we have revealed. So follow it and ward off (evil), that he may find mercy (6:155f.).

The Qur'ān gives us some information about the content of the Torah. It is called the law, and as such it is both a guidance and a light. It is the standard by which the people of Israel are to be judged. The Qur'ān confirms its teaching, but it also suggests that the commands of the law are to be interpreted generously. For example, it reports that the Torah contains the law of retaliation: "... The life for the life, and the eye for the eye, and the nose for the nose, and the tooth for the tooth, and for wounds retaliation." But, the Qur'ān adds, "Whoso forgoeth it [in the way of charity], it shall be an expiation for him" (5:45).

The Qurʾān incorporates many stories, events, and legal prescriptions that are roughly parallel to the Hebrew Bible/Old Testament. Such events include the creation of the world; the story of Adam; Cain and Abel; Noah's ark and the flood; Abraham and the angels; Abraham and the near sacrifice of a son; Jacob's visit to Egypt; the history of Joseph; Moses and Pharaoh; the Israelites in the desert; the manna and quail; Moses striking the rock; the idolatrous calf and Korah; Solomon's judgments and the Queen from the south; Jonah and the fish, and so on.

The Qurʾān also records the uneven response of the Israelites to the revelation that they received. Among them are both believers and unbelievers. The disobedience of the unbelieving Jews has three facets. First of all, they do not apply the teachings of the Book. They are like a donkey that carries around books on its back rather than being obedient to its contents. At other times they are out-and-out rebellious and persecute the prophets. Secondly, they sometimes deliberately distort the message of the Book when speaking to others. Thirdly, they refuse to accept the prophethood of Muhammad even though, the Qurʾān declares, he was foretold in the previous scriptures:

> Those who follow the messenger, the Prophet who can neither read nor write, whom they will find described in the Torah and the Gospel ... He will enjoin on them that which is right and forbid them that which is wrong (7:157).

It is because of their disobedience that God had to send a succession of prophets to the Israelites culminating with ʿĪsā Nabī (Jesus, the Prophet).

2. *Zabūr*: The word *zabūr*, which means "writing," is the ordinary Muslim word for the Psalms. The Book was given to David: "We imparted unto David the Psalms" (4:163). Although very little is said about the actual content of the Psalms, it may be noted that many of the themes in the early Meccan surās of the Qurʾān are Psalm-like in their content and language. It is therefore not surprising that what seems to be the only direct biblical quotation in the Qurʾān is from the Psalms: "Before thee We wrote in the Psalms after the Message (given to Moses): 'My servants, the righteous, shall inherit the earth.'" (21:105).[7]

3. *Injīl*: Muslims accept the Gospel, which was given to Jesus,

as the third of the four "existing" Books that are held sacred by the Muslim community. In the Qurʾān the word refers to both the revelation given to Jesus and its inscripturated form, which is regarded as the possession of Christians at that time.[8] In the same way as the term Torah is extended in everyday use to cover the whole Hebrew Bible/Old Testament, so also the name *Injīl* is commonly used for the whole New Testament. Some Muslims, however, restrict its application to material covered in the four gospels of the New Testament.

The title *Injīl* is an Arabicized form of the Greek word for Gospel, which means good news.[9] The Qurʾān frequently describes the revelations to the prophets as God's good tidings. Although *Injīl* is used only 12 times in the Qurʾān, the Qurānic testimony to its importance is a powerful one. It is reckoned as part of God's covenant with humanity (9:11) and as an aspect of God's gracious guidance of His people:

> And we caused Jesus, son of Mary, to follow in their footsteps, confirming that which was (revealed) before him, and We bestowed on Him the Gospel wherein is guidance and a light confirming that which was (revealed) before him, and We bestowed on him the Gospel wherein is guidance and a light, confirming that which was (revealed) before it in the Torah—a guidance and an admonition unto those who ward off (evil)" (5:46).

The people of the Book are called upon to observe the Law and the Gospel. Such observance will "guarantee" their acceptance by God on the Last Day:

> Say: O People of the Scripture! Ye have naught (of guidance) till ye observe the Torah and the Gospel, and that which was revealed unto you from your Lord ... Lo! those who believe, and those who are Jews and Sabaeans, and Christians—whosoever believeth in Allāh and the Last Day and doeth right—there shall no fear come upon them, neither shall they grieve (5:58f.).

Contrariwise, those who do not observe the demands of the Torah and the Gospel will bear the unhappy result of that decision:

> Let the People of the Gospel judge by that which Allāh hath revealed therein. Whoso judgeth not by that which Allāh hath revealed, such are the evil-livers (5:47).

The references to the *Injīl* in the Qurʾān center on historical events rather than on teachings. These historical occasions include events connected with the birth of John the Baptist, the annunciation to Mary, and events in the life of the Messiah. Further, references to the seed (48:29) and the lighting of lamps (57:3) remind the reader of the Gospel accounts of the parables of the sower and the seed, and the wise and foolish virgins. Another passage holds important prophetical significance for Muslims. The passage (61:6) reads: "And when Jesus son of Mary said: O Children of Israel, Lo! I am the messenger of Allāh unto you, confirming that which was (revealed) before me in the Torah, and bringing good tidings of a messenger who cometh after me, whose name is the Praised One." Since the Arabic for Praised One is *ahmad,* Muslims regard this verse as representing Jesus' own prophecy of the coming of Muhammad after him. In the Ḥadīth and in later Muslim tradition the Qurānic references to the *Injīl* are greatly elaborated, especially in relation to the events of the Last Times.

4. Interrelation of the Sacred Books

Muslims do not regard the interrelation of the sacred books as a dependent one. They are sequentially related, but in terms of content one book is not historically dependent on a previous book. What is involved at this point is the Muslim understanding of revelation. Jesus did not include certain items in the Gospel because of His knowledge of the Torah and Jewish history. Whatever is in the Gospel was directly revealed to him by God. So also the Qurʾān is not dependent on the *Tawrāt* and the *Injīl* for certain materials. Whatever is in the Qurʾān is there because it was revealed to Muhammad through the agency of the angel Gabriel, drawn from the "Mother of the Book" in heaven. Professor George Anawati makes this clear. In commenting on the relation of the Qurānic accounts to the Biblical accounts, and their resemblances, he states,

> For believing Muslims this question presents no difficulties: it is the same God who reveals both, and the Prophet Muhammad, having received the Revelation directly from God had no need to consult, directly or indirectly, the Scriptures in order to reproduce some of the features which are found in them.[10]

However, there is an actual relationship between the sacred books that depends on their common source in God. The book that comes later *confirms* the message of the earlier ones. Again and again, like a litany the words are repeated in the Qur'ān "confirming," "confirming," "confirming." In the Muslim understanding, each revelation that God gave was a focussed one; it included events and established laws related to a particular ethnic or national context. But the *essential* content of each revelation is considered to be common; that is, each sacred scripture proclaimed the unity of God and called on the people of one society to surrender to God alone.

In the same way the Qur'ān confirms that which has gone before, and many passages attest to that function. It does not attempt to repeat everything that is in the previous scriptures, nor to duplicate the special emphases of the *Tawrāt*, the *Zabūr* and the *Injīl*. Rather it is a crystallization of the primary message in all the previous books, a compendium of their fundamental elements. We may say, therefore, that the Qur'ān has an "essentializing" or "encapsulating" function in relation to previous scriptures. But it also has a "universalizing" function. Although the Qur'ān calls itself an Arabic Qur'ān and is directed toward the inhabitants of Arabia, it has a universal aspect that differentiates it from previous scriptures. All previous scriptures were culture-specific and time-bound, but the Qur'ān established what is universal and forever relevant. No further sacred books are needed now by the world community. Therefore the Qur'ān is God's final Word and Muhammad is the seal of the prophets.

5. The Previous Scriptures and the Theory of Corruption

The positive Islāmic attitude toward the previous scriptures, as outlined above, is qualified by the theory of scriptural corruption. The idea arises from the fact that there are differences between the Qur'ān and previous books that need to be explained. Some Muslims suggest that Jews and Christians allowed their scriptures to be tampered with, and this resulted in the development of a corrupt and uncertain text. When the Qur'ān affirms the *Tawrāt*, *Zabūr* and *Injīl* therefore, it affirms the original texts rather than the currently existing ones. The latter are not authentic. Not all Muslims agree on this issue, however. Some will not agree that the Almighty God would allow His books to be falsified. Others decline to regard Jews and Christians as the type of people who would falsify God's Word or allow it to be corrupted.

The concept of corruption is called *taḥrīf*. Two kinds of *taḥrīf* are considered possible. The first kind involves changing the meaning of the words by concealing a portion or by misinterpreting them in oral communication. This is called *taḥrīf al-maʿnawī*. The charge of twisting the words of scripture in this way was levied at the Jews: "And lo! there is a party of them who distort the Scripture with their tongues, when it is not from the Scripture. And they say, 'It is from Allāh,' when it is not from Allāh; and they speak a lie concerning Allāh knowingly" (3:72). The second kind of corruption applies to the actual alteration of the written text. It is called *taḥrīf al-lafẓī*. The Qurʾān says: "Therefore woe be unto those who write the Scripture with their hands and then say, 'This is from Allāh,' that they may purchase a small gain therewith" (2:79).

While many Muslim scholars could be quoted in support of the interpretation that Jews and Christians changed the actual words in their sacred books, others are of the view that there is only a distortion of meaning. Thus, for example, the great Indian Muslim reformer, Sir Sayyid Ahmad Khan, declared, "I do not agree with the statement that Jews and Christians in the sacred books made *taḥrīfuʾl-lafẓī*."[11] On the other hand, Hammudah Abdalati says:

> In principle, the Muslim believes in the previous books and revelations. But where are the complete and original versions? ... For the Muslim there is no problem of that kind. The Qurʾān is in his hand complete and authentic ... It is given to the Muslim as the standard or criterion by which all other books are judged. So whatever agrees with the Qurʾān is accepted as Divine truth, and whatever differs from the Qurʾān is either rejected or suspended.[12]

For Abdulla and Amina the question of the previous scriptures is basically a non-issue. They believe in the sacred books, and they know that the Qurʾān affirms them positively. Yet for them there is only one book that has practical meaning, the Qurʾān. If asked whether you have read the *Tawrāt*, or *Zabūr*, or *Injīl*, the answer would be no. They have close friends among the people of the Book, and they respect their commitments, but they have not had the inclination or occasion to read their scriptures. They are content with the Qurʾān, for them the noblest of books and the greatest of all miracles.

E. The Belief in the Day of Judgment

Muslim belief in the Resurrection and the Day of Judgment go together. The first preaching of Muhammad, as we have seen, was full of references to the Last Times. The warning of the coming Judgment was integral to his message. The Resurrection and Judgment were also personal realities for Muhammad. There is a Ḥadīth that says:

> Hafsa said that when the Prophet wanted to go asleep, he placed his hand under his cheeks, and would then say three times: "O God, guard me from Thy punishment on the day when Thou raisest up Thy servants!"[13]

In recent years I have noticed that my Muslim friends do not greatly emphasize this theme. It is still there, but what has pushed it into the background is a new emphasis on everyday life in *this* world. Within the past 75 years or so there has been a reorientation in Muslim thinking, under the influence of many reformers. Islām is viewed as a practical "worldly" religion. It is true that we must prepare for life in the next world, but now it is the Muslim task to build God's society in this world. As a result there is less discussion of the last times and the world to come. Yet the Judgment Day remains, not only as the fifth basic belief, but as a reality, a Tremor-Producing Reality. Even though Abdulla and Amina do not mention the Day of Judgment very much in ordinary conversation, it is in their consciousness, and they continue to feel what the Prophet Muhammad felt.

The Day of Resurrection and the Day of Judgment are coupled together in sūra 75, and the prospect as presented there is a sobering one indeed:

> Nay, I swear by the Day of Resurrection
> ... Thinketh man that we shall not assemble his bones?
> Yea, verily. Yea, We are able to restore his very fingers!
> But man would fain deny what is before him.
> He asketh: When will be this Day of Resurrection?
> But when the sight is confounded
> And the moon is eclipsed

And the sun and moon are united,
On that day men will cry: Whither to flee!
Alas! No refuge!
Unto thy Lord is the recourse that day.
On that day man is told the tale of that
Which he hath sent before and left behind.
Oh, but man is a telling witness against himself,
Although he tender his excuses ...
Nay, but ye do love the fleeting Now
and neglect the Hereafter.
That day will faces be resplendent,
Looking toward their Lord;
And on that day will other faces be despondent
Thou wilt know that some great disaster is about to fall on them ...
Nearer unto thee and nearer!
Again, nearer unto thee and nearer ... ! (vv.1–35)

There are many passages in the Qurʾān that repeat this throbbing message—the world will come to an end! The end is nearer now, and the final closure will come when all humanity will be raised up and will stand before the Judgment throne of the Almighty. That Day is given other names in the Qurʾān, all of them instructive: the Day of Awakening, the Day of Decision, the Day of Reckoning, the Encompassing Day, the Hour, the Doom of Allāh. The very names are enough to send a chill down any person's spine, but the descriptions of the actual events of the Day, and its conclusion in either Paradise or Hell, are even more graphic. They are designed to remind every human to take this matter seriously. That is why Qurānic exhortations were consistent to the end of the Prophet's career. Thus a late Medinan revelation declares:

O mankind! Fear your Lord! Lo! the earthquake of the Hour (of Doom) is a tremendous thing! (22:1).

Muslims believe that the intent of the message should not be lost amidst the colorful descriptions of Heaven and Hell. The intent is to make humans more aware of their situation, to remind them of the importance of repentance, and to recall them to the true worship of the Almighty. Fazlur Rahman says:

The basic idea underlying the Qurʾān's teaching on the hereafter is that there will come a moment, "The Hour," when every human being will be shaken into a unique and unprecedented self-awareness of his deeds: he will squarely and starkly face his own doings, not-doings, and misdoings and accept the judgment upon them as a "necessary" sequel.[14]

What must be added to this crisp statement of Muslim feeling is the plain fact that the Qurʾān wants its hearers to consider this reality *before* the awful Hour comes, and so do something about their lives in preparation for it.

The Resurrection and the Judgment will be cosmic in scope, but individual in focus. No one can escape it. Every person will be "alone" before God on that Day. There will be no turning to family or friends for help. All that a person will have with him or her are their own deeds. "Now have ye come unto Us solitary, as We did create you at first ..." (6:95). On that day no soul will bear another's burdens, and everyone that has done an atom's might of good shall behold it, and everyone that has done an atom's weight of evil shall behold it. The prospect for sinners—and who is not a sinner?—is a terrifying one.

The Ḥadīth frame the colorful pictures of the Qurʾān with extensive imagery. They include a great deal of material that is not in the Book related to the Last Days, but the sequence of events is not always clear. Following is a summary view of those events. The exact time of the Day of Judgment is not known. It is hidden in the decision of God. "Unto Him is referred all knowledge of the Hour" (41:47). Nevertheless, there will be clear signs of its advent, some of them general in nature and some quite specific. The general signs include such things as a decay of faith in the world, the advance of meanly forces in society, tumults and calamities of different kinds. Following these more general phenomena, there will be specific events that clearly indicate that the end is at hand. They include the following:

1. The Appearance of the Mahdī

The Mahdī is a liberating figure, born from the family of the Prophet and bearing his name. God will send him to establish justice and equity on earth, and to spread Islām. The Mahdī is not a Qurānic idea, but it became a constant factor in later Muslim traditions. Shīʿa Muslims identify the Mahdī with their hidden Imām, the twelfth leader of the Shīʿites. From time to time individuals claiming to be the Mahdī have arisen in different parts of the Muslim world.

2. The Descent of Jesus, the Messiah

Muslim tradition holds that Jesus did not die on the cross, although he was crucified. Someone who resembled Jesus was substituted and died in his place. It has been suggested that this person may have been Judas. At that time God took Jesus to heaven still alive. He will return in the Last Times near the white minaret on the east side of the mosque of Damascus. He will preach righteousness, break all the crosses, kill all the swine, and then—after establishing the rule of God—he will die.

3. The Appearance of Dajjal

Who is the Dajjāl? He is the ally of Satan and the enemy of God. Reddish and one-eyed, on his forehead is inscribed KFR, which implies unbeliever. He will come from the East riding a donkey and driven by clouds of smoke. A great tempter, he will work miracles and will succeed in deceiving many. Thus, for a period he will conquer the earth—except Mecca and Medina—but he will be defeated by the Mahdī or the Messiah. This legendary figure is not mentioned in the Qurʾān, but many stories are told about him.

4. The Appearance of the Beast

This rather obscure being is a compound animal, 75 feet high, who will arise out of the earth near Mecca. He will place identifying marks on the faces of the believers. Once again, this sign is based entirely on tradition.

5. Gog and Magog

These figures, Yājuj and Mājuj, are briefly mentioned in the Qurʾān as the enemies and spoilers of the land. In Ḥadīth it is reported that they will attack Palestine, troubling Jesus and his companions, who will ask God to destroy them.

6. A Miscellany of Other Signs

There are other signs that will occur, preceding the Last Day. The sun will rise in the West, and there will be eclipses, fire, and a kind of volcanic smoke for 40 days. The Qurʾān will be forgotten, the Ka'ba will be destroyed, and many of the earth's inhabitants will become infidels.

It is clear that many of these events that are proclaimed as signs of the Last Times have a legendary quality about them, and many modern Muslims would not accept certain elements as literally true. Everyone, however, would agree that the Last Times will surely be a period of great tumult and unusual events, marked by a fearful struggle between good and evil. Then shall the end come.

7. The Resurrection, the Trial, and the Judgment

Israfīl, the Angel of the Last Times, will blow a blast of his trumpet alerting humanity. This has been called the blast of consternation. At that time all humans shall perish. After a period of 40 years the blast of resurrection will awaken the dead, and the Judgment will commence. Already in the graves the questioning angels will have put everyone through a preliminary hearing, but now the actual trial will begin. All humans will appear before the Almighty, and He will conduct His own questioning. Each individual will be given the books that have recorded his or her deeds. The final account-taking reflects the picture of a great scale. Everyone's books will be placed on the balance; those whose scale is heavy with good will be eligible for Paradise, while those who are heavy with evil will be condemned to Hell. The final step takes place when those who have merited salvation will cross the narrow bridge *(sirāt)* between heaven and hell, but unbelievers and sinners fall into the Fire. The unknown factor is the question of God's will and mercy, and how these will enter into the final decision. Especially the Ḥadīth underline God's right to do what He wishes in this matter. About faithful Muslims, however, there is little uncertainty, nor is there doubt about the fate of unbelievers. But the question of Muslim believers whose sins exceed their good works has been the topic of much discussion. The majority opinion is that they must suffer for a while. One authority says, "Believing sinners, unless forgiven by God, receive their punishment in Hell for some time, after which they are restored to Paradise."[15]

We will take up the description of Heaven and Hell, and further discussion of the ways of salvation, in the closing section of this chapter, which deals with the issue of human destiny.

Mohammad Fadhel Jamāli—an Iraqi philosopher, educator and statesman who signed the Charter of the United Nations in

1945—was sentenced to prison by his country's dictator in 1945, on false charges. He wrote to his son from prison, where he expected death:

> I am a believer in the resurrection after death and in judgment on the Last Day. I have no material proof of this, for none of the dead has returned to tell us what happens to man after death. But this belief of mind is a sequel to my faith in Allāh. His wisdom and justice; My mind tells me that it is not appropriate that the short life of man should end on this earth, and, that with death, all should be over. There must be another life in which man reaps what he sows in this life, for life after death is the real hope of the good man in this world, and without it this life would be like a blind alley without sense and with no goal. Belief in life after death, then gives the individual unlimited hope and it motivates man to do good deeds and prevents him doing evil, for he believes that he will be called to account on the Day of Judgment for each act he performed in this world.[16]

Abdulla and Amina would certainly subscribe to the sentiments of this learned and faithful Muslim. They *know* that the Judgment Day is coming. They *know* that they will be there. They hope that God will be merciful to them in that Hour.

F. The Belief in Predestination

In the classical listing of basic Muslim beliefs predestination was usually added as a sixth required belief. We have discussed the idea of the divine predetermination and control of human actions in connection with the doctrine of God (chapter 4). We noted there that modern Muslims tend to reject this doctrine as a misreading of the Qurʾān. The Qurʾān, in their view, teaches human freedom and responsibility, not fatalism. Nevertheless, the traditional teaching is still current among Muslims, and there are others who espouse a modified commitment to the classical theory. A quotation from Dr. Muhammad Rauf, former Director of the Islamic Center in Washington, D.C., U.S.A., will suffice to make the point:

> Muslims believe that God created the universe as predetermined by Him. This predeterminism is called qadar. Things do not occur haphazardly. The constitution of the human body and the harmonious functioning of its parts; the construction of the heavenly bodies and their movements in space ... all reveal full knowledge and a careful planning of incomparable degree. Muslims therefore believe in God's

eternal knowledge and decreeing all happenings in the universe according to His will and wisdom. Muslims, because of their belief in qadar, are sometimes accused of being fatalistic. This is not correct ... If fatalism means the acceptance of every thing or condition as inevitable, and assumes an attitude of apathy, or implies a denial of human freedom, it is certainly something different from our concept of qadar. We believe at the same time that the universe, being so wonderful and complex and yet running so smoothly, efficiently and accurately, must have been planned and predetermined by God in eternity, according to His wisdom and His will. When some misfortune befalls us, we resign ourselves to it as something coming from God instead of despairing. We also believe in human freedom and the ability of the individual to determine the course of his voluntary acts. God's foreknowledge of what we shall do is not inconsistent with human freedom.[17]

The discussion of this issue is still alive in Islām. Abdulla and Amina, as well as most Muslims, are content to leave the question within the mystery of God. At the same time, their thinking and emotion are deeply influenced by the combination of ideas in the phrases "God is most great!" and "If God wills." This issue joins with others as we ponder the great questions of human destiny. Our consideration leads us next to the Muslim view of sin and salvation.

G. Sin and Salvation

My Muslim friends recognize the problem created by their sins, but they maintain a heavenly hope.

There are at least three distinct ways of considering the problem of sin. One can, for example, begin with the nature of God and ask the questions, What is God's own character like? What is God's relation to the evil of the universe? What is God's attitude toward human sins? Or one can begin from the human side and ask, With what nature was humanity created? What is the moral character, possibility, and goal of a human being? Or one can start with the words of the authoritative scripture, What does it say about sin and sins? In a full study of sin and evil, all of these are involved. However, since we have already touched upon the doctrine of God in Islām in previous chapters, we will deal with this topic by looking at the Muslim teaching concerning the nature of human beings, and then examine what the Qurʾān says about sins.

It should be understood that the beliefs about sin and salvation are not considered essential to the primary beliefs of Islām, and there are varieties of Muslim opinion on the subject.

1. The Nature of Humanity

In Islām, God created human beings to be his surrendering servants. The highest aspiration and true vocation of a man or a woman is to be the obedient servant of God. God, the Lord and Master, prescribes the straight path—both its principles and its regulations—along which human beings should walk. Out of His mercy and compassion He not only provides the necessary guidance for leading a God-pleasing life, but He also makes the path sufficiently easy so that the possibility of obedience exists. In addition, he also makes available the example of noble human beings, especially the great prophets, so that we may be inspired to a life of true *islām*.

Still human beings err and go astray. Why? Is it because God has willed that they do so? Some suggested that solution to the problem. After all, the Qurʾān itself declares in 14:4 and in many other places, "Allāh sendeth whom He will astray, and guideth whom He will." Others say, "No, that approach cannot be the correct view." They assert that God's leading astray is a punishment of human stubbornness and not its cause. The human disobedience comes first, and then God leads recalcitrant humans further astray as a penalty. But that still leaves the question, What accounts for human error? For the answer we have to look at the Muslim understanding of humanity's created nature. We have already touched on this matter in our discussion of creation in chapter 4.

The problem, Muslims believe, arises from the double-sided nature of humanity; that is, human beings are created by God with the capacity for both good and evil. On the one hand, God formed humans with noble qualities, a little higher than angels. He created them with a direction (*fitra*) and propensity toward *islām*, as people who readily and joyfully will surrender to God. Put another way, human beings are made to fear God and to thank Him, to serve God and to obey Him. In addition, God has given men and women a high calling on earth, the vocation to be the vice-regents of God. They are to rule the earth on behalf of God and to make it the abode of Islām. When God said to the angels, "I am about to place a viceroy on earth" (2:30), the angels objected because they sensed that humanity would "mess it up," but God persisted with His decision. As a result, all human beings share the birthright of a natural *islām* and a high calling, and they only become sinful Muslims or unbelievers at a later stage.

The reason that human beings do fall into error is that there is another side to human nature than the one described above. It has a dark side, which is equally a part of the natural human constitution. Human beings are created with frailty as well as nobility, with weakness as well as strength. Every human being has a natural potential for sinfulness as well as for piety. The potential for evil is as much an aspect of the creation as the potential for good. Muslims believe that God intentionally formed human beings in this way so that they would be able to grow and develop through moral struggle. So, the Qurʾān says, "man was created weak" (4:28), with a "hastiness" (17:11) and a "rashness" (70:19) of spirit, which means that humans are destined "for trouble" (90:4). As Joseph said, "The heart is prone to evil" (12:58). Human beings must deal with this created tension. It is their task to educate their positive tendencies and control their negative traits, so that they will walk on the high road of God's straight path. Shabbir Akhtar, a Muslim thinker from England, articulates the Muslim conviction that it is possible to do this. He says,[18]

> The divinely implanted religious seed—providing the knowledge of Allāh's radical uniqueness and of human accountability to the divine—acts as a heavenly counterpoise to man's natural waywardness.[18]

When that waywardness takes control, however, as if often does, men and women fall into error and commit sins.

Ali Shariati (1933–77), a modern Shīʿa thinker, therefore speaks of a human being as "a dialectical being, a binary miracle of God." That is, a human is comprised of two opposites, mud and spirit. "The spirit of God + putrid clay = man." Shariati is reflecting a verse from the Qurʾān that says (15:28f.),

> And remember when thy Lord said unto the angels: Lo! I am creating a mortal out of potter's clay of black mud altered. So when I have made him and breathed into him of My spirit, do ye fall down, prostrating yourselves unto him.

This combination of earth and spirit in the human constitution represents both the problem and the possibility of humanity, and it is the source of moral failure and success. Spirit and mud! These two are in contention, and creative conflict, within the soul of a man or woman. The spirit of God represents goodness, beauty, truth, power, the upper movement toward perfection. Mud or clay represents the downward tendencies, everything that is lowly, ugly, false, and vile. On account of "his dualistic and contradictory nature" the human self "is the stage for a battle between two forces that results in a continuous evolution toward perfection." The striving and conflict are heavy:

> Man is a "choice," a struggle, a constant becoming. He is in an infinite migration within himself, from clay to God.

The goal of that migration is "to take on the characteristics of God."[19]

The first moral casualties in the struggle between good and evil were Adam and his wife. The Qurʾān tells the story of the first human sin. After the creation, God said (7:19-26),

> "O Adam, thou and thy wife in the Garden eat from whence ye will, but come not nigh this tree lest ye become wrongdoers." Then Satan whispered to them that he might manifest unto them that which was hidden from them of their shame, and he said: "Your Lord forbade you from this tree only lest ye should become angels or immortals ..." Thus he did lead them on with guile. And when they tasted of the tree their shame was manifest to them and they began to hide (by heaping) on themselves some of the leaves of the Garden. And their Lord called them (saying): "Did I not forbid you from that tree and tell you, Lo! Satan is an open enemy to you?" They said: "Our Lord! We have wronged ourselves. If Thou forgive us not and have not mercy on us, surely we are of the lost!" He said: "Go down (from hence), one of you a foe unto the other. There shall ye live, and there shall ye die, and thence shall ye be brought forth." O children of Adam! We have revealed unto you raiment to conceal your shame, and splendid vesture, but the raiment of restraint from evil, that is best.

The story provides the essential elements for understanding the Muslim view of sin. God gave clear commands. Satan tempted. Humans erred. In erring, they wronged themselves. God punishes the sinners. They must leave the Garden, and they will experience enmity on earth. Adam and his wife pray for forgiveness and mercy. God, the Relenting One, grants mercy in two forms: a habitation and sufficient provision for a time on earth (2:236) and the promise of divine guidance (2:38f.):

> We said: Go down, all of you, from hence; but verily there cometh unto you from Me a guidance; and whoso followeth my guidance, there shall no fear come upon them, neither shall they grieve. But they who disbelieve and deny Our Revelations, such are the rightful owners of the Fire. They will abide therein.

We will now briefly touch on what the Qurʾān says about sins.

2. Sin and Sins in the Qurʾān

The Qurʾān is full of reference to sins. There are at least 43 words in the Qurʾān for sin, and there are many extended passages that denounce human sinfulness. The most important of the terms used for sin are the following: evil, darkness, error, wrongdoing, disobedience, and transgression. Evil is the most general term. Darkness is synonymous with wickedness. Error involves missing the mark. Wrongdoing is connected with unbelief. Disobedience is the breaking of God's commands. Transgression is the nonobservance of ritual and social laws. Taken together these terms express the attitude and behavior that bring upon humans the judgment and punishment of God. As to attitude, the Qurʾān challenges basic unbelief and rebellion against God. As to behavior, what is criticized is sinful actions; priority attention is given to these rather than to sinful thoughts, although the latter are not neglected. In general, the Qurʾān prefers to speak about sins in the plural rather than about sin in the singular.

From time to time, Muslim thinkers discussed a variety of questions related to the Qurānic teaching about sins. One such question was whether sins can be graded according to their seriousness. A passage such as 53:32 seems to suggest that idea. It says, "Those who avoid enormities of sin and abominations, save the unwilled offences—(for them) lo! thy Lord is of vast mercy." On this basis classical Muslims took the position that it is possible to make a distinction between great and small sins, and a variety of categories were set up to distinguish them.

There is no doubt about the truly great sins. They are *shirk*, associating another being with God, and *kufr*, thankless unbelief. These are really the two "unforgivable" sins. There are two other sins, both directed against God, that are near to them in seriousness, namely, hypocrisy and rebellion against God's will. Other sins mentioned in the Qurʾān have to do with how human beings behave toward other humans. They include covetousness, envy, extravagance, niggardliness, slander, filthiness, and theft. A contemporary listing of major human sins includes the following: murder, theft, extortion, fornication, usury, cheating, lying, backbiting, drinking alcohol, and consuming harmful food or pork.[20]

Muslims today, however, are also paying considerable attention to corporate evils, sins related to the whole society, including such problems as corruption in government, injustice, the oppression of the poor, the breakdown of the family, and various forms of infidelity, ostentatious wealth, and consumption, dictatorship, and other societal crimes of various kinds. Any and all of these may be viewed as forms of disloyalty to the principle of God's sovereignty over life. Abul Aʾla Mawdūdi traces them to this root problem:[21]

> All these are acts of rebellion: false claims to sovereignty and recognition of those claims, both amount to manifest rebellion, and those who are guilty of either of these offences are bound to be punished sooner or later.

God is the ultimate Punisher of sins. Most Muslims today accept human governments as God's punishing agency for social crimes, although a few Muslims take the extreme position that they personally have the right and duty to punish evildoers. But whether the sin is individual or social, in the end God Himself will take account of it and punish it. An immediate punishment may be sorrow and travail of life in this world, but the certain punishment for sins in the future is the horror of hellfire, unless God's mercy intervenes. The Qurʾān does not say that death itself is a punishment for sin, and nowhere does it suggest that Adam and his wife would not have died if they had not sinned. Nor does the Qurʾān teach that Adam's sin has influenced other human beings except as an example of the universal human tendency. Every human being has the same potentiality and the same kind of struggle as Adam and his wife had. Every human being faces the same danger, the same kind of choices, the same range of moral success and failure, and the same possibility of reward and punishment. Moreover, every human being will be held individually accountable by God on the Day of Judgment. The Qurʾān therefore teaches spiritual awareness and a kind of holy fear. God will punish human sins.

Will He punish Muslims? Muslims as we have noted, asked that question. To what extent is a sinful believer punishable? The answer brought into play the concept of greater and lesser sins. It was felt that Muslims who are great sinners but still remain believers must—unless God chooses to forgive them—suffer divine punishment. This feeling introduced the idea of a purgative period in hell, or in a third region between heaven and hell, wherein such individuals would suffer appropriate penalties before entering Paradise. This view continues to be commonly held:

> Those who have firm belief in the oneness of Allāh and in the Prophets of Allāh, but die without atoning for and repenting sins they have committed in this world, will be sent to Hell for a time, from where after receiving due punishment, they will be liberated by the Mercy of Allāh and sent to Heaven, where they will live forever.[22]

The response of a true Muslim, however, to the terrifying fact of sin and punishment must be penitence (*tawba*) and a turning back to God's path. It would be very risky to take sins lightly because of the categories of greater and lesser sins, or because of the hope of God's forgiveness. It may be true that "God forgives minor slips if a man avoids great sins." But it is also true that "God keeps a record of every man's doings ... There will be no one to help man before God ... There is no escape from the consequence of one's actions"[23] Has not the Qurʾān said (18:50):

> And the Book is placed, and thou seest the guilty fearful of that which is therein, and they say: What kind of a book is this that leaveth not a small thing nor a great thing, but hath counted it! And they find all that they did confronting them, and thy Lord wrongeth no one.

Human beings must therefore repent of their sins.

The word for repentance (*tawba*) means the turning of the heart from sin. It implies not only sorrow for sin, but a genuine turning from it. The Qurʾān declares:

> The doom will be doubled for him on the Day of Resurrection ... Save him who repenteth and believeth, and doth righteous work; as for such, Allāh will change their evil deeds to good deeds ... And whosoever repenteth and doeth good, he verily repenteth toward God with a true

repentance (24:69-71).

> O ye who believe, turn unto Allāh in sincere repentance! It may be that your Lord will remit from you your evil deeds and bring you into gardens underneath which rivers flow (56:8).

ʿAlī Zain al-ʿĀbidin, a Shīʿa saint, expressed the true spirit of Islāmic penitence in these words:

> O God, Thou art not veiled from Thy creatures except when sin veils the sight of Thee. He who travels toward Thee is near to Thee except when the burden of sin separates him from thee. O may my prayer for forgiveness make thin the veil of my sin![24]

We have already approached the issue of salvation. Because of the reality of sin, the reality of moral struggle, and the reality of divine punishment, the problem of salvation arises. We turn next to that fundamental question of human destiny.

3. The Idea of Salvation

I recall once proposing a university course in comparative religion that would be named "Types of Salvation." I suggested that it would provide an opportunity to compare different religious views on the basic human problem and its solution. A close friend from Muslim background objected and said that Muslims do not really have a doctrine of salvation. The term salvation, he said, is an imported word that is not natural to Islām.

It is certainly true that in the past Muslims have not used the word salvation with much frequency, but among present-day Muslims its usage is becoming quite common. Illustrating that trend, A. K. Brohi of Pakistan affirms that man "is called by the Qurʾān to seek his salvation."[25] "Seeking salvation" does not imply a theory of *redemption* from sin. That idea is not absent in the Shʿīa tradition of Islām, as Mahmoud Ayoub has shown.[26] In the Sunnī Muslim tradition, however, salvation is primarily concerned with *overcoming* the effect of sins, with a view to heavenly blessing, and with the help of God's guidance. M. A. Quasem of Malaysia illustrates this point when he says, "Every Scripture is guidance for mankind and what this guidance aims at is his salvation, whether in this world or the world to come. This salvation is the central theme of all important Scripture, including the Qur'ān, the Scripture of Islām..."27

Salvation in Islām is very close to being a synonym for heaven. In ordinary language the word is used by Muslims in two ways. The everyday use has to do with life in this world. It refers to release from the problems and pressures of ordinary life that threaten all people. The second usage has to do with the prospect of an untroubled and joyous life in heaven. This is the primary religious usage of the term salvation. Quasem says that it "is found in deliverance from misery or punishments, and attainment of happiness or reward from God. This is the meaning usually understood when the term 'salvation' is used in the Qur'ān and Tradition ... It is the main concern of Muslim devotions."28

That salvation is identical to heavenly deliverance is born out by the term *najāt*, the basic word for salvation in the Qur'ān, whose root meaning is "escape" or "deliverance." It implies escape from the punishment of sins in Hell to the pleasurable life in Paradise. The other terms that are more or less synonymous with salvation, prosperity and success, as well as the word used often in Ḥadīth, namely happiness, underline this essential meaning of salvation. In the Qur'ān, prophetic words contrast salvation and Fire. Muhammad cries (40:41), "O my people! What aileth me that I call you unto deliverance [*najāt*] when ye call me unto the Fire." In another passage (3:182) the Qur'ān repeats the message that being saved is deliverance from the Fire to Paradise:

> Every soul shall have a taste of death: And only on the Day of Judgment shall you be paid your full recompense. Only he who is saved from the Fire and admitted to the Garden will have attained the object (of Life): For the life of this world is but goods and chattels of deception.

Finally, using the same term, the Qur'ān places the issue of saving entry into Paradise into God's hand: "But God will deliver the righteous to their place of salvation: no evil shall touch them, nor shall they grieve" (39:61).29 Muhammad Quasem sums up the teaching when he says: "Salvation is safety from the punishment of sin in the life after death."30 Thus Paradise constitutes the goal of the Muslim search for salvation, and it provides the content of its meaning; salvation is related to sins only in terms of the rescue and escape from their consequences.

This brings us to the question of *how* a Muslim believer shall escape from Hell and enter into Paradise.

4. The Means to Salvation

Muslims have vigorously debated the question of the means to salvation. This debate reflects the variety within the Qurʾān itself, in which there are several distinct emphases, and later Muslims have added other considerations to the discussion. In the following we will deal with six approaches to the issue: salvation as the will of God; salvation as the mercy of God; salvation by faith and by membership in the saved community; salvation by a combination of faith and works; salvation through the grace of intercession; and salvation by the mystical path. These approaches fade into one another and combine in different ways for different Muslims. Each of my Muslim friends will have a personal view of the relative weight to be given to the factors described below and their exclusion or inclusion in the strands of the rope of salvation.

Some Muslims will say that human salvation is hidden in the mystery of God's will. It is controlled by His eternal decree. As one traditional saying puts it: "The pens are lifted up and the pages are dry." In that light, a classical Muslim theologian says, "Allāh is the Creator of all the actions of his creatures, whether or unbelief or belief, of obedience or of disobedience."[31] Those Muslims today who approach the question in this way will argue that it is not quite proper to say, "I am going to Paradise," or "I am saved," but rather one should humbly say, "I am saved, if God wills." Many contemporary Muslims disagree sharply with this approach. Fazlur Rahman declares, "To hold that the Qurʾān believes in an absolute determinism of human behavior, denying free choice on man's part, is not only to deny almost the entire content of the Qurʾān, but to undercut its very basis ... [the] invitation to man to come to the right path."[32]

Some Muslims place the question of human salvation in the arena of God's mercy and grace. God, it is believed, is tender hearted, like the mother of young birds to her young, and more inclined to mercy than to wrath. He has sent His revelations "that He may bring you forth from darkness into light; and lo! for you Allāh is Full of Pity, Merciful" (59:7). Moreover He is named Al-Ghaffār and Al-Ghafūr, the Forgiver and the Very Forgiving

One, who places veils over the sins of humanity, and the Qurʾān mentions His forgiveness hundreds of times. Surely He will also forgive His people who have truly struggled to follow His path. Those Muslims who deal with the question of salvation on this level hope to approach the terrible events of the final Hour "in the name of God the Merciful, the Compassionate."

Other Muslims approach the question of the means of salvation from the human side of the process.

Many believe that salvation is the reward of faith. The witnessing formula of the *shahāda* gives the content of saving faith: "There is no deity but Allāh, and Muhammad is the messenger of Allāh." To that you must assent with your mind, believe in your heart, and confess with your tongue. This does not imply a cold, intellectual faith. Believers are those whose hearts "thrill with fear" or "quiver" when God is named (8:2). No one who believes this way will deny the importance of good works, but there will be insistence that it is faith that makes a person a Muslim, and it is faith that makes one eligible for Paradise. "O ye who believe, be mindful of your duty to Allāh and put faith in His messenger; He will give you twofold of His mercy and will appoint for you a light wherein ye shall walk in, and will forgive you" (57:28).[33] Nominal Muslims may take wrong advantage of the doctrine, but nevertheless, salvation is by faith alone.

The idea of becoming a Muslim by faith merges with the idea of becoming a member of the blessed and sacred community of Islām. Salvation by faith and salvation through membership in the *umma* are therefore closely associated ideas. As a result, membership in the community of Islām virtually becomes a mode of salvation. To have faith means to be a Muslim. To be a Muslim means to be a member of God's chosen community. If you are a member of God's chosen community, you have the opportunity to receive God's guidance and forgiveness. The essential factor, therefore, is to be a member of the community of Islām, even though that membership may be a rather nominal one. This is a very practical idea. Taken literally it implies that everyone who is a Muslim will be saved, even though some may experience penalties for their sins. John W. Sweetman has provided a lucid summary of this approach:

> Thus in Islām salvation is by identification with a community ... Primarily, the institution of the community of Islām, enshrining within it the practice of the Prophet, possessed of the authoritative code

of God in the Qur'ān, presenting a concrete and external unity, composed of members rejoicing in a special divine election, the interim stage of the theocracy never to be superseded, endowed with inerrancy despite apparent differences, is the first means of salvation, and all that follows must be within this framework.[34]

An increasing number of Muslims take an entirely different view. They are displeased with nominalism. They argue that faith and works combined are the only means of salvation. Faith is certainly the basic requirement, and it cannot be dispensed with, but faith alone is not regarded as sufficient to earn salvation. Salvation must be *earned.* Those who uphold this approach point out how again and again the Qur'ān speaks in accents such as these: "And give glad tidings (O Muhammad) unto those who believe and do good works, that theirs are Gardens underneath which rivers flow..." (2:25). Is not the Judgment on the Last Day to be a weighing of the books in which are recorded each person's doings? Does not the Qur'ān say: "And lo! Unto each thy Lord will verily repay his works in full. Allāh loseth not the wages of the good" (11:111, 115)? So, from this point of view there must be a true union between faith (*imān*) and practice (*dīn, ʿibādat*). True *imān*, believing with a fervent piety, and true *islām*, surrendering one's whole life to God, both imply an indissoluble link between faith and works.[35]

> Then, as for those who believed and did good works, their Lord will bring them in unto His mercy. That is the evident triumph (46:30).

Quasem sums up the point by saying: "From the entry into Islām through faith he [the believer] has to make progress and develop the faith through action performed in the light of the Qur'ān and Tradition ... Thus faith and action taken together perfect the life and bring about salvation."[36]

Some Muslims add intercession as a means of salvation and give it great prominence. Since human sinfulness is universal and since God's decisions are unknown, and since it is not clear whether one's own works are sufficient to blot out one's misdeeds, the idea of a helper has been welcomed by some Muslims. This is so despite the fact that the Qur'ān clearly says that the Day of Judgment is "a day on which no soul hath power for any (other) soul. The [absolute] command on that day is Allāh's" (82:19). A sense of deep need, however, produced the idea of the possibility of intercession. As we have seen, the

Qurʾān itself allows for the intercession of angels. Some Muslims have also looked to various saints to fill that role. Shʿiʿa Muslims speak of the intercession of the martyr Ḥusain, the grandson of the Prophet, and the holy Imāms. But the primary helper will undoubtedly be the Prophet Muhammad himself, who will plead for his followers on the Day of Judgment, like an advocate pleads for his clients. God will take account of his intercession. Some traditions say that the Prophet will then take the hands of believers and will lead them across the narrow bridge that separates heaven and hell. We may therefore speak of the intercession of the holy ones as a means of salvation, and this is certainly a factor in popular Islām in many parts of the world.

The final means of salvation is by the mystical path. Sūfi Muslims, the mystics of Islām, not only differ with other Muslims on the means of salvation, but also on the content of salvation itself. The goal of the Sūfi search is not Paradise in its usual sense, but rather it is a union with God, which can be achieved already in this life. The Sūfi strives to become one with God in the closest possible relationship. The means for the achievement of this goal is the Sūfi spiritual discipline. Under the guidance of a Sūfi spiritual mentor, the mystic ascends through a series of stages and states which culminate in a spiritual union with God. The fruit of that union is the vision of the Face of God. Syed Hossein Nasr describes the meaning of that vision:

> On the highest level, the realization of this Face through "self-effacement"—or annihilation (*fanāʾ*), as the Sūfis have called it—means to be already resurrected in God while in this life and to see God "wherever one turns." ... This doctrine represents the highest fruit of spiritual realization, which is to know God and to see Him as He is. The fruit of the spiritual path of Islām is the plenary knowledge of the Divine. He who has gained such knowledge through the means made available in the Islāmic tradition and by virtue of the grace issuing from His Names experiences God as at once transcendent and immanent, as before all things and after all things, as both the Inward and the Outward. He sees God everywhere ... having died to his passionate self. Through his death he has gained access to the world of the spirit and has come to know His Lord, thereby fulfilling the goal of creation and the purpose of the Qurānic Revelation, which is none other than to enable man to know and love God and to obey His Will during this earthly journey.[37]

On the subject of the means to salvation orthodox Muslim theologians tended to move between the twin poles of the will of

God and faith alone. Many ordinary Muslims who are busy about their life in this world, and secularized Muslims, to the extent that they think about this issue at all, look to community membership as a sufficient hope. In popular Islām, folk believers place great emphasis on the intercession of the saints, while Shī'a Muslims look to the intervention of their Imams. But increasingly the pattern of thought among ordinary Muslims on this issue is toward a combination of the Mercy of God, and faith and works. Piety confirms faith and creates a basis for receiving God's Mercy. Nevertheless, ideas and feelings about this issue are intertwined in various ways, and consensus on the subject is still in the making.

Much clearer is the Muslim vision of Heaven and Hell.

H. Heaven and Hell

The Qur'ān portrays Paradise and Hell in very picturesque and material terms. The question arises for Muslims whether to take the pictures literally, to interpret them metaphorically, or both. Many Muslims, including Al-Ghazālī, take the view that both the physical and the spiritual meanings must be accepted, the latter being the higher experience. There are also those who are of the view that the sensual descriptions must be accepted just as they read. Conversely, others regard them all as pure allegories of the supreme blessing of heaven, which is the vision of God, and the supreme curse of hell, which is separation from that experience. The Ḥadīth carry forward and greatly elaborate the already graphic Qurānic descriptions of heaven and hell, emphasizing the literal view.

Paradise is pictured as a place where believers will have silken robes. They will lie on couches, with no sense of undue heat or cold. The trees will be laden with fruits, ready at hand, and there will be plenty of cool, clear water. Handsome youth with green, brocaded costumes, will circulate with the drink of a pure beverage and cups of flowing wine that will have no aftereffects. There will be perpetual virgins (*houris*) available in large numbers, who have large dark eyes and wear pearls. The Gardens will be beautiful and pleasant, and its occupants will have all their wishes fulfilled. A Ḥadīth sums it up:

The lowest place of any of you in Paradise will be that God will tell him to express his wish, and he will wish and wish. He will then ask him if he has expressed his wish, and when he replies that he has, He will tell him that he will have what he has wished and an equal amount along with it.[38]

Some Muslims, however, remembering how Moses saw God on Mt. Sinai (7:139) and considering that the Qurʾān says (75:22f.), "That day will faces be resplendent, looking toward their Lord," consider that not material blessings but the vision of God will constitute the supreme good of Paradise.

Hellfire and its experience is similarly set forth in the Qurʾān in concrete and stirring language. It is like a wretched home that is really a bed in a fire. Boiling water and bloody gore are everywhere. Its occupant must drink tainted water that causes vomiting, and the food will be choking fruit from the bitter tree, al-Zaqqūn. One's clothing will be burning pitch. Liquid pus, serpents and scorpions, and other grievous torments of various kinds will be present. Feelings of death will be experienced, but the suffering will not be released by death. In that terrible fire and torment, "he shall not die, and shall not live" (87:12). There will be seven levels in hell, with different categories of people assigned to each level, ranging from the less severe to the most terrible as follows: unrepentant Muslims; Christians; Jews; Iblis and his cohorts; Magians; idolaters, and Gog and Magog; and finally the bottomless pit for religious hypocrites. The overwhelming impression of hell is calamity, and the Qurʾān uses that very word to sum up its description of the impending punishment for sinners (101:1–3, 11):

> The Calamity!
> What is the Calamity?
> Ah, what will convey unto thee what the Calamity is! ...
> Raging fire!

Under the circumstances, it is not surprising that al-Hajjāj, an early Muslim, was quoted as saying: "Would that God ... when he put us in this world had made us independent of the next [world] and delivered us from anxiety about what would save us from punishment!"[39]

Abdulla and Amina *feel* the issue of sin and salvation, but they hardly discuss it, and neither do they hear their friends talking about it. Their instinct tells them not to engage in fruitless discussion. As one Muslim puts it,

It will be seen that salvation in the one [primary] sense is attainable only in the life to come, and that the decision on it will be made in that life; it is impossible to say anything categorically concerning the ultimate fate of an individual believer, even though some indication of it may be found.

So, although they face the future prospect with mixed feelings of fear and hope, Abdulla and Amina are not preoccupied with the problem. They are much more determined to do what they can to be faithful Muslims in this life. Their determination is spurred on by what is happening in their home. Abdulla's father, Ahmad, is dying, and he must soon face the questioners in the grave. Abdulla and Amina know that, and it reminds them that they too will face that experience. The final decision regarding their ultimate destiny, they realize, is in God's hands, but they believe that its determining factors can be shaped by them. So my friends are giving their attention to the here and now that is under their influence, and to the works that they know will please God.

Let us turn next to those works, the basic practices of Islām.

Notes

[1]*Towards Understanding Islām* (Nairobi: Islāmic Foundation, 1973), p. 99.

[2]Hammudah Abdalati, *Islām in Focus*, p. 13.

[3]*Muqaddima* (El-Mahdi ed.; Cairo, 1930, p. 77), in Jeffery, *Islām*, p. 134.

[4]*Kitāb al-Irshād*, ed. J. D. Luciani (Paris, 1938, pp. 204f.), in Jeffery, *Islām*, p. 133.

[5]Hammudah Abdalati, *Islām in Focus*, p. 27.

[6]I am indebted to various articles in *EI*[1] for traditions related to the prophets.

[7]I have preferred the translation of Yusuf Ali for this verse. Cf. Yusuf Ali, *The Holy Qur-an. Text, Translation and Commentary* (Washington: The Islāmic Center, 1978), p. 816. The Biblical passage is Ps. 37:39, "The righteous shall inherit the earth." Yusuf Ali also sees allusions in Ps. 25, 13; 37, 11; 37, 29; Exod. 32, 13; and Matt. 5, 3.

[8]The Gospel could not have been known in an Arabic version, since to our knowledge there were no translations available at the time of the Prophet. Cf. G. Anawati, *"Indjīl," EI*[2], III, pp. 1205f., for a summary of the latest scholarship on this point.

[9]Εὐαγγέλιον (Greek) or *euangelion*, which means "good news," becomes gospel in English but *injīl* in Arabic, perhaps through Ethiopic.

[10]*EI*[2], III, p. 1205.

[11]*Tasunif-i-Ahmadīyya* (Agra, 1903), Part I, IV, 4, quoted in E. Sell, *Faith of*

Islām (London: S.P.C.K., 1920; repr. 1976), p. 292. Sir Sayyid wrote a famous commentary on a portion of the Bible.

[12]*Islām in Focus*, p. 12

[13]*Mishkat*, II, p. 511.

[14]*Major Themes*, p. 106.

[15]*Islām, Creed and Worship* (Washington: the Islāmic Center, 1975), p. 11.

[16]*Letters on Islām*, p. 36. Jamali's sentence was later remitted, and he become Professor of Philosophy and Education at the University of Tunis.

[17]*Islām, Creed and Worship*, pp. llf.

[18]*A Faith for All Seasons* (Chicago: Ivan R. Dee, 1990), p. 143. Akhbar says (p.147), "Only the Last Day will witness a decisive resolution of a permanently ambiguous destiny vacillating between good and evil..."

[19]Ali Shariati, *On the Sociology of Islām*, pp. 88, 91–96.

[20]Muhammad Rauf, *Islām, Creed and Worship*, p. 13.

[21]*The Road to Peace and Salvation* (Lahore: Islāmic Publications Ltd., 1966; original lecture 1940), p. 16.

[22]Siddiqui, *Elementary Teachings*, p. 21

[23]*Lessons in Islām Series, Book No. 1, Prophets, Angels and Moral Teachings* (Lahore: Sh. Muhammad Ashraf, 1975), pp. 12–16.

[24]*Matālibu ꞌd-dunya waꞌl-ākhira*, in Padwick, *Devotions*, p. 180.

[25]"The Spiritual Significance of the Qurꞌān," in S. H. Nasr, ed., *Islāmic Spirituality* (New York: Crossroad, 1987), p. 15.

[26]Cf. his *Redemptive Suffering in Islām* (The Hague: Mouton, 1978).

[27]*Salvation of the Soul and Islāmic Devotion* (London: Kegal Paul International, 1983), p. 19.

[28]Ibid., p.20.

[29]Both passages, tr. by Yusuf Ali.

[30]Quasem, *Salvation*, p. 18.

[31]Al-Nasāfī, in Elder, *Creed*, p. 80.

[32]*Major Themes*, p. 20.

[33]Tr. by E. H. Palmer.

[34]*Islam and Christian Theology*, Part I, vol. 2 (London: Lutterworth Press, 1947), pp. 216ff.

[35]Cf. Toshihida Izutsu, *Ethico-Religious Concepts in the Qurꞌān* (Montreal: McGill University Press, 1966), pp. 184–92, for a helpful discussion of the relationship between *imān* and *islām*.

[36]Quasem, *Salvation*, p.35.

[37]"God," in S. H. Nasr, ed., *Islāmic Spirituality*, pp. 322f.

[38]*Mishkat*, III, p. 1199.

[39]A. S. Tritton, *Muslim Theology* (London: Luzac & Co., Ltd., 1947), p. 10, quoting *Jāḥiz Bayān.*, I; 145. Al-Hajjaj was a harsh leader, not noted for his pietism.

[40]Quasem, *Salvation*, p. 28. For a more extended treatment of the Muslim doctrines of sin and salvation, cf. Roland E. Miller, "The Muslim Doctrine of Salvation," *Bulletin of the Henry Martyn Institute of Islāmic Studies*, LIX, nos. 1

and 2 (July and October 1960), pp. 33–55 and 11–27.

11

Pillars of Obedience: The Basic Muslim Devotional Practices

It is the month of Ramaḍān and there are a million things to do—yet Abdulla and Amina are deep in discussion. Abdulla has been hoping and planning to go on the pilgrimage, but medical expenses for his father and educational fees for the children have been so heavy that the trip appears to be impossible. He has just shared this information with Amina, and she is deeply distressed. She wonders out loud whether she should give her jewelry to a bank in return for a loan, but Abdulla discourages that step. Amina has always tried to pray five times a day, but now she vows that she will perform extra prayers if only God will bless her husband's intention. But now they must postpone the discussion! It is the month of fasting, and they have to hurry to the night assembly! On their way to the meeting ground, they pass a line of blind beggars who are pleading for help. They go more slowly, and as they pass by, Abdulla places a gift in two or three hands. In the distance they can hear the chanting of *lā ilāha illā Allāh*, and the sound thrills their hearts as they hurry on to join the faithful. Already they are renewing their determination to struggle forward, to the best of their abilities, on the straight path of God.

In one episodic night the life of my Muslim friends has touched on every one of the basic practices of Islām. These are the well-known pillars of Islām: confession, prayer, fasting, almsgiving, and pilgrimage. We may describe them as the pillars of obedience, recognizing that another activity, struggling for God, is also sometimes added to the list. In the following discussion we will consider each of these cardinal duties, and in the succeeding chapter we will take, up the principles of Muslim piety and spiritual struggle.

The Confession of Faith

The first duty of Muslims is to bear witness to the faith. The usual term for the confession of faith is *shahāda*, meaning witness, but sometimes the term *kalima*, which means word, is also used. We have frequently met the confession of faith in earlier portions of this book. A common version of the *shahāda* is *"I bear witness that there is no God but Allāh, and Muhammad is the messenger of Allāh."* The confession is not found in the Qurʾān in these exact words. It is evidently a combination of such verses as 27:26, "Allāh; there is no God save Him," and 48:29, "Muhammad is the messenger of Allāh." More extended confessions may be found, as illustrated by a Ḥadīth:

> The adoration of the tongue, acts of worship, and all good things are due to God. Peace be upon you, O Prophet, and God's mercy and blessings. Peace be upon us and upon God's upright servants. I testify that there is no god but God, and I testify that Muhammad is His servant and messenger. I ask God for Paradise, and I seek refuge in God from hell.[1]

Ordinary Muslims, however, have little interest in longer confessions or in extended creedal statements (*ʿaqīda*). This is partly because of convenience, partly because of hesitation to describe the mystery of God in human language, and partly because there is no authority to prescribe confessions. Moreover, Muslims take great pride in the simplicity and straightforwardness of the *lā ilāha illā Allāh*. They do not feel a need for more.

The confession is the criterion of being a Muslim. If you say these words, accepting them with your mind, believing them with your heart, and confessing them with your tongue, you become a Muslim and a member of the *umma*. Al-Ghazālī says that the confessing person "is not required to penetrate their significance through scrutiny, investigation and research, but only to believe and confess them unequivocally without the least doubt or hesitation."[2] Professor W. C. Smith reminds us that the *shahāda* is more than a belief statement, it is a testimony. Rather than a creed, it is an affirmation and a proclamation. To say that a Muslim *believes* these words to be true is weaker than what is implied in "I bear witness." A Muslim believes in the strongest sense of that term; that is, he or she *knows* it is true, knows it deeply, earnestly and reverently, and gives testimony to what is known.[3]

Drawing on Muslim prayers and poetry as her source, Constance Padwick points to the variety of spiritual benefits that the *shahāda* brings. It bestows divine blessing on the reciter, provides protection against evil, and brings the forgiveness of sins. Its repetition creates a covenant with God, and it serves as "the passport of the soul" in the hour of death. When the believers "wrap (themselves) in the mantle" of the *lā ilāha illā Allāh*, they do not only declare their individual faith in God, but they represent the faith of the community and, in fact, they "verbalize the silent faith" of the whole creation.[4]

As a great Muslim saint, ʿAbd al-Qādir al-Jilānī (d. 1166), has put it,

> My God, there is not a passing wind, nor a drop from the clouds, nor a lightning flash, nor a thunder roll, nor aught in the Throne and the Sea, nor a sign in the Kingdom which does not pronounce the *shahāda* and bear witness that thou art God and there is no God but thee.[5]

What illustrates the importance of the *shahāda* in practical piety is the fact that it is the first religious phrase that Abdulla and Amina taught their children.

B. Prayer

The second aspect of Muslim surrender to God is prayer. My Muslim friends pray a lot. They regard prayer as a crucially important spiritual practice. It is so important that it may be described as the Muslim form of spiritual breathing. There are two kinds of prayer in Islām. The first, called *salāt*, is the formal fivefold daily prayer, accompanied by physical actions, which is the liturgical prayer of Islām. This form of prayer has precedence in Islām and hence, unless otherwise indicated, when the word "prayer" is used we will have reference to *salāt*. There is, however, a second form of prayer called *duʿā*. This is a voluntary form of petition to God, which does not necessarily involve physical movements.

When Muslims think of prayer, they usually have in mind the

salāt. I well recall an occasion when a friend named Ahmad asked me to come to his home, where his 100-year-old mother lay seriously ill. He was hoping against hope that I might be able to suggest a medical solution to her problem, but it seemed to me that my friend's beloved mother was nearing her last breath. I suggested that it was an occasion for prayer to God Whose power is unlimited. Ahmad immediately responded with a prayer. But he did not engage in *duˁā* and call upon God in supplication on behalf of his mother; rather, he immediately turned and performed a cycle (*rakˁa*) of the *salāt.* That to him expressed most profoundly the spirit of prayer.

1. The Spirit of Prayer

The Muslim *salāt* represents an acted out statement of the believer's surrender to God. There are two ideas involved. The first relates to the fact that a human being is both body and soul, and therefore both body and soul must be combined in any symbolic act of surrender. This principle underlies the physical aspect of the prayer. The second idea is that a human being should be frequent in the remembrance of God. This is why at least five daily occasions for prayer are considered appropriate. The twin concepts of wholistic surrender and repeated remembrance are the key motifs in Muslim prayer, and the Qurʾān undergirds their importance:

> O ye who believe! Remember Allāh with much remembrance, and glorify Him early and late (33:42f.).

> Establish worship ... and bow your heads with those who bow (in worship) (2:43).

> So glory be to Allāh when ye enter the night and when ye enter the morning—unto Him be praised in the heavens and the earth!—and at the sun's decline and in the noonday (30:17f.).

The important spiritual concept of intention is interwoven with the action of prayer, for it is the intention of the believer that spiritualizes what would otherwise be only a ritual. The intention must be declared. Before a Muslim sets out to pray, he or she puts that intention (*nīya*) into words, either in the heart or audibly, declaring: "I now intend to pray such-and-such a prayer." The *nīya* has an important psychological function. Its purpose is to focus the mind, to shut out other thoughts, and to concentrate the worshipper on the serious act that is about to take place. A typical *nīya* before prayer is: "I have purposed to offer up to God only, with a sincere heart this morning, with my face toward the *qibla* [direction of Mecca] this prayer." In modern language it would be saying, "I really mean to worship You, O God."

The declaration of intention affects all the basic practices of Islām, not only prayer. A well-known Ḥadīth declares, "Works are in their intention only."[6] So the believer applies the same approach to fasting, almsgiving, and the pilgrimage, declaring: "I intend to fast ...", "I intend to give alms ...", and at the pilgrimage, "I am ready for your service, O Lord." The act of declaring one's intention, like any other religious action, can become habitual, or it may be carelessly omitted, yet it constitutes an important aspect of Islāmic spirituality. Islām does not teach that the omission of the *nīya* makes a religious ritual invalid, but it does teach that by including it the action of the believer is purified. Therefore C. N. Ahmed Moulavi (d. 1993), a South Indian scholar, suggests that the idea of *nīya* should be extended to include all ethical and religious acts, and he affirms that the rewards of those acts will be commensurate with their intention.[7]

2. The Time of Prayer

The *salāt* is comprised of five daily prayers at set times. Those times are really time periods rather than specific hours. This arrangement allows the worshiper some latitude. It is recognized that even then it may be impossible to meet the schedule because of unavoidable circumstances such as travel, sickness, or dangerous situations. If this should happen, the prayers are to be made up later. The following are the five times periods for the prescribed prayers, as established by tradition. (Many Muslims refer to the specific prayer by its Arabic title.)

The First Prayer (*Fajr*)—between dawn and sunrise—two cycles
The Second Prayer (*Ẓuhr*)—just after noon—four cycles
The Third Prayer (*ʿAṣr*)—in the afternoon—four cycles
The Fourth Prayer (*Maghrib*)—after sunset—three cycles

The Fifth Prayer (*ʿIshāʾ*)—before retiring—four cycles

These are the obligatory prayers, but extra cycles of *salāt* are also recommended and commendable. These may be added to the regular prayers or done at other times. Extra prayers are highly recommended for such occasions as going to or coming from a journey, at the celebration of the chief festivals, and as part of the funeral ceremonies. What constitutes one cycle of prayer will be outlined below.

How many Muslims, in reality, pray the required five times a day? There is no clear answer to this common question for, as far as we know, no satisfactory poll or statistical analysis has been done. Muslim friends have told the writer that the great majority of Muslims will pray at least once daily, and perhaps up to 50 percent or more will manage to perform the five daily prayers. It is not easy, in modern contexts, to keep to the schedule, even though one is dedicated, and of course there are Muslims who are only nominal in their practice of the faith. It can safely be said, however, that pious Muslims like Abdulla and Amina will do their utmost to maintain the full cycle of fivefold prayer. The reader may have observed dedicated Muslims at an airport or bus station who have assumed the position of prayer, despite the hustle and bustle of life around them, seeking a moment of quiet to worship the Lord Whose Presence is everywhere, the One Who "both hears and knows."

Friday noon is the occasion when Muslim prayer becomes congregational. All other prayers may be done individually—at work, at home or at school, but on Friday noon Muslims should try to worship and pray together. This service is named the prayer of "Assembling" (*jumāʿa*), the prayer of the gathered community. It is not associated with a concept of "sabbath" rest, for the Qurʾān does not record that God rested on the seventh day. Therefore there is no prohibition of normal activities on Friday, apart from the fact that one must take off time from work and play to join the communal prayer. As a matter of fact, however, most Muslims observe Friday as their day of rest and family time, and in Muslim countries it is an official holiday.

The participation of women in the mosque service varies from culture to culture. There is a difference of opinion among Muslims as to what is appropriate. What is involved is the factor of distraction. The *salāt* prayer, as we have noted, is based on intense concentration that should not be disturbed by physical

215

movements, either for males or females. Therefore, in some societies female attendance at the mosque is discouraged or forbidden, whereas among modern Muslims it is permitted or encouraged. However, even where women are welcome at the mosque service, they often occupy a separate room or curtained area, or they conduct the prayer at the rear of the assembly.

The Friday service is also called the *khutba* service, from a word that means address or sermon, because on this occasion there is a message. The order of service is as follows. The *imām* (prayer leader) first takes his place at the front of the worshippers who are arranged in lines behind him, and he leads the congregation through the normal four cycles of noon prayer. Then he mounts the pulpit or platform to give a message, or another person (*khātib*) will undertake the task. The message ordinarily has two parts. The first section consists primarily of praises to God, prayers of blessing for the Prophet, and an exposition of a Qurānic passage. After this the leader takes a brief rest in a sitting position, then rises for the second part of his sermon, which may be based on any topic of importance. In traditional mosques the sermon is usually in Arabic, often read from older sermon books; in progressive mosques the vernacular language is used, and contemporary issues are addressed. After this, saying the words "the prayer is now ready," the leader takes the assembly through two more cycles of prayer, thus completing the service.

3. The Call to Prayer

The compelling tones of the call to prayer (*adhān*) dominate Muslim culture and daily life. It is, as it were, the ordering symbol of life lived under God's rule. It is given five times daily from the minaret, a tall tower that is attached to the mosque. In great mosques these are high, majestic structures. Within the tower, steps go up to the balcony at the top of the minaret, and at the right time the appointed official (*muezzīn*) ascends and issues the call to prayer. In some places a loudspeaker has now replaced the living voice, but the effect remains magnetic. Five times daily, in powerful Arabic chant, the commanding cry rings out, summoning the community:

Allāh is most great! (repeated four times, once in each direction)

I bear witness that there is no god but Allāh! (repeated once)

I bear witness that Muhammad is the messenger of Allāh (repeated once)

Come to prayer! Come to prayer!

Come to salvation! Come to salvation! [Shīʿa Muslims add: Come to good works!]

There is no god but Allāh! [The dawn call adds: Prayer is better than sleep! The Friday noon call adds: The prayer is now instituted!]

The call is penetrating, stirring, alerting, extremely powerful. It reminds Muslims that they should remember God. It is not surprising that its phrases are whispered into many a Muslim baby's ear at birth. Naturally, when even a powerful call is uttered so frequently and regularly as this one is, it takes on a habitual quality, and some Muslims are able to resist its urgency. But when pious Muslims hear the call, they are moved to participate in the act of prayer. Before they do so, however, the worshippers must pay heed to the factor of purification. Am I ritually clean or not?

4. The Purification

Muslims have a great concern for ritual purification and cleansing prior to engaging in the act of prayer. The need for such purification is mentioned with great frequency in both the Qurʾān and Ḥadīth, and it has become an essential aspect of the worship ritual. The Qurʾān establishes the principle: "O ye who believe! Draw not near to prayer ... till ye have bathed" (4:43), and the traditions greatly elaborate the idea with such phrases as "Religion is built on cleanness" and "Purification is one-half of faith." The physical acts, in their details, are customary. They are to symbolize the cleansing of the heart. Jabir reported God's messenger as saying, "The key of paradise is prayer, and the key of prayer is being purified."[8]

Muslims differentiate between two forms of purification, the lesser and more common ablution (wuduʾ), and the more complex method (ghusl). We will detail the lesser cleansing. Outside most mosques and near to the entrance, one can see a washing area, a shallow pool of water, where the worshipper may perform the required ablution. If the worshippers are at home or at work, they may use whatever facilities are available for cleansing. The stages of the ablution are as follows: Washing the hands to the wrist thrice, reciting one's intention; rinsing the mouth thrice; washing the nostrils thrice: washing the face; washing the hands to the elbows thrice, the water running to the elbow; passing damp hands over the whole head; rubbing wet fingers in the ears, behind the ears, and through the beard; rubbing wet fingers of one hand between the fingers of the other; washing the feet, wet fingers between the toes. When the washing is complete, the believer may carry the Qurʾān, do the prayers, and participate in other spiritual activities. In the rare case when water is not available, a symbolic cleansing with sand is permitted. The greater purification, or *ghusl*, requires a full bath.

The opposite of purification is pollution, which destroys the sacredness that the ritual has produced. When the lesser cleansing has been once completed, it applies to all the five prayers—but it must be repeated if pollution occurs. Polluting acts that call for a repeated *wuduʾ* include the following: bodily evacuations and discharges of any kind; fainting or sleeping; touching the skin of husband or wife; drunkenness or the like. More serious polluting actions that require the *ghusl* bath include such activities as sexual intercourse, childbirth, menstruation, and the handling of dead bodies. A postnatal woman is in the state of pollution for 35–40 days, and a menstruating woman from 3–10 days. Other types of pollution exist, for example, the dire situation created by contact with saliva from the nose of a dog, which requires seven washings. The *ghusl* ablution is also called for on such special occasions as the congregational prayer, the two main festivals, and pilgrimage activities.

Whether it is the lesser or the greater washing, the primary object of spiritual cleanliness and purity should not be forgotten. Therefore this prayer is recommended after the *wuduʾ:* "O Allāh! make me from among those who repent for their sins and from among those who keep themselves pure."9 The worshipper is reminded of this by the *nīya*, the declaration of spiritual intention that should accompany the ablutions.

Another form of purification directly associated with prayer is the covering of the body. It goes without saying that the clothing of the praying person should be clean and the entire body discreetly covered. Footwear must be removed as a mark of respect. The head should be covered during the prayer as a sign of humility before God. The place of prayer should be clean, and if possible a prayer rug should be used. It is not surprising that the design and weaving of prayer rugs has become a beautiful art form in Islām.[10] In wealthier mosques the entire floor may be covered with a series of magnificent carpets, while in poorer mosques there may be only a simple coconut matting. The type of material is not essential to the prayer, but something should be placed between the worshipper and the ground.

Let us now turn to the actual performance of the prayer.

5. The Performance of the Prayer

There are probably very few people who have not seen the images of Muslim masses at prayer—whether on film, TV, or otherwise. It has been called a kind of "visual cliché" of Islām. Nevertheless the sight always causes wonder for the observer; for the participant the wonder is much deeper. Certainly the best way to sense the meaning of prayer for Muslims is to actually observe the solemnity of the performance. My Muslim friends are not self-conscious about praying, and they do not mind being watched if the observance is respectful. While many Muslim mosques are still closed to non-Muslims, an increasing number of Muslim believers are happy to receive non-Muslim visitors to their worship places. Such visitors may seat themselves quietly at the rear of the mosque and observe the progress of the prayer.

Although it is not Friday, Abdulla has decided to conduct one of his prayers in the mosque, and we follow him there. His first essential action after the ablution is to face in the direction of the holy city of Mecca and its sacred House, the Kācba. Amina, who is praying about the same time in her home, also faces in the general direction of the shrine that symbolizes the centrality and the presence of the Almighty. In the mosque the direction (*qibla*) is marked by an indentation in the wall (*mihrāb*). The Qurʾān commands (2:149), "And whencesoever thou comest forth (in prayer) ... turn thy face toward the Inviolable Place of Worship." The spiritual implication is that the direction of one's life must ever be toward God.

It is quiet in the mosque since it is not Friday. There are several worshippers in the room, each following the prayer ritual at their own pace. Abdulla has already spoken the *nīya* and now he begins the first part of the prayer, according to the following steps:

—He raises his hands with his thumbs touching the lobes of the ear and his palms toward the *qibla*; as he does so he says *Allāhu akbar!*

—He lowers his hands, usually crossing them over his chest, the right hand over the left.

—He recites the *al-Fātiha*, the first chapter of the Qurʾān; he may also recall other verses and silently repeat them.

—He puts his hands to his ears again and repeats the *takbīr* (*Allāhu akbar!*).

—He leans forward with his hands resting on his knees; in that position he recites three times, "Glory be to the Almighty God!"

—At this point, if it was a congregational prayer, the *imām* would say, "God hears him who praises him," and the congregation would respond, "O, our Lord!, Thou art praised!"

Now the main physical actions begin. To the observer they seem complicated, but to the participant they are habitual and natural.

—Abdulla now assumes a kneeling position saying *Allāhu akbar!* Quickly he leans forward with his hands outstretched and his forehead touching the ground. In the position he recites the words, "Glory be to the Almighty Lord!"

—After the first prostration (*sujūd*), Abdulla sits back on his left heel and ankle, taking a moment of rest.

—He does a second prostration in the same way.

—This completes one cycle of prayer, or *rakᶜa*.

—After the second prostration Abdulla again sits on his heel.

—In that position he repeats the *shahāda*, utters a prayer of blessing for the Prophet and his family, and repeats a general prayer, or part of a general prayer, such as the following:

O Lord! Forgive us and our parents and ancestors, and our leaders and all the believers who preceded us. O Lord! Absolve all our sins and those we may fall (into) in the future; those open sins and those concealed and all that You know but we may not be aware of. O Lord! Grant us good things in this near life and good things in the life to come, and protect us from the punishment of Fire.[11]

—He turns to the right and to the left saying, "*Salaam aleikum!*" He may add the words, "*And the mercy and blessing of God be upon you.*"

—As a conclusion, he may hold upward the palms of his hands and draw them in toward his body, symbolizing that he has both received and is taking in the blessing of God.

Abdulla has completed his *salāt*. As customary, he greets his friends and makes his way toward his home. In the middle of his forehead people can detect a dark, calloused spot that has developed as the result of his frequent touching the ground in prayer.

6. Voluntary Prayer and Calling Down Blessing

a. Voluntary prayers (*duʿā*) are free, spontaneous petitions, and such prayer is encouraged although it is not a required practice. The Qurʾān has many examples of this kind of supplication since the prophets, led by Muhammad himself, frequently called upon God for help. Muslims often accompany such asking prayers with a vow or with the added plea for the intercessory help of a saint. An example of *duʿā* is the following prayer of al-Tijānī, a noted North African saint and the founder of a mystical order: "O Lord, endow me with a lowly, humble, prostrate heart, and a weeping eye ... and a sincere acceptable repentance."[12]

b. The most common of all Muslim supplications is the calling down of blessing on the Prophet Muhammad and his family (*tasliya*). There is a Qurānic basis for this practice: "Lo! Allāh and His angels shower blessings on the Prophet. O ye who believe! Ask blessings on him and salute him with a worthy salutation" (34:56). Yet it may be said that this practice really flows from the great veneration that Muslims cherish for the messenger of God. In chapter 5 it was pointed out that the ordinary form of this blessing is *salla llāhu alā n-nabī*, that is, "May God bless the Prophet!" Another form is *salla llāhu alaihi wa sallām*, which means "May God bless and preserve him!" The same thought is expressed in one of the recommended *salāt* prayers:

Lord! Grant Muhammad peace; likewise the family of Muhammad,
As you granted Ibrahim and the family of Ibrahim;
And bestow blessing upon Muhammad and the family of Muhammad,

As you blessed Ibrahim and the family of Ibrahim among all worlds.[13]

c. As we conclude our discussion of the Muslim practice of prayer, Professor Rudolf Otto's famous description of the Awesome One as the Mystery that causes both trembling and fascination comes to mind (*mysterium tremendum et fascinosum*).[14] In Muslim prayer it is the liturgical *salāt* that leans toward the aspect of trembling before God, while it is in *duʿā* that we sense an element of fascination, the longing of the Muslim heart for God's mercy and blessing. So we conclude our discussion of prayer with two quotations of Muslim supplications, the first from Sudan:

> O God, I ask forgiveness for myself and for my father; for all Muslims, both men and women; for all believers, both men and women; for those of them who are alive and those of them who are dead.

> Deal with me and with them, whether soon or late, in the faith, in this world and the next, according to What you deserve. Do not deal with us, O Lord, according to what we deserve. For You are forgiving, patient, generous, bountiful, tender and merciful.[15]

And combining both the elements of trembling and fascination is this Shīʿa prayer of the great-grandson of the Prophet, Zayn al-ʿAbidīn:

> O Lord; Thou are the one through whose mercy the erring pray for redress; the one in the remembrance of whose grace the afflicted take refuge; the one in dread of whom the guilty bitterly weep! ... Here I am ready to obey Thee! Here I am at Thy call! Behold O Lord, here I am prostrate in Thy presence.[16]

C. Fasting

Fasting is the third pillar of Muslim duty. My friends enjoy prayer, but endure fasting. It is a rigorous annual physical and spiritual exercise that produces its own satisfaction, a feeling that comes from the knowledge that one has successfully endured in a strenuous effort. In the ninth month of the Muslim year—it is named Ramaḍān—no food or water is to be consumed in the daylight hours, and the believer's attention is to be fully concentrated on the religious life.

Fasting is a practice that is common in the world's religions, and it was known in Arabia in pre-Islāmic times. The Jews in

Medina observed their own fasts, and Christian monks in the area practiced austerities. Muhammad admired those observances, and the Qurʾān endorsed and commanded the practice of fasting. Apparently, at one stage the Prophet had actually conformed to Jewish custom in the selection of fast days, but the Qurʾān then gave a definitive instruction (2:183–185):

> O ye who believe! Fasting is prescribed for you, even as it was prescribed for those before you, that ye may ward off [evil]... And whosoever of you is present, let him fast the month, and whosoever is sick or on a journey, [let him fast the same] number of days. Allāh desireth for you ease; He desireth not hardship for you; and (He desireth) that ye should complete the period, and that ye should magnify Allāh for having guided you, and that peradventure ye may be thankful.

The spiritual purpose of the practice of fasting is clear from the command: the magnifying of God and the giving of thanks. Ala Abūl Mawdūdi, enlarging on these themes, asks, "What is it that makes us voluntarily undergo such rigours?" He answers his own question, "It is nothing but faith in God and the fear of Him and of the Day of Judgment." Fasting, he declares, is a kind of spiritual proclamation and "by our doing so, the supremacy of the law of God" is announced. Furthermore the practice creates "the sentiments of love and brotherhood." But the main function of fasting, he maintains, is spiritual education:

> This consciousness of duty and the spirit of patience that incessant fasting for one full month inculcates in us, help us to strengthen our faith ... [and] our life, during the rest of the year, a life of true subservience to His will.[17]

Let us view Abdulla and Amina as Ramaḍān is about to commence. They are not exactly stressed out, but they are a little tense. Things are in for a change around their household during the coming month. The moment has almost arrived. Their radio is not working, so Abdulla tells Amina, "I'll go to the market and find out." What he is trying to discover is the exact and official moment when the new moon will appear, shaped as a crescent sliver on the horizon just after sunset. That moment will mark the beginning of the month of fasting. After a while he returns and tells Amina, "The moon has been sighted." They look at each other, understanding what they have to do. That night they utter their *nīya*: "I intend to fast tomorrow for the sake of Almighty

God."

The fast (ṣawm) is obligatory on all Muslims, apart from certain exemptions. Young children up to the age of 12, and those who are old and infirm are exempt. The sick, women in an antenatal or postnatal phase, travelers, and those in danger may postpone the fast, but they should try to do compensatory fasts when possible. The actual fast is to be total during the daylight hours, and technically not even saliva is to be swallowed. Sexual. intercourse is forbidden, secular concerns are to be moderated, and passions and temper are to be controlled. Ideally, the practice of the remembering of God should take over. Since most adult Muslims are working and cannot engage in Qurʾān reading or meditation in the daytime, Muslims use the night hours for that purpose. Ramaḍān nights are alive in the Muslim world. Assemblies meet for public instruction, including male and female, especially on the occasion of *lailat-ul-qadr*. This festival on the 27th of Ramaḍān is the traditional date for the descent of the Qurʾān, when 20 cycles of prayers are commended for believers.

Voluntary fasting above and beyond the Ramaḍān requirement is recommended and commendable, and there are various times in the Muslim calendar when such fastings are considered especially appropriate. Vowed fasts represent another type of fasting. These have a specific purpose—to overcome a sin, to pray for the birth of a child, to win a favor, and so on. In short, fasting is considered to be a means to procure God's favor as well as a fine spiritual training.

Because of the intensity of the physical and spiritual experience involved, the Ramaḍān month of fasting is a time of high religious emotion throughout the Muslim world. It may be asked what proportion of the Muslim community is faithful to this demanding requirement and how many Muslims actually observe the fast fully and regularly. That is obviously a difficult question to answer, and Muslims are not eager to pursue such a query. The strict observance of the fast faces some hindrances. It is hard to fast all day and maintain productivity on a job. In some countries the climate may be very hot during Ramaḍān, and going without water is extremely difficult. In industrialized, non-Muslim societies, there is little sympathy for the concept. Secularized Muslims themselves may be indifferent. In some Muslim societies community pressures are exerted to "encourage" obedience to the requirement. I recall drum beating outside restaurants where Muslims may enter to take relief. Nevertheless, a significant proportion of the *umma* makes every effort to observe this basic practice of Islām. For those who do so, there are deep satisfactions. As Muhammad Rauf has put it,

> Fasting is indeed a moral training in the practice of self-control. It is a training in which the rich suffer an experience of the plight of the needy and provokes their sympathy. It is a practice of beneficial advantage to our gastric system. Above all, fasting gives the worshiper a chance to experience a deep inner sense of inestimable spiritual pleasure beyond description by words. During the fasting day, a Muslim feels nearer to his Lord, and this feeds his soul with spiritual calm and immeasurable feelings of satisfaction.[18]

For 29–30 days Amina has prepared the meals for night consumption. Right after sunset the family gathers for its breakfast meal. Again at about 2:00 A.M. or just before dawn—the time varies greatly from place to place—another meal is enjoyed. While this goes on in the home, in Muslim areas of the world the streets are festive. The fast month is a kind of pendulum between the somberness of daylight dedication and the relaxation of night events. In fact, some Muslims criticize the merriment and tendency to extravagance on the ground that they frustrate one of the main purposes of the fasting experience—an identification with the poor and hungry. It is not surprising, however, that the extreme stringency of the fast produces a variety of reactions.

For Abdulla and Amina this particular Ramaḍān has been a very significant time. Their son, Rashid, is far too young to be required to fast, but he has done so anyway. He is very proud of his achievement, and his parents are even prouder. Rashid had made a little deal with his parents. He said, "I will fast Monday to Friday, but I would like to eat Saturday and Sunday!" His parents were more than pleased to make the bargain with their little boy! Abdulla is feeling good also. He has succeeded in making up a disagreement with an angry relative. Ramaḍān, he knows, is the period when the spirit of reconciliation and forgiveness should prevail among believers. He is happy it has worked out that way. The whole family feels good. The family believes that they have truly and wholly *surrendered* to Almighty God.

The month of Ramaḍān is now coming to a close. Once again Abdulla says, "I will go out and find when the new moon is sighted"—but there is no need for him to come back and tell the news. A huge shout erupts in the streets. It is a sound of jubilation. The fast has ended! The feast of ʿĪd al-Fiṭr, the breaking of the fast, has commenced. Another spiritual journey is successfully completed, and Ramaḍān has sanctified the rest of the year for the family of Islām.

D. Almsgiving

The fourth pillar of obedience in Islām is almsgiving. It is commonly referred to by its Arabic name, *zakāt*, which literally means "purification." By giving charity to the poor, believers purify their remaining possessions and, in fact, under the blessing of God the almsgiving will result in an increase of those possessions.

The grace of charity is a primary emphasis in the Qurʾān. The Prophet personally experienced the trials of poverty, and many of the early Companions of the Prophet also were poor people. Therefore the Qurʾān is not subtle on the point, but directly commands the principle of generosity. The word almsgiving is used over 80 times in the Book. It is frequently coupled with expressions of concern for orphans and widows. *Zakāt* is the legal duty that expresses a primary principle of behavior, and through its requirement the *umma* is reminded to take care of its poor and disadvantaged. It is even coupled with worship, as though God does not want to be worshipped by those who forget the poor:

> Establish worship, pay the poor-due, and bow your head with those who bow [in worship] (2:43).

> Establish worship, pay the poor-due, and hold fast to Allāh (22:78).

The message could not be clearer.

A Muslim must therefore pay *zakāt*. While the principle of almsgiving is straightforward, the application is more complex. In the first place, the duty is restricted to those who have the financial ability to give charity. This assumption is built into the operation of almsgiving through the concept of *nisāb*, which means one's basic living income. It is assumed that every Muslim family has a basic right to take care of its own fundamental needs, including food, clothing, shelter, health, and education. The *zakāt* is not to be assessed on this basic amount. It is the income above the *nisāb* that is subject to the requirement of almsgiving.

How much of the excess income is to be given as alms to the poor? That depends on the kind of wealth that is involved. If it is wealth in the form of cash, 2.5 percent is expected. If the wealth is in the form of land, 10 percent of the fruits of watered land must be paid, and 5 percent of the produce from irrigated land. If the wealth is in the form of animals, it may be one animal above 40, two animals above 120, and so on. Modern forms of wealth such as stocks and bonds, or real estate holdings, introduce other parameters, and Muslim legal scholars have expended much effort to try to establish a fair, working system.

In the early days of Islām a great deal of effort was expended to identify categories of individuals who might be recipients of *zakāt*. The alms must be given to people who are really in need of them. The entitlement is established by the Qurʾān (9:60): "The alms are only for the poor and needy, and those who collect them, and those whose hearts are to be reconciled, and to free the captives and debtors, and for the cause of Allāh, and [for] the wayfarers." Thus, the eligible recipients are the poor who do not have a basic *nisāb* income; Muslims in the service of God, whether warriors or pilgrim; inquirers into the faith; and similar categories. Ineligible people include one's own relatives, rich people, and non-Muslims.

A difference of opinion exists among Muslims today as to how to pay the *zakāt*. The disagreement is between those who maintain that the charitable gift must be given directly to the poor person; those who maintain that the *zakāt* or part of it should be used for community job-creation schemes; and those who hold that governments may exact the *zakāt* as a public tax in order to do welfare activities. In some places the issue has produced major confrontations between traditional interpreters and proponents of social change. Traditional interpreters, utilizing legal opinions (*fatwās*) contend that all wealth belongs to God and God, the owner, has commanded direct giving to the poor. Progressive interpreters argue that getting at the root of the poverty problem is a legitimate use of *zakāt* and falls within God's intention for almsgiving. Finally, in Muslim countries it is argued by many that the state has become the welfare agency and therefore should collect and distribute *zakāt*. It is argued that "huge funds wasted on rendering individual help and creating faqirs and beggars can be saved."

All charity should be organized and we should cooperate with each other to eliminate poverty and ignorance, the two great enemies of Islām ... Zakāt—organized Zakāt—honestly collected, honestly distributed, and honestly spent can help Muslims to become real Muslims.[19]

The difference of opinion regarding the collection and distribution of zakāt is not likely to be decided quickly.

There is no difference of opinion, however, regarding the fact that the true spirit of almsgiving must be maintained. As with other religious duties, the intention must be right and the motive honorable. A variety of motives for giving zakāt are commended in the Qurʾān, in Ḥadīth, and in other Muslim writings. They include: the fear of God and the threat of the judgment; the command of God and the sense of duty; love for God and the desire to please God; atonement for evil and the hope of reward; and finally, the strengthening of one's own surrender to God. Abul Alā Mawdūdi states that Muslims are to pay willingly "in the name of Allāh" and "neither expect nor demand any worldly gains from the beneficiaries, nor aim at making our name as philanthropists." Islām, he says, is the sworn enemy of selfish greed and acquisitivism, and zakāt "fosters in us the qualities of sacrifice and rids us of selfishness and plutolatry." God, in turn, blesses the almsgiver. "The more you pay, the greater the reward that Allāh will bestow upon you."[20]

These comments lead us to another form of recommended almsgiving, namely voluntary alms (ṣadaqa). Voluntary alms, like zakāt, are based on the fundamental Qurānic principle of liberality. "Those who spend their wealth by night and day, by stealth and openly, verily their reward is with their Lord" (2:274). Ṣadaqa may be given to anyone, for any godly purpose. It may involve major giving—to build a college or hospital, to finance scholarships for students, or to provide meals for the hungry at the time of festivals. Or it may be something much simpler than these. A Ḥadīth suggests, in fact, that the best of alms are those provided by a person of small means. It may be "smiling in your brother's face." The Qurʾān puts it simply: "A kind word with forgiveness is better than almsgiving followed by injury" (2:263). Related to the principle of ṣadaqa is the practice of creating endowments or trusts, especially of land, the income of which is to be used for godly purposes. Many of the charitable institutions of Islām depend for their existence on such endowments (waqf).

If we were to choose one idea in the Qurʾān that expresses the opposite of charity, it would be usury. The background to the Qurānic castigation of usury is the fact that the rapacious rich people and moneylenders of Mecca were taking advantage of the poor and helpless. Nevertheless, the critique of the Qurʾān is so sharp that it sounds a dominating note in current Islāmic economic theory. Those who devour usury, the Qurʾān proclaims, are devil-touched people who will abide in the Fire. They are people who give miserable arguments such as saying that trade is just like usury. But "Allāh permitteth trading and forbiddeth usury." Indeed, "Allāh hath blighted usury and made almsgiving fruitful" (2:275f.). What makes the prohibition of usury a particular challenge for believers today is the fact that many Muslims identify interest on money with usury (ribā).

In modern society a general distinction is made between two forms of interest on money. The first type of interest is receiving a moderate return on savings and investments. The second type is exorbitant and unfair charges for loans, which is regarded as usury. Some Muslims make the same distinction, and they open savings accounts and participate in the credit system. Other Muslims, however, regard all forms of interest as usury and therefore forbidden by the Qurʾān. This prohibition, in turn, has enormous implications for Islāmic economic theory, and Muslims are looking for fresh ways of doing business in the modern world. One way of doing so is through the establishment of "Islāmic banks," which are now appearing in many places. Since the profit-motive and profit-making are deemed acceptable in Islām, such banks are founded on that principle. Muslims are striving to create an economic system somewhere between the extremes of rugged capitalism on the one hand and extreme socialism on the other hand, the goal being the formation of an Islāmic economic theory based on the spirit of sharing as expressed by both zakāt and ṣadaqa. The goal is elusive, as Muslims face the universal problems of self-centeredness and greed. Against those evils the Qurʾān speaks sharply and clearly:

Lo! Allāh loveth not such as are proud and boastful, who hoard their wealth and enjoin avarice on others, and hide that which Allāh hath bestowed upon them for bounty ... And (also) those who spend their wealth in order to be seen of men ... Whoso taketh Satan for a comrade, a bad comrade hath he. What have they (to fear) if they believe in Allāh and the Last Day and spend (aright) of that which Allāh hath bestowed on them, when Allāh is ever Aware of them (and all they do)?... And if there is a good deed, He will double it and will give (the doer) from His presence an immense award (4:36–40).

Abdulla is heading for the market. It is Thursday, and everyone is bringing their goods for sale. He does the shopping for the family. This week Amina needs quite a large number of food items, so he is hurrying his steps. However, as he draws near to the entrance of the market, his eyes meet a familiar sight. In a row along the entrance path to the marketplace is a group of people begging, many of them blind and handicapped. "Allāh! Allāh! Allāh!" ... the sound goes up. Abdulla is a modern, educated man. He knows that the problems of poverty and human suffering in his nation will take large measures. He dislikes begging in any form, and he is angry with the situations that bring human beings to this pass. He is inclined to Islāmic socialism and believes that governments must intervene to solve the systemic social problems involved in the line of people facing him. Yet he also believes that he understands the meaning of the divine command to give alms. He reaches into his pocket and finds some coins to give to the beggars. In doing so he *feels* that he is surrendering to God.

Now we turn to the culminating act of surrender, the pilgrimage to Mecca.

E. The Pilgrimage

Amina's house is in a happy disarray. Her husband, Abdulla, has just returned from the pilgrimage to Mecca. As a result of the generosity of an uncle he was able to go anyway, despite his financial restraints. He returned safely—and he did not come back empty-handed. He has brought small gifts for Amina and for each member of the family. But far more important are the stories he has to tell of the wonders that he experienced. There is a special look on his face and a light in his eyes as he tries to convey his feelings to his family. The first things Amina said when she met him was: "You're a *ḥāji* now!" She is proud of the fact, as Abdulla is. She hopes to become a *ḥāji* (pilgrimage-returned person) too, when the children get older.

The fifth primary religious duty of Islām is the pilgrimage (*ḥājj*) to Mecca. It is more than a duty, rather the dream of a lifetime. Every Muslim who is of age and has sufficient financial ability not only is required to, but wants to fulfil this obligation if possible. One can confidently say that for most Muslims the pilgrimage represents the supreme spiritual experience in all of Islāmic religion. Let us therefore examine the place that draws such attention, the rites and prayers of the pilgrimage, and the emotion of the pilgrim.

1. The Place of Pilgrimage

The remarkable pilgrimage scene has often been filmed. It is a scene of literally millions of people on the move, and many thousands at a time surging around a central shrine in the great mosque at Mecca. In size, it is the largest annual religious gathering in the world.

The mosque at Mecca and the Ka'ba should not be confused. The mosque is the worship place and the Ka'ba (=cube) is the core shrine that it contains. The mosque is very large, about 250 by 200 yards in size, with nine gates, seven minarets, and large adjoining buildings. Around its circumference are large colonnaded porticos, where religious education and other activities go on. The covered porticos surround a huge unroofed courtyard where the worshippers gather, as many as 600,000 at a time, and seven paths lead to the shrine of the Ka'ba that stands in the middle.

Although the Ka'ba is large in significance, as buildings go it is small—50 feet long, 40 feet wide, and 35 feet high. It is made of stone and is covered with a sloping roof, its surrounding area being paved with marble slabs. The Ka'ba is lined up at an angle, the northeast side having the only door, so that each corner faces a direction. The door is seven feet high and is accessible by a movable wooden ladder. The interior, however, serves no religious function and contains only hanging lamps and wall inscriptions. The exterior of the structure is covered by a black brocade curtain, which is renewed annually. The *shahāda* is woven into the material, and there is a gold-threaded encircling band of calligraphy, two-thirds of the way up, that includes such Qurānic phrases as 3:19: "Lo! Religion with Allāh is al-Islām ..." The famous Black Stone—legend says that Adam brought it from heaven!—is set into the northeast corner, and pilgrims attempt to kiss it as they move about the Ka'ba. Because of the huge crowds very few succeed in the attempt. On one of the several occasions when the Ka'ba had to be rebuilt the rock was broken into three pieces, and it is now held together by a silver frame. Opposite to it in the southeast corner is another smaller rock called the "lucky stone" that pilgrims try to touch.

Surrounding the shrine are a number of sacred areas. One is enclosed by a low semicircular wall near the northwest side of the Ka'ba. It is believed that this enclosure contains the graves of Hagar and Ishmael. Another small depression in the same area marks the spot where Abraham and Ishmael mixed the mortar for the construction of the Ka'ba. In recent years the courtyard of the Ka'ba has been cleared of a number of small buildings that were there in the past, in order to provide more space for the ever-increasing crowds.[21] One of these enclosed the well of Zem Zem. Now two staircases for men and women descend beneath the surface, and the water of the remarkable well is available through taps. Muslims believe that the well has kept flowing since the time of Hagar. Toward the northeast side of the courtyard is a small subsidiary shrine called the Maqām Ibrahīm, which contains two indentations on a rock—said to be the footsteps of the Prophet Abraham. Near to it is a beautifully ornamented pulpit. Outside the mosque but connected to its southern exposure is a long 400-yard covered walkway, where pilgrims go back and forth seven times imitating Hagar's desperate search for water.

The Ka'ba is central to Muslim devotion because, in the first place, the Qur'ān makes it so. It declares (3:96–97):

> Lo! the first Sanctuary appointed for mankind was that at Becca [=Mecca], a blessed place, a guidance to the peoples, wherein are plain memorials (of Allāh's guidance); the place where Abraham stood up to pray; and whosoever entereth it is safe. And pilgrimage to the House is a duty unto Allāh for mankind, for him who can find a way thither ... (3:96f.).

Its validation for Muslims also comes from the practice of the Prophet Muhammad, whose family history is closely entwined with the Ka'ba. With his own participation in the pilgrimage Muhammad confirmed the central significance of the Ka'ba for Muslim devotion. The final element in the Ka'ba tradition is its association with the story of Abraham and his family. The Qur'ān describes its relation to Abraham and later tradition enlarges upon it. Let us look at that story.

Although there is a persistent tradition that runs back to Adam, it is generally believed by Muslims that Abraham built the first

Ka'ba. Hagar and Ishmael, however, entered the scene before Abraham. At Sarah's instigation Hagar was sent away by Abraham, and she and her son Ishmael wandered to the region of Mecca. Their condition became tragic, and they were dying of thirst. In desperation Hagar ran seven time between the hills Safā and Marwah, looking for relief. God mercifully sent the help of an angel who struck the spring of Zem Zem, saving Hagar and Ishmael. Abraham later came to Mecca, and he and his son constructed a simple low-walled, unroofed shrine, the original Ka'ba, and dedicated it to the worship of Allāh, the one God.

Later, however, as we have seen, pre-Islāmic society degenerated and religion became pagan. This continued up to the time of Muhammad whose own tribe, the Quraysh, were the guardians of the Ka'ba. Through the prophetic intervention of Muhammad the shrine of the Ka'ba was finally cleansed and restored to the true worship of Allāh. Muhammad, however, was a purifier and not a destroyer; having cleansed the shrine, he retained many of the rites and customs of the traditional pilgrimage. His performance of the ceremony in the last year of his life is now the model for the Muslim pilgrims that stream to Mecca from every corner of the world.

We now, as it were, travel to Mecca for the rites of the pilgrimage. The territory around the city is forbidden to non-Muslims, and a highway bypass goes from the port of Jedda to Taif so that non-Muslims may not view the sacred precincts. The territory is holy to Islām.

2. The Rites of the Pilgrimage

By land, sea, and air the pilgrims have converged on the outskirts of Mecca. It is the month of Dhū'l-Ḥijja, the twelfth month of the lunar year. The tenth day of the month is the high day, the day when Muslims around the world join with the pilgrims at Mecca in remembering Abraham's sacrifice of his son. The pilgrims start the *hajj* ceremonies earlier, gathering about six miles from the city. From this point we will follow the footsteps of Abdulla. Along with other pilgrims from his country, he has placed himself under the leadership of an expert guide who will see him through the complex procedures.

Abdulla has bathed and put on special clothing, two new white seamless cloths about 6 x 3 1/2 feet in length, which he drapes around his body. One cloth goes around the waist, and the other is thrown over the shoulder. A female pilgrim covers herself with modest clothing, leaving face and hands free. Abdulla has now entered the stage of *iḥrām* (prohibition) when certain things are forbidden, including sexual intercourse, killing, or pollution of any kind, and at a lesser level such affectations as perfumes, shaving, and nail-cutting. He utters his intention (*nīya*) and then starts toward the city intermittently crying out: "*labaika! labaikka!*", that is, "I am ready!":

> I am waiting for thy service, O God!
> I am waiting for thy service, O God!
> There is no partner with thee;
> I am waiting for thy service!
> Verily, thine is the praise, the beneficence, and the kingdom;
> There is no partner with thee![22]

Abdulla has now entered the holy city, and he makes his way to the great mosque, entering through the Gate of Peace. He bathes and then performs his first circuit (*tawāf*) around the Kaʿba, going counterclockwise, three times quickly and four times slowly. He tries to touch the Black Stone and to visit the other sacred places in the area, reciting appropriate verses from the Qurʾān (112; 2,125; 2,158), and he repeats Hagar's race between Safā and Marwah.

The pace of the ceremonies accelerates between the seventh and the tenth days of the month. On the seventh day there is a *khutba*, a sermon in the mosque that Abdulla attends. On the eighth day he goes in an easterly direction to the valley of Minā, eight miles from Mecca, where the famous Treaties of ʿAqaba took place in Muhammad's time and where Adam is said to be buried. Minā plays a great role in the pilgrimage ceremonies. Abdulla has arrived in time to participate in the noon *salāt* as required. There he spends the night in the great tent city that has sprawled across the valley, accommodating hundreds of thousands of pilgrims. The next morning, on the ninth day of the month, Abdulla proceeds another five miles eastward to the hill of ʿArafāt. This 200-foot high elevation is crowned with a platform and pulpit. In the afternoon a vast assembly has somehow gathered around the low "hill of mercy" to hear a message.

Because of the great throng, the cries of *labaika!* that fill the air, the penitential prayers and recitations that resound, and the general tumult, Abdulla can hardly hear the sermon, but he feels its emotion:

> You have come all these miles to ʿArafāt, but that is nothing unless you arrive at the teachings of Islām. Gather together and support God's words. Live by them and be worthy of what you are. Take hold of the rope of God's oneness and haul yours forward. Be generous. Be the nation of Islām.
>
> You came here today to a sacred place. It is safe and secure, and everything is available. It will do you no good to have come all this way if you don't have something worth taking back to others. When you leave, don't forget. Be as you are now, standing here on the Plain of ʿArafāt: remember God before everything else ...[23]

Abdulla takes rest that night at Muzdalifa, an illuminated area midway between ʿArafāt and Minā. He is already exhausted, but there is more to come, as he and his fellow pilgrims draw nearer to the formal climax of their *hajj*.

The pilgrims know that it is the tenth day of the month, and after an early prayer they hasten back to Minā. Minā is the location of three ancient stone pillars, and they take turns casting pebbles at each of the pillars. The latter are said to symbolize evil, and so the pilgrims simultaneously cry out the words: "In the name of the Almighty I do this, and in the hatred of the devil and his shame!" The pilgrimage ceremony now reaches its culmination with the sacrifice of an animal—sheep, goat, cow, or camel. As the sacrifice takes place Abdulla remembers the faith of Abraham who was ready to give up his son. Muslims generally take this son to have been Ishmael, although the Qurʾān is silent on the name. Abdulla's thoughts also fly back for a moment to his own family that is celebrating at the same time this universal festival of Islām. It is a remarkable scene at Minā, and it is not surprising that the Government of Saudi Arabia has had to expend great efforts to provide sanitary facilities and arrangements for the preservation and distribution of the meat.

The sacrifice at Minā concludes the high day and introduces the "first freedom." Abdulla can now shave and remove his special clothing. Before doing so, however, he returns to the Kaʿba and does another circuit of the shrine. He is now a *hāji*, one who has performed the pilgrimage, and henceforth he will be known as Abdulla Ḥāji in his community.

The events of the pilgrimage are not quite over. The music of devotion has risen to a crescendo, but there is still a closing movement. The eleventh, twelfth, and thirteenth days of the month are given over to the task of spiritual disengagement. The pilgrims have to "come down to earth." During these days Abdulla sleeps one more night at Minā. Then, finally, he performs his circuit of farewell around the Kaʿba and retreats from the sacred area, keeping the shrine in view as long as possible. The *hajj* is over. What comes next is his own choice. He decides to do one more action that is commended rather than required, and that is a visit to the city of Medina. He travels the 250 miles from Mecca, observes the great mosque and the hallowed territory where the Prophet Muhammad established Islām, and finally visits the tomb of the Prophet. Content now, he starts on his return journey to rejoin his family.

Although the *hajj* is performed only at the appointed time, it may be noted that there is a "lesser pilgrimage" (*ʿumra*) that can be carried out at any time of the year. The lesser pilgrimage concentrates on the required activities within Mecca, and leaves out the animal sacrifice.

3. The Spirit and Emotion of the Pilgrim

I recall a conversation with a Muslim friend who had gone on the pilgrimage three times. I asked him what he felt and how he felt during the experience. He could not find the words to explain it. At last he simply said: "I felt good." It was his way of expressing the inexpressible.

Various Muslims have made attempts to articulate the significance of the pilgrimage experience in a more explanatory way. Abul Alā Mawdūdī points out how it "inculcates in us goodness and piety." It also "unites the Muslims of the world into one international fraternity." Malcolm X felt the merit of that point. His experience of the color-blind nature of the pilgrimage became a fundamental influence in altering the development of the African-American Muslim movement, enabling the beginning of its integration into the wider Muslim family. Mawdūdī describes the emotional dimension of the experience:

Here his thoughts are concentrated on Allāh, his very being vibrates with the spirit of intense devotion. When he reaches the holy place, he finds the atmosphere laden with piety and godliness; he visits places which bear witness to the glory of Islām, and all this leaves an indelible impression on his mind, which he carries to his last breath.[24]

It is the prayers that are recited by the pilgrims that most clearly express the intensity of the pilgrimage emotion. Following is an excerpt from the prayer for the second circuit:

O God, this House is Thy House,
And this sanctuary is Thy Sanctuary,
And this Security is Thy security,
And this slave is Thy Slave.
I am Thy Slave and the son [or daughter] of Thy Slave.
And in this place of those who taketh refuge with Thee, from the Fire,
Forbid our flesh and our bodies to the Fire.[25]

The prayer for the seventh circuit, which the pilgrim guide reads and his followers repeat, is the following:

O God, I ask of Thee:
Perfect Faith and true conviction,
And Thy boundless bounty,

And a tongue praising Thy Name,
And lawful joys,
And lasting repentance,
And repentance before death,
And tranquillity in death,
And forgiveness and mercy after death,
And pardon on the Day of reckoning,
And that I be rewarded with Paradise,
And salvation from the Fire,
By Thy Mercy, O Glorious, O Oft-Forgiving!

Lord, increase my understanding,
And let me be among the virtuous.[26]

With so many cultic elements, some inherited from the pre-Islāmic period, there is an ever-present danger of superstition taking over the performance of the *hajj*, and rituals such as the kissing of the Black Stone lend themselves to the possibility of lower interpretations. Al-Ghazālī recognized this danger, and to counteract such tendencies he put forward his spiritual-moral interpretation of the various ritual acts. He affirms that the total meaning of the *hajj* must be placed within the principle of surrender. That is, it inculcates the spirit of humility before God.

We honor the House, but at the same time we acknowledge that no House or country can confine Him. The whole world is His mosque.

What about things like stoning pillars? Al-Ghazālī says that God sometimes imposes actions that are not necessarily pleasing intellectually because our obedience to such requirements purifies our hearts and reminds us that there is a mystery in devotional practice. The pilgrimage therefore contrasts with the other religious duties at this point, since they are more rationally understandable and emotionally comfortable. Each event must be taken in its spiritual dimension. Your *tawāf* around the Kaʿba will remind you of the angels circling round the throne of God. The purpose of the *tawāf* is not the circumambulation of the body—it is rather the circling of your heart around the Lord of the House. The touching of the Black Stone symbolizes homage to God. The running back and forth between Ṣafā and Marwah represents your struggle between good and evil and your spiritual movement between punishment and forgiveness. When you stone the pillars, you are not engaging in meaningless play, but rather you are symbolically uniting yourself with Abraham who fought off the devil.

The whole journey of the pilgrimage, al-Ghazālī says, symbolizes the other journey that all believers will take, the journey to God's eternal house where the faithful will be granted the vision of God's face. The pilgrimage should create in us a desire for that greater journey. So settle your affairs and close out all disputes and assume the mantle of repentance. Take only as much provision as you need, for your only true provision is the fear of God; and go as though you will never return. Your special clothing will remind you that some day you will meet God with different garments. And all the other events, experienced amidst the throngs, will cause you to look forward to the pouring forth of humanity on the Day of Resurrection. When the pilgrimage is completed, fear must lodge in your heart and the sincere hope that God will accept your *ḥajj*. In the end, the conviction of your heart will confirm your sense that it is approved by God, but nevertheless, as a true and humble pilgrim, you will pray: "May God protect us from having our pilgrimage rejected."[27]

Abdulla does not have Al-Ghazālī's profound insight and eloquent tongue. He knows, however, that he has had a special experience, one that will continue to mean something important to him for the rest of his days. All his friends are coming to his house to welcome him back and to ask him questions. If he were asked what it all meant to him, he might say: "I felt good."

We now pass from the formal pillars of obedience to the realm of moral piety and spiritual struggle.

Notes

[1]*Mishkat*, I, p. 187.

[2]Al-Ghazālī, *Kitāb al-ʿIlm*, tr. by N. A. Faris (Lahore: Sh. Muhammad Ashraf, 1962; repr., 1974), p. 31.

[3]W. C. Smith, *On Understanding Islām* (The Hague: Mouton, 1981), pp. 31f., and *Faith and Belief* (Princeton: Princeton University Press, 1979), pp. 42ff. The distinction may be subtle, but it helps to underline the depth of the conviction involved.

[4]*Muslim Devotions*, pp. 126–36.

[5]Ibid., p. 251.

[6]A. J. Wensinck, *"Niyya,"* SEI, p. 449.

[7]C. N. Ahmed Moulavi, *Saheehul Bukhari. Malayalam Translation and Commentary* (Calicut: Ansari Press, 1970), p. l. Tr. by R. E. Miller.

[8]*Mishkat*, I, p. 66.

[9]Siddiqui, *Elementary Teachings*, p. 39.

[10]A. H. Christie, "Islāmic Minor Arts," *The Legacy of Islām*, 1st ed.; eds. T. Arnold and A. Guillaume, p. 109, remarks that "Islāmic art had its beginning in the mosque." The Persian mosque carpets rank as one of the highest among the broad-ranging Islāmic artistic achievements.

[11]From the Malikite rite; quoted by Rauf, *Islām*, p. 63.

[12]Quoted in Padwick, *Muslim Devotions*, p. 186.

[13]Rauf, *Islām*, p. 63.

[14]Cf. Rudolf Otto's classic *Idea of the Holy*, tr. by J. W. Harvey (London: Oxford, 1950; 1st ed. 1923), p. 12, *et passim*.

[15]*Al-Rātib*, a book of prayers used by Imam Muhammad al-Mahdi, quoted by Charis Waddy, *Muslim Mind*, p. 8.

[16]*The Sahifat-ul-Kamilah*, tr. by A. A. Mohani (Lucknow: Muayyed-ul-Uloom Association, 1969–70, Supplication No. 16, p. 61; quoted by S. H. M. Jafri, "Twelve-Imam Shiʿism," in Nasr, *Spirituality*, p. 178.

[17]*Toward Understanding Islam*, p.91.

[18]Rauf, *Islām*, p. 100.

[19]*Lessons in Islām Series*, Book No. III, pp. 22f.

[20]Mawdūdī, *Toward Understanding*, pp. 104f.

[21]In 1946 non-Saudi pilgrims numbered only 55,244. In 50 years the number has increased twenty-fold. Cf. Russel King, "The Pilgrimage to Mecca: Some Geographical and Historical Aspects," *Erdkunde*, Band XXVI (1971?), p. 68.

[22]Tr. by John A. Subhan, *Islām, Its Beliefs and Practices* (Lucknow: Lucknow Publishing House, 1938), p. 85.

[23]Michael Wolfe, *The Hadj: An American's Pilgrimage to Mecca* (New York: The Atlantic Monthly Press, 1993), pp. 323f., quoting E. Rutter, *The Holy Cities of Arabia* (New York: G. Putnam's, 1930).

[24]*Toward Understanding Islām*, p. 106.

[25]Ahmad Kamal, *The Sacred Journey* (New York: Duell, Sloan & Pierce, 1961), p. 47.

[26]Ibid., p. 50.

[27]I am indebted to G. E. von Grunebaum, *Muhammadan Festivals* (London: Curzon Press, 1951; repr. 1976), pp. 44–47, where he summarizes Al-Ghazālī's *Ihyā ʿulūm al-dīn* (Bulaq, 1872, I, 252–58). Cf. F. E. Peters, *The Hajj* (Princeton: Princeton University Press, 1994), pp. 114–16, for additional information from the *Ihyā*.

12

Muslim Piety and Spiritual Struggle: *Taqwā* and *Jihād*

The pillars of obedience provide the specific "moments" of a believer's surrender to God. The strong Muslim emphasis on behavior, however, includes considerably more than these rituals. It incorporates much of what is covered by the terms "morality" and "ethics." Muslims express the idea with the words piety or *taqwā*, and striving, or *jihād*. *Taqwā* is doing good; *jihād* is overcoming evil.

We have stated earlier that behavior is a key issue in contemporary Islām. Muslims are discussing the possible distinction between "genuine believer" (*muʾmin*) and "nominal adherent" (Muslim). Some are making the point that in one sense it is easy to be a Muslim, because you can be born as one, and you can remain a casual adherent. It is harder to be a genuine believer, that is, a person who really combines believing and practicing (a *muʾmin*). In short, Muslims are looking for new ways to express the old truth that a religion has to mean something to someone who confesses allegiance.

The old truth, of course, is certainly contained in the word *muslim*, properly understood. A true *muslim* is one who surrenders his whole life to God. In the Qurānic sense the term could never be taken as an equivalent to a nominal adherent. A deeply surrendered person (*muslim*) and a deeply committed person (*muʾmin*) are essentially the same thing. Thus the Qurʾān declares (2:177):

> It is not righteousness that ye turn your faces to the East and the West; but righteous is he who believeth in Allāh and the Last Day and the angels and the Scripture and the Prophets; and giveth his wealth, for love of Him, to kinsfolk and to orphans and the needy and the wayfarer and to those who ask, and to set slaves free; and observeth proper worship, and payeth the poor-due. And those who keep their treaty when they make one, and the patient in tribulation and adversity and time of stress. Such are they who are sincere. Such are the God-fearing.

This famous passage wholistically gathers together faith and ritual, virtue and good works, and declares what it means to be a righteous Muslim.

In the following discussion we will briefly comment on the Muslim regard for piety and its content. The larger part of our discussion, however, will be given over to the more controversial issue of *jihād*.

A. The Principle of Piety

Islām holds that all of life should be the service of God, an idea caught up in the term *ʿibādat*, or worship. In its most narrow sense worship is the adoration of God. In a wider sense it is performing the ritual pillars with a spirit of worship. In its widest sense it is the whole life of piety that the Qurʾān calls *taqwā*. The first revelation of the Qurʾān contains the instruction: "Enjoin piety!"

The noted contemporary Muslim scholar, Fazlur Rahman (1919–88), regards *taqwā* as "perhaps the most important single term in the Qurʾān..."[1] A similar term that captures some of the same meaning is righteousness (*birr*). S. Tahir Mahmood calls attention to "the quadruple principles of *adl*, *rahmat*, *fadl* and *muwaddat*—justice, grace, kindness, affection." He says that these are "to guide all aspects of private and public life."[2]

"All aspects" in essence means only one thing—a Muslim believer is to lead a life that is marked by the fear of God. This is a broad concept, wider than specific precepts, deeper than legal regulations. It is the religious attitude itself, expressed in the totality of life. The spirit of Islām stems from the fear of God, and flows into the life of humanity. You may call it morality and ethics, but it is morality and ethics of a special kind—the kind that recognizes the Lordship of God and the servant status and vice-regent function of human beings. It is thankful *taqwā* and humble *birr*.

Modern Muslim reformers, such as the great Muhammad ʿAbduh (d. 1906) have reminded Muslims that the Qurʾān is much more a preachment of morality than it is a textbook of legal regulations. The Qurʾān declares (3:132–135):

And obey Allāh and the messenger, that ye may find mercy. And vie with one another for forgiveness from your Lord, and for a Paradise as wide as are the heavens and the earth, prepared for thee who ward off (evil). To those who control their wrath and are forgiving toward mankind; Allāh loveth the good, And those who when they do an evil thing or wrong themselves, remember Allāh and implore forgiveness for their sins ... and will not knowingly repeat (the wrong) they did.

The Qurʾān defines success in moral terms (3:104):

And there may spring from you a nation who invite to goodness, and enjoin right conduct and forbid indecency. Such are they who are successful.

The Qurʾān asserts that morality cannot remain as an ideal, but must be expressed in specific acts of piety (17:23–7):

The Lord hath decreed, that ye worship none save Him, and (that ye show) kindness to parents ... And lower unto them the wing of submission through mercy, and say: My Lord! have mercy on them both as they did care for me when I was little. Your Lord is best aware of what is in your minds. If ye are righteous, then lo! He was ever-forgiving unto those who turn (unto Him). Give the kinsman his due, and the needy, and the wayfarer, and squander not (thy wealth) in wantonness. Lo! the squanderers were ever brothers of the devils, and the devil was ever an ingrate to his Lord... Slay not the children, fearing a fall into poverty. We shall provide for them and for you. Lo! the slaying of them is a great sin!

And come not near unto adultery. Lo! it is an abomination and an evil way. And slay not the life which Allāh hath forbidden, save with right ... Come not near the wealth of orphans, save that which is better till he come of strength ... Fill the measure when ye measure, and weigh with a right balance; that is meet, and better in the end. (O man), follow not that whereof thou hast no knowledge. Lo! the hearing and the sight and the heart—of each of these it will be asked. And walk not on the earth exultant. Lo! thou canst not rend the earth, nor canst thou stretch to the height of the hills.

The Qurʾān reminds believers that piety must be accompanied by humility (31:17–22):

O my dear son! Establish worship and enjoin kindness and forbid iniquity, and persevere whatever may befall thee. Lo! that is of the steadfast heart of things. Turn not thy cheek in scorn toward folk, nor walk with pertness in the land. Lo! Allāh loveth not each braggart boaster. Be modest in bearing and subdue thy voice. Lo! the harshest of all voices is the voice of the ass. See ye not how Allāh hath made serviceable unto you whatsoever is in the skies and whatsoever is in the earth and hath loaded you with his favours both without and within ...

Whosoever surrendereth his purpose to Allāh while doing good, he verily hath grasped the firm hand-hold.

And finally, the Qurʾān declares that piety stretches from surrender to God to the remembering of God (33:35):

Lo! men who surrender unto Allāh, and women who surrender; and men who believe, and women who believe; and men who speak the truth, and women who speak the truth; and men who persevere (in righteousness), and women who persevere; and men who are humble, and women who are humble; and men who give alms, and women who give alms; and men who fast, and women who fast; and men who guard their modesty, and women who guard (their modesty); and men who remember Allāh such, and women who remember—Allāh prepareth for them forgiveness and a vast reward.

Mohammed Fadhel Jamali[3] illustrates how Muslim thinkers attempt to interpret the Qurānic call to piety. Based on passages of the Qurʾān he suggests moral virtues and actions that a Muslim must cherish and do, and points to several aspects of immorality that a Muslim must particularly avoid. The moral headings are the following:

piety	work
goodness to parents	striving
doing good	readiness
patience	dignity
philanthropy	brotherhood
truthfulness	unity
fulfillment of obligations	moderation
trustworthiness	humility
justice	contentment
mercy	chastity
restraint of anger	reliance on Allāh
and forgiveness	reading and propagation
cooperation	of learning

The qualities and acts that a Muslim must fight against include:

polytheism	cheating in measurement
injustice	lying
hypocrisy	falsehood
pride and arrogance	treachery

corruption	suspicion and spying
transgressions	backbiting
murder	evil gossip about women
adultery	jealousy
false witness	stinginess
embezzlement	wastefulness
	dispute and disagreement

These headings, says Jamali, point to the spiritual values that Muslim societies should support, and they provide the agenda for the moral education that parents and teachers should undertake.The individual sins and the diseases of society that he lists lead us to the next portion of our discussion, the struggle to overcome evil.

B. Jihād

The word *jihād* means exertion or striving. In itself it is a neutral term, but connected with Islām it signifies striving on God's way or struggling against the evils that God forbids. This activity is sometimes listed with the five primary practices of Islām. Since it has a somewhat different nature than the pillars of Islām, it is not formally included in many lists. Nevertheless, the requirement for Muslims is an inescapable one.

Every Muslim is to be a kind of striver (*mujāhid*), that is, a person who struggles for that which is right, against that which is evil. Majid Khadurri states that Muslim jurists "have distinguished four different ways in which the believer may fulfil his *jihād* obligation: by his heart; his tongue; his hands; and his sword."[4] The ordinary distinction today is between the spiritual and physical forms of striving. Spiritually, it means engaging in a battle against sin and Satan in one's own life. This is called "the greater *jihād*." Applied to the physical realm, the exertion means righteous warfare. This is called "the lesser *jihād*." A well-known Ḥadīth reports that the Prophet Muhammad gave top precedence to the greater *jihād*, humanity's spiritual struggle against evil.

Many Muslims realize that the word *jihād* has become a disturbing term for non-Muslims, who connect it with religious extremism and indiscriminate violence. Muslims do not look at it that way. For them the word signifies a positive religious concept, which may be and frequently is misinterpreted either by Muslims themselves or by non-Muslims. A comparison will make the point clear. The term "crusade" is widely used by many people who see no problems with it and employ it innocently to describe peaceful religious gatherings. At the same time, however, when Muslims hear this word, they experience feelings of distress because it conveys to them an old message of religious violence and suffering. Precisely the same is true with the word *jihād*. Muslims use it in a positive sense to signify an important religious truth, while to many others it carries a message of needless religious violence.

1. Jihād and Violence: The Difference and the Connection

Before taking up *jihād* in detail we will attempt to place it in the context of the wider Muslim view of violence. *Jihād* and violence are two different ideas in Islām. They overlap but have their separate spheres. Because they do overlap the two are sometimes wrongly identified. As we have already noted, however, the "greater *jihād*" has nothing to do with violence. It refers to spiritual development. The overlap comes in connection with the "lesser *jihād*."

In Muslim countries as in any other country the general issue of violence falls under governmental law. Violent criminals are punished and indiscriminate violence is prohibited. But the question arises as to when violence is an option or even a necessity for individual citizens or for the Muslim *religious* community. When does violence become necessary? Muslims are not in full agreement regarding the answer to this question, but there is a growing consensus.

The basic Muslim theory on the subject of violence is that it is always the exception and peacefulness is the rule. There are some situations where the use of violence is, in fact, required, but it must always be regarded as a last resort. The controlling principle is established by the second meaning of the term *islām*, which is peace. Muslims are to be peace-loving and peace-makers. They are not to be aggressors against others. When does that situation change? It changes when violence is used against Muslims, and they are attacked.

Muslims hold that if they are attacked by others two additional principles come into play—God's natural law that allows self-defense, and God's revealed command to oppose evil. On the basis of these two principles Muslims may use violent resistance in the following situations:

1. When one's person is attacked;
2. When one's family or friends are attacked; and
3. When one's nation is attacked.

In such cases the principle of self-defense applies, and Muslims argue that it is highly unnatural not to defend oneself, one's family, or one's nation.

The situations mentioned above have nothing to do with *jihād*. However, reactive violence is also permissible in two other situations, and they are connected with the principle of j*ihād*. These two situations are:

4. When one's religion is attacked; and
5. When oppression must be overcome.

In these two cases Muslims hold that the natural principle of self-defense is combined with the divine principle of resistance to evil. For Muslims, self-defense of one's religion is as important as self-defense for one's country. Furthermore, clear cases of injustice and corruption are contrary to God's will and must be opposed. Every effort short of violence itself must be explored and utilized to solve the problem. Finally, if nothing else works, violence is justified. In this way the ideas of permitted violence and the "lesser *jihād*" come together when religion is involved. The "lesser *jihād*" is righteous war, and violence is the instrument of righteous war.

In classical times some Muslims extended the principle of righteous war to Muslim expansionist military campaigns. This, for some Muslims, became the final permitted use of violence:

6. Violent military action is justified for the spread of Islām.

This interpretation is not common among Muslims today, although occasionally it may be resurrected.

In summary, the current Muslim consensus is that reactive violence is appropriate in the following cases: to defend oneself, one's family, one's nation, one's religion, and the oppressed. The defense of one's religion and the oppressed constitute the active elements of the "lesser *jihād*." The "greater *jihād*" involves the entire moral and ethical thrust of Islām.

2. Jihād and the Qurʾān

When we consider the many different ways in which Muslims have looked at *jihād*, we must turn to the Qurʾān for the basis of Muslim teaching. All Muslim approaches utilize the Qurʾān in support of their positions.

The Qurʾān includes a wide range of emphases on the subject of *jihād*, and we may speak of a development of ideas related to the changing condition of Muslims. At first Muslims were in the position of a persecuted minority, but later they were members of a nation-state involved in subjugating its enemies. The Qurʾān responds to these different conditions, and therefore it reflects a range of ideas on the topic. That range of ideas enables contemporary Muslims to be selective and to emphasize those themes that reason and conscience commend as appropriate for today's conditions. In the Ḥadīth, however, the approach is far less flexible. The Traditions stem from the period when Islām was expanding, and they focus much more on *jihād* as righteous warfare in the interest of territorial expansion than they do on *jihād* as spiritual struggle.

We should also note that the culture context of the Qurʾān is a contributing factor to the early Muslim understanding of *jihād*. The customs of Muhammad's time, related to fighting and warfare, were quite harsh. Violence was a mark of the times. Individual valor and success in tribal warfare were glorified. There were modifying factors such as sacred months when no warfare was permitted, but in general fighting was accepted as a necessary part of life. As fighters, then, early Arab Muslim forces surged into surrounding territories and conquered them. It was natural for these early warriors to interpret *jihād* primarily in terms of righteous warfare, extended to the acquisition of territory and booty. The "lesser *jihād*," as it were, had become the "greater *jihād*," reversing the prophetic emphasis. It was the Muslim ascetics and mystics who kept alive the basic teaching of spiritual struggle.

248

Thus the cultural and the political context of early Islām was an instrumental factor in the interpretation of the broad range of ideas available in the Qurʾān. In the context of today's world the vast majority of contemporary Muslims are choosing to emphasize *jihād* as spiritual struggle. They are seeking to restore the principle of the "greater *jihād*" to its position of primacy in Islām. A small minority of extremists are making the task a difficult one.

When we examine *jihād* in the Qurʾān, we may identify three major groups of passages on the subject. The first group recommends the general virtue of striving. The striving should be a personal struggle for salvation (29:6). It should be a dedicated striving that takes precedence over other loyalties, including family, tribe, and possessions (9:24). Wealth and lives should be sacrificed to the service of God (49:15). The overarching command is 22:78:

> And strive for Allāh with the endeavor which is His right ... He hath named you Muslims ... that ye may be witnesses among mankind.

In these and similar passages the emphasis is on the moral life of believers.

Another group of passages deals with the response to the problem of persecution and oppression. God will allow believers to suffer trials such as these in order to reveal those among them who will remain faithful in striving (47:13). It is permissible to resist the persecutors violently (22:39), but forgiveness is better if the opponents desist (8:38f.) The fighting must cease the moment the persecution is ended (2:193). On no account are Muslims to begin hostilities, for "Allāh loveth not the oppressors" (2:190). In the case of oppression, however, Muslims should always be ready to heed the cries of the distressed (4:75):

> How should ye not fight for the cause of Allāh and of the feeble among men, and of women and children who are crying ... O give us from Thy presence some defender!

The outcome of the Battle of Badr is sufficient to remind all believers that God is with those who defend people against the unrighteous: "Ye Muslims slew them not, but Allāh slew them... Allāh (it is) who makes weak the plan of the disbelievers" (8:17f.)

A third set of passages calls for fighting as a means of establishing the religion of Allāh. Warfare may be distasteful, but it is necessary at times (2:216). So be ready to "fight in the way of Allāh" (2:244). When is fighting required? It is necessary especially in the struggle against idolatry and polytheism. Treaties may be made with polytheists, and they should be honored (9:4), but it must be remembered that the great task of Islām is to uproot idolatry (4:76), and in the absence of treaties idolaters should be slain unless they repent (9:5). All members of the *umma* must be ready to take their share in these struggles (9:40). They should not fear loss, for those slain on the path of Allāh are not to be counted as dead but as living (3:169), and such death is really a victory that brings its own reward (4:71).

Apart from the evil of polytheism, *jihād* does not enter into the issue of interreligious relations. The overriding principle is established by the famous verse: *"Let there be no compulsion in religion"* (2:25). When he began his career in the city of Medina, the Prophet Muhammad provided the model for this principle by establishing a social compact with the Jews and unbelievers. The Qurᵓān declares the words that he spoke: *"Unto you your religion, and unto me my religion"* (109:6).

From these and similar passages the classical and contemporary interpretations of the religious duty of *jihād* emerged. The classical interpretation concentrated on religio-political warfare for the expansion of the Islāmic domain, and dealt with the treatment of religious minorities. The contemporary view has two opposite approaches. The moderate approach de-emphasizes the "lesser *jihād*" in favor of the "greater *jihād*"; that is, it concentrates on spiritual struggle, the theme of justice, and the principle of peace. The contemporary radical view, very much of a minority approach, supports the use of violence as an ordinary method for overcoming evil, whether that be the evil of Muslims or non-Muslims. We will examine each of these interpretations in turn.

3. The Classical Interpretation of Jihād

Muslims in the classical age of Islām emphasized the role of the "lesser *jihād*" in establishing an earthly realm where God's rule would prevail. They believed that Islām had a universal mission to establish such a realm, and that this could not happen without political control which, in turn, required military action. *Jihād* was interpreted as the divinely appointed duty to engage in such aggressive warfare. To underline this theory the world was divided into two entities, the "House of Islām" (*dār al-Islām*) and the "House of War" (*dār al-ḥarb*). At first the "House of War" was interpreted as being anywhere where polytheism reigned, but later its meaning was modified to refer only to places where polytheistic rulers did not allow Muslims to practice their faith freely.

On this basis, although it was applied only intermittently, *jihād* became an accepted instrument of Muslim policy. The principle was frequently abused by cruel and predatory regimes seeking possessions, power, and plunder, often being used by Muslims against other Muslims. This fact, however, did not lessen the classical conviction that *jihād* as righteous warfare was an appropriate concept, even for the spread of Islām. This view is represented by a modern Muslim, Ali Issa Othman, who declares,[5] "The spread of Islām was military. There is a tendency to apologize for this, and we should not. It is one of the injunctions of the Qurʾān that you must fight for the spreading of Islām." Similarly Professor Fazlur Rahman suggests that given the Muslim goal of building a just society on earth: "*Jihād* becomes an absolute necessity. How can such an ideological world-order be brought into existence without such a means?"[6] Thus, classical Muslims accepted the lesser *jihād* as a God-blessed means for establishing the Muslim domain.

In the course of time, jurists such as Al-Māwardī (d. 1058) constructed an ideal theory of valid religious war and laid down detailed rules and regulations for its conduct. Traditional Muslims today take satisfaction in the theory as the most humane expression possible of a necessary evil. Afif al-Tabbarah expresses the viewpoint of many when he says: "Islām permits war but keeps it within the limits of mercy ..."[7] The regulations deal with such issues as the appropriate occasions for *jihād*. The crucial requirement is that only the acknowledged leader of the full and united Muslim community has the authority to call for or declare *jihād*. It cannot be the indiscriminate decision of an individual or a small group.

In addition, the regulations deal with such issues as the relation of fighting to children, the aged, and women (do not harm them), the relation to nature (do not kill animals or despoil crops), the issue of cruelty (avoid it), the question of treaties (keep your promises), the issue of captured territory (it belongs to all

Muslims but is regulated by the caliph), the issue of booty (one-fifth to the general treasury, four-fifths divided), the issue of prisoners (no killing if a safe-conduct is granted), the question of fraternization with occupied peoples (avoid it, and put military camps outside the cities), and the problem of non-Arabs desiring to become Muslims (they must become associate members of an Arab tribe).8 Along with these regulations governing *jihād*, a host of associated regulations regarding the conduct of the ideal Muslim state were also developed.

An important section of the regulations had to do with people of other religions, and the rights of non-Muslims in politically controlled Muslim states. In the case of "people of the book," such believers are to be left alone as long as they pay tribute and do not rebel. Polytheists were to be invited to repent and to accept monotheism prior to engaging them in battle. Gradually, as Islām expanded, its principle of accommodation and toleration was also extended unofficially to include adherents of religions other than Christianity and Judaism. This accommodation was practical and necessary if Muslims were to administrate multicultural and multi-religious societies. Thus, in South Asia for example, Hindus, Buddhists and others were included in a middle territory between the "House of Islām" and "House of War" concepts. The ideological basis of the modification was the idea that the doctrine of the unity of God was implicitly present in these belief systems.

The relation of violent action to religious apostasy is a separate and special issue. Apostasy (*irtidād*) refers to the forsaking of Islām by expressing disbelief after one has become a believer. In the Qurʾān the punishment for such a greatly sinning person is left in the hands of God and is delayed until the Day of Judgment.9 In the Ḥadīth, however, there is a change of approach, and the punishment takes place in this life, with the *umma* responsible for implementing it. Classical doctrine picks up its interpretation from the Ḥadīth rather than from the Qurʾān. Apostasy is viewed as equivalent to blasphemy and treason. The apostate (*murtadd*) is to be given three days to repent and if the individual does not do so, a male is to be killed and a female is to be placed in confinement. If for some reason this is not possible or desirable, social sanctions are to be applied, including divorce, loss of property and inheritance, and the forsaking of family relationships. In the matter of insult against one of the prophets of God, the blaspheming person should be killed. If the person causing the insult later repents, the punishment may be remitted, for "God is the Forgiving, the Merciful."[10] In most Muslim societies today the law of apostasy is set aside, Muslims generally preferring the Qurānic approach that leaves the issue in the hands of God. As one authority puts it,

> "Not only is there no punishment for apostasy provided in the Book, but ... the Word of God clearly envisages the natural death of the apostate. He will be punished only in the Hereafter.[11]

In some areas the traditional law of apostasy, however, remains a factor of considerable consequence, and some voices are still raised in support of its application.[12]

The classical doctrine of *jihād* was related to a specific period and to particular circumstances in early and medieval Islām. Traditional Muslims today accept this legal interpretation of *jihād* as part of the "official" legacy of the community. Since many of its provisions have been bypassed by modern developments, however, much of the material is ignored, even where it is known. It is not formally rejected, but is allowed to stay in the background. In periods of crisis revivalist leaders may attempt to remind believers of certain aspects of the doctrine in the interests of producing a particular response. On the whole, such occasional efforts do not have a long-term effect because the discussion of *jihād* has now moved beyond classical conditions. In dealing with the issue today we may speak of two trends: the contemporary moderate view, and the contemporary radical approach.

4. The Contemporary Moderate View

Many contemporary Muslims emphasize spiritual struggle as "the bottom line" implication of *jihād*. They regard the rules established for the medieval period of Muslim empires as outdated and inappropriate for the needs of contemporary Muslims. In any event, it is not possible to call for a collective holy war because there is no single leader of the Muslim community who has the authority to issue the call. There is no clear mechanism for achieving consensus on the matter, and so-called "Islāmic Jihad" groups have no right to take this authority to themselves. In addition, their extremist methods that involve violence against the innocent have no basis in Islāmic law. In the moderate view *jihād* is still necessary, but it must now be directed toward two issues: the individual's struggle for piety, and society's struggle for justice.

The call to emphasize the "greater *jihād*" of spiritual struggle has been eloquently expressed by a Beirut professor, Yusuf Ibish, who declares,

> The Greater *Jihād* is fighting one's animal tendencies. It is internal rather than external: striving in the path of God to overcome one's animal side. Man shares with animals certain characteristics which, if let loose, make him a very dangerous beast. To bring these passions under control, that is what *Jihād* means. Man has a tendency to overestimate himself—and to underestimate his spiritual potential. He has a tendency to control and exploit his environment and other human beings. *Jihād* is essentially against such tendencies.

> The Lesser *Jihād*—fighting on behalf of the community, in its defense—is a duty incumbent on a Muslim provided he is attacked. A man has the right to defend his life, his property, and he has to organize himself along these lines.

> Of course, one can produce incidents in history and ask whether in fact the principle of self-defense applies. It is true that Muslims have waged wars: wars of conquest, wars in the ordinary sense, often not at all related to religion or faith. But this indicates that some Muslims have not exercised the Greater *Jihād*.[13]

In the same vein Ghulam Parwez, a modern Pakistani exegete of the Qurʾān warns Muslims not to view *jihād* as a fight to gain wealth or dominion, for God wills only that righteousness, fairness, and truth be established on earth. He says: "The believer's total life is *djihād* to bring his human worthiness and spirit on an increasingly higher level."[14]

Sūfi Muslims apply the concept of *jihād* to the internal struggle of the soul (*nafs*) against evil. As part of that struggle the lower self must be killed, and by this internal *jihād* the believer attains the same status as a physical martyr.[15] Al-Jilānī (d. 1166), a famous Sūfi saint (whom we will introduce more fully in a later chapter), put it this way:

> Each time you struggle against your lower self ... and overcome it and slay it with the sword of opposition, God restores it to life and it contends with you again and demands of you desires and delights, whether forbidden or permissible, so that you must return to struggle and compete with it in order to carry off everlasting reward. This is the meaning of the Prophet's saying ... "We have returned from the lesser *jihād* (war) to the greater *jihād* (self-control)." He meant, by this,

struggle with the Self because it is always there, and because of its continuation in lusts and pleasures, its obstinate persistence in rebellion.[16]

This kind of Sūfi thinking on the primary *jihād* is carried over in the reflections of many modern Muslims.

In addition to stressing individual spiritual struggle, the contemporary modern Muslim also argues that there is a legitimate form of social *jihād*—that is, the overcoming of the evils of society. Fighting for the cause of God is the same as fighting for justice, because the cause of God is justice. This should be understood as a peaceful striving, using the structures for change and improvement that are available in any nation.

> The cause of God is the cause of right and justice. Every fight in the cause and support of faith is a fight in the cause of God, and every fight to drive away oppression and support the oppressed against the oppressor, or to support right and justice, is a fight in the cause of God.[17]

From this perspective we see that the interpretation of the cause of God has changed from a struggle for domain to a struggle for justice.

At the background of this moderate view is a high concern to establish Islām as a religion of peace, a Muslim desire that we will come back to again and again. Muslims do not appreciate the stereotype of "fanatic" and "extremist." Quite a few Muslims are reluctantly willing to accept the caricature of "fundamentalism" because they are committed to spiritual fundamentals, but they do not feel that they deserve the other stereotypes. They know that there are some fanatics and extremists in the community, but they do not feel that extremism is only a Muslim problem. They believe that the mainstream of Muslims stands for the principle of peace.

> This is what Islām has always been working for, and the relations of Muslims with others are primarily based on peace and confidence. Islām refuses the killing of people merely because they embrace a different faith, nor does it allow Muslims to fight against those who disagree with them on religious questions.[18]

In this view the concept of peace provides the basic frame of reference for thinking about *jihād*. One of the early representatives of the contemporary moderate approach, Maulavi

Chiragh Ali (d. 1895), gave this interpretation:

> All the fighting injunctions of the Qurʾān are, in the first place, only for self-defense, and none of them has any reference to making war offensively. In the second place, they are transitory in their nature. The Muhammadan common law is wrong on this point where it allows unbelievers to be attacked without provocation.[19]

Maulāna Abūl Kalām Āzād (d. 1958) echoed and expanded on this opinion. He regarded the principles of unity and peace as the most genuine expression of true religion. "If the world would understand the spirit of this message, how could men continue combatting each other only on account of disparity of views on faith and works?"[20] He demonstrated his point of view in India through his companionship with Mahatma Gandhi and his irenic leadership in the multi-religious society of his nation.

5. The Contemporary Radical Approach

The contemporary radical approach involves a small number of Muslims but takes a large share of the world's attention. When in 1994 the foreign minister of a Middle Eastern nation was badly wounded in an attempted assassination he was quoted as saying from his hospital bed, "This has nothing to do with religion." He implied that what had happened in no way represented true Islām. The assassins believed the very opposite. They believed not only that they represented true Islām, but also that they had the ability to recognize those who were not true Muslims, the right to judge them, and the duty to punish them!

In taking this position the present-day radical interpreters of *jihād* are reviving a minor stream of thought that runs through Muslim history and resurfaces from time to time. This point of view calls for separation from evildoers and, if necessary, their destruction. For convenience sake we may refer to them as extremists. They hold that Islām and *shirk* (idolatry) cannot coexist in this world. Human oppressors, whether corrupt rulers or immoral people, are all guilty of *shirk*—placing other things above God and His will—and they must be fiercely opposed. Furthermore *jihād*, which they interpret as legitimate religious violence, is the God-mandated instrument for liberation from corruption and oppression.

These points are aptly summarized by Syed Qutb (d. 1966), the influential Egyptian scholar and revivalist. He views *jihād* in the above sense as a means for liberation and declares,

> Truth and falsehood cannot coexist on earth. When Islām makes a general declaration to establish the lordship of God on earth and to liberate humanity from the worship of other creatures, it is contested by those who have usurped God's sovereignty on earth. They will never make peace. Then [Islām] goes forth destroying them to free humans from their power... This is the constant situation. The liberating struggle of *jihād* does not cease until all religion belongs to God.[21]

Qutb maintains that the ultimate purpose of militant *jihād* is peace. He declares,[22]

> Peace is the eternal principle; war is the exception which becomes a necessity when there is a deviation from the integration exemplified in the religion of the one God [resulting] in injustice, oppression, corruption and discord.

But there must be no hesitation in using force to uproot evil. This is not merely a defensive movement. The attempt to liberate humanity from powerful evil forces and from man-made systems that are contrary to God's will at times calls for an aggressive and revolutionary use of force. The oppressors and evildoers will not voluntarily leave their seats of power. It is clear that to some Muslims, especially the economically depressed, this argument has been a persuasive one.

6. The Internal Muslim Debate over *Jihād*

We have seen that a strong effort is being made by Muslims to reshape the meaning of *Jihād* so as to emphasize the spiritual element and, as much as possible, to eliminate the extremist view.

The extremist view, so well represented by Syed Qutb, has been adopted by a variety of radical groups in contemporary Islām. Some of them are sincere in their Islām, while others are very secular, but all of them are indiscriminate in their use of the term *jihād*. It is being employed to cover a multitude of sins. Most Muslims quietly but firmly resist the extremist point of view. They know that every religion has a problem with that form of mental madness called extremism. They know that Mahatma

Gandhi, Martin Luther King, Anwar Sadat, and Yitzhak Rabin all fell under the attack of extremists in their own religion. They are embarrassed by "The Army of Jihād" movements. They reject their anarchic methods, the harm they bring to the innocent, and the damage to the reputation of Islām. Above all, they oppose the elevation of mindless violence above the spiritual principles of the "greater *jihād*."

The struggle among Muslims to arrive at a new consensus on *jihād* is as intense as it is important. At one end of the spectrum is the militant minority, somewhat increasing in number, which contends that the present atmosphere in the world parallels that of early Islām and that the classical concept of *jihād* as holy war must therefore be revived and employed. At the other end of the spectrum are those who are appalled by the development, vocally resist it, and instead call for a new Muslim *jihād for peace*. In the middle lies the vast body of ordinary Muslims, and it is to them that we turn in conclusion.

Abdulla and Amina represent the relatively silent majority of peace-loving Muslims who dominate Muslim societies in up to a hundred nations of the world. For them *jihād* is basically an ideal religious concept, not a religious activity. It is an approach to life, a feeling for the cause of God. They rarely use the word themselves in their private conversations, although they hear it mentioned in Ramaḍān lectures. It does not enter their daily thinking. It is a theme within their personal faith that they respect, but it is not a flag that they wave in daily life.

Muslims have strong feelings about their faith, however, and when the Prophet Muhammad is maligned or Islām is abused the word *jihād* can be used to arouse their emotions, sometimes to a white-hot fervor. This is the exception, and ordinarily *jihād* remains in the conscience rather than in the conscious mind. Muslims like Abdulla and Amina feel that they should strive on the path of God, and they are trying to do that as best as they know how. They are friendly with the world and the people around them and kind and hospitable to their neighbors. Their neighbors include people of other faiths, but they are equally cordial with them. They strive to express both meanings of the term *Islām*, surrender and peace. The Qurānic verse 41:34 and its high principle expresses their approach:

> The good deed and the evil deed are not alike. Repel the evil deed with one which is better. Then, lo! he, between whom and thee there was

enmity (will become) as though he was a bosom friend.

Our discussion now takes us to the organized path of Muslim behavior, the all-important law of Islām.

Notes

[1]Rahman, *Major Themes*, p. 28.

[2]S. Tahir Mahmood, "Uniform Civil Code and Islāmic Law ," *Religion and Society*, Vol. XXV, No. 4, December 1979, p. 32.

[3]Jamali, *Letters*, pp. 75–79.

[4]Majid Khadurri, *War and Peace in the Law of Islām* (Baltimore: Johns Hopkins Press, 1955), p. 56.

[5]Interview by Charis Waddy, January, 1969, in Waddy, *The Muslim Mind* (London: Longman, 1976), p. 94.

[6]Rahman, *Themes*, p. 63.

[7]*The Spirit of Islām*, tr. by Hasan T. Shoucari; rev. by R. M. Baalbaki (Beirut, 1978), p. 356.

[8]John A. Williams, *Themes of Islāmic Civilization*, pp. 266–74.

[9]Cf. 2:2;7; 3:86-91; 4:137; 5:54; and 9:67. Some Muslim commentators argue that 4:91 and 9:llf. signify punishment on earth. Others argue, from the principle of abrogation, that God has replaced the lenient passages with the stricter ones.

[10]F. A. Klein, *The Religion of Islām* (London: Curzon Press, 1906), p. 181. Cf. W. Heffening, "Murtadd," *EI*², VII, pp. 635f. Heffening cites Al-Shāfiʿi, *Kitāb al-umm*, as a prime source of the teaching.

[11]S. A. Rahman, *Punishment of Apostasy in Islām* (Lahore: Institute of Islāmic Culture, 1972), p. 54.

[12]The Salman Rushdie affair had to do with insult against a prophet; the examples of sanctions against apostates are less notorious but more numerous.

[13]Waddy, *Muslim Mind*, p. 95.

[14]Maʿarif, iv, 489; quoted by J. M. S. Baljon, *Modern Muslim Koran Interpretation* (Leiden: E. J. Brill, 1961), pp. 108f.

[15]Syed Ali Ashraf, "The Inner Meaning of the Islāmic Rites," in Nasr, *Islāmic Spirituality*, p. 129. Islāmic tradition usually speaks of the physical martyr (*shahīd*). The martyr experiences no more pain in being killed than one experiences from a sting. He is forgiven his sins at the first shedding of blood and is admitted directly to Paradise. Thus he is preserved from the questioning in the grave and the ordeal of the Judgment. A ruby crown of honor is placed on his head, and he is the recipient of special heavenly privileges. Ashraf attempts to spiritualize this physical picture. A true Muslim is a spiritual *shahīd*.

[16]John A. Williams, *Themes*, p. 281.

[17]Al-Tabbarah, *Spirit of Islām*, p. 356.

[18]Ibid., p. 353.

[19]E. Sell, *The Faith of Islām*, p. 453. Sell quotes Chiragh Ali's, *Reforms Under Moslem Rule*, pp. 16–17.

[20]Azād, *Tarjumān*, ii, pp. 173f.

[21]Yvonne Haddad, "Sayyid Qutb: Ideologue of Islāmic Revival," in John L. Esposito, ed., *Voices of Resurgent Islām* (New York: Oxford, 1983), p. 82.

[22]Ibid., p. 83.

13

My Muslim Friend Lives by the Law

Recently Abdulla has become rather upset. He and his friends have been carrying on long and sometimes heated discussions over their usual evening cup of tea. Often Abdulla returns home from these conversations with a worried look on his face.

What Abdulla and his friends have been talking about is the critical issue of the Law of Islām, the *sharīʿa*. They have been debating the questions of how to understand it, how to preserve it, and how to apply it in the face of new conditions. The discussions have been so spirited because they know the importance of the *sharīʿa* for Islām. Almost every Muslim knows it because next to the Qurʾān itself the *sharīʿa* is the most precious possession of the Muslim community. There are differences of opinion about the application of the *sharīʿa* in Muslim life, and various approaches are to be found in the Muslim world today. But there is no difference of opinion about its essential significance, and to understand Muslim faith and feeling it is necessary to understand the *sharīʿa*—what it is and how it works. We will begin by discussing the law feeling in Islām.

A. The Law Feeling

Muslims believe that they should regulate their lives according to the Law of Islām. Two attitudes flow together in this belief: the desire to live according to God's will, and the desire for practical and successful behavior in this world. The world is a real place, and one has to live in it practically. At the same time, it is also God's world, and one has to live in it as God wishes. How are these two things to be put together? How can one live in a way that is at the same time pious and practical? Muslims believe that the Law of Islām, the *sharīʿa*, provides the answer. It offers a framework for living in this world that is both pragmatic and God-pleasing. The *sharī'a* is therefore viewed as a special blessing of God. It is a precious possession that Muslims are to respect, adhere to, and guard with the greatest of care.

The Muslim attitude toward the Law of Islām is as much a matter of feeling as it is an element of religious knowledge. Abdulla's wife and children may not be able to explain very much about the *sharī'a* and how it came to be. Abdulla, who is himself a lawyer, has more knowledge. Yet he too is not a *sharī'a* scholar, and he may not be able to provide a full explanation of Islāmic religious law. Nevertheless, the family of Abdulla, like other Muslim families, lives by the law. It does so almost instinctively. Without thinking about it, the members of the family obey its commands and carry out its obligations in their daily life. They, as it were, *feel* the law.

A day in the life of Abdulla will illustrate the point. He rises early at the sound of the morning call to prayer and first takes care of his bathroom needs in the manner *prescribed* by the Law. Then he carefully performs the dawn prayer, as *prescribed*. After breakfast he hurries his children off to the religious education school, again *as prescribed*. On the way to work he remembers that he is short of cash for the shopping he has to do in the evening. So he stops at a bank and makes a withdrawal from a current account; he holds no savings account, for the Law *prohibits* the giving and receiving of interest. The *bismillāh* goes through his mind as he enters his office.

His first case in the morning session of the court has to do with a theft. A man has broken into the house of one of Abdulla's friends and has stolen some jewelry. The court follows civil law and not the *sharī'a* code. But Abdulla knows that the *prescribed* Qurānic punishment for theft is a rigorous one—cutting off the hand—and therefore he is seeking not only the recovery of the stolen property but also a stiff penalty for the robber. After lunch two amiable Muslim friends visit Abdulla in his office, seeking advice on a proposed contract. One man wishes to purchase some coconuts from the other man before they are fully ripe. Abdulla informs them that even though the law of the land permits the deal, the *sharī'a* prohibits such an arrangement, for it violates the principle of mutual satisfaction. After the coconuts ripen, one of the two parties to the agreement will surely be disappointed by the result!

In the evening Abdulla omits his usual tea date with his friends and hurries home instead. An important family matter has arisen. His younger brother, Musa, is visiting him. Musa is the guardian of a young girl, Ayesha, a distant relative. Since a suitable proposal has come, he wants to arrange her marriage, but first he wishes to obtain his elder brother's advice. Abdulla asks Musa many questions. Is the proposed bridegroom really a proper match for Ayesha? The Law *prescribes* that he be a good and righteous man. Is he a Muslim? The Law *requires* it. Is there any impediment to his marriage? If there is an incurable disease, it must be revealed. What is Ayesha's age? The Law does not establish a minimum age, but cohabitation is *prohibited* before puberty. Is the proposed bridegroom a blood-relative and, if so, how near is the relationship? The *prohibited* degrees are clearly laid down in the Law. Carefully Abdulla draws on his knowledge and advises Musa in this important and delicate matter. After the evening meal Musa leaves happily. He is now clear on what he must do. Abdulla is also clear on what he must do before he retires for the night. For the fifth and last time of the day he performs the prayer, as *prescribed.*

Charles Le Gai Eaton, a Swiss-born Muslim, sums up the law feeling of Muslims. Some people, he says, may be puzzled when told that law rather than theology is the principal religious science in Islām.

> But for the Muslim there is no problem in knowing what to believe; his concern is with what to do under all circumstances in order to conform to the Word of God and to walk without stumbling on the road to Paradise.

Therefore, he goes on to say, in Islāmic history "the crystallization of the Qurānic message and the Prophet's example into a body of livable law has been the supreme adventure."[1] Whereas other religious traditions may emphasize an individual's interior faith, Islām is more concerned with providing a unified structure for pious behavior.

> The Law does not invade the privacy of man's inwardness, the relationship of the human soul to God, nor is it concerned with the way in which each individual interprets the basic spiritual teachings of the religion ... But it provides a framework of social and psychological equilibrium within which each individual can follow his particular vocation.[2]

Asaf A. Fyzee (d. 1985), a noted Indian Muslim legal scholar, echoes this opinion. He was naturally enthusiastic about the Law but also in touch with the ordinary Muslim believer's emotion when he suggested that the *sharīʿa* is the soul of the Muslim and the distilled essence of Islāmic civilization. He names it "the central core of Islām."[3]

B. The Law Is the Way of Life

Having made the point that there is a profound law feeling in Muslim hearts, it is essential to add that the Law itself is very real, concrete, and precise. We must define what it is, seek its source, and ask where it is found and what it covers.

1. What is the *Sharīʿa*?

The word *sharīʿa* means "road," "the clear path," "the way to the watering place." The word comes from the Qurʾān (45:18), where God declares:

And now We have set thee ... on a clear road of (Our) commandment, so follow it.

Anwar Qadri translates the same words as "the right way of religion," while A. J. Arberry uses the phrase "the open way of the Command." However it is translated, to the Muslim the meaning is clear. God has graciously demarcated a spiritual path that humans should follow. There is an implicit connection of this verse with the first chapter of the Qurʾān where believers are urged to pray: "Lead us in the straight path, not the path of those who earn Thine anger nor of those who go astray."

Over the years Islām has interpreted the meaning of "right way" by applying it to the realm of human behavior. It has done so by defining a series of rules and regulations that cover a broad range of subjects, including personal, domestic, ritual, civil, and political affairs. All these regulations gathered together and combined with their underlying principles comprise the *sharīʿa*. The *sharīʿa* is thus *an all-embracing code of life*, worked out in meticulous detail. It does not define every individual human action, but it touches on every area of life.

The Law is regarded as having a divine quality. Commonly

when one hears the word "law," what comes to a hearer's mind is the law of the nation. Every land has a set of laws drawn from human experience, accepted by public agreement, and defined in human legislation, which its citizens should obey. Muslims understand the necessity of such national laws and obey them. But they generally do not think of the *sharī͑a* as a human system. Human beings have certainly given the *sharī͑a* language and force and have worked it out in practice, but the religious law of Islām is not viewed by Muslim believers as the product of human wisdom. It is founded on the Word of God and drawn from the example of the Prophet. The *sharī͑a* therefore is *sacred law*, a higher law, the highway of God's guidance along which Muslims should walk. As such, this all-embracing code of life is also a *code of religious duty*. It is not the believer's choice nor the nation's choice, but it is rather the imperative of *dīn*, the following of God's will. We may therefore define the *sharī͑a* as *the Muslim code of religious duty that embraces all of life*.

2. What is the Origin of the *Sharī͑a*?

The source of Islāmic law is clear in the light of our earlier discussion of Muslim beliefs. Both the law feeling and the actual law have a theological origin, a scriptural foundation, a historical development, and a practical source. We will discuss each of these in turn.

The theological origin of the Law is the basic relation between God and humanity that is governed by the twin poles of Command and Obedience. God is al-Rabb, the Creator-Master-Lord-Ruler-Judge Who gives commands to His creatures, and His commands become laws for His creatures. God is the Master, and a master's will is made known in specific instructions. The opposite of master is servant (*abd*). Islām teaches that Muslims are the servants of God, who surrender to His will and obey His command. Moreover, there is an element of human need and divine mercy in the relationship. Servants need directions to guide them on the path of life, and God is a merciful Master Who provides the needed guidance (*hidayat*). The sum of the guidance constitutes the clear road along which God's servants should walk. The ideas of Master-Command, servant-obedience, and guidance-direction combine to produce the strong Muslim sense of religious duty that underlies and gives birth to the *sharī̄ʿa*. Islām is a religion of law. The *sharī̄ʿa* is the formal expression of this reality, and Muslim obedience to the *sharī̄ʿa*, in turn, reinforces the reality.

The scriptural source of the Law is the Qurʾān, but combined with this undeniable fact is the strong tendency that developed among many interpreters to view the entire Qurʾān as a book of regulations. In view of the divine command-human obedience structure of life that we have sketched, this tendency is hardly unexpected. Actually, as it has often been noted, the legal content of the Qurʾān is quite limited, and perhaps below three percent of its verses have to do with actual legislation. The Qurʾān is much more a message of proclamation and admonition, historical reminders, and moral warnings, than it is a book of law. Nevertheless, scholars made every effort to find in it the practical directions that could be used for the conduct of life in accordance with the will of God. That is why Islāmic jurisprudence (*fiqh*) became the first and foremost religious science in Islām. *Fiqh* means understanding and applying, and it signified the task of seeking out the meaning of life's pattern under God and developing the laws for an ordered existence in accordance with the teaching of the Qurʾān.

The third source of the *sharī̄ʿa* is the fertile combination of Ḥadīth-Qiyās-Ijmāʿ applied to the task of defining pious human behavior. This legal development followed that same basic approach that governed the growth of all of Islāmic thought (as outlined in chapter 9). Four "roots" (*usūl*) or sources controlled the development: Scripture, Tradition, Analogy, and Consensus. If the basic Qurānic root required some elaboration, or if a new situation arose that was not covered by it, the next reference point for law was the Ḥadīth. If the holy scripture and the sacred custom of the Prophet were both silent on an issue, or required fresh application, one could use the method of analogy, which resulted in specific legal judgments. To keep order among the individual legal judgments and to allow the community of faith to exert its common will, the final root of consensus came into play, and it continues to be the most powerful factor in the contemporary Muslim discussion of the *sharī̄ʿa*.

The final cause of Islāmic law is the practical orientation of Muslims. That is evident in the historical development of the *sharī̄ʿa*. Islām seeks answers to practical issues, and Muslims want to know how to deal with critical life problems. Therefore there is a pressure on the *sharīʿa* scholars to find pragmatic answers and solutions to problems as they arise. Although this precious code of life, the *sharīʿa*, has been fixed and is viewed by many as a finished product and unchangeable heritage, the pressure of life produces a need and a demand for new applications based on the eternal principles of the Law. The clear road to the watering place needs continuing definition.

Out of this complex of Muslim understandings is born the *sharīʿa*, the Law of the community, which Fazlur Rahman calls "the most central concept of Islām."[4]

3. Where Is the *Sharīʿa* Found?

Here a difficulty arises because there is no single volume called The Sharīʿa as there is one book called The Qurʾān. The *sharīʿa* is more like a law library than a single book. Its regulations are contained in different collections that have developed through Muslim history, and these are summarized in handbooks. From these handbooks Muslim teachers select and teach its basic requirements. Short explanations of the main laws are often published and distributed. Parents in the home train their children in the ritual and domestic regulations, and so the main aspects of the Law become a passed-on possession of the people and part of their everyday life. Even though ordinary Muslims cannot and do not pick up a book called The Sharīʿa and read it, the *sharīʿa* has become the *habit of Islām*. Its intricacies are the concern of specialist scholars who can be called upon in time of need.

4. What Does the *Sharīʿa* Cover?

Muslims refer to the duties related to God as *ʿibādāt*, and they call the regulations that govern human interaction *muʿāmalāt* (lit., "transactions"). Against the background of this broad distinction the legal scholars arrange the various sections of the Law in different ways. For example, a very broad division has three categories: religious duties or *ʿibādāt*; personal and social affairs; and other areas including criminal, constitutional, administrative, and military matters. The religious duties include prayer, fasting, alms-giving, pilgrimage, and purification. The first basic practice of Islām, the confession of faith, is usually dealt with under theology rather than under law.

The following categories are set up by the school of al-Shāfiʿī, one of the four primary schools of law in Islām:[5] religious duties; contracts; inheritance; marriage and family law; criminal law; war and relations with unbelievers; food laws; sacrifice and the killing of animals; oaths and vows; judicial procedures and evidence; and the liberation of slaves. These categories reveal the wide-ranging nature of the *sharīʿa*.

Another arrangement adapted from a modern Muslim legal scholar[6] presents perhaps the clearest picture of the content of the Law:

(a) Religious Law—(Actions concerning conduct toward God): Prayer; fasting; alms-giving; pilgrimage; and purification.

(b) Family Law—(Actions concerning domestic matters and personal status): Marriage; dowry and divorce; parentage and guardianship; family maintenance; inheritance; bequests and donations; endowments; joint ownership; legal capacity and competence.

(c) Private Law—(Actions concerning business matters): Property matters; trade practices; contracts; civil law and liability.

(d) Public Law—(Actions concerning business matters): Theory and conduct of the state; taxation and labor matters; municipal administration; penal laws; and international affairs.

(e) Judicial Law—Courts; council of state; procedure and evidence.

(f) Other Laws—A group of miscellaneous personal and social laws that touch on different aspects of human behavior and manners.

It is the religious law and the family law that constitutes the living heart of this vast legal material, and it is these two areas that dominate Muslim discussion. As an example of ritual duty and family law, we quote the following:

[The fast is broken] if saliva leaves the mouth and one brings it back into the mouth, even if one moistens a thread in one's mouth and then puts it back in the mouth ... If one swallows something, truly forgetting that one is fasting, it does not break the fast, unless one repeats it, according to the soundest opinion.

[The dowry in marriage] is payable to the bride before the consummation of the marriage, unless she has agreed to take the payment of all or part of it at a later time.[7]

Muslims believe that these and the many other individual regulations of the Law are grounded on a set of eternal principles, and we turn next to the consideration of those basic foundations.

C. The Principles of the Law

The superstructure of the *sharīʿa* is the body of regulations. The foundations are the principles. Since the idea of obedience is central to Islām, all Islāmic principles have a relation to the Law. Some of them, however, are particularly important for the understanding of the *sharīʿa*. They include divine sovereignty; inclusiveness; mutuality and equality; moderation and benefit; rights and obligations; or freedom and limits.

1. Divine Sovereignty

The fundamental principle underlying the *sharīʿa* is the idea that God is the Ruler and we human beings are His subjects. As Sovereign Lord, God must rule and does rule. He directly and actively governs His people. This is true both of individuals and the community. He rules through His power by which He exercises lordship over His creation, and He rules through specific commands, by which He provides the needed laws for the correct conduct of life. "Thinketh man that he is to be left aimless?" (75:36). Thus the Sovereign Ruler is also the Supreme Legislator. As Legislator He gives His subjects adequate prescriptions to carry on their personal and social lives. His subjects are dependent on His power and obey His commands. In this way Islāmic society is viewed as a theocracy (God-rule). Muslims differ as to how this principle is to be worked out in practice, but the ideal is accepted.

God, the only Legislator, has shown the way of felicity to the people whom He has chosen and, in order to enable them to walk in that way, He has shown the precepts which are found partly in the eternal Qurʾān and partly in the sayings and doings of the Prophet, transmitted to posterity by the Companions and preserved in the Sunnah—called Sharīᶜah and the rules thereof called Ahkām ... In the whole system of the sacred principles God being the sole Lawgiver is supreme Sovereign or Hakīm ... Who is All-Powerful and Malik-ul-Mulk [King of Kings] or the Rabb-ul-Alimīn [Lord of the Worlds].[8]

2. Inclusiveness

The Law of Islām is all-embracing. In theory, there is no distinction between sacred and secular. Since God is Sovereign over all things, there is nothing that lies outside the scope of His rule. You cannot say that the mosque belongs to God and the marketplace to humans. As the only Lord, there is no area of life that lies outside His jurisdiction or fails to come under His direction. There is none that does not have a religious dimension, or is exempt from religious duty. All of life is sacred because the totality of life is God's domain.

> The principles and institutions of Islām are all-comprehensive. They include the whole of human existence, emotions, thoughts, actions, economic deals, social relationships, bodily urges, spiritual demands, and every other value ... Religion works as a complete code of life. The Muslim life consists of no dichotomy. In what a Muslim has to do in secular transactions, in his actions for social deals, individual interest, national demands, international brotherhood, nay, in contained relations of human civilization, there is a complete direction, contained in the situations which a Muslim follows ... The name given to the whole system is *Shari'ah*.[9]

This does not mean, as we have already noted, that there are laws for everything in Islām. There are many activities of life for which there are no regulations. The *sharīᶜa* does not prescribe whether Abdulla should travel by plane or bus or camel. It does not tell him which newspaper to read, and which soccer team to favor. When we say that the Law of Islām is all-embracing, it means that there is no area of life that is left out. Thus, the *sharīᶜa* is not confined to matters of spiritual practice. It teaches you how to pray, but more than that. There is no part of one's life, individual or social, that is not under God's government.

The principle of comprehension is clear. But something may be true and yet not easy to apply. There is much difference of opinion among Muslims regarding the *application* of this principle in the complex world of today.

3. Mutuality and Equality

We take these two principles together because they are closely related to each other in Muslim thought.

(a) Mutuality
In Muslim writings this is frequently called the principle of brotherhood. If we coined a new word to describe this principle, it might be *ummaity* (from *umma*, community). To community-mindedness belong the ideas of fellowship, helpfulness, and interdependence. The Qurʾān (3:103) advises the members of the Muslim community,

> And hold fast, all of you together, to the cable of Allāh, and do not separate. And remember God's favour unto you: how you were enemies and He made friendship between your hearts so that ye became brothers by His grace ...

The symbolic expressions of this spirit of solidarity include the unified worship of the pilgrimage and the Muslim greeting: *salaam aleikum* or *masalaam*, "peace be with you."

The principle also has application in Muslim law. It implies that mutual help is a religious duty. Every Muslim should be and must be the friend and protector of every other Muslim. This theory is expressed in many specific laws in the *sharīʿa*. Its spirit is summarized in the words of Abū Bakr, the first successor to the Prophet Muhammad, who declared that Muslims are "brothers in the faith, partners in the sharing of booty, allies against the common foe."[10]

(b) Equality
This principle expresses the Islāmic faith that all human beings are the same in the sight of God Who makes no distinctions among them on the basis of race, color, or status. The equality of all humans before God is symbolized by the prayer of Islām. The *salāt* does not only signify submission before the Almighty, but submission together. All foreheads touch the surface at the same time. If there is to be any distinction, let it be in piety! The Qurʾān says (49:13): "Lo, the noblest of you in the sight of Allāh is the best in conduct!"

The only exceptions to this principle are in those areas where the Qur'ān itself has established certain divinely ordained patterns that must be maintained. Such patterns include the relation between husbands and wives; the relation between parents and children; some economic matters including the making of wills and bequests, and the payment of *zakāt*; the punishment of slaves; and the matter of witnesses in court. Apart from these reserved areas, the formal principle of equality is to be observed.

The principle of equality has direct application in Muslim administration of justice. All believers are to have equal access to the means of justice, and all should be treated equally in the courts. 'Umar ibn Khattāb, the second Successor to the Prophet Muhammad, instructed a judge in these terms: "Let them all be equal before thee in respect of thy justice and thy tribunal, lest the powerful put their hope in thy partiality, and the weak despair of thy justice."[11] In order to express this principle, rulers in Saudi Arabia today continue to set apart a time when ordinary people can approach and make known their needs or complaints.

The principles of mutuality and equality are almost as difficult to apply in practice as the principle of comprehension. Social distinctions do exist among Muslims in different cultures, and brotherhood frequently collapses into disagreements and strife between believers. Muslims themselves readily admit that the ideal is frequently broken, but they maintain that the principle remains valid and continues to be the goal toward which humans must strive.

4. Rights and Obligations

The principle of rights and obligations implies that human freedom is not absolute. What limits it is the rights of others. The rights of others not only imply a limitation, but they also impose an obligation or responsibility. In dealing with the principle of rights and obligations/responsibilities, Muslim scholars discuss especially the rights of God and the rights of humans. In recent time, however, the rights of animals and creation have been added.[12] The Muslim discussion insists that the theory of rights is not the expression of natural law, nor a byproduct of human experience, but rather it reflects God's theory, His will as the source of human law. Thus human rights and obligations are set within the framework of moral and religious duty. The religious duty of forgiveness may at times imply the abandonment of what is called a human right.[13]

According to this approach, God Himself has certain rights. He has the right to be believed in, to be worshipped, and to be obeyed. These rights of God, in turn, place upon human beings a reciprocal obligation to carry out the basic duties of religion (*ʿibādat*), owing to God.

Every individual person has certain rights. He or she has the right to fulfill personal needs and interests, to make use of the creation, to seek for prosperity, and to enjoy freedom under justice. These rights result in certain things being allowable, but they also place upon the individual the obligation to respect the rights of other persons.

Groups of humans also have rights. Your family, the community, the whole society—all have rights that involve mutual responsibilities. Only if these rights and obligations are properly regulated so as to assure their observance can general society prosper. It is for this reason that in Islām "obligations are also classified by legal theory."[14]

All God's creatures have rights. In fact, the whole creation itself has rights that cannot be encroached. Those rights involve human beings in limitations and responsibilities. An example will illustrate the point. It is not only a civil disaster for the public to cut down all the trees of the forest, but it is also a sin, for it is a spiritual obligation to creation itself and a religious duty to God to maintain a proper balance in nature. That is the true the service of God's vice-regents.

5. Moderation

For those who are not attuned to the idea of religious law, the *sharīʿa* might seem to be immoderate in its demands. In the Muslim view of the *sharīʿa*, however, a tolerant moderation expresses its spirit. Muslims insist that the *sharīʿa* is realistic, and that it is correctly geared to human nature and human ability. It is at the same time not too demanding and not too slight. The commands of God are geared to the reality that humans have both moral strength and moral weakness. God does not demand what a person cannot do. The Qurʾān says (2:18f), "Allāh desireth for you ease; He desireth not hardship for you..." This verse was revealed in connection with the fast, and it was related to situations where people could not readily carry out the command as required. In Muslim interpretation it is elevated into a general truth, namely, that God does not expect the impossible. At the same time He demands all that a person can do; the commands of God are attainable, but they must be attained. The Qurʾān (64:16) also declares, "So keep your duty to Allāh as best ye can, and listen and obey and spend; that is better for your souls..." Again, it declares (62:11), "...Strive for the cause of Allāh with your wealth and your lives. That is better for you, if ye did but know."

The Qurʾān carries the spirit of moderation into various requirements of religion. It is understood that all Muslims should make the pilgrimage to Mecca, but the poor and the sickly will be exempt from the requirement. Of course, the washing before the prayer needs to be observed properly, but where there is no water a symbolic use of sand-cleansing may substitute. Certainly, fasting is required of all believers, but the very young and the very old must be excused. A passage that is sometimes quoted in this connection is 2:143, which says: "Thus we have appointed you a middle nation." Muslims believe that the Prophet Muhammad also adopted the approach of "the middle way," and they regard the *sharīᶜa* as being constructed on this principle. Its laws take into account the frailty of humans and do not demand what is unnatural, unreasonable, or impractical. The regulations concerning the number of daily prayers illustrate the point. One hundred daily prayers would be impossible, while one prayer would have no challenge; but to pray five times a day is both demanding and possible, and it thus provides a good spiritual discipline.

Briefly put, the *sharīᶜa* is viewed as a practical guide for carrying out God's will in the world, not an impossible ideal. It not only *should* be obeyed, but because of the principle of moderation it *can* be obeyed.

6. Benefit

Closely related to the idea of moderation is the principle of benefit. The *sharīᶜa* is to contribute to human welfare. It is to be utilitarian for human beings, both in this world and for the next world.

To appreciate the idea of benefit it must be linked with the familiar concept of God's gracious guidance. God is a Beneficent Guide and His Law is also intended to be beneficial. To Adam and his wife God had said (20:123), "Whoso follows my guidance he will not go astray or come to grief. But he who turns away from remembrance of Me, his will be a narrow life." The revelation of God's will, expressed in the form of *sharīʿa*, is intended as a favor to humanity, and obedience to it will bring further favor and avert His anger. Therefore Muslims are encouraged to pray (1:5–7): "Show us the straight path, The path of those whom Thou hast favoured, Not (the path) of those who earn Thy anger, Nor the path of those who go astray."

What precisely is the benefit? For this world it provides a structure for successful living, both individually and corporately. The Qurʾān promotes the goal of success and points to the method of achieving it (5:35): "O ye who believe! Be mindful of your duty to Allāh, and seek the way of approach to Him and strive in His way, in order that you may succeed." "His way" is outlined in the clear road of the *sharīʿa*. Under its guidance individuals can lead lives that are balanced and disciplined, families can organize their relationships, and societies can structure corporate life according to God's pattern. Mawdūdī combines the idea of rights and obligations, moderation, and benefit in the following words:

> There is nothing in it [*sharīʿa*] which tends to waste your powers, or to suppress your natural needs or desires, or to kill your normal urges and emotions. Man has the right, and in some cases, the bounden duty, to fulfil all his genuine needs and desires and make every concerned effort to promote his interests and achieve success and happiness—but ... in such a way that not only the interests of other people are not jeopardized, and no harm is caused to their striving for the fulfillment of their rights and duties, but there should be all possible social cohesion, mutual assistance and cooperation among human beings in the achievement of their desires.15

The benefit of the Law is not only this-worldly. Its ultimate, and by far its greatest blessing, has to do with the next world. The Qurʾān lays heavy stress on this point. Again and again it declares that faithfulness to religious duty yields the fruits of heaven:

> He who obeys Allāh and His messenger, and fears Allāh and keeps duty (unto Him), such indeed are the victorious! (24:52)

The passage does not mention the *sharīʿa* per se, but for Abdulla and his friends obedience to the *sharīʿa* is the same as obedience to God's command. Obedience to God, they believe, will bring them to the Abode of Peace. The final destination of God's "right way" is Paradise:

> Whoso believeth and doeth right, there shall no fear come upon them, neither shall they grieve (6:48).

D. The Operation of the Law

How does the *sharīʿa* work in practice? It works by classifying human actions, by providing a system of administration, and by utilizing different schools of legal opinion.

1. The Classification of Actions

The principles of the Law are applied to human actions, and the science of *fiqh* deals with human conduct. Although Muslims recognize the importance of attitudes, emotions and thoughts, the Islāmic Law does not provide legislation for matters of the heart. Since the laws constitute religious duties, it is clear that internal faith and the will to please God are involved in the acts of obedience. The legal system as such, however, restricts itself to actions and has to do with the realm of outward behavior.

In developing appropriate law for outward behavior Muslim legal scholars have chosen to classify human actions. Behind the classification is the concept of freedom and limits. The majority of actions fall into the area of freedom, but some are specifically controlled and others are limited by the principles that underlie the *sharīʿa*. Two types of classification are the twofold division and the fivefold division. The twofold division is well-known to every Muslim. It sets up two major categories of behavior—that which is forbidden (*harām*) and that which is permitted (*halāl*). Thus, it is *harām* to eat meat that has not been slaughtered in the manner prescribed by the Law, and it is *halāl* to consume meat that has been properly butchered. The terms *harām* and *halāl* are very commonly used in everyday Muslim speech. A mother may say to her child: "Don't do that! That is *harām*!" For ordinary Muslims the terms provide a practical frame for their life under the *sharīʿa*.

The fivefold division of human actions is more complex and is preferred by the legal scholars of Islām. It grades human actions according to the following categories:

(a) Obligatory: The action is a duty (*fard*) because it has been expressly commanded by the Qurʾān and patterned by the *sunna* of the Prophet. The performance of the action is rewarded, the omission is punished. Example: prayer.

(b) Meritorious: The action is recommended and desirable. Its performance is rewarded, but its neglect is not punished. Example: Extra fasting.

(c) Indifferent: The action is neutral. You are free to do it or not to do it. There is neither reward nor punishment. Example: Attending a football match. Most human actions fall into this category.

(d) Blameworthy: The performance of the action is disapproved, but it is not subject to punishment. Example: Doing business on Friday noon.

(e) Forbidden: The action is expressly prohibited and is sinful. Its performance is punishable, its avoidance is praiseworthy. Example: Adultery.

This classification, simple as it may seem, requires careful interpretation by the jurists, for depending on the circumstances, a single action may fall into different categories. A traditional example is the ablution before prayer: it is obligatory; if done three times, it is meritorious; if done three times when there is a shortage of water, it is blameworthy. Another example is the football match: it is indifferent; if the expenditure is too high for the family, it is blameworthy; if it becomes associated with beer-drinking, it is *ḥarām*.

In everyday Muslim life the fivefold division of actions is not so much a conscious paradigm of behavior as it is a subconscious awareness that all of life is related to God's moral will, and all human actions should be carried out in conformity to it.

2. The Administration of the Law

The administration of the *sharī̄a* has two aspects, the informal and the formal. Informal administration or self-administration refers to the inherited custom of Muslim families, which we have already discussed. It is limited to the areas of religious law and personal law. Muslim families do not *always* know what to do in these areas, but they can readily consult local religious authorities for assistance. The influence of these authorities depends entirely on the common consent of the community and the willingness of individuals to consult them.

The matter becomes more complicated in formal *sharī̄a* administration. The general oversight of the entire *sharī̄a* requires special knowledge and skill of learned individuals, and the utilization of their skills depends on the situation within different societies. In nations that have only a minority of Muslim population the political, civil, and economic laws will not be *sharī̄a* laws. In such regions the *sharī̄a* system, if it exists at all, has to operate alongside the law of the nation. Muslims in these areas hang on as tightly as they can to the religious and personal regulations of the *sharī̄a*, but large sections of *sharī̄a* law simply remain unapplied.

Formal *sharī̄a* administration comes more strongly into play in population areas where there is a Muslim majority and it is therefore theoretically possible to consider applying the *sharī̄a* across the board. Yet this too does not result in a common pattern. Some Muslim countries are obviously disinterested in implementing the *sharī̄a* in the public realm, preferring other forms of law. One country, Turkey, even abolished the *sharī̄a* in 1926. Others, such as Pakistan, try to integrate it with secular codes of law. With the limited exception of two or three countries in the world such as Saudi Arabia and Iran, nowhere is the *sharī̄a* administration to be found in its full traditional form. What makes the operation of formal *sharī̄a* administration difficult is the fact that it was developed for a different time and situation.

During the period when the *sharī̄a* was taking shape the Muslim world was nominally united in one empire, ruled by one caliph, and managed by one administration. It was possible to formally maintain a single law system for the whole Muslim community. Accordingly the legal scholars of Islām developed a full-scale *sharīʿa* administration, complete with officials, courts, and procedures, which then became the official tradition of Islām. The same situation, however, now no longer exists in the Muslim world of today. There are many different Muslim nations, each with its own traditions, each with its own view as to how the *sharīʿa* is to fit into the legal system of a modern state, each with its own set of policies, many of which change from time to time as old governments die and new governments are born. The great tradition lingers on, however, both as a memory and as a reality, maintained by a large body of legal scholars and clergy, so that *some* elements of the classical procedures remain in every Muslim context. The formal *sharīʿa* administrative system is still available to meet whatever responsibilities Muslim peoples are willing to assign to it.

According to the traditional *sharīʿa* administration there is a religious court conducted by a judge (*qāḍī*), who has wide-ranging power to make decisions. The judge is selected for his learning and piety, either by official action or by community agreement. His justice is to reflect God's attribute of justice, and his administering of the Law is to be appropriately impartial and fair. He may conduct his cases in the mosque or in his home, following procedures that are customary in the courts. In certain cases he has considerable discretionary power. His judgment is final.

The *qāḍī*, however, may feel the need for advice before reaching his decision. Not only is the *sharīʿa* a vast collection of laws, but the application of those laws has also created an immense volume of precedents. He may therefore consult with the learned of the community who are sometimes called ʿ*ulamā*, sometimes *fuqahāʾ* (jurists; skilled lawyers), and sometimes *muftī* ("one who delivers an opinion"; a legal consultant). A *muftī* who is also a *mujtahid*, a recognized "interpreter" of the Law, has the right to blaze a fresh legal trail, whereas an ordinary *muftī* must stick to the precedents. Any one of these learned doctors of the Law will issue an opinion, *fatwā*, which will ordinarily conclude the matter. The number of such *fatwā(s)* is huge, greatly complicating the legal task. It sometimes happens that *fatwā(s)* will be given on both sides of an issue by different scholars—often stated very forthrightly!—and in such cases the consensus of the living community becomes the final factor. *Fatwā(s)* are important to theology as well as to law, for they provide a means by which the Muslim community can deal with new issues as they arise.

The administration of the Law also includes the aspect of penalties, although this is an area where there is wide discretion and flexibility of procedure. The *sharīʿa* gives special heed to Qurānic penalties (*hadd*; pl. *hudūd*) prescribed for criminal and social misbehavior, mainly homicide, theft, sexual indiscretions, wine-drinking, and apostasy. There are differences of opinion among Muslims today as to whether these laws of punishment are still to be taken literally or whether they should be modernized in terms of their primary intention of deterrence. As a result, there is a broad range of applications in various Muslim societies.

When it comes to the area of religious duty such as prayer, the vast majority of Muslims recognize that laws of punishment are impractical and inappropriate. Classical Islām developed the office of *muḥtasib*, a kind of minor guardian of morality, whose task was to investigate violations of the Law and report them to the authorities. Are you attending the Friday mosque prayer or not? Are you drinking tea during Ramaḍān? Are you allowing a lock of hair to escape your veil? If so beware of the *muḥtasib*! On the whole, contemporary Muslims disapprove of this approach, although one or two conservative Muslim societies have resurrected the function. For most Muslims punishment for religious disobedience belongs to God Who will act in His time, and surely at the Day of Judgment. In the meantime, the quiet disapproval of the Muslim community is the greatest sanction levied against impiety, and it provides the greatest pressure to moral conformity.

In carrying out the administration of the *sharīʿa*, Muslim judges and legal scholars utilize the opinions of the major law schools, and we will briefly describe the most important schools.

3. The Major Schools of Law

By the time the Law was more or less fixed, Islām developed a number of law schools, each school (*madhhab*) having its own emphasis. The law schools have come down to the present age, although few Muslims can readily explain the differences between them. Sunnī Muslims recognize four schools, while Shīʿa Muslims have their own *madhhab*, and there are a number of lesser schools. Abdulla and Amina, for example, follow the Shāfiʿī school of law, but many of their friends follow another school. The law schools differ from each other in their approach to legal interpretation, in some of their judgments, and in their instructions regarding the details of certain regulations, for example, the question of the exact position of the folded hands during the act of prayer.

The four chief law schools of Sunnī Islām gathered around four peerless legal scholars, who are highly venerated: Abū Hanīfa of Kufa in Iraq (d. 767); Mālik ibn Anas of Medina (d. 795); Muhammad al-Shāfiʿī of Egypt (d. 820), and Ahmad ibn Hanbāl of Baghdad (d. 855). Their schools of law reflect their names, namely, the Hanafite School, the Mālikite School, the Shāfiʿīte School, and the Hanbalite School.

Perhaps half of the world's Sunnī Muslims follow the legal tradition of Abū Hanīfa. The earliest of the legal scholars, he emphasized the Qurʾān and the use of private opinion (rāʾy) in interpreting its meaning. He was skilled in the use of analogy and was, in fact, called the "master of the art of qiyās." He is noted for his rather liberal concept of "preference" (istihsān), that is, "the discretionary approval of what seems best." This means that where the literal application of the law might produce inequity, the original provision could be adapted in order to ensure that justice would be done.

Mālik ibn Abas was more doubtful than Abū Hanīfa of the role of private opinion in legal judgments, and he felt that its use must be limited to avoid dangers. He lived in Medina where the conduct of the Prophet was living memory, and therefore he placed great emphasis on the practice of Muhammad as it was understood in the collective wisdom of this core Muslim community. Along with that emphasis on the tradition of the community, he stressed that the primary concern of the Law must be the welfare of the public (istislāh). Followers of his school are found in North and West Africa.

Al-Shāfiʿī is regarded as the greatest figure in the history of Muslim law. He was a systematic thinker, interested in consistency and clarity. He sought for a middle position between overdependence on either reason or community authority, and he found it in a combination of respect for Hadīth and for precedents based on Hadīth. It is the sunna of the Prophet based on Hadīth, together with the Qurʾān, that is decisively important because it is removed from human speculation. Systematic reasoning is allowable, but only to apply the clear precedents found in the Qurʾān and Ḥadīth. Analogy and community consensus have a role, but they occupy a secondary place of importance, and the evidence drawn from Ḥadīth reigns supreme. Adherents of the Shāfiʿī School are found in southern Arabia and India, parts of the Middle East, and in the Far East.

Aḥmad ibn Ḥanbal led a vigorous conservative reaction against the ideas of rational and private interpretation. The Qurʾān and the *sunna* of the Prophet dominate his view, while analogy and consensus are inadmissible. What differentiates him most from al-Shāfiʿī is his extreme literalism. That is well expressed by the story that he never ate a watermelon in his life because he could not find an Ḥadīth that said Muhammad did! He is also noted for a great Ḥadīth collection that he gathered. Ibn Ḥanbal represents unquestioning and unswerving loyalty to the literal statements of Qurʾān and Ḥadīth, and his spirit is very much alive in fundamentalist movements in contemporary Islām.

The Shīʿa Muslim community has its own school of law called the Jaʿfari School. It was founded by Jaʿfarl-Sadīq (d. 765), the sixth imam of Shīʿa Islām and a great legal scholar. His interpretation of Law reflects the special doctrines of the Shʿīa Muslims, especially their deep respect for religious leaders. This school therefore gives the broadest scope of all schools to the principle of *ijithād*, the personal interpretation and judgments of pious and learned scholars. This school of law is found wherever the Shīʿa are found—in Iran, Pakistan, North India, and East Africa.

Muslim scholars and administrators of the Law tend to choose their preferred school and then draw on it for their interpretations and judgments, although they may also adopt a composite approach.

The principles, regulations, and operation of Muslim Law create an impression, and rightly so, of great complexity and idealism. How did this complexity come about and how is the traditional *sharīʿa* surviving today?

E. The Forming and Re-Forming of Muslim Law

The *sharīʿa* of Islām passed through a developmental period in which it was crystallized, stabilized, and idealized. The process resulted in a comprehensive and inflexible system of law. In practice, however, this ideal system was influenced and modified by the various cultures it met, and today the impact of modern culture is raising a host of new questions. Muslims are examining these questions with some anxiety as to their implications for the *sharī‘a*. If law can be said to be dramatic, the current time is surely a dramatic moment in the history of the *sharī‘a*. In this section we will look at the formalization of the Law, as well as Islām's informal recognition of other legal traditions and cultural practices. In the following section we will conclude with an estimate of some of today's pressing questions.

1. The Formalization of the Law

In its formation the *sharī‘a* was crystallized, imitated, and idealized. During the first three centuries of Islāmic history Muslim legal experts completed the arduous and complicated task of crystallizing the main elements of Islāmic Law. We might describe it as the creative period of Muslim law making. Great minds were at work, theories were freely expounded, and relevant rules and regulations were developed out of actual life situations. This activity produced a tremendous amount of legal guidance, and by the tenth century much of the work of *sharī‘a* construction was complete. Islām now possessed a vast body of material for organizing individual and corporate life under the Rule of God.

Thereafter the process of imitation (*taqlīd*) took over. By consensus of the scholars it was generally agreed that the formal task of systematic legal reasoning was now complete, and they held that the doors to further constructive developments were closed. From this time forward jurists concentrated on the task of correctly handing down what they had faithfully received, and the Muslim educational system, which was marked by a philosophy of rote learning, reinforced the approach. Jurists had a very high opinion of the scholars who had created the *sharī‘a*. After all, who could match the four Doctors and their followers! Later scholars believed that their task was simply to comment on and to further apply the findings of their honored predecessors. They wrote a vast number of *fiqh* manuals from this point of view, and these helped to harden the Law into the solid structure that we know today. It is true that there were some differences of emphasis in the law schools, and it is also true that through the use of *fatwā(s)* some legal development was still possible, but these could not alter the dominant trend toward a rigid formalism that the habit of imitation produced. This led to increasing complexity, subtlety, and fine tuning, as every possible issue was taken up. As an example, it was ruled that it was not permissible to ride a camel which had drunk wine because of possible contact with the forbidden element through the sweat of the animal![15]

At the same time as this process was going on, the *sharīʿa* also entered a stage of idealization. It was no longer regarded as the product of human legal scholarship, but as an aspect of divine guidance. Not only the principles of the *sharīʿa* were divine, but the human applications in specific regulations were also divine, and therefore immutable. This conclusion made legal change very difficult. As N. J. Coulson puts it: "Classical jurisprudence had thus, by the principle of *ijmāʿ*, consecrated the whole body of doctrine enshrined in the authoritative texts as the complete expression of the divine command."[16] The laws that had come down, in their entirety, were consecrated and identified with the Law of God. Anwar Qadri straightforwardly expresses the point: "The system of the Sharīʿah is based upon heavenly principles, and its institutions are sacred."[17] In summary we may say that the formalizing of the *sharīʿa* included the sacralizing of its detailed rules. As a result, Muslims came to view the developed *sharīʿa* as holy in all its parts. Islām was now both a religion of Law and a code of sacred laws.

2. The Diversifying Influence of Culture

The influence of human culture on the *sharīʿa* and its administration softens the rigidity of the classical *sharīʿa*. Muslim peoples live in a world of many different cultures and conditions. The structured frame of Muslim Law provides a unifying factor to Muslims who live in that diversity. Whether you pray in Yogyakarta, Kano, Detroit, or Mecca, you pray in the same way. In one sense, it is true to say that the *sharīʿa* holds the Muslim world together. At the same time, it is also true to say that local culture has influenced Muslim custom in many parts of the world, and the application of the *sharīʿa* has had to make accommodation with that reality. This led Muslim jurisprudence to the informal acceptance of two other sources of law, namely, *qānūn* and *ʿurf*, which have brought a richness to the tapestry of Muslim behavior.

Qānūn may be defined as nonrevealed administrative law. As Islām spread in its early history, it conquered nations having existing administrative systems. These systems were allowed to continue for some time where they were not in direct conflict with Islām. They were well-established and Muslims were not in a hurry to replace them. Even in later periods, Christian and Jewish communities were permitted to retain their own systems of religious and personal law in some areas. Thus the acceptance of nonrevealed administrative law became part of the unofficial tradition of the Muslim community from very early times. In modern times Muslims have used this principle to introduce a wide range of administrative regulations not found in the *sharīʿa* itself.

The second supplementary source of Muslim law is local custom, which is called *ʿurf* or *adat*.[18] From the beginning of historic Islām, its adherents maintained a generally tolerant attitude toward local custom, and the attitude to their own Arab culture illustrates that fact. The Kaʿba in Mecca was cleansed by the Prophet Muhammad, not destroyed! Regarding the running between two hills—as Hagar did—the Qurʾān says, "It is no sin" (2:158). As Islām spread into different parts of the world, it frequently retained some aspects of the local culture in its everyday practice. Sometimes Muslims retained practices that were actually different from the classical *sharīʿa*; for example, for centuries Muslims in southwest India and in western Sumatra followed the indigenous matrilinear system of inheritance, property passing down through the female rather than through the male line. The process of cultural absorption continues today, and especially in popular and folk Islām there are many colorful varieties. Muslim life in practice is like a broad river. The *sharīʿa* provides its main current, but other waters are constantly joining the stream of life. *ʿUrf* is not so much a quasi-source of Muslim law as it is an acknowledgement of that reality.

There are purification movements in Islām today that are attempting to "cleanse" Muslim behavior of what is regarded as alien influence. So-called "un-Islāmic" behavior is being criticized, and reformers are promoting common patterns that come closer to the classic s*harīʿa*. These efforts, however, face considerable difficulties. The first is the principle of equality that does not encourage cultural dictation. The second is the fact that Muslims appreciate their cultural heritage and do not wish to lose it. The third is that Muslim nations themselves are currently developing along ethnic lines, thereby affirming their traditional cultures. Local custom has been and remains a vital factor in shaping actual Muslim behavior at grassroots levels. Abdulla and Amina have relatives who live in a Western country where Sunday is the weekly holiday. They are asking themselves whether it is possible to join in a *khutba* service on Sunday instead of Friday, since that is the only day they are free. The classical *sharīʿa* says no; but many of their friends are saying yes, since the primary duty is the worship of God. In fact, many mosques in Western countries now conduct worship on Sundays. The dynamic interaction between classical *sharīʿa* and human culture continues today.

F. The *Sharīʿa* Today

Living society and structured Law! A changing world and sacred tradition! Modern freedom and inflexible regulation! Muslims face difficult questions as they strive to adjust the requirements of the *sharīʿa* to the demands of contemporary life. Muslim nations have dealt with the matter in different ways, and individual Muslims have different opinions on the issues. On the whole, most Muslims recognize that many of the administrative areas of the *sharīʿa* are related to another time and place that no longer exists, but Muslim identity is involved in the continuance of religious and personal law. There is no subject more important for Muslims, and the heated debates reflect that importance.

As we conclude our treatment of the law feeling and the law structure in Islām, we close with three points: Re-Visiting Our Definition, Travelling through the Jungle of Terms, and Summarizing the Current Controversies.

Re-Visiting Our Definition

We have defined the *sharīʿa* as the Muslim code of religious duty that embraces all of life. We may now offer a wider, collective definition. Islāmic Law is comprised of

—basic principles and regulations drawn from the Qurʾān and the *sunna*;

—plus additional laws worked out in the first three centuries of Islām on the basis of the Qurʾān and *sunna* and gathered into legal handbooks;

— plus the accepted legal opinions from later times regarding applications of these traditional rules; and finally

— all these are qualified in practice by the influence of local culture or the demands of secular requirements.

What can we say about the *core* of the *sharīʿa* today? The core is represented by laws having to do with the basic practices of Islām: confession, fasting, almsgiving, and pilgrimage, and by laws having to do with personal Muslim behavior, including marriage and divorce, inheritance, family interrelationships, ceremonies related to birth and death, food and festivals, manners and morals.

Traveling Through the Jungle of Terms

The language use of Muslims in regard to the *sharīʿa* has become varied, and the following guidelines may be noted:

—The term *sharīʿa* is sometimes used only for the principles, sometimes only for the regulations, and sometimes for the principles and regulations in combination. The term is even used sometimes as an equivalent for the faith of Islām;

—The *sharīʿa* principles come directly from the Qurʾān. The individual *sharīʿa* regulations are drawn partly from the Qurʾān, partly from the model of the Prophet, and partly they are inferred from the Qurʾān and *sunna*;

—The *sharīʿa* principles and regulations that are directly taken from the Qurʾān are regarded as inspired by God. The regulations from outside the Qurʾān are the product of God's guidance over the human intellect. Some Muslims reserve the word divine for the Qurānic words alone, while other Muslims call the whole *sharīʿa* divine.

Summarizing the Current Controversies

At the beginning of this chapter we found Abdulla and his friends engaged in a heated tea shop discussion regarding the *sharīᶜa.* Similar debates are an everyday thing among members of the *umma.* It is not yet clear in which direction the controversies will finally take Muslim conviction. Let us survey three fundamental questions that Muslims are discussing:

(1) Can the *sharīᶜa* be changed?

No, say traditional believers. It has a divine quality. The Qurᵓān is divine, the principles that come from it are divine, and the rules derived from the principles are divine. What is divine cannot be changed.

Yes, say other believers. The Qurᵓān is the Word of God and the sunna is sacred, but ordinary beings were involved in developing the rest of the Law. If that is true, ordinary human beings today can also be involved in its adaptation.

(2) Can the *sharīᶜa* be updated?

No, say traditional believers. The Law has the quality of timelessness. It is adequate for every age. Innovation is the equivalent of heresy. If new legal situations arise, the Law provides sufficient means for dealing with them.

Yes, say other believers. The Law was developed by scholars of a certain time and place, in the light of conditions prevailing then. It was geared to the situation of early Islām. The present century has brought a whole new set of conditions for Muslims. Let there be a reformed Law that is both true to God's will and suitable for today's conditions.

(3) Can the *sharīᶜa* be supplemented?

No, say traditional believers. The Law has the quality of perfection. Other law codes should not be used beside or above the *sharīᶜa,* which is God's will and sufficient for all requirements. A true Muslim society should have the Qurᵓān as its constitution and the *sharīᶜa* as its law.

Yes, say other believers. Modern life has become very complex, and Muslims are free to use any kind of legislation that will help them to deal with it successfully, as long as it is in harmony with the essential values of Islām. The Qurᵓān (13:12) encourages Muslims to engage in creative change, in anticipation of the blessing of God.

In this confusing situation, and amidst the welter of often bitter controversies, ordinary Muslims are seeking their way forward. Most of them remain quite sure of one thing—the Law of Islām is their inalienable treasure. To endanger it is to endanger that which gives them their identity and unity in the world. To lose it, is to lose themselves. My Muslim friends live by the Law.

Notes

[1]Charles Eaton, *Islām and the Destiny of Man* (New York: State University of New York, 1985), pp. 166f.

[2]Ibid., p. 34.

[3]Asaf A. A. Fyzee, *Outlines of Muhammadan Law* (Delhi: Oxford Press, 1974; 4th ed.; 1st ed. 1949), p. 16. Fyzee echoes J. Schacht, *An Introduction to Islāmic Law* (Oxford: Clarendon Press, 1964), p. 1: "Islāmic law is the epitome of Islāmic thought, the most typical manifestation of the Islāmic way of life, the core and kernel of Islām itself."

[4]Fazlur Rahman, *Islām*, p. 75.

[5]Joseph Schacht, "*Sharīʿa*," *SEI*, p. 256. T. P. Hughes, *Dictionary of Islām*, p. 285, lists as the common division: *Iʿtiqādāt*: beliefs; *ʿibādat*: practices and devotions; *ādāb*: manners and morals; *muʿāmalāt*: transactions; and *ʿuqūbāt*: punishments.

[6]Qadri, *Islāmic Jurisprudence*, pp. ix–xi; sections b. to f. in this adaptation are taken from Qadri.

[7]John, A. Williams, ed., *The Word of Islām* (Austin: University of Texas Press, 1994), pp. 84, 91.

[8]Qadri, *Islāmic Jurisprudence*, pp. 17f.

[9]Ibid., pp. 14f.

[10]David Santillana, "Law and Society," in T. Arnold and A. Guillaume, eds., *The Legacy of Islām*; 1st ed. (London: Oxford, 1931), p. 285.

[11]Ibid., p. 286.

[12]Mawdūdī, *Understanding Islām*, pp. 122–37. Our treatment of rights and obligations is based on Mawdūdī's exposition of this principle.

[13]Schacht, *Introduction to Islāmic Law*, p. 11.

[14]Qadri, *Islāmic Jurisprudence*, p. 243.

[15]N. J. Coulson, *A History of Islāmic Law* (Edinburgh: University Press, 1964), p. 82.

[16]Ibid., p. 85.

[17]Qadri, *Islāmic Jurisprudence*, p. 36.

[18]*Adat* is the term used in Indonesia to describe its indigenous culture, and it is the equivalent of *ʿurf*. The various levels of Indonesian culture and religious tradition are blended with Islāmic allegiance in a unique way.

14

The Muslim Rhythm of Life: Festivals, Family, and Rites of Passage

There are four movements in the Muslim rhythm of life. The first is common to all human beings—eating, sleeping, working and everything else that goes with normal living. The second is the ritual form of Muslim faith—praying five times daily, fasting annually, pilgrimage once in a lifetime, and so on. The third movement stems from the calendar of Muslim festivals. The fourth and final movement is provided by the rites of passage of in Muslim families, from birth to death. These four movements, interwoven with each other, make up the rhythm of Muslim life. In the following section we will examine the festivals and rites of passage that provide the frame for Muslim family life.

A. The Festivals

1. The Muslim Calendar

The Muslim calendar controls the Muslim festivals. The following facts may be noted about the calendar which, as we have noted, is based on the movements of the moon.
—Its beginning point:
   July 16, 622, when the Prophet Muhammad emigrated from Mecca to Medina (the *hijra*).
—Its identification:
   A Muslim year is identified by the phrase "A.H." This means *anno hijra*, "in the year of the *hijra*," or "after the *hijra*."
—Its basis:
   The moon revolves around the sun in 29 1/2 days. The Muslim calendar is based on 12 lunar months, each month starting with the appearance of the new moon. Each month has 29–30 days.
—Its relation to the solar year:

A lunar year of 354 days has about 11 days less than a solar year; every 32 1/2 years of solar time is equal to 33 1/2 years of lunar time.[1] Thus a lunar year does not follow the seasons.

—How can an A.D. date be transferred to an A.H. date?:[2]

The transfer may be made by applying the following calculation in which G equals the Gregorian and solar year, while H equals the Muslim and lunar year:

H = G less 622, plus $\dfrac{\text{G minus 622}}{32}$

—How can an A.H. date be transferred to an A.D. date?:

By applying the following calculation:

$\quad$ G = H plus 622, less $\dfrac{\text{H}}{33}$

—Starting-points:

The year 1416 A.H. began on May 31, 1995;
and the year 1417 A.H. began on May 19, 1996.

2. The Muslim Months and the Chief Festivals

The following are the twelve Muslim months and the chief Muslim festivals:

Muḥarram	1st	New Year's Day.
	10th	Death of Ḥusain at Kerbela
Safar		
Rabīᶜ I	12th	Birthday of the Prophet Muhammad
Rabīᶜ II		
Jamādā I		
Jamādā II		
Rajab	27th	Miᶜrāj, or ascension of the Prophet Muhammad
Shaᶜbān		
Ramaḍān	27th	Lailat al-Qadar, descent of the first revelation
Shawwāl	1st	ᶜĪd al-Fiṭr, festival of the Breaking of the Fast
Dhu ᵓl-Qaᶜda		
Dhu ᵓl-Ḥijja	10th	ᶜĪd al-Aḍḥā, the Festival of Sacrifice

3. Muḥarram, the Martyrdom of Ḥusain at Kerbela

The first day of Muḥarram, the first month of the Muslim year, may be celebrated as New Year's Day when the Prophet's *hijra* is recalled to mind, and it is a time of anticipation in regard to the future. But the month of Muḥarram is really associated with Kerbela.

The 10th of Muḥarram is a time of mourning for all Muslims, but especially for Shīʿa Muslims. The day originally had association with the Jewish Day of Atonement, a time for fasting, and with Islām it became a time for voluntary fasting. Sunnī Muslims may continue that practice remembering all the Muslim martyrs. Shīʿa Muslims, however, remember only Ḥasan and Ḥusain, the grandsons of the Prophet, and especially Ḥusain who fell on that date at Kerbela in the year 680.

For the nine days preceding the culmination of the festival Shīʿas conduct a variety of meetings, both public and in the home (*rawdas*), which are dedicated to the memory of Ḥusain's greatness and the tragedy of his death. During this period the wearing of black garments is a common practice. On the 10th of Muḥarram parades are conducted with devotees carrying replicas of the tomb of Ḥusain. An empty-saddled white horse is part of the mock funeral procession. Ecstatic celebrants engage in self-flagellation, drawing their own blood from chest and forehead in memory of Ḥusain's passion. The highlight of Muḥarram is the theatrical passion play (*taʿziya*) when the whole series of tragic events is portrayed in graphic format. With weeping and lamentation the cries of "Ya, Ḥusain!" go up, as the redemptive suffering of the martyr-saint is celebrated across the Shīʿa world. A verse in the *taʿziya* when sinners give thanks on entering Paradise expresses the emotion, "God be praised! By Husain's grace we are made happy, and by his favor we are delivered from destruction..."[3]

4. *Milād al-Nabī*, the Birthday of the Prophet

The birthday of the Prophet is celebrated by many Muslims in the third month of the year. Love of the Prophet has been a constant factor in Muslim piety, and his veneration has taken many different forms. One of those forms is the commemoration of his birthday, which coincidentally is also his deathdate. The birthday (*milād*; *mawlid*) is an occasion for meetings in mosques, halls, or homes when in speech and song the virtues of the Prophet are extolled. A special lengthy poem called a *mawlūd*, part prose and part poetry, often interrupted with ejaculations of praise, is frequently recited. In different parts of the Muslim world there are a variety of events including fairs, illuminations, processions, feasts, poor-feeding, distribution of sweets, and other expressions of joy. Some Muslims disapprove of too much festivity. They are suspicious of any veneration of human beings, and regard it as an infringement of the rights of God. Such Muslims are content with low-key speeches that call Muslims to fear God and to obey His will.

5. The *Miʿrāj*, the Ascension of the Prophet

In our discussion of the life of the Prophet we have noted the "historical" occasion that lies behind this festival. The Mirʿāj is celebrated by only some Muslims, especially Sūfi Muslims, and it does not constitute a major festival. It recalls the legend of how Muhammad—whether in spirit or physically—journeyed on high where he met prophets such as Adam, Abraham, Moses, and Jesus. Finally he progressed to an ultimate stage, beyond the lotus tree, where even the angel Gabriel could not follow him, and there "he reached very close to the Throne of God Almighty, and attained the utmost nearness to Him."[4] The same kind of events as on *milād al-nabī* may take place, but on a much reduced scale. The chief feature of the celebration is the rehearsal of the mystical events that took place in the original *miʿrāj* that symbolize every Sūfi's spiritual ascent to the divine.

6. *Lailat al-Qadar*, the Revelation of the Qurʾān

The phrase "Lailat al-Qadar," a Qurānic expression, means "Night of Power." It refers to the first of the many revelations given to the Prophet Muhammad. The spiritual concentration that has intensified during the last 10 days of the fasting month of Ramaḍān reaches its peak on this special night. Wherever possible, Muslims assemble together, often in great open-air meetings under the stars. Male and female, they listen with the greatest attention as a religious scholar leads them in reflection on Qurānic themes. For this is the night of nights, the fateful moment when God revealed His power and sent down the first verses of the Qurʾān (2:2–6). The Qurʾān itself (7:2–5) says of this night that it is better than a thousand months, the night when angels and the Spirit descend, the night in which there is peace until the rising of the sun. For every Muslim it is a night of deep emotion.

The Two Great Festivals

7. ʿĪd al-Fiṭr, the Festival of the Breaking of the Fast

In Abdulla and Amina's town it is the last evening of Ramaḍān. The expectancy on the streets and in the homes is almost tangible. Men are wandering up and down and meeting in little groups. Women in the homes are poised for action, and children are alive with excitement. Suddenly there is a tremendous shout—the new moon has been sighted! The fast is over!

The Festival of the Breaking of the Fast is bound to be joyous. For 29–30 days believers have conducted their affairs under rigorous conditions. They have had to fast during the day, carry on their normal work loads, eat at night, and be constant in spiritual activities. Suddenly there is a release. That evening shops and restaurants stay open, and in the homes there are night-long preparations for the morning festival.

In the morning the celebrants don festive garments after bathing and perfumes—the prophet used them—are not despised. They consume the special sweet that mother has prepared, and then they proceed to the place designated for the ʿĪd service. If there is no room in the mosque, it may be an open area, which in South Asia is called the ʿĪd-gah. The worshippers have made arrangements for their voluntary offering for poor-feeding before they assemble for the prayer. The ʿĪd prayer has two rakʿas or cycles. It is similar to the Friday khutba service except for the fact that there are more takbīrs, more cries of Allāhu Akbar! After the service the assembled greet each other with the friendly phrase ʿĪd mubarak!, "a blessed festival to you!" Then they hurry home for happy times with family and friends. Some may visit the cemeteries in respect for the dead, in the course of the 2–3 day festival. While ʿĪd al-Fiṭr is technically considered the lesser of the two major festivals, in actual fact it is the most spontaneously joyful of all Muslim festivities.

8. ʿĪd al-Aḍḥā, the Festival of Sacrifice

The "Great Festival" has many other names by which it is known, including "ʿĪd al-Qurbān," "Bakr ʿĪd" in South Asia, and "Bairam" in Turkey. It is considered the major festival of the Muslim world. At the same time as pilgrims gathered at the pilgrimage in the Valley of Minā celebrate the occasion, elsewhere in the Muslim world believers join them in spirit and in action.

The action is an animal sacrifice commemorating Abraham's near-sacrifice of his son (believed by Muslims to have been Ishmael). Many regulations are laid down governing the sacrifice—for example, a cow for seven families, a sheep for one family, and so on. The sacrifice depends on the income of the family, and the poor are exempt. Because of changing conditions many Muslims do not actually conduct an animal sacrifice, but rather give a spiritual interpretation to the requirement. It means that one should surrender to God's will as completely as did Abraham, Hagar, and Ishmael. Gifts to the poor provided on this special day symbolize that kind of living sacrifice.

The worship service is conducted with the same preparation and format as the ʿĪd al-Fiṭr. In his sermon the mosque preacher usually discusses the meaning of Abraham's sacrifice. Those who offer an animal sacrifice may use the following prayer: "My prayer and my sacrifice, my life and my death, are for the sake of God, the Lord of all the worlds."[5] The Great Festival goes on for three days. The atmosphere is pleasant, relaxed, and kindly, and feasting and friendship fill the time. After the first day of worship, having completed the technical obligations of the festival, the next day is a family time when gifts are given. In many places this is the time when new clothes will be presented to each member of the family. The third day is often spent in going to the wife's family home, or to the homes of other family and friends. The Great Festival is a welcome break in the rush of human affairs that gives rest and joy to the rhythm of life.

In summary, it may be said that the calendar of Muslim festivals provides a kind of spiritual rhythm to the Muslim year. It begins with devotional reflection at Muḥarram, as believers remember the lives of those who have given great sacrifices for the faith. Then the birthday and ascension of the Prophet remind believers that their life must be directed toward God. The Night of Power points to the fact that God's guidance is a gift of grace. The breaking of the fast is a thanksgiving for the strength to meet a spiritual challenge, and for an opportunity to settle differences of opinion and quarrels. Finally the feast of Abraham reminds believers that the life of surrender to God is the life that gives true satisfaction. This is not a conscious rhythm. The rhythm is felt rather than thought about, acted out rather than discussed, but is nonetheless real.

B. The Rites of Passage

The rites of passage in Islām include birth, circumcision, marriage and death. Each of these is marked by appropriate ceremonies, but they vary tremendously in different parts of the Muslim world, where local custom often prevails. In relation to marriage the question of' women's rights will be taken up. The rites of passage provide the fourth movement in the Muslim rhythm.

1. Birth

When a child is born, it is customary for one of the family members or the midwife to whisper into the child's ear the call to prayer. In this way the first sound that a child hears is a godly one: "Come to prayer ... Come to prosperity ... God is great!" In some Muslim societies an elderly member of the family may touch the child's mouth with a drop of fruit juice or honey before the mother actually begins to nurse the baby. The custom goes back to the Prophet himself. A few days after the birth, sometimes on the seventh or the fourteenth day, the baby's head may be shaven. About the same time the family chooses a name, which is frequently, though not necessarily, the name of some great Muslim figure.

Earlier we have noted the Muslim discussion about family planning. In earlier times it was believed that the number of births is a matter of God's will and humans should not interfere. Furthermore, large families provided social and economic protection. Now, however, the advantage of smaller families has become evident, and Muslims themselves are conducting family planning programs. For example, a Muslim physician and director of a family planning project in South Asia utilized popular Muslim song-tunes to convey his information.

One of the songs, "The Message," begins by asking questions:[6]

Why did Ayesha stop with her second birth?
Why did her husband agree?
Were not Adam's descendants to increase?
Was not this the primal approach of the Lord of the Worlds?

The song goes on to point out the problems of large families, and it reminds the listeners that God wants people to be healthy:

Were not Adam's descendants to be well?
Should we not obey the Lord of the worlds?

The answer is a resounding "Yes!" and Ayesha vows to follow a new policy. At a higher level the involvement and leadership of Muslim women in world population discussions has reached a noteworthy stage.

2. Circumcision

The practice of circumcision is common in many societies, and it is present in Islām. It is viewed as a form of purification as well as a rite of passage.

Although circumcision is nowhere mentioned in the Qurʾān itself, it was undoubtedly practiced in pre-Islāmic times and was carried over into Muslim culture. Later Muslim tradition approved it; for example, a well-known Ḥadīth declares: "Circumcision is *sunna* for males and an honorable act for females."[7] In current Muslim practice it is universally observed for males. Where female circumcision is practiced, the custom is related to local culture rather than to Islāmic law, which does not prescribe it. The rite of passage takes place anywhere between birth and the age of 15 years. It has taken on a semi-religious quality, serving as a kind of confirmation of faith, and the celebration is accompanied by Qurʾān readings and festivities of other kinds.

3. Marriage

Marriage customs in Islām, more than any other rite of passage, reflect local culture. Basically, however, marriage arrangements fall into two distinct segments. The first has to do with the signing of the legal contract (*nikāh*), which is the official act of marriage. The second part has to do with the various festivities of the wedding party, which involves family gatherings, meals, music, and celebration.

Marriage is considered to be a social contract rather than a specifically religious activity. In actual fact, however, it falls somewhere between the two. On the civil ceremony side is the understanding that theoretically anyone can perform the marriage, and it can take place anywhere. On the religious ceremony side is the fact that it is usually an *imām* who is in charge of the *nikāh*, and it may be conducted in a mosque. A contemporary scholar says,

> It is not quite accurate, therefore, to designate marriage in Islām as either a secular contract or a religious sacrament; it has elements of both. The approach would seem to be that of a "divine institution."[8]

From the Muslim point of view, a marriage must be entered into carefully. The law books of Islām are full of discussions of the various conditions that should be fulfilled to ensure a proper marriage. The regulations govern such matters as previous marriages (sufficient time must have elapsed between the marriages); the question of the degrees of blood relationship that are allowable (marriage nearer than cousins is forbidden); the woman's right and control over the dowry which the bridegroom provides (she keeps full rights, but may yield part of it if she wishes); and the issue of the religious faith of the two parties. In regard to the latter, the law permits a Muslim man to marry a Jewish or Christian wife, but the reverse is not allowed.

Another area controlled by the law is the number of partners a person may have. A man may have up to four wives, while a woman is restricted to one husband. According to the views of some Muslim reformers the regulations of the law have been weighted in the direction of the male side and represent a misunderstanding of the Qurʾān. They hold that the passages permitting polygamy are stated in such a way that in fact the principle of monogamy is established, except in extraordinary circumstances. The two key passages involved in the discussion are the following:

> And if ye fear that ye will not deal fairly by the orphans, marry of the women who seem good to you, two or three or four; and if ye fear that ye cannot do justice (to so many) then one only ... (4:3).

> Ye will not be able to deal equally between (your) wives, however much ye wish to do so ... (4:129).

It is argued that since no one can treat more than one person equally, this condition makes polygamy impossible. Some Muslim countries have reflected this interpretation in their official laws, and as a result polygamy, which was always the exception to the norm, is on the wane in Muslim culture.

Since the law of Islām is specific on marriage conditions and since marriages are often alliances between families rather than individuals, the details of the marriage contract are worked out prior to the actual signing itself. The *nikāh* is a brief ceremony involving the one who conducts the procedure, two witnesses, and the participating parties. Both the bridegroom and the bride are supposed to have given their agreement in advance, either orally or in writing. The bride may be nearby or she may be represented at the ceremony by her official guardian (*walī*). One of the main conditions agreed to in advance is the amount of the dowry (*mahr*), usually a modest sum, and the time of its presentation. When the group assembles, the *al-Fātiḥa*, the first chapter of the Qurʾān may be recited, or the person in charge may give an admonition such as the following:

> O ye people, make your Lord your shelter, Who created you out of one soul, and created out of its kind spouses, and thus multiplied men and women; and fear Allāh with Whose name you beseech Him, and be mindful of the rights of the relations of the womb. Verily God is watching over you.[9]

After the words of praise and admonition the contract is signed, the *nikāh* is complete, and the marriage is official.

The joyful festivities come next, and they follow many different patterns. In some places the bridegroom proceeds to the home of the bride where a feast has been prepared. Friends and neighbors are invited, and this is the time when well-wishers give their gifts to the couple. The bridegroom may also conduct another dinner for his friends after the marriage has been consummated. In some cultures large amounts of money are spent on weddings, causing some hardship for the poor. Nevertheless, the wedding celebrations are major festive events that linger long in the happy memory of the family.

Marriage leads to the husband-wife relationship that also has religious parameters. Here, however, the human factor takes over. Abdulla's and Amina's relation is unique to them. There is no single pattern that is common to all Muslims. The individual husband-wife relationship is also conditioned by cultural patterns—what part of the Muslim world are we talking about? It is affected by social factors such as education and wealth. It is influenced by the family's religious tradition. Finally, it is affected by the personal equation—what kind of individuals are these two people? Thus every Muslim marriage always becomes a unique thing, involving two unique human beings.

The structure of the *sharīᶜa*, the law of Islām, is placed over these foundational influences. It provides a general frame of reference within which the individual relationship is worked out. There is no area of life for which the *sharīᶜa* has more advice than the area of "personal law," and within personal law marriage is the primary topic. The position of the *sharīᶜa* in regard to the husband-wife relationship, based on traditional interpretations of Qurānic passages, is clear. The wife retains her name and the ownership of her property and is entitled to decent support. It is the duty of the husband to look after the financial and other needs of the family, and the leadership role is his. Legally the husband may demand obedience from his wife, including the privilege of marital intercourse, and if the wife is customarily disobedient, the husband may chastise her in an appropriate way. Fundamentally, however, the relationship between husband and wife is to be understood as an interplay of rights and duties under the guidance of the ethical principles established by God in His Word. The primary charge that God gives is the following:

And of His signs is this: He created for you helpmeets from yourselves that ye might find rest in them, and he ordained between you love and mercy. (30:21).

Islām accepts the possibility that a marriage may not be suitable, and accordingly divorce is allowed under specific regulations. In the traditional interpretation of the Qurānic provisions, a husband does not require formal justification for divorcing his wife, and he may do so through the uttering of the phrase "you are dismissed" three times (*talāq*). The *talāq* form of divorce is to be carried out over a period of time and under certain restraining conditions, but at local levels it has sometimes become a simple one, two, three statement. Muslim reformers have vigorously condemned the latter practice. A woman must justify divorce before the court on such grounds as lack of maintenance, impotency, maltreatment and abuse, long absence, and the like. A woman also has the right to insert protective stipulations into the marriage contract—for example, a husband's prior assent that he will not take another wife—and if that agreement is broken, she may pursue a divorce.

This is an area where considerable change is taking place. In several Muslim societies, at a formal level, women's equal rights in marriage and divorce have been enshrined in national laws, but at popular levels of life older customs frequently prevail.

4. The Family; Women and Children

a. The Family:

All Muslim rites of passage take place within the context of the family. In particular the ideas of marriage and family are closely interlinked. Hammudah Abdalati expresses the connection in this way:

> Islām recognizes the religious virtue, the social necessity, and the moral advantage of marriage. The normal course of behavior for a Muslim individual is to be family oriented and to seek a family of his own. Marriage and family are central to the Islāmic system.[10]

Mohammed Jamali summarizes the Muslim view by declaring that "the individual and the family are the two chief pillars supporting the Islāmic social structure."[11] He goes on to say that Islām honors the individual but it also stresses that responsibility is social, as well as individual. Within the realm of social responsibility the family and its sanctity are paramount.

The concept of the Muslim family tend to the idea of an

"extended" family rather than to a "nuclear" family. While the principle of extended family is not unique to Islām, the custom continues to be maintained within the social context of Islām despite the pressures of modern society. The distinction between brother/sister and cousin, for example, is maintained for legal purposes, but it is overlooked in practice. Muslim families view themselves as a wider unit, and its members rally to each others' needs. The individual relationships of the nuclear family—husband and wife, parents and children—are worked out within this larger context.

Muslims take strong pride in their families, and many of the real joys of Muslim life are experienced within the family circle.

b. The Position of Women:

There is a considerable difference of opinion among Muslims today as to how the Qurānic view of male-female relations is to be understood and applied. The position of women is interpreted differently by traditional Muslims and reforming Muslims.

(1) Traditional Muslims

Generally speaking, at the time of the Prophet Muhammad and the first four Caliphs women had considerable ease in social intercourse and participation in religious affairs. This did not last. In the following two centuries religious scholars chose to interpret the position of women as an inferior one, and the interpretation was crystallized in the law of Islām. The interpretation was buttressed by the accumulation of Ḥadīth that supported the negative view of women's position and role. Without any basis in the Qurʾān, one Ḥadīth went so far as to suggest that "most of the inhabitants of Hell are women and that, 'because of their unbelief'."[12] Notable scholars confirmed this approach, and through the process of tradition it was passed on as the teaching of Islām. Al-Baidāwī (d. 1226), a renowned Sunnī commentator on the Qurʾān and a scholar whose works are regarded as highly authoritative in Sunnī Islām, wrote that since women are inherently weaker than men,

> To men have been confined prophecy, religious leadership, saintship, pilgrimage rites, the giving of evidence in the law courts, the duties of the holy war, worship in the mosque on the day of assembly. They

also have the privilege of electing chiefs, have a larger share of inheritance and discretion in the matter of divorce.[13]

The seclusion (*169*) of Muslim women came as a byproduct of this rigorous approach. Other ideas were added to the belief that women had no natural role in public life. They included such concerns as the discouragement of immorality and the protection of family honor. These ideas combined with cultural factors led to a pattern of seclusion that set back women's progress. Within two centuries of ʿĀʾisha's public role in early Islāmic affairs the practice of separate and secluded women's quarters (*harem, zenana*) had become common. Women ventured forth from seclusion only under certain conditions and for specific purposes. The practice of *pardah* was always modified by economic necessity as Muslim women, especially in agricultural societies, played a major role in the work force, and it was largely confined to the well-to-do. Still the seclusion concept was pervasive as an idea. It did not leave Muslim women powerless, but it confined them to family affairs and to behind-the-scene roles in other matters. Among modern Muslims the practice of seclusion is virtually crumbling as women have emerged from this tradition into the light of a new day. The principle of care and restraint in a woman's relationships with males who are not members of the family is now maintained through modes of behavior and dress, rather than through physical separation.

The issue of seclusion needs to be distinguished from the tradition of female dress customs, including the veil. Many Muslim women choose to cover their heads (*hijāb*), or wear a full-length cloak cum veil (*burqa*) or a wrap cum veil (*chaddar*). These forms of coverage stem from an interpretation of the Qurʾān which encourages modesty in dress (24:30–31). The passage, which applies to both men and women, calls for special care in the matter of eye contact and discreet garb. In the case of women, Muslim tradition interpreted this command to mean a full covering of the body except for face or hands. Many Muslim women today argue that the principle of modesty can be maintained through sensible modern dress. Others compromise with a middle position represented by the wearing of a simple head scarf. In any event, as with men's clothing, women's dress is women's choice, and the elements of fashion, practicality, and tradition all play a part in the final selection.

The traditional Muslim approach to the position of women has been modified by contemporary trends. Although the basic understanding of the respective roles of male and female have not altered, the position is now expressed in moderate and carefully chosen language. One expression puts the traditional viewpoint this way: "The Qurʾān gives a slight superiority to man in the general affairs of life."[14] The many who take this approach quote two passages from the Qurʾān in support of their position:

> Men are in charge of women because Allāh hath made one of them to excel the other (4:34).

> ... And they (women) have rights similar to those (of men) over them in kindness, and men are a degree above them (2:228).

Traditional Muslims regard these passages as a clear and sufficient statement of the principle of "slight superiority."

Others who hold a similar opinion prefer to deal with the issue from the point of view of the doctrine of "orders of creation." The idea is that through creation God has assigned specific functions to males and females that underlie their separate roles. Where passages of the Qurʾān point to male superiority they have reference to such functions and not to fundamental spiritual distinctions or to differences in human rights. From this perspective it is suggested that we may speak of "the instrumental authority" of the male and the "expressive authority" of the female, each having their appointed area; however, it must be remembered that all authority in Islām is "based on equity, guarded by compassion, and guided by conscientiousness."[15] According to this functional approach women have primary responsibility in the realm of the home, while men have similar responsibility in other affairs, including the ultimate decision-making function.

(2) Reforming Muslims

Reforming Muslims believe two things—that the difficulties of Muslim women are still serious and must be redressed, and that a fresh understanding of the Qurʾān is necessary to bring about the required changes.

A female Muslim social scientist enumerates what she considers to be the continuing disabilities of Muslim women: the low level of female education; restriction on the movement of women; male domination in the home; a wife's fear of being quickly put aside, difficulty for a woman to arrange remarriage; and discriminatory regulations in the areas of inheritance, property control, and marriage arrangements. [16] She maintains the position that the problem is not with ideal Islām or the Qurᵓān, but rather it is with the male-oriented interpretation. She says,

Inequalities are appalling ... Although the forces of modernization have made deep inroads into the Muslim community, the women still have to go a long way to achieve an honorable position. Islām regards both men and women as equal and never considers a woman as an impediment in the path of religion. The status accorded to women in Islām is much higher than in any other religion or community ... Despite the elevated position conferred on women in Islām, the various commentators of the Holy Book have over the centuries relegated them to an inferior and obscure position in various spheres, reflecting a perversity of mind ...and male chauvinism and bigotry.[17]

A noted Muslim woman scholar, Professor Riffat Hassan, expresses the emotion of many female intellectuals when she says, "The more I saw the justice and compassion of God reflected in the Qurᵓānic teachings regarding women, the more anguished I became at seeing the injustice and inhumanity to which Muslim women in general are subjected in actual life."[18] A teacher of religious studies, she sees the problem as a theological one, a failure to understand the Qurᵓānic doctrine of creation:

If man and woman have been created equal by God, who is believed to be the ultimate arbiter of value, then they cannot become unequal, essentially, at a subsequent time. Hence their obvious inequality in the patriarchal world is in contravention of God's plan.[19]

Reformers cite the following passages of the Qurᵓān as a basis for a new approach to the position of women:

Lo! men who surrender unto Allāh, and women who surrender, and men who believe and women who believe, and men who obey and women who obey, and men who speak the truth and women who speak the truth, and men who persevere (in righteousness) and women who persevere, and men who are humble and women who are humble, and men who give alms and women who give alms, and men who fast and women who fast, and men who guard (their modesty) and women who guard (their modesty) and men who remember Allāh much and women who remember—Allāh hath prepared for them forgiveness and a vast reward (33:35).

And the believers, *men and women*, are protecting friends one of another; *they* enjoy the right and forbid the wrong, and they establish worship, and *they* pay the poor-due, and *they* obey Allāh and His messenger ... [it., ed.] (9:71).

Lo! I suffer not the work of any worker, male or female, to be lost ... Ye proceed one from another. (3:195).

That He may bring the believing men and the believing women into Gardens ... (48:5).

They believe that all other passages dealing with male-female relations must be interpreted in the light of these fundamental affirmations of equality.

The discussion in the Muslim world on the issue of female rights, marriage and divorce, is an ever evolving one. In many local areas the old traditions are firmly maintained. In other areas, great strides forward have been taken. Abdulla and Amina are progressive in their general attitude and kindly toward each other. They both believe in women's development, but not in a way that threatens their understanding of family patterns and unity. Both have their areas of responsibility and duty, and their areas of power and freedom. We may describe their approach as a form of humane and satisfied traditionalism.

Amina, my friend, is not involved in the intellectual discussions. She is happy in her family situation, and in her relations with her husband and children. She appreciates the fact that she was educated, and she insists that her daughter have the same opportunity. It is her secret hope that Fatima will become a physician. She realizes that Muslim women have some special problems, but she does not spend time analyzing the situation, nor is she revolutionary in her attitudes. She does want to make some changes, however, and she has become a member of the Women's Wing of a community uplift association. She spends a great deal of time at a women's handicraft center, trying to help women from her community and others who are economically backward. She has heard of the great Muslim women who have become heads of state in three different Muslim countries, and she is proud of their achievement. Who knows, she sometimes thinks to herself as she watches Fatima, perhaps she can be a governmental minister some day ...!

(3) The Position of Children

Muslim parents hold their children in high regard. Thereby they reflect natural affection, but in addition they are responding to the tradition of Islām going back to the time of the Prophet who enjoyed children. The Qurʾān says that children are "an ornament of life" in this world (18:47). The Qurʾān intervened in the pre-Islāmic practice of destroying baby girls and gave daughters a new status. It is also full of references to the care and protection of orphans. Since the primary duty of a believer is the remembrance of Allāh (63:9), children in a sense represent a test to parents. The care of children should not take precedence over religious duty (8:28). Apart from that condition, however, parents should gladly assume the responsibilities that God gives them in regard to their children—to the father, responsibility for control, guidance, and sustenance; to the mother, care for the upbringing of children in the home and for their religious development. Like the Qurānic figure, Lukmān, parents should be ready to say to their children,

> O my dear son! Establish worship and enjoin kindness and forbid iniquity, and persevere whatever may befall thee ... Turn not thy cheek in scorn toward folk, nor walk with pertness in the land... Be modest in thy bearing and subdue thy voice. Lo! the harshest of all voices is the voice of the ass (31:17–19).

The lawbooks of Islām contain many regulations concerning children. They discuss such issues as legitimacy, guardianship, maintenance, and adoption.[20] The affect of divorce on children is given careful attention. According to Shāfiʿite law the mother must care for the children up to the age of seven, after which the father becomes responsible for them. One of the most detailed subjects is the law of inheritance.[21] The Qurʾān provides for equal shares in the estate for sons, and half-shares for daughters; the principle, it is explained, is that sons must assume financial responsibility for families, while daughters receive such support after marriage. Additional shares must be given to other members of the family, but the rights of children, including daughters, are clearly protected.

The Qurʾān pays considerable attention to the duty that children have toward their parents. The respect and obedience that they are

307

to give parents is not a time-bound thing, but rather a lifelong obligation. In this case also the duty of children to God transcends their duty to parents. If parents try to turn them from the straight path, they should not follow them. Apart from this exception children should be deeply respectful, thankful, and caring.

> Come, I will recite unto you that which your Lord hath made a sacred duty for you; that ye ascribe no thing as partner unto Him and that ye do good to parents ... (6:16).

> Thy Lord hath decreed that ye worship none save Him, and (that ye show) kindness to parents. If one of them or both of them attain to old age with thee, say not "Fie" unto them nor repulse them, but speak unto them a gracious word. And lower unto them the wing of submission through mercy, and say, My Lord! Have mercy on them both as they did care for me when I was little (17:23–24).

In Ḥadīth there is special stress on reverence toward the mother. The Prophet Muhammad knew his mother for only eight years, but his memory of her was strong and filled with gratitude. A well-known Ḥadīth declares,

> Bahz b. Hakīm, on his father's authority, said his grandfather told that he had asked God's messenger to whom he should show kindness and he had replied, "Your mother." [Some versions repeat the question and answer thrice.] He asked who came next and he replied, "Your father; then your relatives in order of relationship."[22]

In contemporary Islāmic life Muslim parents have tremendous concerns regarding the secularization of society and its effects on their children. They are worried about the temptations of modernity ranging from drugs to immorality; the impact of cinema, TV and videos; the erosion of family values; and the cost of education combined with the struggle to find employment. On their part, Abdulla and Amina share deep concerns for the present and future welfare of Ashraf, Rashid, and Fatima, and they are doing their best to make their religion relevant and helpful to their children as they bring them up in a changing society. They rejoice when their children show an interest in the faith.

5. Death and Funerals

The final rite of passage in Islām has to do with life's ending. Death is called THE CERTAIN in the Qurʾān, for it represents the universal and the inevitable reality.

Unto Allāh will ye all return (5:105).

And serve thy Lord till the Inevitable cometh unto thee (15:97).

Through the various stages of life individual believers are to have a pleasant and helpful relation with each other, and when death comes they are not to become suddenly forgetful. A Ḥadīth sums up what is expected:

He reported God's messenger as saying, "A Muslim has six duties towards another Muslim." When asked what they were he replied: "When you meet him, salute him; when he issues an invitation to you, accept it; when he asks your advice give it to him; when he sneezes and praises God, say, 'God have mercy on you'; when he is ill, visit him; and when he dies, follow him to the grave."23

Muslims frequently attribute illness, suffering, and death to the will of God. This understanding is connected with the high view of God's active role in human life, a view that is most powerfully expressed by the repeated phrase "if God wills!" According to this approach, if one bears sickness as an affliction from God, yet nevertheless praises the Most High, that affliction becomes a cause for the forgiveness of sins and the gift of Paradise. Thus the mystery of suffering bows to an act of faith.

Led by modern Muslims, and especially physicians and development workers, more and more believers are viewing sickness and its causes as a challenge to be met and as an evil to be overcome. It is a problem that can be alleviated and sometimes even solved. However, when the inevitable suffering does come, all Muslims are called upon to be sympathetic with each other. They should visit the sick and bring them comfort. A Ḥadīth states that when someone visits a sick person 70,000 angels invoke their blessings, and he/she gains many credits toward Paradise. Although it is not such a common practice, prayer for healing (duʿā) is also commended. In a Ḥadīth Abud Dardāʾ heard God's messenger say,

If one of you has any complaint or if a brother of his complains of it, he should say, "Our Lord God who art in heaven, hallowed be Thy name. Thy command is in the heaven and the earth. As Thy mercy is in the heaven, so place Thy mercy in the earth. Forgive us our faults and sins. Thou art the Lord of the good ones. Send down some of Thy mercy and some of Thy healing on this pain, and it will be cured."[24]

Abdulla's father, Ahmad, has died. Abdulla had a very close relationship with his father, and so he is *very* sad. Islām teaches the virtue of fortitude, however, and he controls his emotion. He quietly utters the common phrase, "To Allāh we belong and to Him we shall return." The women at the bedside are weeping softly, for wailing is discouraged. Ahmad's face is turned to the direction of Mecca, and the grieving relatives call on him to greet others who have gone on before.

Funeral ceremonies vary considerably in different Muslim societies. In some modern settings traditional customs have often been adapted or even abandoned as impractical. Abdulla's family, however, observes the inherited practices. The preparation of the body is a sacred act of caring. There is a full washing, frequently by a professionally competent person. After the necessary preparations, the body is shrouded in two sheets of white cloth. It is then taken on a bier to the place where the funeral prayer is recited—praying over the dead and for the forgiveness of the dead person is commended. Both in this prayer and at the graveside the sounds of the *al-Fāṭiha*, the *shahāda*, and the *Allāhu akbars* may be heard.

From the place of the funeral prayer the mourners carry Ahmad's bier to the cemetery. As the bier passes by, people stand in respect, for the Prophet commanded such honor for the departed, Muslim or non-Muslim. In the procession Ahmad's friends walk in single file, most of them behind the bier. As they walk, one solemn word issues in unison from their lips: Allāh ... Allāh... Allāh. The chant expresses both the profound mystery of death and the helplessness of humans before that mystery. Only God can help us. At the cemetery the body is laid in the grave facing Mecca. There the recital of holy passages may also include sūra 112 and sūra 20:55 which says: "Thereof We created you, and thereunto We return you, and thence We bring you forth a second time." Earth may be sprinkled on the body with the sad words, "All thou hast from the world is this handful of dust."[25]

After the grave is filled a simple stone is placed at its head and foot. Traditionally there is to be no adornment, no writing, and no structure that allows sitting. A low brick surround with a pebble covering of the enclosure is considered adequate. The great mausoleums of kings, saints, and wealthy persons show how this practice can be ignored, but generally Muslim cemeteries represent a plain and simple sight.

Abdulla and his family have returned home. In the next days he and Amina will revisit the cemetery. Visiting the graves of the departed is considered a meritorious act for both men and women, but women have made this custom their particular practice. ʿĀʾisha, whose own quarters became the burial place for Muhammad, Abū Bakr, and ʿUmar, once asked the Prophet what she should say when she visited a grave. He told her to say,[26] "Peace be upon the inhabitants of the abodes, believers and Muslims, and God show mercy to those who go before and those who go later. If God will, we shall join them." After Abdulla has said goodbye to the friends who came to express their condolences, he reflects on the words of the Qurʾān:

To Thee is the end of all journeys ...

Our Lord! lay not on us a burden greater than we have strength to bear. Blot out our sins, and grant us forgiveness. Have mercy on us. Thou art our Protector; help us against those who stand against Faith (2:285–86).[27]

Abdulla now sends Rashid and Fatima to bed. Before they go he tells them that they should never forget their grandfather. There is no more oil in this lamp. Now they must light their lamps and burn brightly.

Notes

[1]G. S. P. Freeman-Grenville, *The Muslim and Christian Calendars* (London: Rex College Ltd., 1977), p. 2.

[2]M. Hodgson, *The Venture of Islām* (Chicago: University of Chicago Press, 1974), vol. I, p. 21.

[3]G. von Grunebaum, *Muhammadan Festivals* (London: Curzon Press, 1951), p. 94; quoting T. Pelley, *The Miracle Play of Ḥasan and Ḥusain* (London, 1879), II, 335–48.

[4]Rashid Ahmad Chaudhry, *Muslim Festivals and Ceremonies* (London: International Publications Limited, 1988), p. 34.

[5]Ibid., p. 32.

[6]Miller, *Mappilas*, p. 320. The translation is the writer's; from Malayalam.

[7]Aḥmad ibn Ḥanbāl, quoted in A. J. Wensinck, "*Khitan*," *EI²* , V, p. 21.

[8]Hammādah ʿAbd al-ʿAṭi, *The Family Structure in Islām* (Indianapolis: American Trust Publications, 1977), p. 59.

[9]Chaudhry, *Festivals*, p. 39.

[10]Abdalati, *Islām in Focus*, p. 114.

[11]Jamali, *Letters*, p. 55.

[12]Bukhārī, Saḥīḥ, xi, 13, quoted in Reuben Levy, *The Social Structure of Islām* (Cambridge: Cambridge University Press, 1962), p. 130.

[13]Ibid., p. 99.

[14]*Lessons in Islām Series. Book No. 5* (Lahore: Sh. Muhammad Ashraf, 1976), pp. 181f.

[15]Abdalati, *Family Structure*, pp. 181f.

[16]Puma Iftikhar, "Indian Muslim Women: Plight and Remedy," *Muslim Women in India*, ed. by Mohini Anjum (New Delhi: Sangam Books Ltd., 1992), pp. 135f.

[17]Ibid., p. 134.

[18]"Equal Before Allāh? Woman-Man Equality in the Islāmic Tradition," in *Harvard Divinity Bulletin*, vol. XVII, No. 2, May 1987, p. 2.

[19]Ibid., p. 4.

[20]Cf. "The Status of the Child in Islām," Levy, *Islām*, pp. 135–49.

[21]The sixth sūra "Women" contains many of the regulations on inheritance.

[22]Tirmidhiī and Abū Dāwūd, *Mishkāt*, III, p. 1027.

[23]Muslim, *Mishkāt*, I, p. 320.

[24]Abū Dāwūd, *Mishkāt*, I, p. 325.

[25]Kenneth Cragg, *The Dome of the Rock* (London: S. P. C. K., 1964), p. 213. I am also indebted to Professor Cragg for the proverb, "There is no more oil in this lamp."

[26]Muslim, *Mishkāt*, I, p. 370.

[27]The translation is by Yusuf Ali.

15

History and Heroes: My Muslim Friends Are Proud

In this chapter we will concentrate on Muslim heroes. Muslims are immensely proud of their heroes. Their stories are constantly repeated, and they represent additional models for Islāmic behavior. It has been suggested that the theme of the hero in art and architecture is "one key to understanding both what is Islāmic about the Islāmic world and what is unique to any one local setting."[1] The same could be said about all of Muslim history. My Muslim friends are proud of their history—but when they think about it, they remember first their heroes. A number of factors account for this emphasis. The main one is the importance the Muslims give to people, to human engagement, and to personal relations.

When Abdulla goes to the marketplace for shopping, he loves to bargain. The bargaining is a kind of game. Who will win, seller or buyer? The goal of course is a "no win, no lose" result, that is, a final price which is about right and to which both can agree. At times the game becomes almost more important than the item purchased. Abdulla has just bought a fish after some hectic bargaining. There is a kind of twinkle both in his eye and in the vendor's eye. They did not merely do business together. In the process of the pseudo-heated discussion there was a human engagement. The fish changes hands, quite unaware of its role in a minor human drama.

The illustration points to the fact that Abdulla and Amina tend to be people-oriented. That does not mean they have no interest in owning things. All along we have insisted that Muslims are ordinary people who share the dreams and desires common to all humans. If they have the means, they obtain and enjoy material blessings like everyone else. In fact, one of the most common complaints that Muslim reformers make today is that Muslims are succumbing far too readily to the temptations of materialism!

Having recognized that, we may also make the point that Muslims give some priority over acquisitions to human relations. For men it is the tea shop and the coffee shop that are the symbols of a deeply cherished pleasure—engaging in conversation with friends. For women the same holds true, as they share with each other in their homes, and in the privacy of "women-only" occasions.

In terms of Muslim history this basic people orientation extends into hero respect. Little Rashid is heading for the *madrasa*. His mother makes sure that he has taken along his copy of a small booklet on the great heroes of the faith. Studying the heroes is one of the highlights of the *madrasa* experience. It is then that the faith comes alive for the children.

The personal emphasis runs through Muslim literature of all kinds. It was the stature of the narrators that validated the authenticity of a Ḥadīth. Epic "song-stories" that tell of human exploits or romantic events are enjoyed in many parts of the Muslim world, and their balladeers are greatly admired. Muslim historiography is above all biography, and the biography that is regarded as most important is the life of a devout saint or scholar. The *mawlūds* are recitations of a great individual's personal history, frequently narrated on that person's birthday. Finally, Muslims take strong interest in genealogies and read them with fascination. In the past, scholars prepared large encyclopedic dictionaries of esteemed individuals, and the production of photographic bibliographies is common today. For Muslims, history and heroes flow together.

There is a final consideration. The people orientation and the respect for great individuals are linked with the factor of Muslim nostalgia. The great individuals whom Muslims admire most are mainly persons from the past. Contemporary Muslims share the widespread global suspicion of modern leadership. Occasionally some individual like the boxer, Muhammad Ali, will capture the universal admiration of Muslims, but those people who are most highly revered by the faithful are generally from the earlier eras of Islāmic glory and achievement.

We may even suggest that Abdulla and Amina live in a mental world of powerful memory and persistent nostalgia. They look back to what is for them a grand religious saga and to a company of glorious heroes. They cannot stay in memory lane because they have to live in the here and now, and they have to spend most of their time and energies on survival issues. Muslim nostalgia therefore exists side by side with Muslim pragmatism. Abdulla and Amina are wise enough to know that they cannot constantly be looking backward. Yet perhaps more than any other people Muslims revere the past. They sometimes idealize it, and they are certainly nostalgic about it. The past tells a story of achievement that many Muslims wish could be replicated in the present age.

A. Original Greatness: The Heroes of Early Islām

When Muslims look back, they love to remember the first 30 years of Muslim history. That is the time when things went very well for Islām, the time when it all began. It was then that the first followers of the Prophet, who knew him personally and shared his vision, built upon what he had done and established the community of faith. It was at that time that the greatest victories occurred. And there, in Medina, was the glory and pattern of Islām. All Muslims look back and look up to these beginnings. Their common knowledge of those stirring events unites them. Their hearts beat with pride as they consider the splendor of those days. Their spirits feed on the remembrance of men like Abū Bakr, ʿUmar, ʿUthmān, and ʿAlī, and women like Khadīja, ʿĀʾisha, and Fāṭima.

Certainly what happened in those years from 632–61 is startling and important, not only for Muslims but also for the whole world. Four leaders followed the Prophet, and before their brief careers were finished, the state of humanity was dramatically altered. The four, with their dates of rule, are

Abū Bakr	632–34
ʿUmar ibn Khaṭṭāb	643–44
ʿUthmān b. Affan	644–56
ʿAlī b. Abi Tālib	656–61

These admired figures are called the "rightly-guided" leaders by Sunnī Muslims. Shīʿa Muslims, on the other hand, give precedence to ʿAlī. The first leaders are also called caliphs, a word that means successors, the "deputies" of the Prophet. Caliphs were temporal leaders who also had a spiritual function. As temporal leaders their task was to administrate the Muslim *umma* and to expand its borders. Their spiritual function was to be the custodians of the sacred things of Islām—Qurʾān, *sunna* of the Prophet, and later the Law. They had no spiritual authority of their own to reinterpret the faith or to lord it over fellow believers. They were leaders among equals, and their guardian task was to enable Muslims to live in a Muslim context. In so doing, they undoubtedly believed that they were continuing the work of the Prophet.

Nevertheless, the first four leaders were not selected without some confusion, because there was no agreed-upon method of appointment. Abū Bakr was a consensus leader, chosen immediately after the Prophet died. He soon nominated ʿUmar as his successor, and fortunately so since Abū Bakr died early in his term as caliph. ʿUmar arranged an appointment committee that chose ʿUthmān as his successor. When ʿUthmān was killed, ʿAlī came to the fore, almost by a process of natural selection. Shīʿa Muslims argue that he should have been the first of the successors, since he was from the Prophet's family—and on that issue rests the great division in Islām between Sunnīs and Shīʿas. At any rate, his turn finally came but as we shall see even then his caliphate did not go uncontested.

There are other famed "Companions" (ṣaḥāba) of the Prophet, who are highly honored by Muslims. Six of them join the four to comprise a group who are promised the highest place in Paradise: Talha, Zubair, ʿAbd al-Rahmān b. ʿAwf, Saʿd b. Abi Wakkās, Saʿid b. Zaid, and Abū ʿUbaida b. al-Djarrāh. Their virtues are extolled in the Ḥadīth, and when their names and the names of other noble Companions are mentioned, the phrase "May Allāh be pleased with them" is to be added.[2] In the following discussion we shall limit ourselves to the first four Sunnī caliphs, adding three great women of Islām, namely, Khadīja, ʿAʾisha, and Fāṭima.

1. Abū Bakr

Abū Bakr led Islām during the first two critical years after the death of Muhammad (632). Two years younger than the Prophet, Abū Bakr was his staunch friend. So unshakable was his faith and loyalty that he was given the name al-Ṣiddīq, "the Reliable one." He was a merchant and a man of means, but he spent his wealth for Islām. Personally devout, he sometimes wept when the Qurānic revelations were recited, and he would frequently purchase the freedom of slaves. He was nearly always with the Prophet and accompanied him on his campaigns. He was "the second of the two, when they were in the cave, and when he said to his comrade, "Grieve not! Lo, Allāh is with us" (9:40); that is, it was Abū Bakr who accompanied the Prophet in the successful escape and emigration to Medina. His relationship to the Prophet was strengthened by the betrothal of his daughter, ʿĀʾisha, to Muhammad.

In Medina Abū Bakr continued his stalwart supporting rule that had begun in Mecca. When Muhammad was sick or absent, he led the prayers in the mosque. In 632 a greater responsibility was thrust upon him. At the death of the Prophet there was great confusion, and it was indeed a perilous time for Islām. Could it survive the shock? The majority of the Muslims, led by ʿUmar ibn Khaṭṭāb, looked to Abū Bakr for leadership. ʿUmar addressed the assembly and declared, "God has placed your affairs in the hands of the best one among you ... So arise and swear fealty to him."[3] Abū Bakr reluctantly accepted the challenge and spoke these words:

> O people, I have been appointed to rule over you, though I am not the best among you. If I do well, help me, and if I do ill, correct me ... obey me as long as I obey God and His Prophet. And if I disobey God and His Prophet, you do not owe me obedience. Come to prayer, and may God have mercy on you.[4]

Thus al-Ṣiddīq became the first deputy of the Prophet and Islām survived its first crisis.

Abū Bakr proved to be the right man for the moment. His two years of rule were not easy ones. Now that the Prophet was gone, there were a number of tribes who did not see the need for paying taxes to Medina and obeying its directions. Some even had other "prophets" they wanted to follow. Abū Bakr held firm. He made a wise choice of generals, including the brilliant warrior, Khālid b. Walīd, whom Muhammad had named "the Sword of Islām." After two years of struggle the Arabian peninsula was united again under Islām, and Abū Bakr had even started to send his forces to the borders of Syria and Persia. At his death in 634 he was succeed by ʿUmar, a simple, powerful man of great integrity.

2. ʿUmar

ʿUmar was the organizational genius who directed the early Muslim expansion and brilliantly administered the new Muslim possessions.

The dramatic story of ʿUmar's conversion has already been told. He was a vigorous 26 years old when that event took place, and thereafter his enthusiasm was a powerful influence upon the young Muslim community. As strongly as he had once opposed Islām, so fervently he supported it after his conversion. He threw all of his considerable energies into the task of advancing the faith. He had great will power, and by sheer force of personality he dominated those around him. The Prophet recognized his unusual abilities. There is a Ḥadīth that says,[5] "If God had wished that there should have been another Prophet after me, ʿUmar would have been he." On his part, ʿUmar loved the Prophet dearly. He refused to believe that he had died, and only Abū Bakr could persuade him of the truth. When he found that it was so, he fell to the ground in great anguish. His loyalty matched his simplicity. He showed no ambition for power and no envy toward Abū Bakr, whom he supported in an appealing manner. Even at the height of his own rule, he led an austere, ascetic life. Many are the stories told of this "ruddy, tall, bald and ambidextrous man" who "walked as though he was riding"[6] and who often, carried a leather whip in his hand. He struck fear into the hearts of evildoers. ʿUmar was married to Hafsa, the daughter of the Prophet.

When ʿUmar succeeded Abū Bakr, he adopted the title, *amīr al-muʾminīn*, the "Commander of the Faithful," and under his leadership the energies of the believers were directed outward. By the close of his 10 years of rule, Syria, Egypt, and Persia had all fallen before the Muslim armies. Damascus opened its doors to Khālid in 635, and Jerusalem in 638. Ctesiphon in Persia fell to Saʿd b. Abī Waqqāṣ in 637, and Alexandria to ʿAmr b. al-ʿĀṣ in 642. There are many factors that play into the speed of this development, but the towering personality of ʿUmar played an important role.

ʿUmar was a master at controlling and handling personnel. Who else could have dismissed the independently minded General Khālid, the politically active General ʿAmr, and the wealth-struck General Saʿd? More important, he had a natural instinct for policy development. The major political institutions of Islām had their origin in this period, including arrangements for the governor (*dīwān*) system; the founding of military centers; the registering of Muslims and their income; the establishment of regulations concerning non-Muslims; the institution of a system of judges (*qādī*), and so on.

The conquest of Jerusalem revealed his attitude toward Christians. The Christian inhabitants were granted security of life and property. Churches could remain, and Christians were granted freedom of worship. In return, they were to pay a tax (*jizya*) in lieu of military service. Similar arrangements were made in Persia. However, ʿUmar did not want his soldiers to obtain land in alien surroundings and settle down with native populations. His troops went out from Arabia and returned there, laden with wealth, thus spurring on other expeditions. Those who had to remain behind for administrative or security reasons were housed in specially constructed military towns. Some of these later became large cities and centers of future dynasties.

The stamp that ʿUmar placed on it all was his simple Islāmic faith. He is considered a model of virtue, and long are the lists of his merits. The story is told of how he sought for a place of worship in Jerusalem. He did not disturb existing sanctuaries. He found the place he wanted amid the deserted ruins of the temple area on Mt. Moriah. Clearing some rubble on that sacred spot of Abraham, he erected a small mosque. This was the site where a successor ruler, ʿAbd al-Malik, in 691 built the majestic monument, the Dome of the Rock, as well as the mosque of Al-Aqsa. The initial small structure really typified ʿUmar's understanding of Islām. Before he died at the age of 52 in 644—unfortunately, murdered by a Persian slave—ʿUmar had appointed a six-member committee to choose his successor. That successor was the third in line of the "rightly-guided" caliphs, and another contrasting personality.

3. ʿUthmān

Abū Bakr and ʿUmar were leaders of incomparable quality, and in their time the Muslim ship of state was lifted high by the waves of success. The gentle ʿUthmān b. ʿAffān was not so forceful a pilot, and he experienced stormy weather as well as favorable winds.

ʿUthmān was one of the earliest converts to the cause of Islām. Although the majority of the first believers were poor, ʿUthmān was a member of the leading Ummayad family and was a wealthy merchant. He was very careful of his grooming and presented a fine appearance. A courteous and considerate man, he did not like to say "no," and he loved his family. As loyal to the Prophet as his two predecessors, he suffered with Muhammad through the early years of persecution. At least once he helped lead a group of believers into Ethiopian exile. His marriage to Rukaiyya, the Prophet's daughter, ended in her early death; but the affection of the Prophet for ʿUthmān became clear when he gave him a second daughter, Umm Khultum. Perhaps this close association with the Prophet helped to determine the selection of ʿUthmān as caliph, even though there were other capable leaders among the surviving companions of the Prophet. The choice of ʿUthmān had great impact on the history of Islām. It meant that the Ummayad family, which included many of the Prophet's early opponents, had come to the fore, and the Hashimite family of the Prophet felt left out. This ancient family division has remained a constant factor in Muslim affairs.

During ʿUthmān's time the Muslim forces continued their forward march, probing into North Africa and what is now called Turkey. The advance was less rapid now, and economic problems began to raise their head. The latter had to do with the distribution and management of the vast accumulation of wealth that resulted from the conquests. The wealth itself brought inevitable corruption. In addition, as the expansion slowed down, there was greater acrimony over the distribution of the spoils.

ʿUthmān's greatest achievement was to direct the production of the official edition of the Qurʾān. We have noted that story earlier. This action involved some difficulty because a few areas such as Kufa resented the destruction of their own versions. However, ʿUthmān successfully implemented this all-important decision despite vigorous opposition in some quarters.

Things did not go well for ʿUthmān in the second half of his reign, and it finally ended in disaster. His administrative policies led to his assassination, which ruptured the unity of Islām. The story is a sad one. Like ʿUmar, ʿUthmān too had appointed governors for the conquered territories, but there were two major criticisms of his policies. First, it was alleged that he favored family members in his appointments. Secondly, it was charged that he failed to exercise strong enough control over the governors who ruled as they pleased. Certainly it must have been an almost impossible challenge to find an adequate number of skilled and loyal administrators for such a far-flung empire. Matters came to a head when a group of disaffected soldiers from Egypt brought their list of grievances to ʿUthmān. They were patiently heard out by the kindly leader and left with apparent satisfaction. However, in the confusion that followed, feelings turned in the other direction, the home of ʿUthmān was besieged, and finally some hotheads dared to lay hands on the unresisting and aged caliph. He was stabbed to death. Legend holds that his lifeblood stained the pages of his beloved Qurʾān, which he was reading at the time of the assassination. The event represents one of the truly traumatic moments in the history of the Muslim family. After all, the assassins were led by a son of Abū Bakr! The curtain of Islāmic unity was irreparably torn.

The tragedy at Medina plunged Muslims into gloom and created serious divisions. The powerful Muʿāwiya, a son of Abū Sufyān, had been appointed as the governor of Syria by the Caliph ʿUmar. He was also the cousin of ʿUthmān. Having heard of the caliph's approaching difficulties, Muʿāwiya had sent forces to assist him, but they were too late and returned. Where were the "Companions" of the Prophet, and why was it not possible for them to save their leader? No one really knows, but suspicion filled the air. Muʿāwiya himself never forgave that failure, and his deep resentment colored later events. The effects of the tragedy unfolded during the next five years in the reign of the fourth hero-caliph, ʿAlī ibn Tālib, cousin and son-in-law of the Prophet Muhammad.

4. ʿAlī

ʿAlī is revered by Sunnī Muslims as the fourth of the "rightly guided" caliphs and by Shīʿa Muslims as the first true successor of the Prophet. Thus a great deal of controversy revolves around the life and career of this unique leader.

ʿAlī was involved in the destiny of Islām from its historic beginning. There was an intimate relation between him and the Prophet Muhammad. ʿAlī's father and Muhammad's father were brothers, and the former, Abū Talib, was Muhammad's great protector. ʿAlī was like a younger brother to Muhammad, and later he married Fāṭima, Muhammad's daughter. One of the first three converts to Islām, he was the Prophet's loyal assistant. When Muhammad left Mecca by night, it was ʿAlī who slept in his bed, thereby deceiving the enemies. He stood beside Muhammad at the terrible struggle of Uhud, sustaining 16 wounds in his body, and like the lion for which he was named, he fought in almost all the early campaigns.

As great as his military prowess, so great was the fame of ʿAlī's piety. He was called "the friend of God" (*walī Allāh*). He cared little for the things of this world, gave away most of his possessions, and owned hardly anything when he died. He is reported to have said, "Blessed are those who have renounced this world, and only aspire to the life to come."[7] Others regarded him as an authority on the faith of Islām and frequently consulted him as to its meaning. He is pictured as short and heavy, with large dark eyes and a broad smile. He left 14 sons and 17 daughters; among them Ḥasan and Ḥusain, who were born to Fāṭima, took precedence.

Despite this formidable record, ʿAlī had been passed over in the earlier selections to the leadership role. For whatever reason—was the cause in him or in others?—he could not rally sufficient support for his claims. He now became caliph when ʿUthmān died, but even then the choice was disputed. Muʿāwiya for one did not agree with it. He was disturbed over ʿAlī's alleged "failure" to rescue ʿUthmān, and perhaps more important, he wanted the position himself. It was not only Muʿāwiya, however, who resisted the clear choice of the Medinans. Two old Muslim companions, Talha and Zubair, persuaded ʿĀʾisha to join them in opposition to ʿAlī over the issue of the punishment of ʿUthmān's murderers. Their forces met ʿAlī near Basra in the "Battle of the Camel," in 656, the first open warfare between Muslim believers. ʿAlī won out in the struggle as Talha and Zubayr perished. ʿĀʾisha was captured, but ʿAlī treated her with the greatest care and respect and sent her back to Medina.

ʿAlī then transferred his capital to Kufa at the borders of Iraq, where the believers had solidly supported him. He now turned his attention to Muʿāwiya, who had hung on to his governorship in Damascaus. ʿAlī's army and Muʿāwiya's Syrian forces met at the Battle of Siffin in 657. After heavy fighting, ʿAlī's opponents tricked him into accepting arbitration by placing leaves of the Qurʾān upon their lances and crying, "Let the Qurʾān decide!" but the final result was a stalemate. Muʿāwiya maintained his power in Syria and soon controlled Egypt with the help of the wily ʿAmr al-ʿĀs. The Caliph ʿAlī had to be content with ruling Iraq and Arabia. "Not every archer hits the mark," he said. It was not possible for him to reign over the whole Islāmic empire, and from that time forward political division was a constant factor in Muslim history.

ʿAlī's most trying struggle came with a group of Muslim believers called Khārijites (i.e., *khawārij* = "seceders"). They were religious puritans who did not like the fact that ʿAlī engaged in arbitration with Muʿāwiya whom they regarded as an unworthy pretender. They viewed ʿUthmān's murder as a legal execution, and ʿAlī could not be faulted for not pressing charges against the attackers. They felt, however, that by accepting arbitration he had abandoned his moral position and he had forfeited his right to be their leader. Thus it was time for them "to go out." Muslims must be pure, and it is un-Islāmic to follow an impure leader. How ironic that the pious ʿAlī was charged with a form of impiety! Since the Khārijites chose to oppose him with violence, much of ʿAlī's time and effort had to be expended in the task of overcoming their resistance. In the end, however, it was an extreme Khārijite who in 661 assassinated ʿAlī while he was at prayer in a Kufan mosque. That distressing event evokes great sadness in Muslim hearts. Three of the four "rightly-guided" caliphs had fallen by the sword, but the last of them was a member of the Prophet's own family!

It is not surprising that there should have been veneration for the family of the Prophet among early Muslims, and that veneration continues today. All over the Muslim world believers love to trace their descent to the Prophet, and if they are successful in doing so they are known as *sayyids* or *sharīfs*, and they are sometimes given special honor. Now that ʿAlī had died, the veneration passed forward to Ḥasan and Ḥusain, his sons through the Prophet's daughter. We will consider their story below. In concluding the story of ʿAlī it may be mentioned that many legends gather around his name and memory. By some, and especially by Shīʿa Muslims, he is regarded as "the king of saints," his wisdom equals that of Solomon, and his special powers have resulted in many miracles.

We turn next to three prominent women in the history of early Islām, namely, Khadīja, ʿĀʾisha, and Fāṭima. Their names are regularly given to Muslim girls.

323

5. Khadīja

Khadīja b. Khuwayhid (555?-620) was an important member
of the Quraysh tribe, the first wife of the Prophet Muhammad, his
first convert, and his comforter in distress. When she was age 30,
her father died and she became a career woman in merchandise.
She managed her family affairs and business very well, becoming
wealthy and achieving a high social position. This formidable
woman was impressed by Muhammad's competence and
character, and she gave him a job in connection with her trading
business.

The relationship soon became a closer one. Khadīja had been
married twice and had previous children, but she was now either
widowed or divorced. Through a friend she made an overture to
Muhammad, suggesting, "What would you think if a woman such
as Khadīja would propose a marriage?" When the reply came
back positively, the marriage was arranged, and it turned into a
warm and loving alliance. Khadīja shared with Muhammad her
wealth and standing.

When the Prophet began to go to Mt. Hira for meditation
purposes, Khadīja did not complain, and she sometimes
accompanied him. After the first revelation she accepted it as
genuine and reassured Muhammad. She continued that service in
later years and stood by the Prophet's side until her death two
years prior to the Hijra. Saadia Chishti says of Khadīja, "In the
Prophet's first wife, Khadījah, the Muslim wife finds her best
example ... She is known for her untold sacrifices in order to
spread the message of Islām, while maintaining a household,
serving her husband, and leading her family in accordance with
the tenets of Islām."[8] For this reason many call her *umm
al-muᶜminīn*, "mother of the faithful."

6. ᶜĀᵓisha

After Khadīja died the six-year-old ᶜĀᵓisha (613–78), daughter
of Abū Bakr, was betrothed to the Prophet Muhammad. Early
betrothal was common in Arab custom, and the arrangement
cemented an important alliance. The marriage was consummated
after the Hijra in 623. ᶜĀᵓisha was very becoming, and she had

considerable influence with the Prophet. She almost lost that influence in an unfortunate event. At the age of 15 she was accidentally left behind at a stopping place on a caravan trip, but was rescued and brought to Medina by a youth. This caused some scandal, and various individuals including ʿAlī suggested a divorce. At this time, however, a revelation (24:11ff.) was received by the Prophet, decreeing that a charge of adultery must be sustained by four witnesses. This incident helps to explain the later antipathy between ʿĀʾisha and ʿAlī.

ʿĀʾisha was devoted to Muhammad, and when he was dying the Prophet requested that he be taken into her chamber. Thus at the age of 18 ʿĀʾisha was left as a childless widow; however, she never remarried, and instead threw her energies into the affairs of the *umma*. She became as involved in politics as Khadīja had been involved in business.

ʿĀʾisha was not pleased with the Caliph ʿUthmān's management of Muslim affairs, but she was even more displeased with ʿAlī and his alleged failure to deal with ʿUthmān's killers. As we have noted above, together with Talha and Zubair and a thousand warriors, she aggressively challenge ʿAlī at Basra. The struggle is called the Battle of the Camel because some of the heaviest fighting surged around her litter as she sat on her great camel. After ʿAlī sent her back home she withdrew from active politics, and later became reconciled to both ʿAlī and Muʿāwiya.

Because her life crossed both Muhammad's career and the great events of early Islām, ʿĀʾisha became the source of hundreds of traditions.[9] She was noted for her fiery personality and strong views. She was said to have been eloquent, literate, poetical, with some knowledge of theology and law. She was also called a "mother of believers," but perhaps the title that most aptly captures the essence of this heroine of Islām is "the Truthful One."

7. Fāṭima

Fāṭima (605–33) was the youngest of four daughters of Muhammad and Khadīja, the others being Zaynab, Rukaiyya, and Umm Khultum. The daughter of Khadīja's old age, she was greatly loved by her parents. At her mother's death Fāṭima was disconsolate, and Muhammad comforted her by saying that a wonderful pavilion was prepared for her mother in heaven. As a young girl Fāṭima cleaned off the dirt that was thrown on her father's head in Mecca, while he was praying. Later in Mecca she tended his wounds after the defeat of Uhud, and she used to pray at the graves of Muslim martyrs.

Fāṭima was married to ʿAlī, and she bore the Prophet's grandsons, Ḥasan and Ḥusain. After Muhammad's death she supported ʿAlī's claims to the caliphate, but to no avail. She soon found herself in disagreement with Abū Bakr regarding the disposal of a piece of Muhammad's property. Fāṭima claimed the right over a certain oasis, but Abū Bakr decreed that the Prophet had willed its possession to the entire community as his voluntary alms. She fought off both Abū Bakr and ʿUmar with an Arab woman's ultimate weapon, the threat to unloose her hair in public![10] The young Fāṭima sickened and died a year after the Prophet's demise, and there are stories that she became reconciled to Abū Bakr before her death.

For all Muslims Fāṭima represents the image of a hardworking and helpful woman, who is also the defender of her family's rights. Shīʿa Muslims endlessly elaborate on her graces and miracles. Among her many titles is al-Zahrāʾ, "The Light," and she is regarded as "the model of ideal womanhood," and even as Mother-Creator" and "virgin."[11] She, it is believed, will be the first person to enter Paradise after the Resurrection, where she will appear with Mary, the mother of Jesus, as a true *sayyida*, or saint of God. A female Muslim scholar declares,

> Muslims unanimously recognize her as the fountainhead of female spirituality in Islām, because she occupied herself with the purity of the Oneness and Unity of God and was confirmed in her absolute sincerity in the practices of the beliefs and tenets of Islām ... expressing her spirituality of the highest order through her role as a daughter, wife and mother.[12]

From the story of these heroines of Islām we turn to the last of our selected group of Muslim heroes, namely, Ḥusain, the son of ʿAlī and the grandson of Muhammad. After his untimely death the stream of Muslim history broadens into a wide delta of people and events.

8. Ḥusain

Ḥusain ibn ʿAlī (627–80) is the epitome of the Muslim hero-saint. Annually on the tenth day of Muḥarram the Muslim world remembers his tragic death and grieves.

Ḥusain's sorrowful history is intertwined with the triumphant rise of Muʿāwiya that took place after the death of Caliph ʿAlī. The bold and able Muʿāwiya succeeded him as the fifth Caliph of Islām (661–80). Furthermore, he became the founder of the first great dynasty of Islām, the Ummayad dynasty, named after his family, which lasted from 661 to 750. It resulted from the decision of Muʿāwiya to introduce the hereditary royal principle of leadership into Islām. Up to that point Sunnī Muslims had argued for the qualifications of piety and ability, while Shīʿas spoke up for the Prophet's family. Muʿāwiya chose to assign the caliphal succession to his loose-living son, Yazīd, and thus the theory of kingship entered Islāmic history.

A natural leader, Muʿāwiya aggressively pursued Islāmic expansion westward toward Algeria, eastward toward Central Asia, and with newly organized seapower he moved against Byzantium. He took Islām ever further along the path from a simple Arabian kingdom to a multicultural empire. Muʿāwiya established his capital at Damascus in the heart of his power base of Syria. Thereby he moved the base of authority from the center of Arabian Muslim piety in Medina to the center of Greek-Syrian-Christian culture, and in so doing he began a major transformation in Muslim culture and civilization. During his rule the Muslim *umma* was more or less at peace and relatively united. Nevertheless, many Muslims remember his reign as much for the tragedy of Ḥusain which immediately followed it, as for his impressive achievements.

Hasan ibn ʿAlī, Muhammad's oldest grandson, had chosen to withdraw from political affairs and had died at Medina around 670. Ḥusain succeeded him as the leader of the party of the Prophet's family. When Muʿāwiya I died in 680 and his son Yazīd presumed to the caliphate, Ḥusain stepped forward and accepted the invitation of supporters at Kufa to challenge Yazīd. In 681 he led a small band of family members and followers, perhaps as few as 70, on a trek to Iraq. There the promised support melted away as General Ubaidullah's army surrounded his tiny force and followed it to Kerbela. At Kerbela an ill-fated struggle resulted in the death of Husain, and all but five of the direct descendants of the Prophet Muhammad. Husain himself was not only killed but beheaded, much to the horror of the uncomprehending Muslim world. Husain, the flesh and blood of the Prophet Muhammad, had been struck down! Everywhere sincere Muslims shuddered and wondered how such an event could transpire in the household of Islām. Yazīd became the prototype of the anti-hero in Islām, and the term "Yazīd" is the greatest expression of contempt in Muslim vocabulary. The death of Husain crystallized the Muslim division into the majority Sunnī and the minority Shīʿa segments, a division that exists today.

The personality of Husain is lauded in Muslim biography. He is remembered as the boy whom Muhammad loved. He was not a power-hungry person and came forward only by the persuasion of others. Not a violent man, he refused to strike back at the soldiers who attacked him. He is regarded as a pious and saintly person who in no way deserved his persecution and death. Shīʿas in particular extol his saintly virtues and seek his intercession on their behalf. "Ya, Husain" is a common Shīʿa cry. He is not only a hero-saint, but also a martyr-savior, whose self-denial and suffering was undertaken on behalf of his people and their sins. His bloody sacrifice is therefore widely commemorated in the passion plays of Shīʿa Islām.[13] But Husain also—and especially in contemporary times—symbolizes the struggle against tyranny and the necessity to accept suffering as the price of liberty from the oppressor. Husain is quoted as saying,

> He who sees a cruel governor violating God's law, breaking his covenant, acting in contrast to the Tradition of the Prophet, mischievous and suppressing people, then he does not try to change that ruler by action or speech, indeed God has promised with an appropriate place in hell.[14]

The shrine of Husain in Kerbela, after Mecca and Medina, is the most important pilgrimage center in Islām. Abdulla and Amina's Shīʿa friends travel there with the same pleasure as Abdulla and Amina go to Mecca. Their mixed emotion of reverence and pathos symbolizes the Muslim attitude to Islāmic history in general.

Islāmic history is like a broad river that has its beginning in a spring and a narrow brook in the high mountains. The spring is the revelation of Allāh through the Prophet Muhammad. The narrow brook is the first 30 years of Islām after Muhammad.

From this point the river broadens out as Islām spread to become the world religion as we know it today. It was a remarkable expansion, but a history that included tragedy as well as heroism. We turn to that story next.

Notes

[1]John Renard, *Islām and the Heroic Image* (Columbia: University of South Carolina, 1993), p. 1.

[2]"Al-ʿAshara ʾl-Mubashshara," and "Ṣaḥāba," *SEI*, pp. 46, 488.

[3]John Williams, *Themes*, p. 79.

[4]Guillaume, tr., *Ibn Isḥāq*, p. 661.

[5]G. Levi della Vida, "ʿUmar," *SEI*, p. 601, quoting al-Muḥibb al-Tabarī, Manākib al-ʿAshara, i., 199.

[6]Ḥadīth descriptions quoted by B. Lewis, *Islām*, Vol. 1 (New York: Harper & Row, 1974), p. 12.

[7]C. Huart, "ʿAlī," *SEI*, p. 31.

[8]Saadia Chishti, "Female Spirituality in Islām," S. Nasr ed., *Islāmic Spirituality*, p. 205.

[9]M. Seligsohn, "ʿĀʾisha," *SEI*, p. 26, suggests that perhaps 1210 Ḥadīth can be traced to her; M. Watt, "ʿĀʾisha," *EI²*, I, pp. 307f., notes that 300 traditions in Bukhārī and Muslim find their source in her.

[10]L. Veccia, "Fāṭima," *EI²*, II, p. 842.

[11]Moojan Momen, *An Introduction to Shiʿi Islām* (New Haven: Yale University Press, 1985), pp. 235f.

[12]Saadia, Chishti; Nasr, ed., *Islāmic Spirituality*, pp. 207f.

[13]Cf. Dwight Donaldson, *The Shiʿite Religion* (London: Luzac & Co., 1933), pp. 341–43, for descriptions of this aspect of the veneration of Ḥusain.

[14]Yusuf Fadhl, *Imam Ḥusain's Revolution* (Teheran: Muslim Youth Association, 1970), p. 34.

16

Muslim History Unfolds: The Shaping of Islām and Its Memories

Abdulla's town is in a valley, surrounded by hills. He and Amina see the beauty of their lovely valley, but they cannot see beyond. They do travel occasionally and know that there are other things to see, but they like home best.

The metaphor illustrates Abdulla's relation to Islāmic history. Abdulla's faith and feeling are not based on a strong knowledge of Islāmic history. Islām spread and became a global, multicultural religion. As it spread it experienced many ups and downs, great achievements and also human failures. That unfolding Muslim story with its repeated rise and fall, its oscillation between heroes and anti-heroes, and its steady movement forward to the status of the second largest religion in the world, is beyond Abdulla's and Amina's range of sight. Like most Muslim believers they know about their own culture, but their knowledge of other Muslim cultures is limited, and their awareness of Muslim historical events is cursory.

That situation is now changing. One factor is the increase in education. More and more Muslim students are studying Islāmic history in colleges and universities. A second factor is the increasing travel among Muslim nations. In the first centuries of Islām there was tremendous mobility in the Muslim world. Then for a long period of time it was only the pilgrimage that brought Muslims together. Now Muslims are traveling again, and the experience is culturally enriching. Finally, the mass media and literature distribution aid the process, as new Islāmic information services spread their materials. Nevertheless, there is a lot of ground to be made up before Muslims as a whole become more knowledgeable about the history and culture of various parts of the widespread Muslim world.

This being the case, can we omit a discussion of Muslim

history from a study of Muslim faith and feeling? We do so at some risk. The first reason is that the shaping of the wider Muslim world affects Abdulla and Amina where they are. The second reason is that Muslim feelings are very much tied up with Muslim memories. We have taken note of the fact that Muslims are nostalgic about their heroes. There are also other feelings that they carry forward from the past. They are proud of the rapid growth of Islām and the achievements of Muslim civilization, as far as they are aware of them. They are not proud of the divisions and tragedies that are also a part of that history. However, they are especially depressed and angry when they recall their plight as helpless colonies under western nations, and, conversely, they are bouyant and hopeful over recent history, especially since the discovery of oil and the recovery of political power.

We may summarize by saying that, although Abdulla and Amina do not know the intricacies of the Muslim story, they do know the names of some of its main characters, they resonate to some of its events, and they glory in the high points of its cultural splendor. Their knowledge is episodic and selective, and on the whole they prefer not to think of the tragedies that took place. In what follows, therefore, we will note only some of the high spots of Muslim history that helped to give shape to the Muslim world of today. We start with the early spread of Islām.

A. The Spread of Islām

The rapid spread of Islām is one of the marvels of human history. Its beginning in Arabia was small, and it was surrounded by powerful and seemingly well entrenched religio-political empires. Yet Islām burst out from that small beginning and within a century encompassed many territories and large populations. In the view of Muslim believers, this remarkable advance confirmed and fulfilled the promises of God to His people. However, we may also point to tangible human factors that help to account for this astonishing development. They include the following:
— The simplicity of the Muslim message had a power in it. In that regard it compared favorably with the more complex religious messages of the day.
— The religious zeal of the Muslim believers who were ready to die as martyrs (*shahīds*) for the faith was a factor; the

promise of immediate entry into the joys of Paradise, provided a strong stimulus to those who struggled for the faith.

— Coupled with that, the concept of *jihād* was gradually interpreted as a divine mandate to expand the Islāmic domain beyond the borders of Arabia; this provided another form of incentive and a unifying principle.

— The natural hardiness and courage of Arab Muslim warriors enabled them to overcome formidable hardships, including their long distance from the home base.

— The strong leadership of the Muslim forces, their fast-moving cavalry, and their ability to maintain military momentum helped Muslims win against superior enemy forces.

— The desire for booty provided a major motivation for the rapid Muslim advance; the poverty-level Arab *badwā* were suddenly coming into possession of vast wealth, a portion of which they were able to retain.

— Observers have frequently pointed out the fact that the natural Arab energy had been bottled up within the confines of the Arabian peninsula and had never found a real opportunity for release; now, under the banner of Islām, it exploded on the world scene.

— The power vacuum left behind in the wake of the terrible struggle between the two world powers, the Eastern Roman Empire (Byzantium) and Persia, was unquestionably a primary factor in the fast-moving Muslim advance. Their two armies had fought each other to virtual exhaustion, and they were not able to resist the driving new force that emerged from Arabia.

— The weak state of the religions was the final factor in the context. In particular the weak state of Christianity facilitated the Muslim advance. Christians at that time were divided ethnically and theologically, and there were many fierce controversies; at grassroots levels Christian learning was often superficial; and at court levels there was a great deal of corruption. In Persia the ruling Zoroastrian religion was weakened by its struggles with a form of communism (Mazdakism) and gnosticism (Manichaeism). The great religions were in no condition to effectively resist the dynamism of the Islāmic force.

All these factors combined to enable the rapid spread of Islām ranging from the Atlantic Ocean to the China Sea in less than a century. But we must still ask, *how* did Islām advance? That is, what was the method by which its advance was achieved? The answer is important because the disinformation in this area is considerable, and it causes resentment among Muslim friends. It is important to distinguish two questions:

How did Islām advance territorially?
How did Islām advance numerically?

Islām advanced territorially in two ways—through military conquest and through peaceful methodologies. Military conquest was the dominant approach in the early period, but peaceful methodologies eventually replaced it. Sometimes these two methods went on side by side, sometimes separately.

The military expansion of Islām took place primarily in the Middle East, North Africa, Central Asia, North India, and Europe. Although there must have been many Muslims interested in spreading the *faith* of Islām,[1] the early expansion was largely an attempt to acquire territory, power and control, and wealth. It was not in the first place a drive to win converts for Islām. New adherents to the faith, especially if they were from Arab tribes resident in conquered lands,[2] were obviously welcome. This, however, could not have been the first concern. The religious populations in the areas where Islām initially expanded were mainly Christian, Jewish, and Zoroastrian, and the Qurʾān had recognized these as "people of the book" with a special status. It was also not in the best interests of the conquerors to pressure or compel the conversion of these populations, for the large non-Muslim groups provided a strong tax base for the conquerors. There were some zealous Muslims who violated the policy, especially when rebellions occurred, but on the whole the principle was maintained.

The second method of Muslim territorial expansion was the peaceful approach of emigration and immigration, trading contacts, and intermarriage. The emigration pattern started very early, beginning in Iraq, as Arab Muslims settled abroad. The reverse immigration pattern was just as important, as non-Muslim tribes, especially Turkish tribes and Mongols, moved into Muslim territories and accepted the faith of their host cultures.[3] The trading contacts had already been there in pre-Islāmic times, but they increased and extended with the acceleration of Muslim power. The intermarriage of traders and soldiers abroad was an ordinary practice. This peaceful methodology characterized the Muslim advance into South India, Southeast Asia, China, and Sub-Saharan Africa. Commerce was the vehicle, and lay Muslims carried their faith with them. This took place in a natural manner as they did business with indigenous people. (Until recent times Islām has not had a professional missionary class, and Muslims have not considered the religious mission of Islām (*daᶜwa*) to be a specialized task; the closest to this concept were itinerant Sūfī saints whose example and message had wide impact, and Ismāᶜīlī missionaries.) Through the peaceful modalities of commerce, immigration, and intermarriage territories became at least partially Muslim in an entirely different way than the militant method. The contrast is well illustrated from India where Arab traders brought Islām peacefully to the Malabar coast of South India, while Muhammad ibn Qasim brought Islām militarily to Sind in northwest India, both in the same early period.

The question of how Islām spread *numerically* reflects the situations described above. In captured territories where Muslims exercised military and political control, a process of Islāmicization took place, as native populations gradually became Muslim. Either the inhabitants of the captured regions were persuaded of the merits of the new faith, or they desired the social and economic advantages of being Muslim. For them it was largely a matter of free choice. As we have noted, Muslims, despite certain restrictions, maintained a live and let live policy over against other religions, and forced conversion was the exception. Once again, this fact is well illustrated from the history of events in South Asia where Hindus, though considered polytheists, were nevertheless granted the same status as people of the book on a *de facto* basis. It is noteworthy that only a small minority of South Asians were Muslim even after five centuries of Muslim rule. L. Bevan Jones sums up the issue as follows:

> The Khalīfa ᶜUmar seems to have been favorably inclined toward Christians, and when he conquered Jerusalem he treated the Christians very fairly ... More than one Christian historian says that the Christians in Syria preferred the Muslim rule to that of the Romans, under whom they had suffered such persecution for the Jacobite form of their Christian faith. Under the Ummayads the Christians undoubtedly suffered a certain amount of persecution, but we must confess that at least some of those persecutions were stirred up by complaints made to the Muslim authorities by one Christian against another ... From what

little information we have, it appears that in the early days of the Khilāfat those Christians who adopted Islām did so of their own accord. Probably many nominal Christians became Muslim in order to avoid paying the *jizya* [tax on non-Muslims]. At a later time, from about the ninth century onwards, the economic position of the Christians may have led some of them to embrace Islām ... It is probable, from the time of the first Muslim conquests, many Christians were convinced by the success of the Muslim armies that Islām was approved by God.[4]

The issue of religious equality which, as Thomas Jefferson pointed out, transcends even the issue of religious toleration, is a perennial one for all societies, especially religious societies. Abdulla and Amina believe that the record of early Muslims on this point is better than has been often portrayed, and compares favorably with other religious societies of that period. In fact, the model of Caliph ʿUmar represents a pattern that many educated modern Muslims admire and even put forward as a rebuke to intolerant Muslim groups.

From the early spread of Islām, we now turn to its dividing. The heroes of early Islām had led the community outward in a generally unified expansion, a heroic history. Now the profile of Islāmic history takes on a different form.

B. The Muslim World Divides and Expands

As Islām spread, the Muslim world grew bigger. As it enlarged, it divided. The division, in turn, resulted in further advance. However, it was impossible to keep up the pace of the original growth. The period of rapid advance merged with a period of settlement, consolidation, and slower extension. Settlement and consolidation brought all the problems associated with the management of an empire. Moreover, people other than Arabs were now involved in the community of Islām, and a complicated period of cultural adjustment was under way.

Although it grew more slowly after the hectic first century, the world of Islām continued to expand. By the end of the 16th century Islām had penetrated to the boundaries of Asia, Africa, and Eastern Europe. In contemporary times it has moved into Western Europe, the Americas, and Australia, thus completing the saga of becoming a world religion. Under the pressure of this globalization, the ideal of one great pan-Islāmic society under one commonly accepted leader has faded away, to be replaced by the concept of a family of Muslims, a spiritual *umma* that remains emotionally one despite its national divisions.

We must briefly view the greatest of the Muslim empires and subempires that dominated the Muslim scene in the course of this development. The various names and places seem distant, but they make up a knowing Muslim's image of a partly heroic history. There is much in the total development that Muslims themselves regret—dictators and cruelty, schisms and wars, and a whole range of un-Islāmic behavior. But it is common to forget the roughness of an age and to remember the greatness of its civilization. Muslims celebrate their societal achievements, even as they deplore periodic failures. At one end of the Muslim world a believer stands in wonder before the arabesque splendor of the Alhambra Palace in Grenada, Spain, "a Mecca for all sensitive minds."[5] In the geographical middle of that world he/she may gaze in admiration at the intense blues of the great mosque in Isfahan, Iran, or view the monumental symmetry of the Taj Mahal in Agra, India. At the other end the viewer may wonder at the pagoda-like forms of the ancient mosque in Sian, China, or marvel at the brilliance of *wayang* puppetry in Yogyakarta, Indonesia, that utilizes the eternal theme of human struggle between good and evil. In a very real sense, Muslim history itself represents that struggle.

The two foundational dynasties of Islām are the Ummayads and the Abassids.

1. The Ummayad Dynasty (680–750)

Muʿāwiya I founded the Ummayad dynasty under which Islām became relatively unified. The dynasty, centered at Damascus in Syria, was Arab-oriented, monarchical and secular. On the one hand, it instituted the Arabicization of the Muslim empire, in administrative language and coinage, which appealed to the pious Muslims of Medina. On the other hand, it drew the wrath of many believers because of its overwhelmingly imperial style that contradicted the principle of Muslim equality, its casual and often careless attitude toward religion, and the scandalous behavior of many of its caliphs. An exception was ʿAbd al-Malik (685–705), the only major Ummayad caliph known for his piety. He and his son started the mosque-building tradition. He was responsible for the Dome of the Rock and Al-Aqsa in Jerusalem; his son, Walīd, demolished the Church of John the Baptist in Damascus and constructed the now ancient mosque in its place. With the help of his quite ruthless general, al-Hajjāj, Caliph ʿAbd al-Malik unified the empire that had been divided by warring Arab factions, including a rival caliph, Ibn al-Zubayr who had ruled Mecca for nine years.

In the Ummayad period Islām moved westward—Carthage in North Africa falling in 697—through Spain and into southern France. There the exhausted Muslim forces were finally defeated at Poitiers in 732, marking the end of the Muslim military advance to the west. Eastward Muslims penetrated to Central Asia, Eastern Persia, and the borders of Afghanistan and India.

2. The Abbasid Dynasty (750–1258)

Opposing the growing secularization, Muslims everywhere were calling for a return to a pure Islām, and against that background the Abbasids came into power. They claimed to be a new moral force, a "blessed dynasty,"[6] with divine sanction and support. The Abbasids were named for an uncle of the Prophet, and they were sympathetic both to the Prophet's Hashimite family, from which they claimed descent, and to a higher role for religion in the state. The first Abbasid caliph was appropriately named ʿAbūʾl-ʿAbbās (d. 754). The Persian-Iraqi Muslims now came to the fore and, symbolizing the eastward orientation, the city of Baghdad was founded as the new capital at the juncture of the Tigris and Euphrates rivers. Culturally the Abbasids produced the magnificent Golden Age of Islāmic civilization, which included vast achievements in mathematics and astronomy; medicine; architecture; geography, commerce, and industry; philosophy, law, and theology. Their rulers supported the development of religious studies, but they were as imperial as the Ummayads, and the behavior of the kings was not much different. The names of Harūn al-Rashīd (d. 809) and al-Maʿmūn (d. 833) rank with those of the greatest rulers of all time.

The second half of the Abbasid dynasty witnessed the breakup of the unified Muslim empire. The rule of one caliph over a fairly united body of Muslims really lasted only to the mid-900s, after which it was replaced by territorially based governors (*amirs*) who would give nominal allegiance to the caliph at Baghdad.[7] In addition to the growing independence of the emirates, the advent of the Christian Crusades (1095–1270) compelled Muslim leaders to think of defense rather than expansion. Nevertheless Islām continued to extend its influence eastward. The primary expansion was among the Turkish peoples of Eastern Anatolia and Central Asia, beginning around 875. Access was gained to China along the great Silk Route across Central Asia. By sea, on wings of trade, Muslims pushed eastward from Malabar in South India toward Malaysia and Indonesia. However, in 1258 in a catastrophic event, the Abbasid dynasty and its capital city fell before the great Mongol invasion.

3. Spanish Islām (756–1492)

A Spanish branch of the Ummayads continued in Spain after the dynasty's fall in the Middle East. There an almost incredibly rich Muslim, Christian, Jewish/ Spanish-North African blend of cultures developed. The development began with violence and ended in tragedy, but in between "Moorish" Islām became a jewel in the crown of Muslim civilization.[8] The depth of its philosophy and the delicacy of its architecture have rarely been matched. Here are located the exquisitely decorated pillars and arches of the great mosque in Cordoba, which became a Christian cathedral in 1236, and from here the preeminent philosopher, Ibn Rushd (Averroes), influenced the West. When Christian Spain under Ferdinand finally recaptured full control of the country in the late 1400s, many Spanish Muslims were compelled to become Christians (Moriscos), and were then punished under the laws of the Inquisition; thousands of others were forced to flee as refugees to North Africa.

4. Berber Islām (750–1269)

The Berbers of North Africa were early converts to Islām, but they maintained their distinct culture and tribal organization. Their two major dynasties were the Almoravids (1059–1125) and the Almohads (1147–1269). Both dynasties were heavily involved in Spanish affairs, often militantly. The Almoravids were noted for their puritan simplicity. The founder of the Almohads, Ibn Tumārt (d. 1130) is the prototype of Muslim reformers who strive to restore Islām to a pure monotheism, using the Prophet Muhammad as their example. He called himself the Mahdi, the expected Deliverer of Islām. Nevertheless, mystical and philosophical movement flourished under the later Almohads. These contrasting approaches—puritanism and liberalis—remain as a distinctive feature of North African Islām today.

5. The Fatimids (901–1174)

The Fatimids were Ismaʿīlīs, the smaller of the two major groups of Shīʿa Muslims. They take their name from the granddaughter of the Prophet, their heroine Fāṭima. The Fatimids vigorously opposed the Abbasids and Sunnī Islām. They embarked on a revolutionary attempt to install their own caliph-imam as the head of Islām. From their base in Yemen they first took control of North Africa, and then of Egypt where they built Cairo as their capital. From this power base they sent Ismaʿīlī missionaries into every part of the world, proclaiming Ismaʿīlī tenets. Theirs was a brilliant culture stretching from Tunisia to Syria to Mecca. In memory of Fāṭima in 972 the Fatimids established Al-Azhar at Cairo, which is now the most influential *Sunnī* religious school in Islām. The Fatimids were weakened by internal divisions and fell before Saladin, the Sunnī leader from Syria.

As part of the Abbasid breakup that the Fatimids helped to produce, other dynasties arose in this period, including the Buwayhids (Buyids) in Persia, the Hamdanids in Syria, and the Ghaznavids in Afghanistan.

6. The Seljuks and Ayyubids (1055–1243)

The Seljuks were the first Turkish Muslims, and they became

the major dynasty within later Abbasid Islām. They were the "saviors" of Sunnī orthodox Islām against an increasingly dominant Shīʿism. The Seljuks built a network of *madrasas*, sponsored the advance of religious learning, and constructed many great mosques. One of the greatest of all Muslim prime ministers, Nizam ul-Mulk (d. 1092), fostered the work of the greatest of all Muslim theologians, al-Ghazālī (d. 1111). The Seljuks enthusiastically embraced Persian language and culture, and during this period they became the primary language and culture of Abbasid Islām.

The Seljuks also encouraged the immigration and settlement of newly converted nomadic Turkish tribes in Asia Minor, thus furthering both the Turkification and Islāmicization of that region. Their victory against Byzantine Christian forces at Manzikert in 1070 facilitated this process. The emboldened Seljuks established a major subdynasty in inner Asia Minor (Anatolia), which was called the Sultanate of Rum and which was marked by a relatively just and tolerant administration of the interreligious and multicultural population of the area. The region and period produced Jalāl al-Dīn Rūmī (d. 1273), the great Muslim mystical poet of love, whose epic work (*mathnawī*) has been called "the Qurʾān of the Sūfis."[9]

During the Seljuk time the Kurdish Ayyubids wrestled Egypt away from the Fatimids and also ruled Syria, led by the able warrior, Saladin (d. 1193). Zealous for the conversion of both Shīʿa Muslims and Christians, as well as for the restoration of Sunnism, they wielded strong influence during their period of power (1173–1250). Saladin's recapture of Jerusalem from the hands of the Crusaders was a vital moment in Muslim history.

Today 89 percent of the world's Muslims are Sunnīs. For at least a century as Shīʿa dynasties dominated the scene there could have been ample doubt that this would be the outcome. It may be suggested that it was in these years that Sunnī orthodoxy turned the tide in its favor and set the course of Islāmic history.

7. The Mongols (1258–1506)

The Mongols from inner Mongolia were the rulers of the widest empire in human history. Surging westward, they captured

Baghdad in 1258 and ended the Abbasid dynasty. They also engulfed much of eastern Europe. The last Abbasid caliph was killed, and a shadow caliphate was set up in Cairo, which transferred to Istanbul in 1517. The concept of a unified *umma* was still an emotionally powerful idea, but the disaster of Baghdad had turned it into an empty dream. The Mongol conqueror, Hulagu Khān, and other shamanist and Buddhist Mongols had a leaning toward Christianity—it is said that Hulagu's wife was a Christian—but when the Mongol leader, Ghāzān, chose Islām as his faith in 1295, the die was cast. The action was instrumental in determining that in the end Central Asia and Western China would become predominantly Muslim. The Mongols adopted settlement patterns and gradually followed their leaders into Islām. Although the Mongol period was not devoid of cultural achievement, it was a time of great instability. Tīmūr (d. 1405), sometimes known as Tamerlane, a cruel Turkish-Mongol tyrant, ruled from Mongolia to the Mediterranean, and from Moscow to Delhi (1380–1405). But from his capital in Samarqand the bigoted ruler destroyed much of the Muslim world and its culture and systematically massacred Christians. He has been called "one of the worst enemies to whom Islāmic civilization ever fell a victim."[10] If Saladin is a hero of Sunnī Islām, Tīmūr is an anti-hero.

A survivor of the Timurid dynasty, named Babur, founded the Mughul Empire in India in 1525.

8. The Mamluks (1250–1517)

The Mamluks represent a remarkable phenomenon in Muslim history, namely, the slave-soldier rulers. Slaves were recruited, Islāmicized and trained in the military arts. Thereupon their generals became powerful and took effective control of their societies. The Mamluks were Turkish and Circassian slave-soldiers who broke off from the Ayyubids and made themselves the masters of Egypt and Syria. They maintained the caliphate as an office in Cairo but paid little or no attention to its incumbents. After 1517 Egypt was a province of the Ottoman empire, but the Mamluk slave-soldiers succeeded in penetrating even the Ottoman administration and keeping some power. Perhaps the greatest contribution of the Mamluks was the fact that they successfully stemmed the tide of the Mongol advance to the west. They also completed the defeat of the Crusader kingdoms.

The Mamluks continued the process of making Cairo the grand center of Arabic-Muslim civilization. They supported many literary and building projects, not the least of which were the impressive tomb-mosques of the city. The two intellectual heroes who emerged from the Mamluk period were Ibn Taimīya (d. 1328), a great reform theologian whose influence on modern Muslim puritan movements is a towering one, and Ibn Khaldūn (d. 1406), the seminal Muslim "philosopher of civilization" who tried to understand Muslim history and its relation to human history as a whole.[11]

The Mamluks lost their power before the twin pressures of the Ottomans on the one hand, and on the other hand the Portuguese who now emerged on the scene as the vanguard of renewed European power.

9. The Safavids (1501–1722)

The Safavids were the great Persian dynasty that established Shīʿism as the state religion of Iran. Shīʿism constituted the faith of the majority of Persians, but to that time it was never established as the state religion. The Safavid rulers used the pre-Islāmic title of Shāh and continued the Persian pattern of grand imperial kingship. It was the long reign of Shāh ʿAbbās (1588–1629), one of the great world monarchs of the age, that brought the dynasty to the peak of its power. He established his capital at Isfahan and made it a center of architectural beauty. The splendor of all Muslim dynastic capital cities is well illustrated by the fact that Isfahan had 162 mosques, 48 colleges, 1802 inns, 273 baths, and over a million inhabitants.[12] The making of Persian rugs, textiles, and ceramics reached their highest perfection.

The Safavid dynasty technically fell before Afghan invaders, but its fall was really due to the legendary cruelty and corruption of the royal court.

10. The Ottomans (1326–1683–1924)

The Ottomans who were named after a Turkish ruler, Osman,

rose out of the interior of Turkey, in the midst of the struggle between the Mongols, the Mamluks, and Byzantium (Constantinople). Inspired by a warrior (*ghāzī*) spirit and later utilizing trained soldiers from converted captives and slaves (janissaries), they conquered Anatolia. Defeated by the forces of Tīmūr in the east, they pushed westward toward the centers of Christian power, and into the Balkans. In 1453 they captured Constantinople (Istanbul), and in that dramatic moment the Eastern Christian Empire finally fell. By the year 1517 the Ottomans had conquered Egypt and Arabia. It was under Sulaymān the Magnificent who ruled 1520–66 that the Ottomans became a world power and a heavy player in European affairs. In alliance with Francis I of France against Charles V of Spain, Sulaymān's armies advanced to the siege of Vienna in 1529. From 1521–1683 the Ottomans constituted one of the greatest empires in the history of the world, their rule extending from Algeria to Hungary to Mecca. Their defeat at Vienna in 1683 began the ebbtide. It ended in the dismantling of the Ottoman empire by the Allied powers after World War I. The brilliant general Kemal Atatürk (d. 1938) restored the fortunes of Turkey, and as part of his secularizing approach he formally ended the Muslim caliphate in 1924. The action created dismay in the Muslim world among the many who did not sympathize with the drastic decision.

The six centuries of Ottoman achievement cannot be easily summarized. The Ottomans had a genius for administration and organization, with power funnelling down from the sultan. In addition to the *sharīʿa* which provided the principles of administration, the Ottomans developed *qānūn*, practical civil regulations not directly related to religious law. They also created the *millet* system, which allowed non-Muslims great autonomy to conduct their own affairs apart from the reserved areas of tax and security. The Ottoman cultural accomplishments reflected their blend of Turkish, Arab, Persian, and European elements, and the intertwining of the Muslim and Christian civilizations. The symbol of that interaction was the Hagia Sophia or Aya Sofya, the oldest religious building in Europe. First built by a son of Constantine the Great in 360 and rebuilt by Justinian as a cathedral in 562, the huge structure was converted into a mosque in 1453 and a museum in 1935. The city of Istanbul reflects the glories of Sulaymān's reign and the brilliance of its chief architect,

Mimar Sinan (d. 1588). Sinan's dramatic use of the dome may be seen in many of its buildings. In modern times the Ottomans, turned to western learning. Ziya Gökalp (d. 1924) became Turkey's philosopher of modernization, arguing that Islām and modernism were friends not enemies, and his views are the vision of that nation today.

11. The Mughuls (1526–1706–1857)

The Mughuls are the preeminent dynasty of South Asia. Islām came to South India peacefully through Arab traders immediately after its birth in Arabia. It came to North India through a series of Arab-Persian-Afghan-Turkish invasions. From 1210 a succession of Muslim sultanates ruled North India from Delhi, but none could compare with the Mughuls who governed a vast population and created a great Indo-Saracenic culture.

Beginning with Babur who founded the empire (1525) the Mughuls ruled as absolute monarchs, touched with elements of both cruelty and humanitarianism. The peak of the dynasty was Akbar the Great who ruled 1556–1605 as one of the great potentates of the ages. He reigned brilliantly over his religiously pluralistic society, banning religious intolerance and extending the *ahl-kitāb* ("people of the book") concept to Hindus. After the revivalist emperor Aurangzeb (d. 1706) had extended his control over most of the subcontinent the Mughul empire began to disintegrate. In the beginning it broke into a series of smaller dynasties who gave only nominal allegiance to the Mughul emperor, but it soon fell entirely before the onslaught of the European powers. When the last Mughul emperor was deposed by the British in 1857, the greatest Urdu poet, Ghalib (d. 1869) wrote, "The stars weep tears of blood to hear it told."[13] And to those who were caught in the cauldron of animosity that surrounded the moment he penned a line of undying significance:

Bow down and ask for God' s forgiveness,
Where'er you do so, there His threshold is.[14]

Under the Mughuls the composite Indian Muslim language of Urdu became the vehicle of a flourishing body of prose and poetry. Mughul achievement in miniature painting, music, and the applied arts is rightly celebrated. While Akbar is famed for his capital city, Fathepur Sikri, it was the emperor Shāh Jāhān ("King of the World," d. 1666) who built the Taj Mahal in Agra as a tomb for his beloved wife, Mumtāz Mahal, and the large Jāmiᶜa Mosque in Delhi. Religiously the Mughuls ran the spectrum from liberal to conservative, but their practical rapprochement with Hindus represents a high point in the Muslim contribution to interreligious harmony, whether based on natural law (Akbar) or Islāmic law (Shāh Jāhān). The illustrious theologian, Shāh Wali-Allāh (1703–1762) bridged the classical and modern periods, pointing to the creative outburst of fresh religious thinking that was to be the contribution of modern Indian Muslim thinkers, ranging from Sir Sayyid Ahmad Khān to Sir Muhammad Iqbāl, from Syed Ameer ᶜAlī to Maulāna Abūl Kalām Āzād.

12. Malaysia, Indonesia and China (1200 forward)

In the early Islāmic centuries Muslim traders, especially from Gujarat and Malabar in India, brought Islām to Southeast Asia. The peaceful development produced the largest Muslim nation in the world, Indonesia. Islām moved gradually from the coastal trading centers inland. The Malacca dynasty in Malaysia (1404–1511) was instrumental in supporting the Muslim advance through the archipelago, while the Aceh dynasty in Sumatra (1524–1600s) encouraged Islāmic learning. The spread of Islām was also sparked by the work of Sūfis, Islāmic mystics, whose teachings found a ready home in the hospitable syncretistic environment of the area. In the 1500s Mataram in Java became a Muslim dynasty replacing the Hindu Majahapit rule, and from that time the growth of Islām moved rapidly. Indonesian Islām, overlaid upon forms of animism, Buddhism, and Hinduism, is known for its composite culture, respect for indigenous values (*adat*), and religious tolerance. Malaysian Islām, in a contrasting history, has emphasized a more traditional approach and renewed Islāmic learning. The symbol of Malaysian commitment is the architecturally brilliant new mosque in the capital of Kuala Lampur.

Islām came to China at a very early period by the medium of Muslim trade across Central Asia, Muslim trade by sea to Canton, and by Arab and Persian soldiers in Mongol armies. The result was two great streams of Chinese Islām, the first being the Hui Muslims, who stem from the dominant Han culture of China and who speak Chinese, and the second being the Muslim Turkish minorities of Sinkiang in Western China, who retain their own language and culture. The contrast between the two traditions is a striking one.

Southeast Asian Islām and Far Eastern Islām illustrate the tremendous cultural variety in the Muslim world and the differences of religious approach. It is the *shahāda*, the common allegiance to the Qurʾān, elements of the *sharīʿa*, and the *muezzin's* call to prayer that constitute the chief unifying factors for the far-flung world of Islām.

13. Sub-Saharan Africa (650 and 750 forward)

In east Africa, coastal regions met Islām at a very early date. Ethiopian Christians welcomed Muslim refugees, as we have seen, while the Prophet Muhammad was still in Mecca. Further south the process of Islāmic penetration along the Eastern African coast culminated in the development of the distinctive Swahili Muslim culture and the great Zanzibar dynasty of the 19th century, founded by the Sultan of Oman, Saʿīd ibn Sultān, in 1832. In central and western Africa various other factors influenced the development. Berber and Moroccan traders came from the north at a very early date; Songhai Sudanese influence came from the East; the activities of Sūfi missionaries were an important factor; the impact of chiefs who became Muslims strongly affected the process; and intermittent *jihāds* played their role. Common elements in both East and West Africa were the slave trade that carried Islām into the interior of the continent and the policies of the European colonialists that paradoxically favored Islāmicization of the people.

By the 16th century a series of small Islāmic states, which never consolidated, were spread across Sub-Saharan Africa. As a result of the modern independence movements, the Muslim presence is now incorporated into a number of nation-states. From Kano to Khartoum, from Cairo to Capetown, African Islām now includes 27 percent of the Muslim world. Culturally Sub-Saharan African Muslims maintain a close linkage with their traditional tribal values; as a result, there is a range of custom (sometimes called "folk Islām") not common to the Arabicized culture of North African Islām.

14. Europe and the Americas

Finally, in our brief survey, we turn to Europe and the Americas. As we have seen, Europe has had a long contact with Islām. In the southern areas of the former U.S.S.R., Islām became the dominant religious force and remains so in the new nations of the region. In the Balkans (known to Muslims as "Rumelia") from 1354 the Ottomans brought Islām in the process of their empire building, and Bosnia and other areas became Muslim. North African Muslims captured and controlled Sicily from 965–1080, and we have seen the history of Spain. Islām left an important cultural impact on Europe, but in medieval times Islām virtually disappeared with the exception of Albania and the area of former Yugoslavia. The situation did not change in the modern period of European dominance. Since 1945 and the end of World War II, however, a new situation has arisen. The Muslim presence has now been dramatically renewed in Europe, this time through the process of immigration. Whether it be Turkish and Kurdish Muslims in Germany, Indonesian Muslims in the Netherlands, Algerian, and other North African Muslims in France, or South Asian Muslims in the United Kingdom, European Islām has become a numerical and cultural reality of significant proportion. The number of European Muslims is variously estimated between 9 and 11 million.

Islām in North America resulted primarily from two forces—immigration and the conversion of African-American Christians. The immigration has been a steady process from the 19th century, and immigrant or immigrant-descended Muslims represent about two-thirds of North American Muslims. The conversion process has largely taken place within the last half century. The result has been significant in the U.S.A., where about one-third of American Muslims have emerged from this development. Although the estimates of Muslim population in the U.S.A. start as low as 1 1/2 million,[15] most authorities prefer the figure of 4–6 million or nearly two percent of the population. It appears that Islām is moving to become the second largest religion in North America. Muslims in North America face many challenges, including the task of cultural integration between two streams, various issues related to minority living, and the desire to maintain relationships with the wider Muslim world. Central and South America include about one million Muslims, largely the result of immigration. Suriname is the nation with the largest Muslim population (20 percent) in the western hemisphere.

C. Contemporary Muslim History

Today Muslims are creating a new history. The question of what kind of Muslim community can be shaped in today's world is a vital one for thoughtful Muslims. The story of modern Muslim history, however, is another saga that we will not attempt to tell here. The elements of that story are very diffuse. They do not yet constitute a common heritage. Modern Islām is a heritage in the making. The history that we have presented in the foregoing—with all its lights and shadows—is a heritage that Muslims can deal with. In general they are proud of it. What they are creating now is what Muslims in years to come will look back to. Will future Muslims be proud of the past that is now in the making? The answer lies still unresolved in the hands of millions of Muslims around the world.

In the 18th–20th centuries Muslims went through a period of depression as western powers colonized their territories. That onslaught produced a residual distrust in the "West." Since 1945 Muslims have recovered their strength, but not their unity. The Muslim family is now even more fragmented than in the dynastic period as a result of the formation of many Muslim national states. Muslims are therefore laboring at the task of furthering the unity and the commonality of the Muslim family. Most have given up on the idea of political oneness. Some emphasize the concept of spiritual oneness that allows for both loyalty to national interests and allegiance to the *umma*. Others think that the unity can be maintained by keeping the *sharīʿa* principle alive, to whatever extent that is possible. Still others would impose a stricter doctrinal interpretation of true Islām, a concept associated with various forms of fundamentalism. Many simply favor the idea of letting the river of Islām flow freely through its various channels. Finally, especially younger Muslims are really excited about the task of building a brave new Muslim world that is modern, bold, creative. They remember the stirring words of Sir Muhammad Iqbal:

Rechisel then thine ancient frame,
and build up a new being![16]

They are in search of that kind of community that reflects both the best things of the Islāmic past and nurtures the new things that make life possible in the modern world.

Abdulla and Amina are quite practical. As far as the future is concerned, they will agree to almost anything that is reasonable, that makes life better, and that is true to Islām. At the same time, they are happy to take pride in the Muslim achievements of the past, and that gives them confidence for the days ahead.

Notes

[1] F. M. Donner, *The Early Muslim Conquests* (Princeton: Princeton University Press, 1981), p. 271, suggests that "the true causes of the Islāmic conquests ... will probably remain forever beyond the grasp of historical analysis."

[2] Many of the first Muslims regarded Islām as an Arab religion. New converts from other ethnic backgrounds were therefore required to become associate members of an Arab tribe. They were called *mawāli* or "clients." When Persians started to become Muslims, they deeply resented the requirement, which produced considerable tension. Later the Muslim principle of equality overtook this early ethnic bias.

[3] Cf. Dominique Sourdel, *Medieval Islām*, tr. by J. M. Watt (London: Routledge & Kegan Paul, 1983), pp.41–56 for a careful analysis of the phenomenon.

[4] E. Bevan Jones, *The People of the Mosque* (Calcutta: Baptist Mission Press, 1965), p. 44.

[5] Miguel Sanchez, *The Alhambra* (Grenada: Marino Antiquierra, n.d.), p. 5.

[6] P. Holt, A. Lambton, & B. Lewis , eds., *The Cambridge History of Islām*, Vol. 1A (Cambridge: Cambridge University Press, 1970), p. 104.

[7] The important implication is that a fully unified Islāmic state existed for only about 200 years of Muslim history, whereas political diversity is the characteristic of over a thousand years of Muslim history.

[8] The confusing term "Moor" stems from *mauri*, a word that Romans used for the dwellers of Mauritania, and later it was applied to "Moroccans." Thus it was a natural term to describe the mixed Berber-Spanish Muslims of Andalusia. It finally became the common medieval Christian word for Muslim; through Spanish influence it remains extant today in the "Moros" of Mindanao in the Philippines.

[9]Fazlur Rahman, *Islām*, p. 200.

[10]B. Spuler in P. Holt, et al., *Cambridge History of Islām*, Vol. 1A, p. 170.

[11]Kenneth Cragg, *The House of Islām* (Belmont, Calif.: Wadsworth Publishing Col., 1975), p. 207.

[12]*Cambridge History of Islām*, Vol. 1A, p. 420.

[13]Ralph Russell and Kurshidul Islām, *Ghalib, Life & Letters* (Cambridge: Harvard University Press, 1969), p. 138.

[14]Ibid., p. 146.

[15]A City University of New York, National Survey of Religious Identification, 1994, lists 0.4 percent Muslim population or 1.4 million, a remarkably low figure, which conflicts with other major sources. Cf. Appendix A.

[16]Muhammad Iqbāl, *Javid Nama*, in *The Reconstruction of Religious Thought in Islām* (Lahore: Sh. Muhammad Ashraf, 1962 repr.), p. 199.

17

Glimpses of Muslim Thought: *Sunnī, Shīʿa, and Sūfi*

Muslim thought is a tapestry of differing views on important issues, and it is a mosaic of distinctive groups. Taken together it is a rich and complex heritage, and its development continues to unfold today. In this chapter we provide some glimpses into a wide and dazzling world of theology, philosophy, and mysticism, of doctrines and divisions, of movements for renewal and reform. We might have titled the chapter, "Some Questions Asked, Some Answered." The Muslim mind has explored many channels, and new questions continue to arise from the living experience of contemporary believers. Some Muslim friends are looking at the old for inspiration and help in dealing with the new.

There is a hum of controversy in Abdulla's town and district. Two leading religious teachers have taken opposite sides on a certain issue. Both of the leaders happen to have the same name, Abū Bekr, and so in order to distinguish them their supporters use their initials: "E.K." and "A.P." The "E.K." Sunnīs are arguing that religion and politics cannot be divided. The "A.P." Sunnīs are maintaining that it is time to distinguish the two realms. In the heat of the debate both leaders have made caustic remarks about each other. They have gone so far as to call each other *kāfir*, a term that is usually reserved for non-Muslims. In this instance the word does not mean unbeliever, but rather "a wrong-headed and wrongly-teaching Muslim."

Some of Abdulla's friends are smiling at the controversy. They are saying that the true issue is not doctrine at all, but rather represents a personality conflict. Others say that it is a power issue. Still others suggest that there is a financial factor involved. Many people, however, are taking the matter seriously and are lining up on one side or the other. The problem is, Who will decide who is correct? The fact that in Sunnī Islām there is no official court of appeal means that Muslim believers have the privilege of enjoying personal opinions and living with a variety of views. The dilemma that arises is that conclusions on important issues can be reached only through the slow process of consensus-building. Until that time, or until people tire of it, controversies may rage on. In the "E.K."-"A.P." debate Abdulla prefers not to be associated with either party. He thinks that there are more important things that Muslims should be worrying about, especially the task of improving the educational and economic level of the *umma*. The majority "E.K." Muslims are conducting a mass meeting in his town, but he will not attend, even out of curiosity.

This real-life incident suggests the manner that Muslim doctrine has developed over the centuries. It did not emerge from a very systematic process. Scholars did not sit down to study the Qurʾān, then make organized presentations which the general body of believers would vote to accept or to reject. This was never the Muslim way. Certainly the scholars of Islām engaged in studies. Expositions were set forth. Community decisions were taken. But the whole process was informal and life-related. It was informed by the quite unique combination of Islāmic principles that includes a tilt to the practical, the principle of spiritual equality, and what has been called "a genius for moderation."[1]

We may describe the moderation as a kind of intellectual toleration. Behavior can be ordered, but Islāmic thought is, technically, "uncontrolled." Muslims are more interested in how they should act than in how they should think. Islām has creeds, but no confession is *required* except the *shahāda* itself. It is obvious that this approach would end up in a diversity of thought in Islām, and so it did. About four centuries after the death of the Prophet Muhammad, Muslim religious leaders (*ʿulamā*) came to the conclusion that this was not a healthy situation. The religious scholars succeeded in forcing upon Islām the principle of tradition (*taqlīd*)—that is, whatever was received from the past up to that time and accepted by the majority of Muslims was to be respected, held in faith, and handed on intact. The crucial decision resulted in an apparent unity of ideas, but it also had the effect of inhibiting further intellectual development. In the late 19th and 20th centuries Muslim thinkers have broken out of this narrow clerical position and are once again exercising the inherent Muslim freedom of interpretation (*ijtihād*). This has produced waves of reform and a variety of crises among contemporary Muslim believers.

What we have outlined above is the background for viewing

the panorama of Muslim thought. The mosaic of opinion is as vast as could be expected of a world religion with a history of almost 15 (Muslim) centuries of development. Ideas richly abound. Theologians, philosophers, and mystics crowd the scene. Issues are addressed, opinions are voiced, and controversies are ever-present. Ideological movements of many kinds and even outright divisions mark the surface of Islāmic unity. In this history Muslims have faced, and dealt with, many of the major intellectual and spiritual questions common to all humanity.

Abdulla and Amina have a rather distant relation to this vast body of learning. Like ordinary members of any religion, they have a limited knowledge of its theology. They did attend the *madrasa*, but their experience there gave them only the basics of the faith, its ritual, and duties. They have heard the name of al-Ghazālī (d. 1111), the most well-known Muslim theologian, but they have never read any of his works. They know the name of al-Jilānī (d. 1166), the eminent Sūfi saint, but they have probably never heard the name of Ibn Rushd (d. 1198), arguably the greatest Muslim philosopher, who came to the West as Averroes. Abdulla and Amina and their children are one family, in one place, at one point in time. They are Sunnī Muslims, conservative in faith, pragmatic in orientation, moderate in their relationships, liberal in their support of progress, and forward-looking in their general outlook. They are people of the present. They have a sense that a great deal has transpired in Muslim thought in the past, but much of their tradition is like a mine waiting to be quarried. They are well aware of the major distinctions in the Muslim world—Sunnī, Shīˤa and Sūfi—but they are interested in current issues rather than the past. Nevertheless, al-Ghazālī, al-Jilānī and Ibn Rushd belong to them and have helped to determine what they are today.

A. Muslim Thought: An Overview

When Islām was born in seventh century Arabia, it began its history in an intellectually unsophisticated environment. The Qurʾān brought new ideas, but at this stage the Arabs were not interested in—perhaps not capable of—reflecting and writing on the meaning of these ideas. They were practical, survival-oriented folk. The questions of what to do rather than what to believe preoccupied them. What they were to believe appeared straightforward: "There is no god but Allāh, and Muhammad is His messenger." What they were to do seemed more complex and required more decisions. Thus, as we have seen, it was *sharīʿa* and *fiqh*, the sciences of behavior, that became the first and the dominant sciences in Islām, and law continues to hold first place.

It did not take very long, however, for the Muslim mind to become more active. As Muslims spread out beyond the borders of Arabia, they met the great thought worlds of their time. There was the Greek philosophical world, the Christian theological world, and the Zoroastrian religious world. The encounter was on. Sometimes it took the form of rejection, sometimes of acceptance. The Caliph ʿUmar ordered his soldiers to stay outside the cities they captured to avoid the alien influences. That was only temporarily successful. As people of these thought worlds became Muslim they brought their ideas with them into Islām. Now the encounter became an intra-Muslim engagement. Questions emerged that challenged the simple faith of the *shahāda*, especially as Muslim thinkers developed their fascination for Plato and Aristotle, and the intellectual products of Greek thought were translated into Arabic. The Muslim family had to deal with them. Intellectual issues as well as behavioral and ethical problems had to be faced. Muslim theology and philosophy emerged from this encounter. A little later mysticism came in to complete the scene, partly out of the desire for nearness to God, partly as a reaction to the formality and coldness of law, theology and philosophy.

The "Golden Age" of the Islāmic intellectual Renaissance lasted from the 700s to the 1200s. During that time Muslim doctrinal positions were established on many issues, and the main outline of Muslim sectarianism became visible. The straitjacket of *taqlīd* harnessed further development until the 1700s when reform from within and the encounter with "Western" learning produced the new spiritual and intellectual surge that goes on today. We turn now to some of the main issues and movements that dominated the scene. We will follow the theme of practical questions, intellectual questions, and spiritual questions as outlined in the illustration, starting with the practical issues.

Islamic Thought

Practical Questions

Who is the true leader?

Shīʿism
Ismāʿīlism

Who is a true Muslim?

Khārijites
Murjites

How should we behave?

law
sharīʿa

Intellectual Questions

What should we believe?

regarding free will — Qadarites

regarding unity and justice,
reason and revelation — Muʿtazilites

Al-Ashʿarī and
orthodox theology

philosophy

Al-Ghazālī

Spiritual Questions

How should we relate to God?

ascetics
Sūfis
saints

Revivalism **Modern Reform** **Orthodox Islam** **Popular Religion**

As Professor Gibb has put it,

> The first questions and difficulties with which the growing Muslim community was faced ... were not dogmatic and theological but practical. They were problems of personal relationships within the new organized society... in a word, ethical problems.[2]

Muslims today continue to observe the same priority.

B. The Practical Questions

The first two questions that Muslims addressed were the following:

1. Who is the true leader for Muslims?
   The Shīʿas of Islām emerged from that issue.
2. Who is a true Muslim believer?
   The answer that resulted was this: A Muslim is someone who confesses the faith, not one who reaches a certain standard of behavior.

1. The Leadership Issue and Shīʿa Muslims

Leadership is a crucial issue in all of life, and certainly in religion. The controversy over leadership in Islām produced the major divisions in the Muslim community today: Sunnī and Shīʿa.

Sunnī Muslims believe that the Qurʾān and Muhammad's *sunna* (custom) hold the key to the leadership question. The Qurʾān commands piety, and Muhammad's life is its pattern. All believers are essentially equal and are obligated to follow God's commands. If there is to be any priority among believers, then let it be in the realm of piety. Muslims should look for their leaders among people who understand this. Islām teaches earned leadership, not inherited leadership.

Moreover, for Sunnī Muslims the functions of human leaders are carefully limited. In civil matters a leader's duties are qualified by the fact that he is only a first among equals, while in spiritual matters a leader is only a guardian of the practice of the Prophet. In no sense is the leader a sacred or charismatic figure. He has no power to interpret God's Word or to legislate new moral laws. It is this regard for the *sunna* of the Prophet and the consensus of the community that lies behind the name "Sunnī." In theory the

Sunnī approach meant that almost anyone could become the community's leader. In practice, however, the choice of leader depended on all kinds of personal, cultural, and political factors, and quite often leaders were corrupt dictators rather than able and godly individuals.

Who is the true leader of the Muslim community? There was, and is, another answer to the question in Islām. That is the one given by Shīʿa Muslims. The word "Shīʿa" means "follower" or "partisan" of the Prophet's family. Shīʿas, who represent about 11–12 percent of Islām,[3] add a fundamental requirement to the Sunnī qualifications for the Muslim leader. In addition to being able and righteous he must be a direct blood descendant of the Prophet Muhammad through the family of ʿAlī and Fāṭima. Shīʿa emotion is loaded into this belief. Why should we not look to "the household of God" for our leaders? That is not only respectful but it also guarantees the grace of God that a leader needs; for not only does the Prophet's family have a divine right to leadership, but it is also the channel for God's favor and illumination.

Shīʿas have consistently maintained this position down to the present. We have traced the story of ʿAlī and his son Ḥusain. Despite the trauma of their assassinations, Shīʿas courageously went on with their struggle. In the early days of Islām the struggle was often marked by tragedy because the Shīʿas were generally a persecuted minority. This history of persecution and martyrdom has been an important factor in the shaping of Shīʿa emotion. From this context there emerged two main Shīʿa groups, the Ithna Ashariyya or "Twelvers," Who represent the main body of Shīʿas, and the Ismāʿīlīs or "Seveners."[4]

a. The Twelvers

The central point in all Shīʿa teaching is the doctrine of the Imāmate. This is the idea that certain designated Imāms have a distinctive role and position in Muslim life. The word "imām" has a confusing breadth of meaning. Basically it means leader, but the religious use of the term is more specific. The first and simplest meaning is prayer-leader. He is the person who stands at the head of the worshipping congregation on Fridays. Since that individual is usually a "clergy" person, a Muslim clergyman is sometimes called imām. In an enlarged sense the word is used for the first four caliphs of Islām and for the founders of the four law schools.

Implied in this usage is the idea of being a model for others. In the Shīʿa tradition, however, the term has a very special meaning. It refers to the twelve designated successors of the Prophet starting with ʿAlī and ending with the "Hidden Imām," the legitimate leaders of Muslims.

The Shīʿa view is that appointed spiritual leaders are necessary for the Muslim community, and God provided them as an aspect of His mercy to humanity. Shīʿas hold that there must be someone available to guide God's people along the straight path. God would not leave His people rudderless after the time of the prophets. There must be someone to interpret the Qurʾān, to apply it carefully to current situations, and to save Muslims from confusion. There must also be someone to guide governmental leaders to the true Islāmic pattern. What Ayatullah Khomeni did in Iran was to add one idea to the latter point, namely, that the God-guided religious leaders should actually conduct the political affairs of a Muslim community. Up to his time that idea was not popular among Shīʿa religious leaders.

Shīʿas go to the Qurʾān for support of their views on leadership. For them a key passage is 2:124:

> And remember when his Lord tried Abraham with His commands, and he fulfilled them, He said: Lo! I have appointed thee a leader for mankind. (Abraham) said: And of my offspring will there be leaders? He said: My covenant includeth no evil-doers.

Shīʿas also have their own body of Ḥadīth, and they cite many in support of their position. They maintain that Muhammad confirmed there should be a succession of leaders, and he himself began the appointment process with ʿAlī. "It is inconceivable that the Prophet should have died without appointing someone as his successor, a guide and leader to direct the affairs of Muslims and to turn the wheels of Islāmic society."[5] In making provision for the succession, Muhammad turned to his own family, and Muslims should follow this precedent. Thus, in Shīʿa understanding, the Qurʾān and the family of the Prophet are inseparable authorities until the Day of Judgment, and through them both God provides for the needs of believers.

In Shīʿa view, God affirms the high status of the Imāms and assures their leadership abilities by providing them with special graces. We will mention four. The first is the gift of illumination. Prophets receive the light of revelations (*waḥy*), while the Imāms receive an emanation or ray of that original light (*ilhām*). That is enough to give them a special aura, a power of understanding. This leads to the second grace-gift which is knowledge. Through the quality of *ilhām*, the Imāms can penetrate to the inner meaning of Qurānic passages and provide correct legal and theological judgments. The third grace is sinlessness. Only this infallibility can ensure that God's guidance through the Imām will remain pure. The final charisma is guardianship (*walāyat*). As God's friend (*walī*), the Imām possesses "the power of initiating men into the Divine Mysteries"[6] and can safely direct the human spiritual journey.

These qualities undergird the authority of the Imām. It is not the authority of a prophet, but rather the authority of an interpreter and a renewer. At the same time, this is a very powerful authority. Obedience to the Imām is essential, and this alone ensures prosperity. He who does not know the Imām of the age cannot be saved, for in addition to his functions as interpreter and renewer the Imām also intercedes for sinners. Mullā Bāqir Majlisī (d. 1699), a great Shī^ca thinker and collector of traditions, reported the following Ḥadīth. The Messenger of God said to ^cAlī:

> There are three things that I swear to be true. The first is that you and your descendants are mediators for mankind, as they will not be able to know God except through your introduction. The second is that you are to present to God those who may enter Paradise, i.e., those who recognize you and those whom you recognize. The third is that you are the absolute mediators, for those who will go to Hell will only be those who do not recognize you and whom you do not recognize.[7]

The same message comes through an appointed shrine prayer:

> Those who have known them have surely known God;
> And those who are ignorant of them are ignorant of God.
> Those who take them by the hand, and commit themselves to them
> Have given their hands to God:
> But those who abandon them have truly abandoned God.[8]

The Twelver Shī^cas believe that each Imām, beginning with ^cAlī designated his successor. One by one they died a martyr's death. You may see their shrines in Iran and Iraq, including the great shrine of the eighth Imām, ^cAlī al-Rida, at Meshhed in Iran, a huge complex of buildings. The eleventh in the chain of Imāms was Hasan al-ʿAskarī, whose son (b. 868), Muhammad, the twelfth Imām, disappeared.

The belief developed that the twelfth Imām, the "Master of the Age" and the "Proof of Islām," had gone into hiding because of the hostility and threats of his enemies. This is called the period of "the lesser concealment." It was the normal lifetime of Imām Muhammad, and he exercised his authority from hiding through four agents (*bābs*). Then in 941 he withdrew further into an opaque region where he remains alive to the present. This is the period of "the greater concealment" from which he continues to direct Shīʿa faith and life. His warmth and light filter through the clouds of concealment by means of the guidance given by the Shīʿa clergy who are his representatives. In the last times of this world he will return as the Mahdi, the awaited Deliverer, paving the way for the coming of the Messiah, the Resurrection, and the Day of Judgment.

Against this background it is easy to understand the prestige and power of Shīʿa clergy which have become quite evident in contemporary affairs. They are not to be confused with the twelve Great Imāms whom we have described above. They are imāms in a derivative sense, as representatives of the Hidden Imām. This prestige does not apply to the lower clergy called "mullās," but to the higher clergy called "mujtahids," who have the authority to render spiritual guidance. That authority has also been extended to civil affairs. They are not only representatives of the Hidden Imām, but they share a fragment of the ray of spiritual illumination. Shīʿas therefore pay special reverence to their religious leaders. The senior leaders are also given the name "āyatullāh," which means the "sign of God." By consensus one among them frequently reaches the status of "Reference Point" (*marja al-taqlīd*) who is the chief Shīʿa interpreter of God's will for our time.

Apart from the Imāmate, Shīʿa beliefs and practices do not differ radically from the Sunnī tradition. To the confession of faith the phrase " ... And ʿAlī is His Walī" is added. In theology an emphasis is placed on God's unity, and on the concepts of His justice and human free will. Exegetically, Shīʿas tend to look for the inner meaning of Qurānic passages, and they claim the right to *ijtihād*, fresh interpretation. Ritually, the pilgrimages to Shīʿa shrines are considered meritorious. There is a natural interaction with Islāmic mysticism. Certain practices are unique to Shīʿas. They include the permission to hide one's faith in times of persecution, the provision of possibility for temporary marriage, and the payment of a special 10 percent tax on certain categories (*khums*) to the religious establishment.

More significant is the emotional distinction of Shīʿas. The veneration of the Imāms, particularly Ḥusain, has given impetus to a double psychology: On the one hand, patient endurance under suffering, and on the other hand the willingness to engage in revolutionary activity to overcome evildoers. Both aspects of the psychology are visible in modern situations. At the same time those who have suffered and died for the faith are granted the capacity to intercede for sinners. In this world they give support to our prayers to God, and in the future they will speak on behalf of their friends on the Day of Judgment.

The relationship between Sunnīs and Shīʿas is an ambiguous one. Most Muslims have a sense of difference. Sunnīs for their part are unhappy when Shīʿas deny the legitimacy of Abū Bakr and ʿUmar. Shīʿas on the other hand are not pleased when Sunnīs reject the concept of the Hidden Imām. Separate mosques symbolize the difference, and from time to time there are open disputes. At the grassroots level, however, there is a strong trend to live and to let live, a feeling that what unites is greater than what divides. There are many Muslims, Abdulla and Amina included, who discount the differences, simply saying:,"We are all Muslims." It is certainly a fact that both Sunnīs and Shīʿas revere the pious ʿAlī, and together they celebrate the Muharram festival that commemorates the death of Ḥusain, the martyr-saint of Islām.

b.. The Ismāʿīlīs

Over the course of their history the Shīʿas have suffered many divisions. The largest subgroup are the Ismāʿīlīs, the "Seveners," who number 15–16 million adherents.[9] The Ismāʿīlīs have a basic difference of opinion with the Twelver Shīʿas. They believe that Ismāʿīl, who was the firstborn son of Jaʿfar, the sixth Imām, died before his father. Thereupon Jaʿfar named as his successor Muhammad, the son of Ismāʿīl and his own grandson. The Twelver Shīʿas believe that the line passed on through a younger son of Jaʿfar named Mūsa Kāzim.

Some Ismāʿīlīs hold that Muhammad, the son of Ismāʿīl disappeared, and he is the true Hidden Imām. Others say that he passed the Imāmate on to designated successors. Two major lines of Ismāʿīlī succession emerged. The Mustʿalian line claims that the last legitimate Imām went into occultation in 1132. Thereafter his representatives called *dāʿīs* or missionaries have led the community. They are found in Yemen, India (Bohras), the Persian Gulf, East Africa, and elsewhere. The other line, the Nizāris, hold there has always been a successor or living Imām down to the present. This leader is named the Aga Khan. The Nizāris are found in Pakistan, India (Khojas), Afghanistan, Central Asia, and many other areas including North America.

The teaching of the Ismāʿīlīs is maintained in privacy. It is founded on a distinction between outer knowledge (*zāhir*) and inner knowledge (*bāṭin*). The external religion is similar to Shīʿa Islām in general, although Ismāʿīlīs pray only three times a day. The inner knowledge, however is a form of medieval Islāmic philosophy and science that combines Neo-Platonism, mystical interpretation, and the use of the number seven. There are seven cycles in the current era: Adam, Noah, Abraham, Moses, Jesus, Muhammad, and the Imāmic manifestation of today. The Imām interprets the meaning of the Law for his time and passes it on to the instructed Ismāʿīlīs. Its core principle is that there has been a series of emanations from God, Universal Intelligence, and the believer in turn must return to God through a series of contemplative stages.

Historically the Ismāʿīlīs were known for their missionary zeal, and some had a reputation for violent methods. That period has long ended. In modern times Ismāʿīlīs are best known for their commitment to education, social service, and business skill under the leadership of the Aga Khan.

c. Shīʿa Offshoots

At the edges of Shīʿa Islām there are a variety of sectarian groups distantly related to the Twelvers or Seveners. Most of them are marked by a near-heretical veneration of a human leader, including theories of incarnation, thus taking Islām far from its simple separation of Creator and creature. ʿAlī especially is elevated to a position of near-divinity. Typical of this phenomenon are the ʿAlawis of Turkey and Syria, and the Druze of Lebanon. Sunnī Muslims and orthodox Shīʿas consider these movements to be heterodox. Bahai, a separate religion, is a modern offshoot from Shīʿa Islām.

d. A Sunnī Offshoot: the Ahmadiyyas

An entirely different development not directly related to the Shīʿas but involved with the leadership question is the Ahmadiyya movement. Founded by Mirza Ghulam Ahmad (1839–1908) in India, the Ahmadiyyas have grown rapidly to a membership of about five million.[10] Ahmad claimed to be a renewer, a prophet, the Mahdi, and the Promised Messiah. The crucial factor in his claims was the assertion to prophethood, which conflicts with orthodox Muslim teaching that Muhammad is the final Prophet. He rapidly gained followers who formed a dedicated community of believers. After his death they split into two groups. The main branch, the Qadiani group, has its headquarters at Rabwah, Pakistan, while the smaller Lahori segment is centered in London, England. Through its aggressive missionary activity and the use of apologetic literature Ahmadiyyat has expanded throughout the world and is very active in the West. The sect is ruled by its own elected Caliph.

The Ahmadiyya teachings are basically those of orthodox Islām. The variations include the concept of prophecy, the interpretation of *jihād* as a peaceful methodology, and the view of Jesus (ʿIsa Nabī). Instead of the orthodox view that Jesus ascended to heaven alive, Ahmadis hold that he traveled to Kashmir in South Asia where he preached to the supposed 10 lost tribes of the Jews. He is said to have died there and is buried at Srinagar. Because Ahmadis have denied the finality of Muhammad's prophetic vocation, the main body of Muslims has rejected them. They have suffered social ostracism and frequent persecution. In 1984 the government of Pakistan declared the movement to be non-Muslim, the action underlining the absolute significance of the Prophet Muhammad's leadership for Islām.

2. Faith Or Works: The Khārijites and Murjites

The second practical question faced by early Muslims was the issue of faith or works. The question was, Is a Muslim required to be a pious Muslim in order to be counted as a believer? Does faith make me a Muslim or is it a combination of faith and works? If works are required to be a true Muslim, how many works are needed and who will decide whether my standard of performance is adequate?

This quite basic religious issue was intensified when ʿAlī, the fourth Caliph, agreed to arbitration in his dispute with Muʿāwiya. What seemed like a sensible idea to him came as a rude shock to some of his followers. They could not believe that the epitome of Islāmic virtue had agreed to human arbitration in a matter that was controlled by the divine guidance of the Qurʾān. Many of his most loyal and very puritanical followers were appalled. They withdrew from ʿAlī and thus received the name Khārijites (Khawāridj) or separatists.

To understand the Khārijites we must look more closely at the issue that lay behind their separation. The Khārijites believed firmly that true Islāmic allegiance must be marked by purity of behavior. A Muslim's behavior must be consistent with his confession, and his life must be governed by the dictates of God's Word. True religion is more than lip service. It is not mere belief that makes a Muslim a real Muslim, but rather the combination of faith and piety. There can be no compromise with personal desires or secular interests. If you call yourself a Muslim, prove it by your life!

Together with this principle, the Khārijites linked the leadership question which, as we have seen, was a primary issue for early Muslims. The Khārijites were basically democrats. For them leadership is a moral issue; it is related to conduct. It is not tribal membership, nor social status, nor family or gender but rather behavior that is the key factor.

The Khārijites had deeply emotional feelings about the issue of Muslim behavior. So do many faithful Muslims today. Some would resonate favorably with the words of the Khārijite leader who spoke from the pulpit of Muhammad's mosque in Medina after the capture of the city (747); Abu Hamza declared,

> I counsel you in fear of God and obedience to Him; to act according to His Book and the *sunna* of His Prophet, to observe the ties of kinship, and to magnify the truth which tyrants have diminished, and to diminish the falsehood that they have magnified, to put to death the injustice they have brought to life, and to revivify the just laws they have let die—to obey God. Those who obey Him disobey others in obedience to Him, for there is no obedience to a creature who disobeys its Creator ...

We did not become Khārijis lightly or frivolously, in license or for play, or to overthrow the empire wishing to immerse ourselves in government, or in revenge for what had been taken from us. We did it when we saw that the earth had been darkened ...[11]

Despite the attractiveness of their appeal the Khārijites surrounded it with two attitudes that made them a very difficult group for Islām. The first was their spirit of judgmentalism. They made themselves the monitors of Muslim behavior. Greatly sinning Muslims are really non-Muslims (kāfir), and they are subject to hellfire in the same way as unbelievers. The only thing to do is to withdraw from them as the Prophet withdrew from Mecca to Medina. Their anger turned into bitterness that deeply affected their relationships, even with one another.

There was a second negative factor and that was their militancy. Moderate Khārijites were willing to make truce arrangements with fellow Muslims, though erring, but extreme Khārijites considered it their duty to punish them. Obviously, not every sinful individual could be dealt with, so they concentrated their attention on "corrupt" leaders. The climax came when a Khārijite assassinated ʿAlī while he was at prayer in a Kufan mosque. The position of the Khārijites gradually become more radical. They decided that a true and pure divine community on earth had to be established, and the only way was to enforce the standards, if necessary, through violence. Along the way they developed the idea of religious war and applied it to fellow Muslims.

In order to survive, the Muslim *umma* had to deal with this matter, and it did. The Khārijite position was rejected. It was too dangerous, it did not conform to common sense, and it threatened to break up the community. A loose counter movement developed called the Murjites (*murjiʾa*). The Murjites held that the Qurʾān puts primary emphasis on faith. It is faith expressed in the *shahāda* that makes you a Muslim. Pious behavior, which the Qurʾān demands, makes you a good Muslim. Impious behavior, which the Qurʾān condemns, makes you a bad Muslim. However, it does not make you a non-Muslim! God will certainly punish a gravely sinning Muslim—perhaps in this world, perhaps in an interim space between hell and heaven—but in the end a Muslim who believes and accepts the Islāmic way of life will be blessed.

The term Murjite really means to observe restraint. That is what they counselled Muslims. Believers should maintain a live-and-let-live policy toward each other. Good behavior must be commended, but judgmentalism is out of place. External obedience must be ordered but the heart cannot be legislated, and punishment is God's business not ours. Their position became the position of orthodox Islām. It allowed Islām to go on as a relatively unified community. It enabled Muslims to pray behind an *imām* who was not a model citizen. It permitted Muslims to live under the authority of tyrants without advocating revolution. It allowed the state to punish criminals without declaring them to be non-Muslims. In short, it made social life possible. The Murjites disappeared as a distinct group because their position became the official one. The extreme Khārijites divided and subdivided until by the close of the eighth century they had eliminated themselves as an influential party.

3. Fundamentalism and Extremism

Let us turn for a moment to modern Muslim fundamentalism and extremism. In contemporary Islām there is a revival of the Khārijite spirit that is presenting a new challenge to the Muslim community. I would like to call it "neo-Khārijism." It has the same double side: moderate and extreme. In its moderate form it is frequently given the name "fundamentalism." Most Muslims have great trouble with this term that stems from Western culture. Abdulla would be one of these. He would argue that if the term fundamentalism implies believing in basics such as God, Qurʾān and *sunna*, then I am a fundamentalist. Similarly, if fundamentalism means a sincerely believing Muslim who holds that Islām has to mean something to adherents, that nominal religion and secularism are equally to be deplored, and that condemning the good and prohibiting the evil are important, then too I am a fundamentalist. For such a committed believer, however, Muslims prefer another term, namely *muʾmin*, that is, one who strives to combine faith and piety.[12]

What the vast majority of Muslims object to within their communities is what they call *extremism*, which corresponds to the extreme Khārijites of the early period. These are people who advocate the same things that Islām once rejected: separation from the community, militant overthrow of corrupt leaders, and the indiscriminate use of violence that harms the innocent. These are all the meanings that are bundled up in the term "terrorism." Muslims rejected this approach once, and in their own way they

are fighting it today. They recognize the problem, but they deeply
resent the identification of mainstream Islām with extreme
neo-Khārijism.

C. Intellectual Questions

The need to deal with intellectual questions produced Islāmic
theology and philosophy. In earlier chapters we introduced the
first debate—the issue of free will and predestination. That
discussion led to further questions. Behind them all was the
fundamental problem of the relation of human reason to divine
revelation. The problem surfaced with the Muslim intellectual
revolution that began in the eighth century.

What is the relation of reason and revelation for religious
believers? Does reason stand above revelation since we use it for
interpretation? Or does it stand by revelation as an equal partner?
Or is it subject to revelation, with a supporting role? These
questions are still not answered in Islām to everyone's
satisfaction, and each approach has its supporters. The point of
view taken determines the approach to such heavy issues as the
following: What is the relation of divine unity to the divine
attributes, in particular the attribute of speech? What is the relation
of human concepts of justice to God's unlimited power? What is
the relation of the divine will to human freedom? The questions
were profound, the answers complex. The discussions tended to
be far from the instinctive Muslim preference for simplicity and
acceptance (*naql*), and to many they seemed to open the door to
reckless human innovation (*bidʿa*). Yet there was no stopping the
questions!

The questioning was led by a group called Muʿtazilites. They
emphasized the role of human reasoning power (*ʿaql*) in Islāmic
thought. They did not fear it but rather admired it, maintaining that
it has a high and legitimate role in interpreting Islāmic truth.
Called "the people of unity and justice," the Muʿtazilites wielded a
tremendous influence on Islām for three centuries. Contemporary
Muslims who contend that religion must be reasonable and who
try to harmonize human rationality and divine revelation are
sometimes called "Neo-Muʿtazilites."

The Muʿtazilites were preceded by a development known as the
Qadarite movement. The implication of the term "Qadarite" is that
God restrains His own power in dealing with human beings. He

does this to preserve both His own justice and human responsibility. He gives humans enough freedom and power to assure that they are responsible for what they do. Hence God can justly reward and punish on the basis of the commands that He gives. People can do good or reject it, they can pursue evil or abandon it. In neither case does God compel them or author their acts. The much-admired al-Hasan al-Basrī (624–728) led the charge for moral responsibility:

> Oppression and wrong are not from the decrees of God; rather His decree is His command to do good, justice and kindness, and to give to relatives. He forbade abomination, evil and injustice ... God would not openly prohibit people from something and then destine them to do it secretly ... If that were so, He would not have said in the Qurʾān 41:40, "Do what you wish."13

The Muʿtazilites shared the moral concerns of the Qadarites, but they emphasized the *intellectual* necessity of the idea. Anything less than human free will and moral responsibility would be *unreasonable*. To be unreasonable is the same as being un-Islāmic because God *is* Intelligence. The Muʿtazilites had learned this concept from the Greeks, and now they brought it into Islām. In fact they opened the door to the insights of Plato and Aristotle, and above all the mystical philosophical movement called Neo-Platonism. Serious Muslims, they accepted the basic Islāmic doctrines, but they discussed them with language drawn from Greek philosophy and required that they be explained rationally.

In regard to God's justice the Muʿtazilites argued that eternal principles of justice and goodness exist, and God's will reflects them. Orthodox thinkers could not agree that God might be placed *under* the constraints of human concepts, noble though they were. That would limit the majesty and power of God and put Him at the mercy of human thinking. The Muʿtazilites, however, did not hesitate to take that position. Moreover they drew its logical conclusion. Since God is just, He is bound to do that which is best for His creation. There is necessity in God. He will not arbitrarily condemn humans to hell. Furthermore He will provide the guidance needed for humans to make moral decisions. Human destiny in turn depends on the free human response to God's initiative.

With regard to God's unity the Muʿtazilites adopted a very rigorous view. Nothing must compromise the absolute Unity of

God! They concluded that the whole question of divine attributes needed to be reviewed. The personal descriptions of Allāh in the Qurʾān must be dealt with carefully. They do not signify human qualities, and above all they do not point to independent characteristics that are outside God's essence. The way orthodox Muslims were talking about God made God look like a human being on the one hand, and on the other hand like a bundle of separate things. God is not a human being and God is not a multiplicity. The attributes are only metaphors. We must cling to the Unity, the *tawhīd* of God.

The issue came to a head with the idea of God's Speech. God speaks and therefore, the orthodox had said, God has Speech. Moreover the Speech that He has is the Qurʾān. To the Muʿtazilites this meant the breaking up of God's unity for, now there are two eternities, God and Qurʾān. This cannot be. It is *shirk*. Therefore the Qurʾān must be viewed as a created book. Not only did the Muʿtazilites hold this doctrine, but they were also very aggressive in demanding compliance of others. For 150 years their view became the official teaching of the Islāmic state, and it was enforced. Even such a great teacher as Aḥmad ibn Hanbal who opposed their doctrine was clapped in jail. The Muʿtazilites were rationalists, but they were definitely not liberals!

The Muʿtazilite positions distanced them from ordinary people. Because it was difficult for them to talk about God with other than negative language, their Allāh seemed cold. He was different from the Living God of the Qurʾān. The same problem was true of other Muʿtazilite teachings. For example, they denied the possibility of miracles. As to the prospect of seeing God in Paradise, which many Muslims hoped for, the Muʿtazilites declared: impossible, irrational, unacceptable! Although they were remote from common Muslims and always a minority, the Muʿtazilites served as the womb of both Islāmic theology and Islāmic philosophy.

1. Islāmic Theology

Islāmic theology in the formal sense emerged in the period of the Muʿtazilites. It is called *ʿilm al-kalām*, the knowledge of the word, or more simply *kalām*. Theology in the sense of the accumulated beliefs of the community was already present in

Islām before kalām made its appearance. The controversy with the Muʿtazilites compelled its formalizing at certain points. In formalizing their position the theologians rejected the principles of the Muʿtazilites but accepted their language and methodology. This process produced the technical body of theological thought called *kalām*.

The first stage in the reaction was led by Ibn Hanbal (780–835) of Baghdad. He was both ardent in defending the orthodox tradition and fearless in challenging the philosophical theology of the Muʿtazilites. He, as it were, asked the simple question, Where is God's Word in all of this? Let us return to it and take it seriously. Let us put a stop to rationalizing and allegorical interpretations, to idle speculation. We must take the words of scripture *literally* as they stand. If God "sits on a throne," it means exactly that. Do not ask how, but rather accept and believe "without how" (*bilā kaif*). Islām is not a rational system of beliefs and practices but a body of moral convictions, and the important thing is obedience. What is essential for a believer is sincerity of spirit and the willingness to relinquish what one desires in favor of what one fears.

To the Muʿtazilites Ibn Hanbal was an intolerant literalist and sectarian, but to the masses he was a hero, and when he died there was a huge outburst of emotion. His stern influence is evident in forms of Muslim "fundamentalism." Orthodox Muslim theology, however, did not follow Ibn Hanbal; it took a more moderate road. It was Abuʾl-Ḥasan al-Ashʿarī (873–935) who blazed that trail.

This was the problem faced by Muslim thinkers: Is there nothing between the rationalism of the Muʿtazilites and the literalism of the Hanbalites? We cannot speak of a longing for something in the middle, but that would not be surprising for Muslims who take pride in being "a middle nation." That something was born with the appearance of *kalām*. It may be argued that *kalām* was not really in the middle, that it was closer to Ibn Hanbal than to the Muʿtazilites, but it has satisfied many Muslims.

Al-Ashaʿrī placed a virtually indelible stamp on Muslim thought. Muslim tradition records the story of his famous conversion from rationalism to orthodoxy. Imagine for a moment the drama of the occasion. One of Islām's greatest teachers is mounting the *mimbar*, the pulpit in a Baghdad mosque. He is a proud Muʿtazilite scholar, that author of perhaps 200 works, the son-in-law of al-Jubbāʾī, a famous thinker. From the pulpit al-Ashaʿrī announces that he can no longer continue as a rational theologian because reason does not satisfy! Whether the events described were historical or not, what is sure is that al-Ashaʿrī threw himself into the task of providing a new theological basis for the orthodox faith.

Al-Ashaʿrī argued that there is a place in religion for one important aspect of reason, and that is the art of logical deduction. You cannot use reason to *establish* religious truth, for the understanding of truth comes from revelation and the consensus of the community, and is received by faith. But you can use logic to *prove* what is believed and to *defend* it. He pointed out that the Qurʾān itself uses the deductive method when it points to the wonders of creation as the signs of God. Al-Ashaʿrī would not go farther than that. He abandoned the ideas of Greek philosophy but kept the method that had been received from Aristotle. To this day the study of logic is an important item in the syllabus of conservative Muslim theological institutions. Thus al-Ashaʿrī founded scholastic theology, which continues to be the heritage of the Muslim *madrasa* and through its educational program the theological thought world of most ordinary Muslims.

We will not expand on the teachings of al-Ashaʿrī that are represented in many of the traditional doctrines we have outlined. He started and ended with an emphasis on the unlimited power of God, calling people to His fear:

> I enjoin you, O servants of God! the fear of God, and warn you against the world; for it is fresh and sweet, and it deceives its inhabitants ... Labor for the abiding life and for endless eternity ... Know that you are mortal and that you return to your Lord ... Therefore be diligent in your obedience to your Lord.[14]

He held that God's attributes are real; the Word of God is uncreated; the actions of human beings are decreed and created by God the only Creator, moment by moment, and in some way acquired by humans; goodness is commended and evil is prohibited; the events of the Last Days are literally true, and God will be visible to the sight. Al-Ashaʿrī succeeded in bringing order and structure into Muslim thinking. In that task he had an important partner in another part of the Muslim world, al-Maturīdī (d. 944) of Samarqand, whose teachings were not significantly different.[15] Despite the importance of both al-Ashaʿrī and al-Maturīdī to Muslim thought, Islām had to wait for al-Ghazālī before it found its ultimate theologian and the one who breathed life into the dry statements of the *kalām* theologians.

Muʿtazilite thought led in one direction to Muslim theology. In the other direction it led to Muslim philosophy, and we now turn briefly to that subject.

2. Islāmic Philosophy

The complex story of Muslim philosophy is beyond the scope of this volume. In classical Islāmic thought the term philosophy (*falsafa*) covered the whole range of human knowledge including the natural sciences. Muslim philosophers took interest in medicine, law, mathematics, physics, and frequently music in addition to theology and philosophy. They were monumental figures attracted to the whole span of human learning, and in particular Greek learning.

The Muslim philosophers were more interested in the *ideas* of the Greeks than their logical method. That is what differentiated them from the theologians. They believed that what Greek philosophy taught was really Islāmic thought in essence, and so they combined the two. It took some time for the bulk of Greek thought to circulate through the Muslim world, but as the number of translations increased, much of Plato and Aristotle came to the attention of the Muslim thinkers. What was most influential in their thinking, however, was Neo-Platonism, a movement of thought that blended ideas from Plato and Aristotle with the mystical thinking of Plotinus. As part of that process the *Theology of Aristotle*, which was really a compendium of the writings of Plotinus, became a primary source of ideas for Muslim thinkers.

What did the philosophers say, and why in the end did orthodox Islām reject their teachings? They were fascinated with two ideas that run through their writings—the Greek ideas of being and intelligence. Essentially, they believed, God is an indescribable and unknowable Being, the Absolute One and the Utterly Beyond. However, within God, or as the first expression of God, is the principle of Active Intelligence (*ʿaql*). The Active Intelligence expresses itself through a series of emanations, the first of which is World Soul. Like a rock thrown into a pond, the waves of emanation continue to go out, producing heavenly beings, human souls, and matter. Human souls are trapped in matter, far from God. They yearn for God and must return to Him by reversing the process of emanation. They accomplish that through rational reflection and mystical contemplation. The ultimate sin is ignorance, and salvation comes through knowledge. Professor Fakhry sums up Islāmic Neo-Platonism in these words:

> [They taught] the utter transcendence of the First Principle or God; the procession or emanation of things from Him; the role of Reason as the instrument of God in his creation and... the source of the illumination of the human mind; the position of Soul at the periphery ... and finally the contempt in which matter was held as the basest creation or emanation from the One and the lowest rung in the cosmic scale.[16]

All along the line these ideas differed profoundly with orthodox Muslim teaching. What was the place in this picture for scriptural revelation and for religious practice—all the things that ordinary Muslims believe and do? As far as the philosophers were concerned, revelation and ritual religion are intended for the masses who cannot reflect at their level and who need symbolic language to motivate moral living. Philosophers, on the other hand, are able to follow the path of independent wisdom through the reasoning powers that God gives them. This path leads to the higher truth that orthodox belief and practice only symbolize. This position did not endear the philosophers to the theologians. More importantly, the theologians trembled for the survival of the faith, and they resisted this approach. As far as ordinary Muslim believers were concerned, they were barely aware of the debates.

Nevertheless, the Muslim philosophers were mental giants, and among educated Muslims their names are known and they are respected for their love of learning. Among them at least four persons must be mentioned:

a. Al-Kindi (801?–866)
   The first Arab Muslim philosopher and a bridge figure, he tried to keep a basic loyalty to traditional Muslim thinking even while he disseminated his vast learning in many fields. He was the author of up to 242 works.

b. Al-Fārābī (870?–950)
   Of Turkish descent, al-Fārābī set much of the agenda for

Muslim philosophic discussion, maintaining firmly that Greek philosophy held the answers for Islāmic issues. The world would be a better place, he believed, if it were run by philosophers. Al-Fārābī received the honored title, "The Second Teacher," the first being Aristotle.

c. Ibn Sina (980–1037)

A person of immense intellectual and physical energy, Ibn Sīnā (Avicenna) ranks with Ibn Rushd as the preeminent Muslim philosopher. A Persian who wrote encyclopedic works on philosophy, medicine, and science, his great *Canon of Medicine* held the field for centuries. Although he turned Islāmic philosophic thought into a mystical mode, Ibn Sīnā believed that a person of knowledge must also be a man of action, and he was heavily involved in politics. No one worked harder, and no one exceeded his range of knowledge.

d. Ibn Rushd (1126–1198)

A Spanish-Moroccan physician-judge-philosopher, this penetrating mind was known as Averroes in the West. He was a great lover and interpreter of Aristotle, and through his commentaries he transmitted Aristotle's teachings to Jews and Christians. Ibn Rushd respected the *sharīʿa*, but he argued that it was the task of philosophers to reveal its inner meanings. He vigorously defended philosophy against the attacks of the theologians, including al-Ghazālī, but he was accused of heresy for such teachings as the eternity of matter and continuous creation. This peerless thinker was the last of the great Muslim philosophers.

Philosophy almost died in Islām after Ibn Rushd. Al-Ashaʿrī had thrown a heavy blanket over religious freethinking, and the theologians of tradition (*taqlīd*) had followed his lead. After al-Ghazālī added his severe criticism of philosophy, its supporters further diminished in number. The attacks of the Mongols that culminated in the capture of Baghdad crushed the centers of Muslim learning and strengthened the trend to defend tradition. A few of the ideas of the philosophers did enter the thinking of later *kalām* theologians and left some mark, but philosophy had to look for another home. It found it in mystical thought, with which it had affinity through Neo-Platonism, and it retreated to that more hospitable environment. In the process, however, it lost the power of its rationalism; in finding Soul, it lost its soul. As Professor Rahman describes it:

> Its character was radically changed through the influence of mysticism. From a rational endeavor to understand the nature of the objective reality, it became a spiritual endeavor to live in harmony with that reality.[17]

Certainly Islām as a whole also lost something as a result of the decline of philosophy—and that was its intellectual drive. While it lasted, it had helped to create the atmosphere that produced the Islāmic Golden Age with its vast range of intellectual achievements. The memory of that remarkable period is high in Muslim consciousness.

In modern times Muslim thought is recovering its interest in intellectual exploration. That recovery is sparked by its engagement with scientific thought, the foundations of which Muslims regard as their gift to the West. Muslims are now tremendously interested in technology, and this rather than philosophic thinking occupies the Muslim imagination. The free exploration of human reason into religious questions is more delicate, but it too is on the rise through the application of the Islāmic principle of *ijtihād*. It is directed more toward moral questions than to speculation regarding ideas. It is clear that Muslims are reaching out for an intellectual revival, and possibly to a second Golden Age. Most Muslims are convinced that the only way of achieving that revival is through education, the right kind of education that does not dispense with Islāmic values. Fadhel Jamali, Professor of Philosophy of Education at the University of Tunis, expressed the view of many:

> The Muslim world today faces a crisis in regard to education. Muslim teachers need a new educational philosophy: one which will bring about a renaissance among the peoples of Islām—a renaissance that is scientific, social and economic as well as spiritual and moral.[18]

Abdul Ghafoor, a physician and founder of the Muslim Education Society in Kerala, India, put the matter in more trenchant language that has its echo in many parts of the Muslim world today. He declared that we are "going forward to create a revolution of the mind."[19]

In the market in his town Abdulla picks up a set of books that has been approved for Muslim school libraries. He wants to have them available for his children. They indicate what Muslim religious thought means for a family at the grassroots level:

Vol. I: Prophets, Angels, and Moral Teachings
Vol. II: Faith and Deeds, Prayer and Fasting
Vol. III: Charity and Hajj, Duties to the Community
Vol. IV: Constitution, Law, Social and Economic System;
          Duties of Parents, Children, Kinsmen, Neighbors
Vol. V: Marriage, Divorce, Sex Equality

Neither *kalām* nor *falsafa* are listed. The practicing religious thought of many Muslims is very much *sharīʿa*-oriented, and Muslims continue to walk the simple road of obedience to God. "A man can get close to him only by doing good deeds"[20] is what the first book says, and Abdulla heartily agrees. He respects what he knows of theology and philosophy, but he lives by the law.

The phrase "getting close to God" points to a great spiritual issue that arose in Islām, and we turn to that next.

D. Spiritual Questions

Abdulla and Amina are definitely not mystics. "Getting close to God" for them means obeying God's law. The same is true for most Muslims. Nevertheless Islām developed a major mystical movement! What lay behind the development was a very important spiritual problem. It was a question that arose very early in Muslim history: How should I draw near to God? As we have seen Islāmic thought centered on three fundamental questions. The first one, how should I behave, produced Islāmic law. The second one, what should I believe, produced theology and philosophy. The third question, how should I draw near to God, produced Muslim mysticism which is called Sūfism. Both the last question and its answer represent a kind of Islāmic surprise.

1. The Sūfis

The development of Sūfism is a surprise because the central teachings of Islām seem to have little room for it. There is, after all, a very sharp distinction between Creator and creature, Master and servant. The separation is expressed in the words *islām*, surrender, and *ʿibādat*, service. Orthodox Muslims do not want to blur that difference. Blurring it gives rise to the greatest sin of *shirk*, association with God. How then could a Muslim speak of drawing near to God or experiencing God?

Yet the question did arise. We may suggest some reasons. The primary factor is the fundamental human desire to have some relationship with Ultimate Reality. In every religion, in one way or another, poets have sung the theme that the human heart thirsts for the living God. Traditional Muslim teaching had gone far in the opposite direction, emphasizing the transcendence of Allāh. The Muslim heart, however, sensed another side—the merciful nearness of God. The Qurʾān had spoken about it, affirming that God is our Friend and that He is nearer to us than our jugular vein.

The discussion of the human relation with God was hastened by the intellectual coldness that had gripped Islāmic thought. The formalism of law, the dryness of theology, and the abstruseness of philosophy did not satisfy the human spirit. The heart did not throb to these drums. The warmth and emotion were missing. The legists, theologians, and philosophers of Islām had not intended this result. Yet it was inevitable that some Muslims would look for something more, a deeper spirituality. What is called Sūfism emerged from this context. The Sūfis said, There is another way of thinking—let us follow a spiritual path that leads to a loving union with God. A preeminent Sūfi, al-Junayd (d. 910) stated the matter simply: "Sūfism is that God should make thee die away from thyself and live in Him."[21]

Sūfism did not develop overnight. It went through stages, took many different forms, and flowed through countless channels. Sometimes it seemed to be within orthodox Islām, sometimes on the edge, and sometimes outside. Its historic beginning is fairly clear. It did not start with the nearness debate but rather with a prior concern: *How can I live a pure life before God? How can I live truly in the fear of God?* The people who were thinking about these questions were dedicated to expressing a more ethical religion. They were, as it were, the Abdullas and Aminas of their time, who believed that doing God's will was the primary spiritual concern. We Muslims must engage in personal *jihads* against the evil of our lives, pray and fast, and strive to make ourselves worthy of God.

In sum, these first-stage Sūfis were spiritual ascetics, living very simply, struggling against worldly and material attractions. Their primary spiritual goals were repentance, renunciation and absolute trust (*tawakkul*) in God. Their efforts were spurred on by the sight of the gross materialism and corruption that had infected Muslims. It was saints like Ḥasan al-Basrī who represented their ideal. The rough wool cape that they wore is the probable source of the term "sūfi."

The second stage in the development of Sūfism came when these pious devotees began to form spiritual circles to remember God. Within their circles they engaged in a variety of spiritual exercises to help their devotions. There was a movement now from the fear of God to a new emphasis on the love of God. God is merciful and wants us to remember Him. The best way to remember Him is to repeat His Name, to recite the Qurʾān, and to utter other spiritual phrases such as "Glory be to God!" They called their ritual *dhikr*, the remembering of God. God in His mercy remembers us and reminds us that He is ever near to us. We in turn remember God, and remind each other of His love for us. In the end *dhikr* took many different forms, becoming the special liturgical and prayer life of Sūfis. Its primary focus was a system of meditation that would allow one to reach *maʿrifa*, the experiential knowledge of God and loving union with Him.

At first the Sūfis carried on their spiritual exercises in the mosque. Traditional Muslims, however, began to frown. Is this the Islām we know, the religion of surrender to the Almighty and obedient devotion to His service? Or is it heresy? In reaction, Sūfis began to form their own separate groups. They looked for support in the Qurʾān and found it in passages such as these:

Wherever you turn, there is the face of God (2:109).
A people whom he loveth, and who love him (5:59).
And those who believe do love God the stronger (2:106).
We are nearer to men than the vein of his neck (50:15).
Allāh is the Light ... and guideth unto His Light whom He wills (24:35).

They also reminded others of how the Prophet Muhammad himself used to go to Mt. Hira for meditation, and how he experienced God in his miraculous ascension (*miʿrāj*). The mystical Muhammad is the model for all Sūfis.

There were attractive elements in Sūfism. Moreover the Sūfis were often very missionary in their approach; not only did they draw fellow Muslims to the Sūfi way, but they also attracted non-Muslims to Islām in various areas of the Muslim world. There were other elements in Sūfism, however, that troubled perceptive Muslims and placed orthodoxy in a quandary. To some it seemed as though the religion of mystical relationship was taking Muslims away from the basic religion of pious obedience. The distance between the two approaches widened as the Sūfis further refined their spiritual methodologies and began to form separate organizations under saintly leaders.

The transition from pious asceticism to love mysticism took place between the years 750–850. It is the great female saint, Rabīʿa al-ʿAdawiyya (d. 801), who often receives the credit for introducing into Sūfism the aspect of selfless and flaming love. The full development of the *dhikr* ritual and the Sūfi orders came later. "The basic rules of mystical education were elaborated during the 11th century, and in a comparatively short time—beginning in the 12th century—mystical fraternities that included adepts from all strata of society were emerging."[22] For two centuries thereafter Sūfism continued its lively progress but from the 1400s forward the majority of scholars agree that it entered a declining stage.

What is the spiritual methodology of the Sūfis? It is known as the path (*tarīqa*). The path is dedicated to leading the seeker to clear spiritual goals that include the perfecting of the individual's piety; the development of a blazing awareness of God the One, and the desire to know Him more nearly; and the attainment of the experienced knowledge of God called *maʿrifa*, the path culminating in a union with God (*fanāʾ*). These spiritual goals are often expressed by Sūfis in the language of longing desire and passionate love. So, for example, Dhuʿn-Nūn (d. 861) declared,

I shall die, but never can die the heat of my love for Thee.
Daily and hourly my work I neglect for the sake of my love.
Thee I desire, the only desire of my heart is for Thee.
Thou with Thy riches alone canst meet this poor one's need.
Thou art my highest desire, the goal of all my longing,
The place where my troubles I tell, the hidden world of my soul.[23]

When the Sūfi longing is finally fulfilled in the experience of the seeker, the relationship with God becomes extremely intense, and Sūfis have differed in its description. A sharp dispute arose of the implication of idea of "union with God." Did it mean uniting with God in the sense of having a near relation with God? Moderate Sūfis took this approach, and orthodox Muslims, though swallowing hard, were able to accommodate the idea. Extreme Sūfis took the idea of union farther. It signifies "becoming one with God" in the sense of an identity of being. The distinction between the Lover and the Beloved is wiped out. This blurring of the separation between God and a human produced tremendous objection. The most famous example is al-Hallāj (d. 922) who was crucified in Baghdad on the charge of having claimed to be God. His ecstatic cry, "I am the Reality!" (*ana'l-Haqq*) was one of the proofs of his heresy.

The Sūfi path is a technique to reach the goal of union. It includes some essential elements that are common to all shades of Sūfism. The first is the requirement of a spiritual master, someone who has already followed the path and reached the goal. It is the seeker's task to place himself or herself under the complete control and guidance of the Sūfi master (*shaikh, pīr*). The second requirement is a knowledge of the stages (*maqāmat*) through which you must pass. These are ethical stages that constitute a growth in piety. There are different lists of the recommended virtues ranging from seven to twenty in number. All begin with conversion and repentance, and end with reliance on God. Every seeker (*murīd, dervish, faqīr*) must travel this road of virtues.

It is at this point that an apparent conflict begins with the straight path of orthodox Islām. Orthodoxy regards reliance on God (*tawakkul*) as the ultimate goal of true religion in this world. It is to that which a pious Muslim should aspire, and there cannot be more. Sūfism, however, regards *tawakkul* as only the *starting point* for the final portion of a seeker's spiritual journey. From the stages the mystic proceeds to the states (*ahwāl*). These are a series of psychological moods: nearness, fear, hope, intimacy, tranquillity, contemplation, certainty, knowledge, and love. The final end of the process is indescribable. Hence Jalāl al-Dīn Rūmī, Islām's poet of love and the founder of the Mevlevīyya Sūfi order, spoke eloquently about silence:

> When it comes to love, I have to be silent ...
> To describe Love, intellect is like an ass in a morass;
> The Pen breaks when it describes love.[24]

As Sūfism spread, encouraged by its reception in other cultures from Persia to Indonesia, Sūfis organized themselves into orders. There is now a large number of such orders in Islām. They naturally developed out of the relation between the Sūfi master and the students. Both lived together in retreat centers that were usually endowed by patrons. Each master developed his own form of initiation and *dhikr*. Eventually individual groups began to link up and the great orders came into existence. Each is presided over by a successor (*khalīfa*) of the original saint. Both professional and lay Sūfis are attached to the retreat center. The professional Sūfis live in the lodges and engage themselves in meditation and teaching, while lay members attend ritual performances on set occasions. In conservative Sūfi orders the *dhikr* is relatively restrained, emphasizing silence rather than sound; other orders use a greater variety of methodologies including bodily motions, music, and even hypnotic effects. The four great foundational orders of Sūfism are the Qādirīyya, Suhrawardīyya, Shādilīyya, and Mevlevīyya orders, but other orders may be more influential in different regional settings.

The noblest representatives of Sūfism, through their love for God and longing for His fellowship, produced a tremendous impact on Islām. There was, for example, the deepest respect for a saintly individual like Rābiʿa who said,

> O God! whatever share of this world Thou hast allotted to me, bestow it on Thine enemies, and whatever share of the next world Thou hast allotted to me, bestow it on Thy friends. Thou art enough for me.

> O God! if I worship Thee in fear of Hell, burn me in Hell; and if I worship Thee in hope of Paradise, exclude me from Paradise, but if I worship Thee for Thine own sake, withhold not Thine everlasting beauty.[25]

At their best the Sūfis of Islām gave warmth and spiritual beauty to their faith. They were a powerful answer to the question, How shall I draw near to God? and their overall impact on Islām is incalculable.

In the end, however, there were three things about Sūfism that most deeply troubled the larger family of believers. The first was its trend to extremism. The most famous representative of Sūfi extremism was Muhyī al-Dīn Ibn ʿArabī (1165–1240) of Spain, whom some Sūfis call "the Great Master." His system of thought, named "the unity of being" (*waḥdat al wujūd*), ended up in the idea that "Everything is He." This kind of theosophical pantheism brought extreme Sūfism to the outer edge of Islāmic tolerance. The second problem was the authoritarianism and exclusivism of the movement. That had to do with the absolute power of the Sūfi *shaikh* and the secrecy of the orders. The final difficulty was the development of superstitious practices that became a prominent characteristic of later Sūfism. These practices permeated and merged with popular Islām, often helped by Sūfi adaptation to local religious cultures.

As a result of these difficulties Sūfism—even while it was tolerated—came under the steady criticism of orthodox Muslim reformers. The conservative Egyptian theologian, Ibn Taimīya (1263–1328), a follower of Ibn Hanbal, asserted that the Sūfi spiritual objectives—fear, reliance, love of God—are in fact the objectives of traditional Islām. Moreover, you cannot obtain a personal relation to God through mystical union. Rather, you must be content with the knowledge that God gives about His will in His Word, and on the basis of the *sharīʿa* live a life of dedicated service to God. Beyond that a Muslim cannot and should not try to go. Four centuries later Muhammad ʿAbd al-Wahhāb (1703–87) in Arabia, himself a former Sūfi who was influenced by Ibn Taimīya, levied a devastating attack against Sūfi corruption and superstition, and his influence continues to be powerful today. In more recent times Sir Muhammad Iqbāl (1876–1938) the eloquent philosopher-poet-revivalist of Indian Islām, made one final charge against Sūfism—he criticized its escapism. As a poet he had affinities with Sūfi ideas, but, in his view, Sūfis are struggling for release from this world when instead they ought to be engaged in an active life of change-making in this world. Finally, the activity of militant Sūfi orders in such areas as Africa has brought criticism from peace-loving Muslims.

It is not too much to say that within Islām the Sūfi movement suffered deterioration and fell on hard times. The pragmatism of much of contemporary Islām leaves little room for a revival. Despite many eloquent Sūfi voices that continue to be raised, as a movement Sūfism is far less influential today than it once was. Nevertheless, *as an idea*, it continues. The great mystical theologian, al-Ghazālī, brought the idea into the orthodox faith and practice of Islām (see below), and for many modern intellectual Muslims it has renewed appeal. Weary of formalism, they seek meaning in religion. They find it in both sides of the Sūfi equation—our drawing near to God and God granting His nearness as a gift. A Sindhi Sūfi sums it up:

Not only the thirsty seek the water,
but the water seeks the thirsty as well.26

2. Saints in Islām

Muslim saints belong to the Islāmic surprise. With the exception of a few areas, all over the Muslim world one may see the shrines of Muslim saints. Often the shrine is a simple tomb in a pleasant shady grove, but elsewhere it may be a huge complex of buildings in a bustling urban center. Muslims attend the shrines to get a boon, to make an oath, to experience the *baraka*, the mysterious spiritual power of the saint, or simply to feel the energy and excitement of the great crowds at festivals of the saints. The "surprise" stems from the fact that Islām, from one point of view, does not seem to be very congenial to the idea of saints.

Abdulla and a visitor are having an argument. Tempers are flaring and voices are rising. Rashid whispers to his mother, "What's wrong?" His mother commands him to hush. Abdulla and his friend emerge from their room with flushed faces, and he tells his wife, "We are going to M_____ ." Now Amina understands the problem. Abdulla has almost completed a major business deal with the visitor, but the visitor refuses to sign the legal contract. Instead he wants to go the shrine of his saint and swear to the agreement in the name of the saint and before his grave. Abdulla is so angry because he is opposed to the idea of saints. But on this occasion he is forced to agree, and so they leave together and head out for the shrine.

Sunnī Muslims have always resisted any elevation of human beings that would threaten the Transcendence of God and that would lead to the sin of *shirk*, association of partners with God. Their extreme carefulness in this matter is an important aspect of the Muslim heritage. There are no pictures in a mosque. That Kaʿba in Mecca is empty. In Medina, Muhammad's grave is visited, but not as a shrine. Reformers in the Muslim world are steady in their criticism of the saint-veneration that has crept into Islām. Despite all this, Muslim saints play a huge role in everyday popular Islām in many places.

There are at least three reasons for this unexpected development. The first is the natural respect that human beings pay to someone who is regarded as extraordinarily pious. The second is the esteem for religious leaders that in different ways characterizes both Sunnīs and Shīʿas. The third is the pressing nature of one more spiritual question: *Who will intercede for me with God? Who will help me?* Every Muslim declares, *Allāhu akbar!* God is very great. He is very great indeed, in a sense beyond my reach, distant and removed. Who will take my needs and prayers and assure that they receive divine attention? Who will speak for me in my final hour when the books are opened and my account is taken?

Who will help us? It was natural for Muslims to look for help to the saints who were near at hand and who were God's friends (*walī*; pl. *awliyāʾ*). Cannot they be our benefactors? People believed that they could. They further decided that the *walīs* received a special blessing from God that gave them the power (*karamāt*) to do miracles; this was true not only in their lifetime, but the power also carried over after their death. Finally, people came to believe that God would heed the prayers of these holy ones on their behalf. The pressure of popular faith could not be bottled up, and the phenomenon of saints erupted in Islām and spread to every corner of the Muslim world.

It continues today. Many Muslims who very well recognize that the veneration of saints has led to the development of abuses and superstitions in Islām are nevertheless not quite ready to give up their saints. Even as Muslim reformers levy their scathing attacks against saint veneration, mass meetings are also held in defense of the saints. It cannot be as easily offset as many reformers wish because saint veneration, in a sense, represents the Sūfism of the masses. Are not the Prophet Muhammad, the pious ʿAlī, and the Messiah ʿĪsa true saints? Why, then, is it not possible or proper for there to be other saints, even though they may be less great than these? Why is it not valid for a Muslim to plead, "O Muiuddīn, pray for me!"? So argue the pious defenders of the saints.

ʿAbd al-Qādir al-Jilānī (1077–1166), the founder of the Qādiriyya order of Sūfis, is a representative saint. In one person al-Jilānī illustrates the overlapping and interacting nature of the various movements of thought that we have discussed. He was at the same time a Hanbali jurist and theologian, a preacher and a teacher, a moderate mystic and a saint. People thronged to hear his sermons, and their collections still circulate the Muslim world. He called for both piety and nearness to God:

Be with God, the Mighty, the Glorious, as if no creation exists. And

384

be with the creation as if there is no self in you. And when you are with God, the Mighty, the Glorious, without the creation you will get Him and vanish from every other thing, and when you are with the creation without yourself you will do justice and help the path of virtue and remain safe from the hardships of life. And leave everything outside the door while you are entering in your solitude and enter therein alone. And when you have done so, you will see your Friend in your solitude with your inner eye and will experience what is besides the creation, and then your self will vanish and in its place will come the command of God and His nearness. And at this point your ignorance will be your nearness and your silence will be your remembrance of God, and your bewilderment will prove friendship.27

What is represented in al-Jilānī is a pious, humble form of Sūfism, but his followers made of him a power-laden saint. Even during his lifetime people narrated the stories of his miracles —and after his death, legends upon legends were attached to his name and career. From the beginning of his life when he refused his mother's breast during the fast of Ramaḍān, to the end of his days when a student asked him what had made him a saint and he replied, "I have never lied in my life," the highest spiritual ethics and miraculous powers are attributed to him. 28 The following is a prayer dedicated to his memory and his family:

Peace, peace be upon the Shaykh, the Teacher ... O You, refuge hidden in space, help us from your abundance and quench us from your cup of salvation. O lineage of Jilānī!, help us with our vows. Your nobility is like the prophet's family ... Prayers and best wishes for Mustafa, the holy Prophet, his family, his companions, and for our Jilānī.29

Not many other Muslims come near to al-Jilānī for global influence, and he is called "the Sultan of the Saints."

Not all the saints of Islām are such great and splendid figures. Many are local *walīs*, not known beyond their immediate area. Amina's mother, Zaynaba, has come home for her visit to a local saint. Amina is definitely not happy with what her mother has done, for like her husband she has rejected what she believes to be un-Islāmic superstitions. Zaynaba, however, has been diagnosed with tuberculosis, and she has gone to a nearby living saint for help. In return for a gift the holy man has written a Qurānic phrase on a small piece of paper, has blown on it in a mysterious way, and has presented it to her. The charm is now in an amulet that Zaynaba has tied around her upper arm to ward off the disease. Tomorrow she is going to the government hospital to start modern treatment for her disease. She is living in two worlds at the same time. It is true to say that many Muslims, like Zaynaba, live in similar worlds. The are looking for all the help that they can get in the constant human struggle against Satan and evil, pain and suffering in this life.

3. Imām al-Ghazālī

We conclude our discussion of Muslim thought by turning to Abū Hamīd Muhammad al-Ghazālī (1058–1111), "the most original thinker that Islām has produced and its greatest theologian."[30]

Muslims refer to al-Ghazālī as "Imām al-Islām," the Teacher of the Faith. He came along when the rivers of Islāmic thought were flowing swiftly but in different directions. Al-Ghazālī entered into that situation not only with his spiritual depth and intellectual clarity, but with an unusual ability to integrate ideas. Perhaps because he was himself a legist, a philosopher, a mystic, and a theologian all rolled into one that it was possible for him to bring some harmony into Muslim thought. His legacy continues today.

In modern times there are many great thinkers who have contributed fresh ideas and left their stimulating mark on Islām. They have dealt courageously with some of the wide range of issues that preoccupy Muslims today: change and reform, problems of modernization, religion and politics, creating a Muslim society or state, justice and gender issues, problems of wealth and poverty, educational uplift of Muslims, secularization, and the like. Together they represent a great honor roll of Islāmic intellectual leadership:

> Jamāl al-Dīn al-Afghānī (1839–1897) who cried, "Wake up, Muslims!", and who epitomizes political revivalism. Countless Muslims responded to his stirring call.
> Muhammad ʿAbduh of Egypt (1845–1905) who said that faith and reason go harmoniously together because they occupy different spheres, and whose conservative reforming principles have spread through the Muslim world.
> Sir Sayyid Ahmad Khān of India (1817–1898) who believed that the principles of modern knowledge were in conformity with the original "bright face of Islām."
> Sir Muhammad Iqbāl of India-Pakistan (1876–1938) who asked

Muslims to be co-creators with God, and to engage in an intellectual and social revolution.

Abul Kalām Āzād of India (1888-1958), who said that the essence of Islām is the spiritual mind, and who lifted up beauty, love and tolerance as primary teachings of the Qurʾān.

Syed Abūl Mawdūdī of Pakistan (1903–79) the advocate of "theodemocracy" and Islāmic revivalism, whose books may be more widely read than any other modern Muslim publications.

Syed Qutb of Egypt (1906–66) whose theology of liberation has spurred on Muslim revivalism and also forms of religious extremism.

ʿAlī Sharīʿati of Iran (1933–77), who called for self-giving sacrifice in the constant human struggle between good and evil, mud and spirit.

Other names could be added to this list of great Muslim thinkers, but despite their prominence none has supplanted the place of al-Ghazālī as the Teacher of Islām.

Al-Ghazālī's life and career represent an extraordinary story. Everyone knew he was brilliant, and at the age of 33 he was appointed *shaikh al-Islām*, the chief Sunnī authority in law and theology. He was also a master of the philosophic thought of al-Fārābī and Ibn Sīnā. He could not aspire to a higher position. But as he went about his duties at Baghdad, doubt assailed him and he lost his faith. Law and theology, as he knew them and taught them, had become arid and lifeless to him. Their dependence on human authority seemed like trusting "a broken reed." Nor could he find satisfaction through intellectual activity. Reason, he discovered, travels down dead-end streets, and leads to no certainty about anything. His spiritual sufferings, recorded in his revealing *Confessions*, produced severe psychosomatic symptoms. He could not lecture; he could not even talk. In desperation he abandoned his high position, and traveled widely in his search for truth. His final hope was to become a contemplative mystic, and in the ancient mosque in Damascus the corner is still shown where he sat and meditated.

To abbreviate the story we will simply say that al-Ghazālī's experience as a Sūfi seeker led to the recovery of his faith. "God at last deigned to heal me of this mental malady," he wrote.[31] The experience was so moving and revealing for him that he spent the rest of his days trying to harmonize orthodox thought and mysticism. He went at the task systematically. He first cleared the deck by showing the perils of either authoritarian or imitational religion. Then he made his famous attack on philosophy in his work, *The Incomprehensibility of the Philosophers*. Finally he addressed himself to the constructive task of setting forth an understanding of Islāmic religion that would allow for both an ethical interpretation of the faith and the spiritual experience of God.

Al-Ghazālī outlined his teaching in his great work, *The Revival of the Religious Sciences* (*ihyā ʿulūm al-dīn*). The *Ihyā* has 40 books in four quarters. Ten books deal with the life of piety, ten with social custom, ten with vices or faults that lead to perdition, and ten with virtues or qualities that lead to salvation. His ethical concern in the *Ihyā* is clear. It is a guide for human conduct, for purification of the heart, and for advance forward on the path of God that will both end and begin with knowing God.

God, for al-Ghazālī, is a loving God who wants intercourse with his creatures. On their part, human beings also desire fellowship with God. It is God who enables that to take place. Men and women, however, must do their part by spiritual discipline—here is where the Sūfi path plays its role—until the seeker has attained to the vital experience of God. That experience is marked by the remembrance of God, a feeling of longing for God, affection for all of God's creatures and activities, and a sense of spiritual tranquillity. Al-Ghazālī particularly liked 87:27–30 in the Qurʾān:

> O thou comforted soul! return unto thy Lord,
>   well-pleased and well-pleased with!
> And enter amongst my servants, enter my Paradise!

One who has found a mystic's Paradise, however, cannot remain in that ecstatic state, but rather that person must return to "the real world" and translate his/her experience into the concrete realities of life. What does that translation mean? It means doing exactly those things that the Qurʾān and the Law of Islām have prescribed, but now doing them from the heart. Every command of God has a heart meaning, and ethical depth to it. What true spiritual mysticism does is to show the heart meaning of God's commands, but it does not lead to any other religion than the prophetic religion which God has revealed in His sacred Word. In short, you *must* walk around the Kaʿba, but walking around the Kaʿba symbolizes your placing God at the center of your life and circling about Him at all times.

In this way, al-Ghazālī, as it were, tried to make orthodoxy mystical and mysticism orthodox, to show the ethical dimensions of the Law, and to answer the question of nearness to God. Many observers have noted that he was not entirely successful in his efforts, but there is no doubt that he spiritually revitalized Islām. At the same time, his attack on rationalism encouraged the imitationism that he deplored.

Al-Ghazālī had a great sense of the wonder and destiny of humanity. He wrote,

Know, O beloved, that man was not created in jest or at random, but marvelously made for some great end. Although he is not from everlasting, yet he lives forever; and though his body is mean and earthly, yet his spirit is lofty and divine. When in the crucible of abstinence he is purged from carnal passions, and in the place of becoming a slave to lust and anger becomes endued with angelic qualities. Attaining that state, he finds his heaven in contemplation of Eternal Beauty.[32]

He further said,

Many claim to love God, but each should examine himself as to the genuineness of the love which he professes. The first test is that he should not dislike the thought of death, for no friend should shrink from going to such a Friend.[33]

His own last words as he placed the shroud over his eyes were, "I hear and obey the command to go unto the King."[34] Another version says, "Most gladly do I enter into the Presence of the King."[35]

Al-Ghazālī's prayer is the ideal and hope of all Muslim believers as they go through the rhythm of life.

Notes

[1] I have taken this phrase from Ilse Lichtenstadter, *Islām and the Modern Age* (New York: Bookman Associates, 1958); for her view of the Islāmic "creative genius" in accommodating ideas, cf. pp. 22–30.

[2] H. A. R. Gibb, "The Structure of Religious Thought in Islām," *Muslim World*, vol. XXXVIII, 1948, p. 185.

[3] The spelling "Shī'a" is used throughout this work. The number of Shī'as in the world is about 120 million.

[4] The Zaydis, a smaller group of Shī'as, are found especially in Yemen. They trace their lineage to the son of the fourth Imām. In their doctrinal emphases among the Shī'as they are closest to the Sunnīs.

[5] M. H. Tabatabai, *Shiite Islām*, tr. by S. H. Nasr (Albany: State University of

New York Press, 1975), p. 175.

[6]Ibid., p. 79.

[7]*Hayatu'l-Qulūb*, III, Chapter i, section 7, in Dwight M. Donaldson, *The Shiite Religion* (London: Luzac & Co., 1943), p. 344.

[8]Majlisi, *Tuhfatu'z-Za'irin*, pp. 360ff., in Donaldson, *The Shiite Religion*, p. 346.

[9]David Barrett *World Christian Encyclopedia* (Nairobi: Oxford, 1982), p. 5. Few scholars will commit themselves on Ismā'īlīs statistics.

[10]Ibid. Ahmadiyyas themselves claim a much higher figure.

[11]Al-Ṭabarī, in J. Williams, *The Word of Islām*, pp. 174f.

[12]Some Muslims reverse the usage and for "true Muslims" use the phrase *hakīm muslīm*.

[13]"The Letter of al-Hasan al-Basri," in A. Rippen and J. Knappert, eds., *Textual Sources for the Study of Islām* (Chicago: University of Chicago Press, 1986), p. 117.

[14]*Al-Ibānah 'an Usūl ad-Diyānah*, tr. by W. C. Klein (New Haven: American Oriental Society, 1940), p. 46.

[15]His views may be found in the commentary of al-Taftazānī (d. 1390) on the creed of al-Nasāfī (d. 1142), in E. E. Elder, tr., *A Commentary on the Creed of Islām* (New York: Columbia University Press, 1950). He differs from al-Ash'arī by adding the phrase "not with His pleasure" to the affirmation that God creates the evil acts of human beings.

[16]Majid Fakhry, *A History of Islāmic Philosophy* (New York: Columbia University Press, 1983), p. 31.

[17]Fazlur Rahman, *Islām*, p. 115.

[18]M. F. Jamali, "Towards a Unity of Educational Thought in the Muslim World," Tunis, 1972, Introduction; quoted in Waddy, *The Muslim Mind*, p. 136.

[19]R. Miller, *Mappilas*, p. 218.

[20]*Lessons in Islām Series. Book No. 1* (Lahore: Sh. Muhammad Ashraf, 1975), p. 6.

[21]Martin Lings, *What is Sūfism?* (Berkeley: University of California Press, 1977), p. 1.

[22]Annemarie Schimmel, *Mystical Dimensions of Islām* (Chapel Hill: University of North Carolina Press, 1975), p. 231.

[23]*Hilija* 9:390, in Tor Andrae, *In the Garden of the Myrtles* (Albany: State University of New York, 1970), pp. 118f.

[24]Annemarie Schimmel, *As Through A Veil* (New York: Columbia University Press, 1982), p. 101.

[25]R. A. Nicholson, *The Mystics of Islām* (New York: Schocker Books, 1975; repr. of 1914), p. 115.

[26]Shāh Latīf quoting Rūmī (Māthnawī 1:1741), cited in Schimmel, *Mystical Dimensions*, p. 392.

[27]*Futuh al-Ghaib* ("The Revelations of the Unseen"), tr. by Aftab-ud-Din Ahmad (Lahore: Sh. Muhammad Ashraf, 1973), p. 203.

[28]A. Rippin and J. Knappert, eds., *Textual Sources*, p. 163.

[29]Ibid., p. 165.

[30]D. B. MacDonald, "Al-Ghazālī," *SEI*, p. 110.

[31]*The Confessions of Al-Ghazālī*, tr. by C. Field (Lahore: Sh. Muhammad Ashraf, 1978), p. 20.

[32]*The Alchemy of Happiness*, tr. by C. Field (London: The Octagon Press, 1980), p. 15.

[33]Ibid., p. 119

[34]Claud Field, "Introduction," *The Confessions*, p. 10.

[35]Margaret Smith, *Al-Ghazālī, the Mystic* (Lahore: Hijra International Publishers, 1983; repr. of 1944), p. 36.

18

My Friends Have Fears and Hopes

As we conclude our introduction to Muslim faith and feeling, we remember that our friends have fears and hopes. In this work we have attempted to set forth Abdulla and Amina as representative Muslim believers. They represent the Muslim middle, the silent majority. They consider themselves to be faithful in their religion, progressive in their approach, and friendly in their outlook. There are Muslims at either end of the spectrum of faith and life whom they do not accurately represent. Such is ever the case. No generalized description of a religion, and no personalized portrayal of an adherent can ever be fully representative. Against the typical background we must always come to know individual believers as they are. For the writer, Abdulla and Amina are "real" people, and as real people they have both fears and hopes.

Like al-Ghazālī and all Muslims, Abdulla and Amina must look ahead to their meeting with the King, the One Who "summoneth to the Abode of Peace" (10:26). In that connection they have both fears and hopes—fears in regard to the Judgment, hopes in regard to the Mercy of God. This reality remains a constant presence. At the same time, the Muslim tendency today is to give major attention to the fears and hopes associated with life on this earth. Muslim believers do not forget or discount the Day of Reckoning, but they believe that their faith and obedience will be rewarded in the end in the heavenly Abode of Peace. They must await God's decision. In the meantime they feel that they have to give priority to their lives in this world, both as families and as a community.

Abdulla and Amina are doing their best as they concentrate on and engage in the daily struggle of life. Their attempt is to find in the here and now a portion of the peace that comes from surrendering to God, the fulfillment of which will come later. Their confidence in their striving comes from the second part of Qurānic word that we have cited (10:26): "And Allāh leadeth whom He will to the straight path." God does not only invite to the Home of Peace, but He also gives guidance on the path that will lead to it. Thus the realms of the temporal and the eternal have merged in the unity of faith.

Muslims in general welcome true friends as they make their way along life's path. My wife and I have been invited to the home of Abdulla and Amina for a special "high" tea. We have been looking forward to the occasion not only because Amina will provide many food delicacies—as we have come to know—but mainly because of our close friendship. We are greeted at the door with happy smiles, and "salaam aleikums" are exchanged. Amina and my wife immediately begin sharing information about each other's children. We are warmed by Abdulla's and Amina's spontaneous and genuine interest in our family. The evening has already fulfilled its promise.

There is a family photo on the wall facing us. It is a new one and we comment on its beauty. The family is arranged in a conventional style. Abdulla and Amina are seated, with Ashraf, Rashīd, and Fatima standing behind them. Abdulla has a steady, determined expression on his face as he looks into the camera. The appearance of Amina's face is a mixture of pensiveness and pride. The children are alert and carry a sense of the future. Beyond that we cannot guess at their feelings. There is only so much that can be learned from a photograph.

A human relationship is more revealing, and it is there that one experiences the interplay of faith and feeling. As the evening goes on Abdulla and Amina share the problems facing them and their aspirations for the future. Their feelings are a blend of fear and hope. Their fears and hopes are not "religious" ones in the narrow sense. They are confident of their Islām and content with their faith as Muslims. Their emotions relate rather to the totality of life, and especially to their concern for their family. These are not apart from God. Their frequent references to God's intention ("If God wills!") and God's blessing ("may God help us!") in our conversation shows that they see faith and life as a whole. They are not able to see all the connections, but it is faith that is expressed and not knowledge. They habitually but not lightly declare that God is great, and they are sure that God will also see them through their situation. The evening of sharing seems to help them, as it has helped us, and when it is over it is hard to part ways.

There is another photograph hanging on the wall of the home.

Abdulla is a member of the Muslim Education Association in his area, and the people in the photo, including himself, are its leaders. Abdulla has fears and hopes not only in regard to his family but also in relation to his community. The many problems that the Muslim *umma* is facing at times produces stress and acrimony, and even fears about its future. Abdulla, however, believes that it is much better to actively address the problems than to worry about them. He has therefore committed himself to the task of doing something to uplift his community. He is quite excited over what the Association is doing, and is positive about the future. The other individuals in the photo are a university president, a physician, and a newspaper editor. The people in the picture do not look doubtful and worried, but rather express firmness and confidence. Again a photo can only reveal so much. There is no doubt that behind the scene there are some worries about the big task that they face.

In his courageous book, *Islām, the Fear and the Hope,* Habib Boulares, a Tunisian educational and cultural leader, speaks of the "unbearable process of cultural uprooting that all humans and also Muslims are experiencing." That struggle, as he describes it, is for "a modernization that does not separate man from his roots and does not create a gulf between him and his fellows."[1] This is the challenge for Muslim society—to stay true to Islam and to humanity at the same time, to overcome fear and fear-creating, and to establish hope and hope-creating. He says,

> If today Islam is ready to give itself new meaning, what can this new meaning be if not to establish the greatest possible communication among men? Every Muslim believes, in fact, that his religion addresses itself to all men, and that it is valid for all time and places. The challenge that the modern world hurls before Islam is quite simply for Islam to prove it.[2]

Boulares is convinced that Muslims can meet the challenge successfully, though not easily. By returning to the Qurʾān and understanding it according to the needs of this century, by inculcating "magnanimity and generosity of the soul," and by applying its "universalist vision, its morality, and its appeal to human intelligence" Islam can give meaning to its claims. Boulares typifies Muslim believers who are attempting to deal creatively with their fears and hopes for Muslim society.

My Muslim friends have fears and hopes, sorrows and joys. They struggle between the two. In that they are like all humans.

Their distinctiveness is in their faith and feeling that the straight path of Islam will lead to the Abode of Peace, and that Allāh's blessing will make that possible. This conviction is summed up by al-Ghazālī's comment on the first sura prayer, "Guide us along the straight path":

> The words of God, "Guide us along the straight path," are a prayer which is the marrow of worship ... These words of His make man aware of the need for entreaty and supplication to Him (may He be exalted!) which form the spirit of servitude and also make man aware that the most important of his needs is guidance along the straight path. For it is by following this path that advancement toward God (may He be exalted!) is accomplished.[3]

To that Abdulla and Amina say *Āmīn* ... Amen. A Muslim scholar would add

"but God knows best!"

Notes

[1]Habib Boulares, *Islam, the Fear and the Hope* (London: Zed Books, 1990), p. 116.

[2]Ibid., p. 113.

[3]*The Jewels of the Qurʾān*, tr. by M. A. Quasem, p. 71.

Appendix A

Muslim Population

	1995 Pop in 1000s	Percent of Muslim Pop	1995 Muslim Pop in 1000s	Percent of Annual Increase	World Pop in Year 2000	Muslim Pop in Year 2000	World Pop in Year 2020	Other Muslim Percentages NG	MAK	GNP Per Capita US Dollars
WORLD	5,817,000	19.3	1,122,661	1.8	6,920,000	1,195,480	8,228,000		25.0	3,470

Notes:

1. World and Country statistics are from the *1990 World Population Data Sheet* (Washington: Population Reference Bureau Inc., 1990), calculated to 1995. Basic religious statistics are drawn from the *1990 Encyclopedia Britannica Annual (EB)*, which is a compilation of several sources including David Barrett, *World Christian Encyclopedia (DB)*. Use is also made of M. A. Kettani, *Muslim Minorities in the World Today* (London: Mansell, 1986), A Muslim source (*MAK*) and the *National Geographic* maps (*NG*).

2. *EB* estimates the Muslim percentage of world population at 18.7%; *DB* at 17.8%; and *MAK* at 25.0%. The estimate of 19.3% used above represents a compilation of several sources, including country statistics, and is the author's figure.

3. The figure for Muslim population in the year 2000 is calculated on the basis of the annual global increase of 1.8%. If the preferred figure of 2.5% for Muslim population increase is used, the Muslim population in the year 2000 may be estimated at 1,265,879,000 (Cf. John I. Clarke, "Islamic Population: Limited Demographic Transition," *Geography*, 1985, p. 119).

COUNTRY	1995 Pop in 1000s	Percent of Muslim Pop	1995 Muslim Pop in 1000s	Percent of Annual Increase	Country Pop in Year 2000	Muslim Pop in Year 2000	Country Pop in Year 2020	Other Muslim Percentages		GNP Per Capita US Dollars
								NG	MAK	
[North Africa]										
Algeria	29,150	99.1	28,888	2.7	32,700	32,405	45,600	99.0	99.0	2,170
Egypt	61,850	91.0	56,283	2.9	69,000	64,929	101,900	90.0	92.0	630
Libya	4,900	97.0	4,753	3.1	5,600	5,432	8,500	98.0	99.0	5,410
Mauretania	2,350	99.4	2,336	2.8	2,700	2,683	4,500	96.0	100.0	490
Morocco	28,500	98.7	28,129	2.5	31,400	30,991	43,300	97.0	99.0	900
Sudan	28,854	73.0	20,863	2.9	32,508	23,732	54,600	72.0	90.0	420
Tunisia	9,050	99.4	8,996	2.2	10,001	10,039	13,800	92.0	99.0	1,260
West Sahara	225	100.0	225	2.5	250	250	400	90.0	—	390
[West Africa]										
Benin	5,650	15.2	859	3.0	6,600	1,003	11,700	16.0	40.0	380
Burkino Faso	10,800	43.0	4,644	3.3	12,500	5,375	23,000	22.0	60.0	310
Cameroon	12,800	22.0	2,816	2.6	14,500	3,190	23,500	15.0	60.0	1,010
Central African Rep	3,300	5.9	194	2.6	3,700	218	5,900	—	40.0	390
Chad	5,600	44.0	2,464	2.5	6,200	2,728	9,400	50.0	80.0	190
Ivory Coast	15,550	20.0	3,110	3.5	18,500	3,700	35,400	25.0	35.0	790
Gambia	950	95.4	886	2.6	1,100	1,049	1,700	90.0	98.0	230
Ghana	17,700	15.7	2,779	2.0	20,400	3,202	33,900	19.0	33.0	380
Guinea	8,250	85.0	7,012	2.6	9,200	7,820	14,400	65.0	85.0	430
Guinea-Bissau	1,100	30.0	330	2.0	1,200	360	2,000	30.0	70.0	180
Liberia	3,200	13.8	442	3.2	3,700	510	6,500	15.0	45.0	450
Mali	9,400	90.0	8,460	3.0	10,700	9,630	19,200	60.0	90.0	260
Niger	9,000	80.0	7,200	3.3	11,100	8,880	20,600	85.0	90.0	290
Nigeria	139,800	45.0	62,910	2.8	160,800	72,360	273,200	47.0	60.0	250
Senegal	8,500	91.0	7,780	2.8	9,700	8,827	15,200	82.0	90.0	650

COUNTRY	1995 Pop in 1000s	Percent of Muslim Pop	1995 Muslim Pop in 1000s	Percent of Annual Increase	Country Pop in Year 2000	Muslim Pop in Year 2000	Country Pop in Year 2020	Other Muslim Percentages NG	MAK	GNP Per Capita US Dollars
Sierra Leone	4,800	39.4	1,891	2.7	5,400	2,127	8,900	30.0	60.0	200
Togo	4,450	12.1	538	3.7	5,200	629	9,900	—	25.0	390
[East Africa]										
Comoros	550	99.7	548	3.5	600	598	1,000	—	99.0	460
Djibouti	500	94.0	470	2.9	600	564	1,000	94.0	100.0	450
Ethiopia	61,250	31.4	19,232	2.9	70,800	22,231	126,000	40.0	60.0	120
Kenya	29,850	6.0	1,791	3.8	35,100	2,106	60,500	—	30.0	380
Madagascar	14,103	1.7	239	3.2	16,579	282	27,190	—	10.0	230
Malawi	10,500	16.2	1,701	3.4	11,800	1,811	22,000	—	40.0	180
Mauritius	1,150	13.0	149	1.4	1,200	156	1,300	—	20.0	1,950
Mozambique	18,050	13.2	2,383	2.7	20,400	2,692	31,900	—	45.0	80
Somalia	9,400	99.8	9,381	2.9	10,400	10,379	18,700	99.0	100.0	170
Tanzania	31,250	33.0	10,312	3.7	36,500	7,409	68,800	27.0	55.0	120
[Asia: Middle East]										
Bahrein	600	85.0	510	2.3	700	595	1,000	95.0	90.0	6,360
Cyprus	750	23.0	172	1.0	800	184	900	18.0	24.4	7,050
Gaza	700	99.0	693	4.4	800	792	1,400	—	44.0 ⎤	590
West Bank	1,397	71.7	1,002	3.9	1,685	1,208	2,400	Pales.	⎦	1,200
Israel	5,000	13.9	695	1.6	5,400	750	7,000	10		9,750
Iran	65,650	98.8	64,859	3.3	75,700	74,186	130,200	98.0	99.0	2,320
Iraq	23,000	95.8	22,034	2.7	27,200	26,057	50,900	95.0	97.0	4,410
Jordan	4,900	93.0	4,557	4.1	5,700	5,301	9,700	93.0	95.0	1,730
Kuwait	2,500	91.5	2,287	3.0	2,900	2,653	4,600	97.0	90.0	13,680
Lebanon	3,700	53.0	1,761	2.1	4,100	2,173	5,800	51.0	65.0	1,425

COUNTRY	1995 Pop in 1000s	Percent of Muslim Pop	1995 Muslim Pop in 1000s	Percent of Annual Increase	Country Pop in Year 2000	Muslim Pop in Year 2000	Country Pop in Year 2020	Other Muslim Percentages NG	MAK	GNP Per Capita US Dollars
Oman	1,800	86.0	1,548	3.8	2,100	1,806	3,800	100.0	99.0	5,220
Qatar	600	92.4	554	2.5	700	646	1,100	100.0	95.0	9,920
Saudi Arabia	16,500	98.8	16,320	3.4	22,000	21,736	42,200	99.0	95.0	6,230
Syria	15,300	89.6	13,709	3.8	18,000	16,128	32,600	87.0	85.0	1,020
Turkey	62,800	98.0	61,544	2.2	69,000	67,620	93,800	98.0	99.0	1,360
United Arab Emirates	1,800	99.4	1,699	2.7	2,000	1,888	2,600	92.0	90.0	18,430
Yemen	11,700	99.5	11,641	3.5	13,600	13,532	25,900	99.0	100.0	640
[Asia: Central]										
Afghanistan	19,404	99.0	19,210	2.6	25,400	25,146	43,000	99.0	100.0	220
Azerbaijan	7,260	78.0	5,663	2.1	8,324	6,503	10,072	—	83.2	870
Kazakhstan	17,218	44.0	7,576	1.3	18,261	7,155	23,009	—	42.5	1,680
Kyrgizstan	4,578	67.0	3,055	2.2	4,921	3,297	7,086	—	65.3	810
Tajikistan	5,356	84.0	4,499	3.3	6,766	5,683	11,232	—	86.3	480
Turkmenistan	3,918	80.0	3,134	2.6	4,904	3,923	7,454	—	82.6	1,270
Uzbekistan	21,641	81.0	17,529	2.8	22,812	18,477	35,587	—	85.2	860
China	1,199,950	2.4	28,799	1.4	1,280,000	30,720	1,496,300	—	10.5	360
[Asia: South and Southeast]										
Bangladesh	130,700	86.6	113,186	2.4	146,600	124,610	201,400	85.0	85.0	180
India	947,950	11.3	107,118	2.0	1,042,500	114,675	1,374,500	—	12.0	330
Maldives	250	100.0	250	3.7	300	300	600	99.0	100.0	420
Myanmar	45,707	3.8	1,747	2.1	51,567	1,960	73,225	—	10.7	400
Pakistan	131,800	96.7	127,450	3.0	149,100	144,627	251,300	97.0	97.0	370
Sri Lanka	18,300	7.6	1,391	1.5	19,400	1,474	24,000	10.0	7.6	430

COUNTRY	1995 Pop in 1000s	Percent of Muslim Pop	1995 Muslim Pop in 1000s	Percent of Annual Increase	Country Pop in Year 2000	Muslim Pop in Year 2000	Country Pop in Year 2020	Other Muslim Percentages NG	MAK	GNP Per Capita US Dollars
Brunei	337	63.4	214	2.5	375	238	400	60.0	70.0	14,120
Indonesia	197,586	86.9	171,702	1.8	214,410	186,322	287,300	85.0	90.0	490
Malaysia	18,650	52.9	9,866	2.5	21,500	1,373	27,300	50.0	54.0	2,130
Philippines	67,099	4.3	2,889	2.3	74,555	3,206	108,850	—	12.2	770
Singapore	2,850	16.0	456	1.3	3,000	480	3,400	15.0	17.0	10,450
Thailand	59,700	4.2	2,507	1.3	63,700	2,675	78,100	—	12.0	1,170
[Euromerica]										
Albania	3,613	20.5	741	1.9	2,660	779	4,700	70.0	75.0	2,150
Bulgaria	8,950	7.5	675	0.1	9,000	675	9,100	11.0	19.3	3,200
Russia	151,870	3.8	5,771	0.8	157,944	5,982	183,215	—	—	3,220
Guyana	753	8.7	66	1.6	813	71	1,073	—	15.0	330
Suriname	418	19.6	82	1.7	454	98	543	—	35.0	3,690
Trinidad-Tobago	1,249	6.6	82	1.9	1,304	86	1,799	—	13.0	3,620
United States	259,800	1.9	4,936	0.8	268,300	5,044	294,400	—	1.3	21,100

Notes:

1. For Egypt, the MAKING figure is used in preference to EB. For Russia the figure of 3.8% Muslim population is extrapolated from the old USSR figure of 17.1% (NG), less Muslim populations lost through the formation of the independent republics. For Balkan nations, especially Albania and Bulgaria, the EB percentage is used, which prefers a comparatively low percentage taking into consideration Marxist affiliation.

2. Accurate religious statistics for former Communist territories are notoriously difficult to obtain. What is involved is how one deals with secularized, non-religious populations. Albania is an example of the problem. The number of Muslims is estimated to be between 20-75 percent. In this case I have chosen the lowest percentage, following DB, but EB (1994 Annual) prefers 64.9 percent or 2,220,000 adherents. The figures for the Central Asian Muslim republics are estimates only, which have been drawn from various sources with preference for the figures of the Europa Year Book.

Appendix B

Glossary

The following glossary lists only terms that are used in this work.

ʿabd—servant; a believer in Islām is viewed as the servant of God.

Allāhu akbar!—God is greater; this common Muslim expression of praise is called the *takbīr*.

adhān—the call to prayer, issued five times daily.

adat—indigenous cultural tradition in Indonesia; the equivalent term elsewhere is *ʿurf*.

adl—justice.

ahl al-dhimma—people of protection; Jews and Christians, who deserve the protection of the state are called *dhimmīs*.

ahl al-kitāb—people of the book; religious people, such as Christians and Jews, who in Muslim view have received a legitimate scriptural revelation from God.

aḥmad—the praised one; a short form for Muhammad.

al-Fātiḥa—the opening; the first chapter of the Qurʾān.

al-ḥamdu lilāhi!—praise to God!; an ejaculation of praise frequently repeated in everyday speech.

ʿalīm (pl. *ʿulamāʾ*)—a learned person; one who possesses *ʿilm*, knowledge; religious scholars, equating clergy.

amir al-muʾminīn—commander of the faithful; from Caliph ʿUmar's time, a title for the community leader; amir alone may stand for governor.

ansār—helpers; the people in Medina who welcomed and assisted Muhammad after the *hijra*.

ʿaqīda—statement of belief; creed.

ʿaql—reason, intelligence; a term widely used in philosophy, applied to both God and humans.

arkān—pillar; the pillars of Islām are confession, prayer, fasting, alms-giving, and pilgrimage.

asbab al-nuzūl—occasions of descent; the particular events that marked the giving of Qurānic revelations.

āya (pl. *āyāt*)—word or sign; a verse of the Qurʾān.

āyatullāh—sign of God; a leading religious figure in Shīʿa Islām.

bāb—door; used in the theological phrase *bāb al-ijtihād*, the door of private interpretation.

badwā—Bedouin; the nomadic country people of Arabia.

401

baraka—blessing.

bāṭin—the inner meaning of a Qurānic passage; allegorical, esoteric.

bidᶜa—innovation; used negatively for change that is deemed Islāmically unacceptable and heretical.

birr—righteousness.

bismillāh—in the name of God; the first part of the phrase "in the name of God, the Merciful and Compassionate"; the latter stands at the beginning of every chapter of the Qurʾān except the ninth; sometimes written *basmala*.

bilā kaifa—without how; the idea that believers should accept the human descriptions of God in the Qurʾān without inquiring into or pressing their meaning.

burqa—a full-length woman's cloak with veil; a term used in South Asia.

chaddar—a full-length woman's cloak with veil; a term used in Iran, chador.

dār al-ḥarb—house of war; the non-Islāmic world inimical to the faithful.

dar al-islām—house of Islām; territory under Islāmic sovereignty or areas where Islām is secure.

dār al-ᶜulūm—house of studies; a term used for educational institutions, especially higher theological schools.

daᶜwa—calling people to faith in Islām; mission activity.

dāᶜīs—missionaries and community leaders in the Ismaᶜīlī branch of Shīᶜa Islām.

darwīsh—or dervish, a member of a mystical order; saintly person; mendicant.

dhikr—the remembering; the remembering of God in Sūfi liturgy; also a synonym for the Qurʾān.

dīn—in its narrow sense the practices of Islām, namely, prayer, fasting, alms-giving and pilgrimage; in its wider sense it equates "religion" and "Islām"; in the phrase *yawm al-Dīn*, it means Day of Judgment.

duᶜā—voluntary prayer and supplication.

faḍl—grace.

faqīr—or fakir, a member of a mystical order; an ascetic or poor man (=dervish).

fanāʾ—passing away; the Sufi experience of mystical union with God.

fard—a required duty.

fatwā—a legal or theological opinion by a learned scholar.

falsafa—philosophy; philosophers are falāsifa.

faqīh (pl. *fuqahāʾ*) legal scholars, religious lawyers.

fiqh—jurisprudence; the art of applying *sharīᶜa*, the religious law.

fiṭra—disposition; the inclination of the heart toward God.

furqān—discrimination or distinction; al-Furqān is a term for the Qurʾān.

ghusl—the major ablution before prayer that does away with pollution.

hadd (pl. *hudūd*)—a legal punishment according to the *sharīʿa*.

Ḥadīth (pl. *aḥadīth*)—a story or tradition; the sayings and doings of Muhammad that constitute a second source of faith in Islām; also the sayings and doings of the first companions of the Prophet.

ḥafīz—one who memorizes the entire Qurʾān; a professional reciter.

hajj—the pilgrimage to Mecca.

ḥājī—one who makes the pilgrimage; the term is often added to a pilgrim's name after returning.

halāl—that which is permitted; often applied to food or drink.

ḥanīf—one who turns away; the worshipers of Allāh in Arabia who had already turned away from polytheism before the time of Muhammad.

ḥarām—that which is forbidden.

hidāyat—guidance, especially the guidance of God.

hijāb—a woman's scarf or head-covering.

hijra—emigration; the escape of Muhammad from Mecca to Medina in 622; also the starting point of the Muslim calendar.

ḥūrī—a virgin woman in Paradise.

ʿibādat—service; worship as service; the required duties as service; the whole life of service to God.

Iblīs—a Qurānic name for the fallen angel, the devil.

ʿīd—festival; *ʿīd mubarak!*, have a happy festival!

ʿĪd al-Aḍha—the feast of sacrifice; it commemorates Abraham's near-sacrifice of his son; the first of the two major Muslim festivals, it is called Bakr-ʿĪd in South Asia and Büyük Bairam in Turkey, and occurs on the 10th of Dhuʾl-Ḥijj.

ʿĪd al-Fiṭr—the breaking of the fast; the second major festival that starts in the evening of the last day of the fast month of Ramaḍān.

iḥram—the condition of sanctity that a pilgrim to Mecca enters into before approaching the city of Mecca.

ijmāʿ—the consensus of the community.

iʿjaz—the miraculous nature of the Qurʾān.

ijtihād—the right to the personal interpretation of the Qurʾān through the application of reason.

ilhām—illumination; spiritual enlightenment enjoyed by a saint or a Shīʿa religious authority.

imām—leader; a leader of the weekly mosque prayer; a community religious leader; in Shīʿism, one of the designated successors of the Prophet.

īmān—the attitude of faith; the five basic beliefs.

Injīl—the Gospel; understood as a sacred book revealed to ꜥĪsā (Jesus).

irtidād—apostasy; the sin of leaving Islām in favor of membership in another faith.

ꜥĪsā—Jesus; usually designated as ꜥĪsa Nabī, Jesus the Prophet, or ꜥĪsa Masīḥ, Jesus the Messiah, or simply as Jesus, the son of Mary, Ibn Maryam.

isnād—chain; the chain of narrators for an Ḥadīth.

istiḥsān—equity or justice; the interpretation of the law in the light of what seems prudent.

istiḥslāh—welfare; the interpretation of the law in the light of community well-being.

jāhiliyya—darkness or ignorance; the unenlightened age in Arabia before Muhammad.

jihād—struggle; the greater jihād is personal striving for spiritual purity; the lesser jihād is militant striving for God and community.

jinn—spirits, good and bad, who are lesser in power than angels or devils.

jizya—the tax required of people of the book under Muslim rule in return for governmental protection and exemption from military service.

jumāꜥ—assembly; the "Jumā prayer" is the Friday congregational prayer. *jāmiꜥ* is a term for a major mosque; *jāmiꜥa* is used for a society or organization.

kāfir—an unbeliever; a heretic.

kalām—word or speech; the Speech of God; classical dialectical theology.

kalima—the confession of faith, "there is no god but Allāh, and Muhammad is the messenger of Allāh."

karāmāt—the wonders produced by saints.

khalīfa—successor or deputy; the successors of Muhammad; the title (caliph) of the religio-political leader of the united Muslim community; the caliphate was only an ideal concept after 1258 and ended in 1924.

kharāj—land tax paid by conquered people.

khums—a Shīꜥa religious tax above the *zakāt*, paid to the religious establishment.

khatīb—the preacher in the mosque service.

khutba—the sermon in the mosque service.

kitāb—book, scripture; al-Kitāb is a synonym for the Qurʾān.

kufr—ingratitude; unbelief.

lā ilāha illa Allāh, wa Muhammadu rasūl Allāh—the confession of faith; "there is no god but Allāh, and Muhammad is the messenger of Allāh."

lailat al-qadr—the Night of Power; the night in Ramaḍān when the Qurʾān was first revealed.

lawḥ maḥfūz—the preserved tablet; the repository of God's revelations in the seventh heaven, from which the angel Jibra il transmits God's words to the prophets.

madhhab—a school of law; one of the four primary schools in Muslim jurisprudence.

madrasa—a religious education school; in some areas a lower school is called a *maktāb*, and *madrasa* is reserved for higher level religious education.

mahr—dowry; an amount paid by the bridegroom to the bride and retained by her.

Mahdī—the guided one; an end-time figure who will come to restore Islām.

malāk—an angel.

malik—a king or ruler.

maqām—standing-place; the Maqām Ibrahīm is a stone where Abraham stood when he built the Kaʿba.

maʿrifa—mystical knowledge; the direct awareness of God espoused by Sūfis.

marjaʿ al-taqlīd—the primary religious scholar and authority in Shiʿa Islām.

masjid—a place of prostration; the mosque.

matn—the content of an Ḥadīth.

mawāli—clients; early non-Arab Muslim converts who had to associate with an Arab tribe.

mawlūd—the biographical ballad sung at the birthday (*mawlid*) of a prophet or saint.

mawlavī—a clergy scholar in South Asia; the West African equivalent is *mallam*.

miḥrāb—the niche in a mosque wall that marks the direction of Mecca.

milād al-nabī—the birthday of the prophet; a festival.

mimbar—the raised platform or pulpit in the mosque.

minār—or minaret, the mosque tower from which the call to prayer is issued.

miʿrāj—the mystical ascension of Muhammad to the heavens.

muezzīn—the person who gives the call to prayer.

muftī—a learned scholar who is able to deliver a legal or theological opinion.

mujāhidīn—those who struggle on the path of God; often applied to militants.

muhājirūn—the emigrants who went from Mecca to Medina with Muhammad.

muhtasib—a minor functionary sometimes appointed to oversee morals.

Muḥarram—one name of the festival that occurs on the tenth day of the month of Muḥarram, memorializing the death of Ḥusain at Kerbela.

mujtahid—one who interprets the Qurʾān; in Shia Islām a major religious leader.

mulla, or *mullah*—a Muslim divine, in most areas with lesser training and of a lesser stature than an *ᶜalīm*.

muʾmin—a true believer.

munāfiqun—hypocrites; people in Medina who resisted Muhammad and Islām.

murid—the disciple of a Sūfi shaikh or teacher.

muslim—one who surrenders to God; a follower of Islām.

parda, or *purdah*—curtain or veil; it may refer to women's seclusion or women's dress.

pir—a Sūfi master.

qadar—power: the powerful and eternal decrees of God are His *taqdīr*.

qāḍī—a judge in the system of *sharīᶜa* administration.

qanūn—administrative law drawn from nonreligious sources.

qibla—direction; the direction of prayer towards Mecca.

qiyas—reasoning by analogy; a source for Islāmic law and theology.

Qurʾān—the recital or reading; the sacred scripture of Islām.

Rabb al-ᶜālamin—the Lord of the Worlds; a name for God in the first chapter of the Qurʾān.

Rahmān and *Rahīm*—the Merciful and Compassionate; names for God in the *bismillāh* at the head of Qurʾānic chapters.

rakᶜa—a cycle of prayer.

Ramaḍān—the ninth month of the lunar year; the time for the annual fast.

rasūl—messenger; apostle of God, usually applied to Muhammad.

rawda—the recitation of the passion of Ḥusain, the grandson of Muhammad, among Shīᶜa.

raʾy—free opinion in legal or theological matters.

ribā—interest on money, forbidden in Islām.

rūḥ—spirit.

ṣadaqa—voluntary charity.

ṣāḥib—honorable person; an expression of respect; *ṣaḥāba* are the companions of the Prophet.

sahih—correct; the sound and authoritative collections of Ḥadīth.

salaam aleikum—peace be to you; the normal Muslim greeting.

salāt—the fivefold prayer.

salla ʾallāhu alaihi wa sallām—may God give him (the Prophet) peace!

salla ʾllāhu ᶜalā ʾn-nabī—may God bless the Prophet!

ṣawm—fasting.

sayyid—a descendant of the family of Muhammad; a term of respect.

shahāda—the witnessing; the primary term for the confession of faith.

shahīd—a witness; primarily one who is a martyr.

shaikh—chief or leader; head of a Sūfi order; an important teacher.

shaikh al-Islām—the religious scholar whose opinion was held the highest in Sunnī Islām, especially in Ottoman times; in practice there is now no such universally accepted individual.

sharīʿa—the clear road; the entire body of religious law; the code of Islām.

sharīf—noble person; a descendant of the Prophet.

Shaytān—Satan.

shirk—associating a partner with God; an idea that combines polytheism and idolatry; the greatest sin in Islām.

Shīʿa—partisan; the party of the family of the Prophet; the minority section of Islām, centered in Iran; cf. *Shīʿi* and *Shīʿite.*

shukr—gratitude.

sīra—the biography of the Prophet.

subhāna ʾllāhi—glory be to God!; a common expression of praise, especially used in prayer.

sujūd—prostration; the culmination of prayer, with the forehead touching down.

sunna—the custom of Muhammad drawn from Ḥadīth.

sunnī—one who follows the custom of the Prophet; a term for the majority Muslim community.

sūra—chapter; one of the 114 chapters of the Qurʾān.

tafsīr—exegesis and commentary on the Qurʾān.

tahrīf—corruption of the scriptures.

talāq—dismissal; the phrase used by a man in divorcing a woman.

tanzil—the descent; the coming down of the Qurʾān; al-Tanzil is a name for the Qurʾān.

taqlīd—handing down tradition and imitating the past; a simple acceptance of religious authority; theological traditionalism.

taqwā—piety.

tarīqa—path; a Sūfi order.

tasliya—the calling down of blessing on Muhammad.

tasawwuf—mysticism; Sufism.

tawāf—the circling around the Kaʿba during the pilgrimage.

tawākkul—the spiritual quality of reliance on God alone.

tawba—penitence and repentance.

tawhīd—unity; a central theme in the doctrine of God and the theory of Muslim society.

tawrāt—the revelation of God to Moses; the Torah.

taʿziya—consolation; a Shīʿa procession taken out at the memorial festival for Ḥusain in Muḥarram.

ʿulamāʾ—religious scholars; clergy.

umma—community; the family of Muslims, locally and worldwide.

umm al-muʾminīn—mother of believers; Khadīja.

umma al-kitāb—the mother of the book; a term for the totality of revelation, kept in heaven and progressively revealed.

ʿumra—the lesser pilgrimage; a voluntary activity, without the sacrifice.

ʿurf—local culture and custom; a secondary source of law.

uṣūl—roots; the foundations of law and theology, namely scripture, tradition, analogical reasoning, and community consensus.

waḥdat al-wujūd—unity of being; a mystical concept.

waḥy—the prophetic capacity to receive the inspiration of God; revelation.

walī (pl. *awliyāʾ*)—nearness; friend of God; saint.

walāyat—guardianship; a key concept in Shia theology.

waqf—a religious financial trust or foundation.

wuḍuʾ—the lesser washing before prayer.

Zabūr—writing; the Psalms revealed to the Prophet David.

zakāt—legal almsgiving.

ẓāhir—the external and literal meaning of Qurānic passages.

zenana—female and children's quarters in a Muslim home, a South Asian usage; elsewhere the term harem is common.

Bibliography

A. Books Cited in This Work

Abdalati, Hammudah. *Islam in Focus*. Aligarh: Crescent Publishing Co., 1973.

_____. *The Family Structure in Islam*. Indianapolis: American Trust Publications, 1977.

Abdulkarim, K. K. Muhammad. *Introduction to Moyinkutty Vaidyar, Badar Pāda Paṭṭ*. Parapanangadi, India: Bayaniyya Book Stall, 1971. Malayalam.

Abul Kalam Azad. *The Tarjuman al-Qurʾān*. 2 vols. Trans. by Syed Abdul Latif. Bombay: Asia Publishing House, 1962.

Ahmed Moulvavi, C. N. *Pariṣuddha Khurān—Paribhāshayom Wyākhyānawom* ["The Holy Qurʾān. Translation and Commentary"]. 6 vols. Perumbavoor, India: Abdul Majeed Marikar, vols. I and II; Calicut: By the Author, vols. III–VI, 1951–61. Malayalam.

_____. *Saheehul Bukhari. Malayalam Translation and Commentary*. Calicut: Ansari Press, 1970.

Akhtar, Shabbir. *A Faith for All Seasons*. Chicago: Ivan R. Dee, 1990.

Al-Ghazālī, Abu Hamid M. *The Alchemy of Happiness*. Translated by Claud Field. London: The Octagon Press, 1980.

_____. *The Confessions of Al-Ghazali*. Trans. by Claud Field. Lahore: Sh. Muhammad Ashraf, 1978.

_____. *The Jewels of the Qurʾān*. Trans. by M. A. Quasem. London: Kegan Paul, 1983.

_____. *Kitab al-ʿIlm* ["The Book of Knowledge"]. Trans. by N. A. Faris. Lahore: Sh. Muhammad Ashraf, 1962.

_____. *On the Duties of Brotherhood*. Trans. by Muhtar Holland. Woodstock, N.Y.: The Overlook Press, 1976.

Al-Jilānī, ʿAbd al-Qādir. *Futuh al-Ghalib* ["The Revelations of the Unseen"]. Trans. by Aftab-ud-Din Ahmad. Lahore: Sh. Muhammad Ashraf, 1973.

Al-Ashʿarī, Abū Mūaā. *Al-Ibānah ʿan Usūl ad-Diyānah* ["The Elucidation of Islam's Foundation"]. Trans. by W. C. Klein. New Haven: American Oriental

Society, 1940.

Al-Tabbarah, Afif. *The Spirit of Islam*. Trans. by Hasan T. Shoucari; revised by R. M. Baalbaki. Beirut, 1978.

Andrae, Tor. *In the Garden of the Myrtles*. Albany: State University of New York, 1970.

_____. *Mohammed, the Man and His Faith*. London: George Allen & Unwin, 1936.

Anjum, Mohin, ed. *Muslim Women in India*. New Delhi: Sangam Books Ltds., 1992.

Arberry, A. J., tr. *The Koran Interpreted*. New York: Macmillan, 1944.

_____., ed. *Islam, Muhammad and His Religion*. New York: The Liberal Arts Press, 1958.

Arnold, Thomas and Guillaume, Alfred, eds. *The Legacy of Islam*. London: Oxford University Press, 1931. First edition.

Ayoub, Mahmoud. *Redemptive Suffering in Islam*. The Hague: Mouton, 1978.

Baljon, J. M. S. *Modern Muslim Koran Interpretation*. Leiden: E. J. Brill, 1961.

Balyuzi, H. M. *Muhammad and the Course of Islam*. Oxford: George Ronald, 1976.

Bell, Richard. *Introduction to the Qurʾān*. Edinburgh: The University Press, 1953.

Boulares, Habib. *Islam, the Fear and the Hope*. London: Zed Books, 1990.

Chaudhry, Rashid A. *Muslim Festivals and Ceremonies*. London: International Publications Ltd., 1988.

Coulson, N. J. *A History of Islamic Law*. Edinburgh: The University Press, 1964.

Cragg, Kenneth. *Alive to God. Muslim and Christian Prayer*. London: Oxford University Press, 1970.

_____. *The Dome of the Rock*. London: S.P.C.K., 1964.

_____. *The House of Islam*. Belmont, Calif.: Wadsworth Publishing Co., 1975.

Donaldson, Dwight. *The Shī'ite Religion*. London: Luzac & Co., 1933.

Donner, F. M. *The Early Muslim Conquests*. Princeton: Princeton University Press, 1981.

Eaton, Charles. *Islam and the Destiny of Man*. New York: State University of New York, 1985.

Elder, E. E., tr. *A Commentary on the Creed of Islam. Sa'd al-Dīn al-Taftāzānī on the Creed of Najm al-Dīn al-Nasafī*. New York: Columbia University Press, 1950.

Esposito, John L., ed. *Voices of Resurgent Islam*. New York: Oxford University Press, 1983.

Europa World Year Book, 1991. Vol. II. London: Europa Publications Ltd., 1991.

Fadhl, Yusuf. *Imam Husain's Revolution*. Teheran: Muslim Youth Association, 1970.

Fakhry, Majeed. *A History of Islamic Philosophy*. New York; Columbia University Press, 1983.

Farūqī, Isma'īl and Farūqī, Lois. *Cultural Atlas of Islam*. New York: Macmillan, 1968.

Freeman-Grenville, G. S. P. *The Muslim and Christian Calendars*. London: Rex College Ltd., 1977.

Friedlander, Shems. *Ninty-Nine Names of Allah*. New York: Harper & Row, 1978.

Fyzee, Asaf A. A. *Outlines of Muhammadan Law*. Delhi: Oxford University Press, 1974.

Gätje, Helmut. *The Qur'ān and Its Exegesis*. Trans. and ed. by A. T. Welch. Berkeley: University of California Press, 1976.

Grunebaum, G. E. von. *Muhammadan Festivals*. London: Curzon Press, 1951.

Guillaume, Alfred, tr. *The Life of Muhammad. A Translation of Ibn Ishāq's Sīrat Rasūl Allāh*. Lahore: Oxford University Press, 1967.

Hamidullah, M. *The First Written Constitution in the World*. Lahore: Sh. Muhammad Ashraf, 1975. Third revised edition.

Haykal, Muhammad. *The Life of Muhammad*. Translated by Isma'īl R. A. Farūqī. Plainfield, Ind.: American Trust Publications, 1976.

Hodgson, Marshall G. S. *The Venture of Islam*. 3 vols. Chicago: University of Chicago Press, 1974.

Ibn Isḥāq. See Guillaume, Alfred, for entry.

Iqbāl, Sir Muhammad. *The Reconstruction of Religious Thought in Islam*. Lahore: Sh. Muhammad Ashraf, 1962.

Jamali, Mohammad F. *Letters on Islam*. London: World of Islam Festival Trust, 1978.

Jones, L. Bevan. *The People of the Mosque*. Calcutta: Baptist Mission Press, 1965.

Kamal, Ahmad. *The Sacred Journey*. New York: Duell, Sloan & Pierce, 1961.

Keddie, Nikki, ed. *Scholars, Saints and Sufis. Muslim Religious Institutions in the Middle East Since 1950*. Berkeley: University of Calif-ornice Press, 1972.

Kettani, M. A. *Muslim Minorities in the World Today*. London: Mansell, 1986.

Khadduri, Majid. *War and Peace in the Law of Islam*. Baltimore: Johns Hopkins Press, 1955.

Klein, F. A. *The Religion of Islam*. London: Curzon Press, 1906.

Lessons in Islam Series. Books I–V. Lahore: Sh. Muhammad Ashraf, 1975.

Levy, Reuben. *The Social Structure of Islam*. Cambridge: Cambridge University Press, 1962.

Lewis, Bernard. *Islam*. 2 vols. New York: Harper & Row, 1974.

Lichtenstadter, Ilse. *Islam and the Modern Age*. New York: Bookman Associates, 1958.

Lings, Martin. *What is Sufism*. Berkeley: University of California Press, 1977.

Mahmud, S. F. *A Short History of Islam*. Karachi: Oxford University Press, 1960.

Mawdudi, Syed Abul ʿAlā. *Toward Understanding Islam*. Nairobi: Islamic Foundation, 1973. First revised edition, 1960.

_____. *The Road to Peace and Salvation*. Lahore: Islamic Publications

Ltd., 1966. Original lecture, 1940.

McGiffert, A. C. *A History of Christian Thought*. 2 vols. New York: Charles Scribner's, 1932.

Moomen, Moojan. *An Introduction to Shīʿi Islam*. New Haven: Yale University Press, 1985.

Nasr, Seyyed Hossein, ed. *Islamic Spirituality*. New York: Crossroad, 1987.

Otto, Rudolf. *Idea of the Holy*. Trans. by J. W. Harvey. London: Oxford, 1950. First edition, 1923.

Padwick, Constance. *Muslim Devotions*. London: S.P.C.K., 1961.

Palmer, E. H., tr. *The Koran (Qurʾān)*. London: Oxford University Press, 1900.

Peters, F. E. *The Hajj*. Princeton: Princeton University Press, 1994.

Pickthall, Marmaduke, tr. *The Meaning of the Glorious Koran*. New York: New American Library. Mentor edition, 1953.

Qadri, Anwar. *Islamic Jurisprudence in the Modern World*. Lahore: Sh. Muhammad Ashraf, 1973. Second revised edition.

Quasem, Muhammad A. *Salvation of the Soul and Islamic Devotion*. London: Kegan Paul International, 1983.

Rahbar, Daud. *God of Justice*. Leiden: E. J. Brill, 1960.

Rahman, Fazlur. *Islam*. New York: Anchor Books, 1968.

_____. *Major Themes of the Qurʾān*. Chicago: University of Chicago Press, 1980.

Rahman, S. A. *Punishment of Apostasy in Islam*. Lahore: Institute of Islamic Culture, 1972.

Rauf, Muhammad. *Islam, Creed and Worship*. Washington: The Islamic Center, 1975.

Renard, John. *Islam and the Heroic Image*. Columbia: University of South Carolina, 1993.

Rippin, Andrew and Knappert, Jan, eds. *Textual Sources for the Study of Islam*. Chicago: University of Chicago Press, 1986.

Rodinson, Maxime. *Mohammed*. Trans. by A. Carter. London: Penguin, 1971.

Russel, Ralph and Islam, Kurshidul. *Ghalib, Life and Letters.* Cambridge, Mass.: Harvard University Press, 1969.

Sanchez, Miguel. *The Alhambra.* Granada: Marino Antiquierra, n.d.

Schimmel, Annemarie. *And Muhammad is His Messenger.* Chapel Hill: University of North Carolina Press, 1985.

_____. *As Through A Veil.* New York: Columbia University Press, 1982.

_____. *Mystical Dimensions of Islam.* Chapel Hill: University of North Carolina Press, 1975.

Sell, Edward. *The Faith of Islam.* London: S.P.C.K., 1920; reprint, 1976.

Shariati, Ali. *On the Sociology of Islam.* Translated by H. Algar. Berkeley: Mizan Press, 1979.

Smith, Margaret. *Al-Ghazālī, the Mystic.* Lahore: Hijra International Publishers, 1983. Reprint of 1944.

Smith, Wilfred Cantwell. *On Understanding Islam.* The Hague: Mouton, 1981.

_____. *The Meaning and End of Religion.* San Francisco: Harper & Row, 1978.

Sourdel, Dominique. *Medieval Islam.* Trans. by J. M. Watt. London: Routledge and Kegan Paul, 1986.

Stade, Robert. *Ninety-Nine Names of God in Islam.* Ibadan: Daystar Press, 1970.

Subhan, John A. *Islam, Its Beliefs and Practices.* Lucknow: Lucknow Publishing House, 1938.

Sweetman, John W. *Islam and Christian Theology.* 4 vols. London: Lutterworth Press, 1947.

Syed Abdul Latif. *The Mind al-Qurᵓān Builds.* Chicago: Kazi Publications, 1983.

Tabatabāᵓī, M. H. *Shiᶜite Islam.* Translated by S. H. Nasr. Albany: State University of New York Press, 1975.

Tritton. A. S. *Muslim Theology.* London: Luizac & Co., Ltd., 1947.

Updike, John. *Rabbit at Rest.* New York: Fawcett Crest, 1990.

Waddy, Charis. *The Muslim Mind*. London: Longman, 1976.

Watt, W. Montgomery. *Muhammad, Prophet and Statesman*. London: Oxford University Press, 1961.

_____. *Islamic Philosophy and Theology*. Edinburgh: The Edinburgh University Press, 1962.

Weitbrecht-Stanton, H. U. *The Teaching of the Qurʾān*. London: S.P.C.K., 1919.

Williams, John A., ed. *Themes of Islamic Civilization*. Berkeley: University of California Press, 1971.

_____. ed. *The Word of Islam*. Austin: University of Texas Press, 1994.

Wolfe, Michael. *The Hadj: An American's Pilgrimage to Mecca*. New York: The Atlantic Monthly Press, 1993.

Wolfson, H. A. *The Philosophy of the Kalam*. Cambridge, Mass.: Harvard University Press, 1976.

Yusuf Ali. *The Holy Qur-an. Text, Translation and Commentary*. Washington: The Islamic Center, 1978.

B. Journal Articles Cited in This Work

Barakat Ahmad, Syed, "Non-Muslims and the Umma," *Studies in Islam*, XVIII, 2, April 1980.

Gibb, Sir Hamilton A. R., "The Structure of Religious Thought in Islam," *Muslim World*, XXXVIII, 1948.

Haneef Juwaid, "Muslims and the Uniform Civil Code," *Religion and Society*, XXVI, No. 4, December 1979.

King, Russel, "The Pilgrimage to Mecca: Some Geographical and Historical Aspects," *Erdkunde*, Band XVI, 1971[?].

Miller, Roland E., "Sin and Salvation in Islam," *Al-Basheer, The Bulletin of the Christian Institutes of Islamic Studies*, Vol. V (Jan.–Dec. 1982), pp. 152–96.

Riffat Hassan, "Equal Before Allah? Woman-Man Equality in the Islamic Tradition," *Harvard Divinity Bulletin*, XVII, No. 2, May 1987.

Smith, Wilfrid Cantwell, "Comparative Religion. Whither and Why?" *The History of Religions, Essays in Methodology*, ed. by Mircea Eliade and

Joseph Kitagawa. Chicago: University of Chicago Press, 1959.

Tahir Mahmood, S., "Uniform Civil Code and Islamic Law," *Religion and Society,* XXV, No. 4, December 1979.

C. Reference Works

The Encyclopedia of Islam. Leiden: E. J. Brill, 1954. Second edition, 8 of 10 volumes complete (1996). The best reference. See also *The Encyclopedia of Islam,* 4 vols. and supplement; first edition, 1913–38. *The Shorter Encyclopedia of Islam,* ed. by H. A. R. Gibb and J. H. Kramers. Leiden: E.J. Brill, 1953, has selected articles on religion from the first edition of *EI.*

Esposito, John L. ed., *The Oxford Encyclopedia of the Modern Muslim World.* 4 vols. New York: Oxford University Press, 1955.

Hughes, T. P. *A Dictionary of Islam.* London: W. H. Allen, 1953. A revision and reprint of the 1885 edition.

World Christian Encyclopedia, edited by David Barrett and others. Nairobi: Oxford University Press, 1982.

Ede, David, ed. *Guide to Islam.* Boston: G. K. Hall, 1983.

Geddes, Charles L. *An Analytic Guide to the Bibliographies on Islam, Muhammad and the Qurʾān.* Denver: American Institute of Islamic Studies, 1973.

Haddad, Y. Y., Voll, J. O., and Esposito, J. L. *The Contemporary Islamic Revival: A Critical Survey and Bibliography.* New York: Greenwood, 1991.

Holt, P. M., Lambton, A. K., and Lewis, B., eds. *The Cambridge History of Islam.* 4 vols. Cambridge: The University Press, 1978.

Hourani, Albert. *A History of the Arab Peoples.* Cambridge, MA.: Harvard University, 1991.

Kassis, H. E. *A Concordance of the Qurʾān.* Berkeley: University of California, 1983.

Pearson, J. D. *Index Islamicus.* Cambridge: Heffer, 1958, and subsequent supplements.

Schacht, J., and Bosworth, C. *The Legacy of Islam.* London: Oxford University Press, 1974. Second edition.

Weekes, Richard V., ed. *Muslim Peoples: A World Ethnographic Survey,* 2 vols.; Connecticut: Greenwood, 1984. Second edition.

D. A Selection of Additional Introductions to Islam

The following introductions are supplementary to those listed in the bibliography of works cited. For an insightful review of some of the many introductions to Islam cf. Willem Bijlefeld, "Introducing Islam: A Bibliographic Essay," I and II, in *Muslim World,* LXIII, Nos. 3 and 4, July and October 1973. For a full, categorized bibliography on Islam cf. Caesar Farah's listing in his work, *Islam, Beliefs and Observances.* The following include only some basic monographs. There are many helpful chapters in general encyclopedias and various introductions to world religions.

Ahmad, Kurshid, ed. *Islam, Its Meaning and Its Message.* London: Islamic Council of Europe, 1976.

Calverley, Edwin. *Islam, an Introduction.* Cairo: American University at Cairo, 1958.

Cragg, Kenneth and Speight, Marston, eds. *Islam from Within: Anthology of a Religion.* Belmont, Calif.: Wadsworth Publishing Co., 1980.

Denny, Frederick. *Islam and the Muslim Community.* San Francisco: Harper, 1987.

Esposito, John. *Islam, the Straight Path.* New York: Oxford University Press, 1992. Second revised edition.

Farah, Caesar E. *Islam, Beliefs and Observances.* New York: Barrons, 1944. Fifth edition.

Faruqi, I. R. al-. *Islam.* Niles, Ill.: Argus, 1979. See also his *Tawhid: Its Relevance for Thought and Life.* Plainfield, Ind.: International Islamic Federation of Student Organizations, 1983.

Gibb, H. A. R. *Muhammedanism.* London: Galazy Books, 1962. Second edition.

Goldziher, Ignaz. *Introduction to Islamic Theology and Law.* Trans. by Andreas and Ruth Hamori, and annotated by Bernard Lewis. Princeton: Princeton University Press, 1981. The first German edition was in 1910.

Guadefroy-Demombynes, Maurice. *Muslim Institutions.* Translated by J. P. MacGregor. London: George Allen & Unwin, 1950.

Hitti, Philip. *Islam, A Way of Life.* Chicago: Henry Regner Company, 1970.

Martin, Richard C. *Islam: A Cultural Perspective.* Englewood Cliffs: Prentice-Hall, 1981.

Morgan, K. W., ed. *Islam, the Straight Path.* New York: Ronald Press,

1958.

Nasr, Seyyid Hossein. *Ideals and Realities of Islam*. London: George Allen & Unwin, 1966.

Schimmel, Annemarie. *Islam, an Introduction*. Albany: SUNY, 1992.

Smith, Wilfrid C. *Islam in Modern History*. Princeton: Princeton University Press, 1957.

Journalistic Surveys

Lippman, Thomas W. *Understanding Islam*. New York: New American Library. 1982.

Ruthven, Malaise. *Islam in the World*. London: Penguin, 1984.

Introductions with Inter-Faith Reflection

Braswell, George. *Islam: Its Prophet, Peoples, Politics and Power*. Nashville: Broadman & Holman, Publishers, 1996.

Cragg, Kenneth. *The Call of the Minaret*. Maryknoll, N.Y.: Orbis, 1985. Second edition, revised and enlarged.

Guillaume, Alfred. *Islam*. Baltimore: Penguin, 1956. Second revised edition.

Martinson, Paul O., ed. *Islam, an Introduction for Christians*. Translated by S. O. Cox. Minneapolis: Augsburg, 1994.

Speight, Marston. *God is One: The Way of Islam*. New York: Friendship Press, 1989.

Index

Roland E. Miller, currently Visiting Professor and Coordinator of the Islamic Studies Program at Luther Seminary in St. Paul, Minn., is also Director of the seminary's Global Mission Education Program. A Canadian, he is on a three-year leave from his position as Professor of Islam and World Religions at Luther College, University of Regina. From 1953 to 1976, as an ordained Lutheran missionary in India, he participated in a variety of evangelistic, medical, literary, administrative, and other church-related activities. His wife, Mary Helen, a social  worker, received wide recognition for her global citizenry, especially in refugee services. She, Dr. Miller, and their children resided in the Muslim-majority community of Malappuram in Kerala State. They continue their long involvement with India through a variety of agencies and projects.

Dr. Miller holds an M. Div. degree from Concordia Seminary, St. Louis. He received his M.A. and Ph.D. in Islamic studies from the Hartford Seminary Foundation. An internationally known Islamicist with a specialization in Indian Islam, he is regarded as the leading authority on the Mappila Muslims of Kerala. He is the author of several books and many articles in the fields of Islamics, India studies, and missiology. He has frequently been called upon to lecture in various forums around the world and has twice been a visiting scholar at Harvard University. In 1993 he was given the University of Regina's master teacher award for excellence in undergraduate teaching. He founded the Summer Centre for International Languages at the University of Regina and headed the major bilateral Indo-Canadian project, "The Computerization of Indian Universities." As the international consultant for the Division of Global Mission of the Evangelical Lutheran Church in America he directed the planning for its current "Focus on Islam." He has been invited to establish the first graduate Islamic studies program in a Lutheran theological institution on this continent.

Dr. and Mrs. Miller have five children, two in the U.S.A., two in Canada, and one in India.